MOL
Atlantic Canada

A GUIDE TO THE CLASSIC TRAILS

SARAH L. HALE AND JODI E. BISHOP

*Dedicated to Ruthie and Evangerswish,
who were always prepared for what we did not expect.*

© 1999 by Sarah L. Hale and Jodi E. Bishop
All rights reserved
Printed in Canada
Copublished by Menasha Ridge Press and Vanwell Publishing
First edition, first printing

Library of Congress Cataloging-in-Publication Data:
Hale, Sarah L., 1970-
Mountain bike! Atlantic Canada: a guide to the classic trails/
Sarah L. Hale and Jodi E. Bishop.
p. cm. —(America by mountain bike)
Includes bibliographical references and index.
ISBN 1-55068-096-X
1. All terrain cycling—Atlantic Provinces Guidebooks.
2. Bicycle trails—Atlantic Provinces Guidebooks.
I. Bishop, Jodi E., 1969-
II. Title III. Series: America by mountain bike series.
GV1046.C22A864 1999
917.504'4–dc21   99-29364
                              CIP

Photos by the authors unless otherwise credited
Maps by Steve Jones
Cover and text design by Suzanne Holt
Cover photo by Dennis Coello

Menasha Ridge Press
700 South 28th Street
Suite 206
Birmingham, Alabama 35233

All the trails described in this book are legal for mountain bikes. But rules can change—especially for off-road bicycles, the new kid on the outdoor recreation block. Land access issues and conflicts between bicyclists, hikers, equestrians, and other users can cause the rewriting of recreation regulations on public lands, sometimes resulting in a ban of mountain bike use on specific trails. That's why it's the responsibility of each rider to check and make sure that he or she rides only on trails where mountain biking is permitted.

CAUTION

Outdoor recreational activities are by their very nature potentially hazardous. All participants in such activities must assume the responsibility for their own actions and safety. The information contained in this guidebook cannot replace sound judgment and good decision-making skills, which help reduce risk exposure, nor does the scope of this book allow for disclosure of all the potential hazards and risks involved in such activities.

Learn as much as possible about the outdoor recreational activities in which you participate, prepare for the unexpected, and be cautious. The reward will be a safer and more enjoyable experience.

CONTENTS

Ride Location Map   vi-vii
Map Legend   viii
List of Maps   ix
Acknowledgments   xi
Foreword   xii
Preface   xiv
Ride Recommendations for Special Interests   xxiii

INTRODUCTION   1

   Trail Description Outline   1
   Ride Configurations   3
   Topographic Maps   4
   Trail Etiquette   5
   Hitting the Trail   6
   And Now, a Word about Cellular Phones . . .   8

NEW BRUNSWICK   11

    1 Archer's Alley   16
    2 Bunker's Hill   22
    3 Odell Park   28
    4 Woolastook   32
    5 Le Sentier Petit Temis   37
    6 Mont Farlagne   40
    7 Porter's Pacer   44
    8 Mount Carleton Recreational Loop   50
    9 Mount Carleton Summit Trail   54
   10 Sentier NB Trails: Whites Brook–Mann Siding   59
   11 Restigouche River   62

12 Sugarloaf Mountain 68
13 Caraquet 72
14 French Fort Cove 76
15 Kouchibouguac 81
16 Bouctouche 85
17 Sentier NB Trails: Sackville–Port Elgin 88
18 Beaumont 94
19 Centennial Park 99
20 Hillsborough 102
21 Goose River 106
22 Marven Lake 110
23 Bennett Brook 114
24 Poley Mountain 118
25 Cripps Hill 123
26 The Mighty Salmon 129
27 Tour of Lisson Settlement 135
28 The Fundy Trail 139
29 Rockwood Park 143
30 Sentier NB Trails: West Saint John–Musquash 147
31 Grand Manan/Southern Head 151

PRINCE EDWARD ISLAND 156

32 Tignish–Alberton Confederation Trail 160
33 French River 164
34 Homestead Trail 168
35 Anne's Land Heritage Roads 172
36 Brookvale 175
37 Charlotte's Shore Heritage Roads 180
38 Bonshaw 183
39 Morell–St. Peter's Confederation Trail 186
40 Souris Confederation Trail 189
41 Elmira Confederation Trail 192

NEWFOUNDLAND 197

42 Pippy Park 202
43 Torbay Coast 206
44 Pouch Cove 211
45 South Side Hills 219
46 Freshwater Bay 224
47 Petty Harbour 227
48 Shoal Bay 231
49 Kenmount Hill 235
50 La Manche Bay 239
51 Come By Chance 244

52 Sunnyside   248
53 Clarenville   254
54 Dunphy's Pond   258
55 Trailway Provincial Park: Gander   261
56 Marble Mountain Summit Trail   264
57 Massey Drive   268
58 Pinchgut Lake   273
59 Lady Slipper Road–12-Mile Dam   277
60 Stephenville   281
61 Trailway Provincial Park: Cape Ray   285

NOVA SCOTIA   289

62 Clyburn Valley   294
63 Lake of Islands   298
64 Money Point   302
65 Trous de Saumons   307
66 Pembroke Lake   310
67 Cape Mabou   315
68 River Denys Mountain   320
69 Eigg Mountain   325
70 Wentworth   330
71 Cape Chignecto   335
72 Martock   340
73 Grand-Pré Dikes   346
74 Annapolis Valley Time Trial Loop   350
75 The Gorge   355
76 Black Rock   359
77 Delap's Cove   364
78 Fire Tower Trail   369
79 Mushpauk Lake   372
80 Liverpool–Summerville Rail Trail   376
81 Jimmy's Roundtop   380
82 Lakes Loop   385
83 Shad Bay   391
84 Wrandees   394
85 Lawrencetown Beach   400

Appendix: Metric Conversion   405
Glossary   407
Index   413
About the Authors   422

MOUNTAIN BIKE! ATLANTIC CANADA

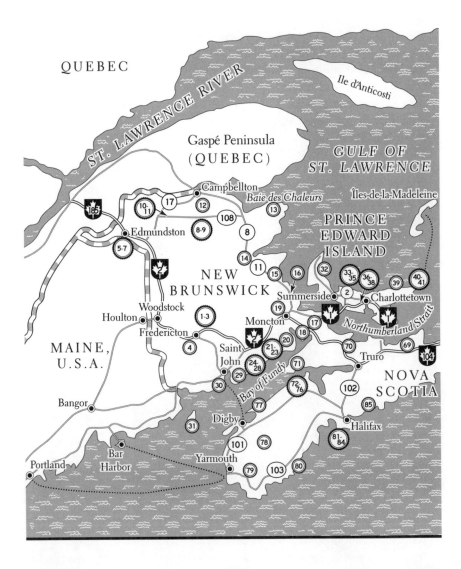

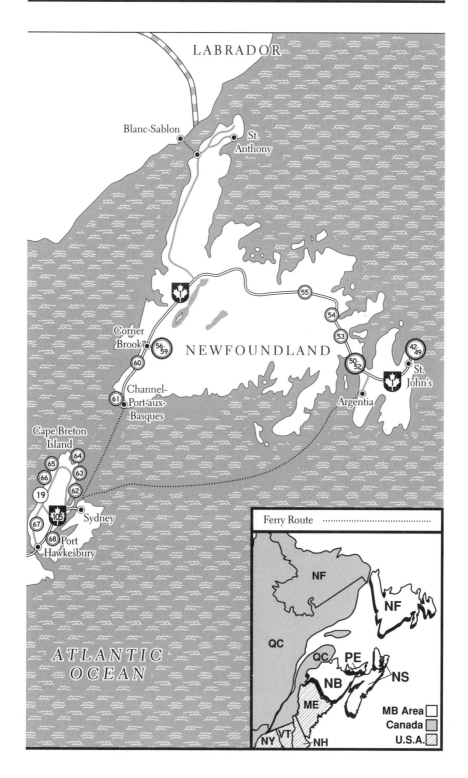

AMERICA BY MOUNTAIN BIKE   MAP LEGEND

LIST OF MAPS

1   Archer's Alley   17
2   Bunker's Hill   23
3   Odell Park   29
4   Woolastook   33
5   Le Sentier Petit Temis   38
6   Mont Farlagne   41
7   Porter's Pacer   45
8   Mount Carleton Recreational Loop   51
9   Mount Carleton Summit Trail   55
10 Sentier NB Trails: Whites Brook–Mann Siding   60
11 Restigouche River   63
12 Sugarloaf Mountain   69
13 Caraquet   73
14 French Fort Cove   77
15 Kouchibouguac   82
16 Bouctouche   86
17 Sentier NB Trails: Sackville–Port Elgin   89
18 Beaumont   95
19 Centennial Park   100
20 Hillsborough   103
21 Goose River   107
22 Marven Lake   111
23 Bennett Brook   115
24 Poley Mountain   119
25 Cripps Hill   124
26 The Mighty Salmon   130
27 Tour of Lisson Settlement   136
28 The Fundy Trail   140
29 Rockwood Park   144
30 Sentier NB Trails: West Saint John–Musquash   148
31 Grand Manan/Southern Head   152
32 Tignish–Alberton Confederation Trail   161
33 French River   165
34 Homestead Trail   169
35 Anne's Land Heritage Roads   173
36 Brookvale   176
37 Charlotte's Shore Heritage Roads   181
38 Bonshaw   184

LIST OF MAPS

39 Morell–St. Peter's Confederation Trail   187
40 Souris Confederation Trail   190
41 Elmira Confederation Trail   194
42 Pippy Park   203
43 Torbay Coast   207
44 Pouch Cove   212
45 South Side Hills   220
46 Freshwater Bay   225
47 Petty Harbour   228
48 Shoal Bay   233
49 Kenmount Hill   236
50 La Manche Bay   240
51 Come By Chance   245
52 Sunnyside   249
53 Clarenville   255
54 Dunphy's Pond   259
55 Trailway Provincial Park: Gander   262
56 Marble Mountain Summit Trail   265
57 Massey Drive   270
58 Pinchgut Lake   274
59 Lady Slipper Road–12-Mile Dam   279
60 Stephenville   282
61 Trailway Provincial Park: Cape Ray   286
62 Clyburn Valley   295
63 Lake of Islands   299
64 Money Point   304
65 Trous de Saumons   308
66 Pembroke Lake   311
67 Cape Mabou   316
68 River Denys Mountain   321
69 Eigg Mountain   326
70 Wentworth   331
71 Cape Chignecto   336
72 Martock   341
73 Grand-Pré Dikes   347
74 Annapolis Valley Time Trial Loop   352
75 The Gorge   357
76 Black Rock   361
77 Delap's Cove   365
78 Fire Tower Trail   370
79 Mushpauk Lake   374
80 Liverpool–Summerville Rail Trail   377
81 Jimmy's Roundtop   381
82 Lakes Loop   386
83 Shad Bay   392
84 Wrandees   395
85 Lawrencetown Beach   401

ACKNOWLEDGMENTS

Beyond the topography that supports this collection of rides there are the people. First of all, we would like to thank the people who offered to be our guides and who shared their trails and stories with us: Brian Adams, Richard Archer, André and Francine Arpin, Nancy Austin, Colin Banks, Greg Cashin, Dr. and A. J. Cleary, Paul Cyr, Cory and Damian, Brian Gillet, Stéphane Hamel, Chris Jarret, Dave MacDonald, Doug Miller, Terry Morrison, a New Brunswick warden, Pete-the-tooth-man Ollerhead, Outside Expeditions, John Porter, Sean Ritchie, and Patrick Sewell. For their generosity and wholehearted welcome, we also extend our sincere thanks to our hosts: Larry and Ida Adair, the Clearys, Harold Earle, Andrea Mortson and Eric Edson, Bea Murphy and family, Charlie Traverse and family, and Woolastook Park. There are also individuals for whose support of and unique contributions to this project we shall always be grateful: Irvin Leopold and Joey O'Brien, Deputy Minister Wilson, Alexander and Keith from Pembroke Lake, Arnold Kearney (for getting the ball rolling), The Sweet Guy Paul Martin, Mr. Protégé, and Luke Roy. For enhancing our research and travels with exceptional equipment, we also thank Madden Mountaineering and Casio Canada.

Finally, a special thanks to Hugh and Mary Bishop, John and Valerie Hale, and Doris Murphy and Cynthia Pernice, for their unconditional support, invaluable contributions, and lasting friendship. We shall always remember our angels, Strength and Efficiency, and we shall forever be grateful for the countless, random acts of kindness we encountered on our travels and the wonderful truth that you never know who you're going to meet on the trail . . .

FOREWORD

Welcome to *America by Mountain Bike*, a series designed to provide all-terrain bikers with the information they need to find and ride the very best trails around. Whether you're new to the sport and don't know where to pedal or an experienced mountain biker who wants to learn the classic trails in another region, this series is for you. Drop a few bucks for the book, spend an hour with the detailed maps and route descriptions, and you're prepared for the finest in off-road cycling.

My role as editor of this series is simple: First, find a mountain biker who knows the area and loves to ride. Second, ask that person to spend a year researching the most popular and very best rides around. And third, have that rider describe each trail in terms of difficulty, scenery, condition, elevation change, and all other categories of information that are important to trail riders. "Pretend you've just completed a ride and met up with fellow mountain bikers at the trailhead," I told each author. "Imagine their questions, be clear in your answers."

As I said, the *editorial* process—that of sending out riders and reading the submitted chapters—is a snap. But the work involved in finding, riding, and writing about each trail is enormous. In some instances our authors' tasks are made easier by the information contributed by local bike shops or cycling clubs, or even by the writers of local "where-to" guides. Credit for these contributions is provided, when appropriate, in each chapter, and our sincere thanks goes to all who have helped.

But the overwhelming majority of trails are discovered and pedaled by our authors themselves, then compared with dozens of other routes to determine if they qualify as "classic"—that area's best in scenery and cycling fun. If you've ever had the experience of pioneering a route from outdated topographic maps, or entering a bike shop to request information from local riders who would much prefer to keep their favorite trails secret, or if you know how it is to double- and triple-check data to be positive your trail info is correct, then you have an idea of how each of our authors has labored to bring about these books. You and I, and all the mountain bikers of America, are the richer for their efforts.

You'll get more out of this book if you take a moment to read the Introduction explaining how to read the trail listings. The "Topographic Maps" section will help you understand how useful topos will be on a ride, and will also tell you where to get them. And though this is a "where-to," not a "how-to" guide, those of you who have not traveled the backcountry might find "Hitting the Trail" of particular value.

In addition to the material above, newcomers to mountain biking might want to spend a minute with the glossary, page 407, so that terms like *hardpack*, *single-track*, and *waterbars* won't throw you when you come across them in the text.

All the best.

Dennis Coello
St. Louis

PREFACE

The foundations of this book were laid during the summer of 1992, far from Atlantic Canada and before either of us owned a mountain bike. During eight weeks of cycling through France and the northeast coast of Spain we discovered that riding can be a way of exploring a landscape intimately, at a pace that fosters a true appreciation of the unique topography and characteristics of different regions. We came to cherish cycling as a sport through which differences in language and experience can be bridged among people with nothing more in common than the bikes they ride. Furthermore, we discovered qualities within ourselves that would see us through unforeseen circumstances and propel us toward unknown destinations, as well as a common passion for outdoor activity and exploration.

Returning to our respective American and Canadian homes, we pursued post-university lives that would coincidentally introduce us both to the world of off-road biking in the same year. For Sarah, the adventure began while researching trails for *Mountain Bike! Maine* (also published by Menasha Ridge Press), while Jodi hit the trails of western Canada, exploring Alberta and parts of British Columbia. It was this happy coincidence that prepared us both for what became a celebration of the fifth anniversary of our first cycling trip: an offer to research and write a guide book to mountain biking in Atlantic Canada.

Mountain Bike! Atlantic Canada is the product of two summers of research and riding, the culmination of an exhilarating journey that allowed us to experience again the wonders of riding and traveling. We began the project with the realization that the question of mountain biking in Atlantic Canada did not have an easy answer. There were almost no books to consult and no trail maps to scrutinize. Our journey began with only the most general of missions to guide us: to find the best places to mountain bike in New Brunswick, Prince Edward Island, Newfoundland, and Nova Scotia. In every province this mission was advanced through the people we met: the guides who showed us their favourite trails; the mechanics who coaxed extra miles out of our bikes; and our many hosts, who shared not only their homes but also their stories and knowledge of an area relatively new to both of us. In our travels we discovered all the reasons that mountain biking can be an ideal way to see and experience the diverse landscape and warm hospitality of Atlantic Canada.

The mud, guts, and glory of mountain biking in Atlantic Canada.

It is our hope that this book, which has given us the opportunity to turn our experiences into a resource for other adventurers, will inspire both experienced mountain bikers and newcomers to the sport to pick up their bikes and explore the many wonderful trails that lead to the heart of Atlantic Canada.

THE HISTORY AND PEOPLE

It is thought that the first inhabitants of this part of North America were nomads who crossed the Bering Strait at the end of the ice age. Several native nations have been identified in the human history of the area. Of these, the Mi'kmaq were the largest and still make up a portion of Atlantic Canada's diverse population. An area that now forms part of southern New Brunswick was home to the Maliseet and Passamaquoddy native peoples. Additionally, the Inuit and the Montagnais still inhabit regions in Labrador. Only traces of the existence of the other three nations remain: the Maritime Archaic, the Dorset, and the Boethuk, believed to have been the predominant Indian nation in Newfoundland at the time of European contact. Over the course of European settlement these native populations were forced to retreat inland. Weakened by the depletion of the natural resources they depended on for survival, they eventually succumbed to various illnesses and are now extinct.

The first record of European exploration of the area is found in archeological evidence of a Viking settlement at L'Anse aux Meadows on the tip of the Northern Peninsula of Newfoundland. It is believed that the Norse established this settlement around A.D. 1000. However, it was not until much later that the Europeans established a permanent presence in the area. Basque fishermen probably set up the first temporary camps on the coast of Newfoundland in the 1400s. Anxious not to betray the source of their huge catches, these fishermen never claimed any land. As a result, John Cabot (Giovanni Caboto) is credited as being the first to discover the region in 1497, in his efforts to find a passage to the Indies.

The French first made their mark on the area with Jacques Cartier's voyage in 1535, when he named the river and the Gulf of St. Lawrence. This and subsequent explorations brought increased attention to the profitable fishing waters surrounding what is now Atlantic Canada. In 1605 the first permanent colony in the area was founded by the French in Port Royal (Nova Scotia). This colony was called Acadia and led to further settlements on the shores of the Bay of Fundy. This development also marked the beginning of a long struggle between the French and the English for control of the area. Throughout the late 1600s areas claimed by each country were regularly contested.

In 1713 the Treaty of Utrecht settled the status of Acadia as a British colony and forced the French to withdraw from Newfoundland as well. To offset this strong British presence on the Atlantic Coast the French developed Ile Saint-Jean (Prince Edward Island) and Ile Royal (Cape Breton Island). Between 1713 and 1755 the Acadians who had been forced to accept British authority were able to maintain a certain independence, refusing to pledge allegiance to the Crown and declaring themselves neutral. However, in 1744 war was declared in Europe between France and England. By 1755 the hostilities had intensified and spread to the colonies, and all the descendants of the original French settlers who refused to take a loyalty oath to Great Britain were expelled.

Between 1755 and 1762 most Acadian villages were destroyed and nearly 7,000 Acadians were deported. The Seven Years War (also known as the French and Indian War) filled the years between 1756 and 1763. The Treaty of Paris finally ended the war and asserted, once and for all, British claim to the area. France relinquished all of its North American holdings, with the exception of the islands of Saint-Pierre and Miquelon off the coast of Newfoundland.

After the Treaty of Paris several different groups moved into the region. Loyalists from New England turned to Atlantic Canada after the Revolutionary War, and in the early 1800s English speaking emigrants—predominantly Irish and Scottish—moved to the area in large numbers. The influence of these groups is seen in the musical and literary culture of the area as well as in place names. Irish and Scottish traditions are most pronounced on Cape Breton Island, where fiddle music, ceileighs, and highland farms still thrive. Many Irish settled on the east coast of Newfoundland. New Brunswick, also, is peppered with distinctively Irish personalities and reminders of the distinct Protestant and Catholic communities that settled along the shores of the Bay of Fundy. As you explore the rides we have included in this guidebook, you will find yourself on trails that retrace historic footpaths and lead to the remains of early settlements and forts that are evidence to the history of the conflict and development of the region.

THE LAND

Today, Atlantic Canada is renowned for its warm hospitality and is made up of four peaceful provinces: New Brunswick, Prince Edward Island, Newfoundland and Labrador, and Nova Scotia. Although the region represents only 2.5% of the Canadian land mass, it covers an impressive 539,105 square kilometres (about 208,148 square miles). This area makes up the far eastern corner of North America and is almost literally a mosaic of land and sea, comprised of peninsulas and islands surrounded by the Atlantic Ocean. Our research took us through every province and every region. with the exception of Labrador.

Geographically, Atlantic Canada is part of the Appalachian Region, forming the north end of a long belt of old mountains running northeasterly along most of the Atlantic seaboard of North America. The highest point in the region is Mount Carleton, which climbs to 820 metres (2,690 feet) above sea level in northern New Brunswick. Other mountainous regions include Newfoundland's Long Range Mountains and Nova Scotia's Cobequid Mountains and Cape Breton Highlands.

While the mountains provide some of the more spectacular scenery in the region, the valleys, plateaus, and low-lying areas provide most of the region's wealth. In New Brunswick the heavily forested mountain valleys in the north and plateau areas atop the cliffs of the Bay of Fundy have been a boon to the lumber industry. Similarly, the west coast and interior of Newfoundland has supported a large timber industry centred around Corner Brook. On Prince Edward Island the rolling flatlands have sustained generations of potato and dairy farmers, while Nova Scotia's Annapolis Valley produces a wealth of fresh fruit. Fossil fuels and metallic and non-metallic ores have been discovered off the shores of Newfoundland, in Labrador, and in areas of New Brunswick, attracting the captains of industry into once pristine wilderness and marine areas.

FLORA AND FAUNA

The relatively moist climate of the Atlantic region produces conditions ideal for forest cover. Newfoundland is situated in the largest vegetation zone in Canada, the boreal forest. The dominant tree species in this zone are the white and black spruce. Balsam fir and jack pine are also common, and other species such as white birch (known locally as tuckamore) and tamarack are also found. Cape Breton Island in northern Nova Scotia features similar forest cover. Heathlands, or barrens, make up much of the non-forested areas in Newfoundland, along with two types of peatland—bog and fen. The other provinces are characterized by Acadian forest, a typically mixed forest where softwoods are found in poorly drained areas and hardwoods dominate drier areas. Softwoods typical to the area include red, white, and black spruce; balsam fir; and lesser proportions of red and white pine and hemlock. Hardwoods include red maple, sugar maple, yellow birch, and white birch.

Each of the Atlantic Provinces is also home to a variety of wildflowers. Although spring and early summer tend to feature the brightest and showiest display of flowers, trailsides in all the provinces have flowers to share throughout the riding season. Lupine are common in the grassy verges of open and sunny trails, along with varieties of wild rose, thistle, and several varieties of vetch. Fireweed and Queen Anne's lace are plentiful as well. In Newfoundland the forest undergrowth includes bunchberries and pink lady's slipper, whereas more open, barren areas feature the magenta flowers of rhodora, sheep laurel, and Labrador tea. Newfoundland also provides prime habitat for the pitcher plant, a distinct carnivorous plant that feeds on insects and is found in peatland areas. Many of the rides included in this book also pass by ponds and lakes where aquatic plants flourish, particularly different varieties of water lily.

By far our favourite species of plant life are the berry-producing ones! Blueberry bushes and tangles of raspberries and blackberries can be found and enjoyed throughout the Atlantic Provinces. These precious plants offer an abundance of fruit that is simply the best trailside snack available. In Newfoundland the choice of fruit is even greater, including the bake-apple (or cloudberry) and tart partridgeberry (or mountain cranberry).

Wildlife in the Atlantic Provinces includes moose, caribou, black bear, deer, lynx, timber wolf, marten, beaver, porcupine, and rabbit. In our experience, moose, deer, and porcupine are the creatures you are most likely to spot from your bike, while rabbits will certainly make an appearance if you do any camping. To our delight and surprise we also stumbled into a controversy surrounding the cougar, a rare and majestic creature. Sightings of this nocturnal hunter spark conviction among those who claim to have seen its long tail or huge paws and doubt among those who do not believe it inhabits the woods on the east coast. Though hesitant to enter the debate, we can certainly vouch for the existence of at least one large catlike creature in the woods along the coast of New Brunswick.

Though mountain biking is an exclusively land-based activity, one of the greatest rewards of the sport in Atlantic Canada is the sighting of whales and seals from the many tremendous viewpoints offered by the rides in the region. There is simply nothing more awe-inspiring than the view of any of these marine mammals as they fish the waters of a protected cove or bask on the rocks near the shore. Among the numerous species of whales that visit Atlantic Canada's coastal waters, fin, humpback, minke, and pilot whales are the most often spotted. Whales are most often seen inshore from May to September, when capelin (their primary food source) are abundant.

In addition to the variety of wildlife that inhabits Atlantic Canada's woods and waters, a rich diversity of bird life thrives. Of note is the loon, the great blue heron, and the Canada goose. Eagles and osprey can be spotted in some areas, and colonies of puffins and gannets can be observed from the coast of Newfoundland. Of course, not to be forgotten among flying creatures are the blackflies, mosquitoes, and midges that sometimes fill the air. In general, June is the worst month for these pests. Although they do not really present much of a physical threat, these insects can certainly be counted among the possible psychological hazards of mountain biking in the region. In addition to insect repellents of both the herbal and high-test varieties, wearing light-coloured clothing can help to reduce their impact on your riding experience.

THE WEATHER

Atlantic Canada is coloured by the erratic moods of distinctly maritime weather patterns. This climate demands respect from all outdoor enthusiasts: changeable and unpredictable conditions can be dangerous to anyone traveling through the wilderness without the proper clothing, adequate food, and plenty of water. Precipitation in the Atlantic Provinces is plentiful throughout the year, especially around the coasts. Coastal areas are also the most likely to be shrouded in fog and exposed to the worst of high winds. The sunniest and driest places are the central, inland areas. Although spring and early summer are the driest seasons over the entire region, strong winds, changeable temperatures, and occasional thick fog banks can threaten at any time of year.

In general, the best riding conditions in the region are from June through September. These months typically feature the most moderate temperatures. In July and August temperatures can be quite warm, offering the best conditions in which to enjoy the swimming opportunities available along many of the trails. In addition to your swimsuit, it is advisable to always carry extra clothing (especially raingear) when riding in any of the Atlantic Provinces, taking particular care to pack for variable conditions in the spring and fall. We have included warnings and specific recommendations for individual rides where exposed terrain, isolated areas, or extreme conditions are likely to impact the riding.

HITTING THE TRAILS

At the time of our research, mountain biking in Atlantic Canada was just advancing into its second generation. Veterans of the sport, who were among the first to race or discover how to use a chainsaw and map out a trail, were passing on their knowledge and encouraging participation among riders of all ages. The

Throughout Atlantic Canada, there are trails waiting to be explored by mountain bikers who possess a strong spirit of adventure.

greatest increase in new riders is among teenagers, who are competing in any possible category at local and regional races. This group is also active in assisting with the construction of new trails and is among the most enthusiastic about laying the first set of tire tracks on fresh-cut single-track.

Three of the four provinces have vast areas of wilderness that are littered with informal trails and seemingly endless kilometres of dirt roads worthy of exploration. Prince Edward Island (PEI) is the exception here, where riding is characterized by more restricted trail access. Footpaths, former coach and cart tracks, abandoned rail beds, and logging or forestry roads form the base of many rides contained in this guidebook, and there are many more awaiting discovery by adventurous riders who are reasonably adept at reading a topographic map. Exploring on your own you are likely to discover that many trails have resisted overgrowth by alders, are in good condition, and are often easily navigable thanks to regular use and signage by all-terrain bike riders and snowmobile clubs.

Back on the beaten track you will find that most of the single-track exists in and around major urban centres, although there are a few that you may come upon by chance in the locales of small but ambitious groups of riders. An even smaller percentage of trails in the region enjoy the luxury of signed trailheads, services of any kind, regular maintenance, or distribution of detailed maps. Those that do are likely to be found in national and provincial parks or as part of the Trans-Canada Trail initiative. Trail development in all four provinces has recently been anchored by the progress in development of the tremendous vision of the Trans-Canada Trail. While converted railroad bed is not generally favoured amongst mountain bikers, its role in luring unsuspecting riders off-road by making it accessible to everyone cannot be underrated. For that reason, several sections of the Trans-Canada Trail and provincially related initiatives have been included in this guide.

Mountain biking in Atlantic Canada is about more than hitting a few good trails; it is an opportunity to explore and meet people and literally become part of what is the foundation-setting time for the sport in this region. It is an exciting time, when riders still enjoy the freedom to ride their favourite trails without encountering fierce opposition. Here, the spirit of the sport is still about experiencing the beauty of the landscape and celebrating the adventure of the unexpected. It should also be acknowledged that with the freedom to explore vast expanses of wilderness comes some responsibility: every person who rides must work to preserve it. Atlantic Canada is a place where the work every individual contributes to the sport of mountain biking is noticed, recognized, and truly makes a difference. It is a place where residents and visitors alike can contribute positively to the development of the sport.

USING THIS BOOK

The format of this guidebook comes from our knowledgeable editor and publishers at Menasha Ridge Press. Their categories and trail description content requirements ensure thorough coverage of regions and individual trails. While informative and enjoyable don't always go hand in hand, we have striven to accomplish both by peppering our trails with personal anecdotes from our experience of both the ride itself and the research process. We hope that you will appreciate the epic-length trail descriptions that occur occasionally even for seemingly short rides. These are often the result of many, many twists and turns and few obvious landmarks. In preparing the descriptions, we have also painstakingly converted distances from metres to feet and kilometres to miles to accommodate readers and riders on both sides of the border. Most important, these measures have been taken to help you avoid getting lost and to prevent you from losing your sense of humour on the trail.

To help you make your way through the guidebook, you will also find a section titled "Ride Recommendations for Special Interests." This section, immediately following this one, will help you choose rides based on your own preferences for land or sea, or for easy or difficult rides. We have also included categories in this section that highlight some of the unique features of mountain biking in

Atlantic Canada (i.e. Coastal and Wilderness, both of which deliver exactly what they promise). Finally, because we have documented many rides that have not previously been recorded, we have also taken the liberty of naming some of the trails. Often we have used predominant geographical features or, in the absence of such a reference, have had the opportunity to create names that we think aptly describe the ride. In some cases we have unabashedly used the real names of the masterminds behind the trail.

The result is a guidebook that is not just a collection of trail descriptions, but also the story of our experiences exploring Atlantic Canada, meeting people, and riding into previously unexplored territory or along never-before documented trails. We hope it will both guide riders to places where riding will not erode the beauty of the region and encourage people to celebrate and share in the vision of an ever-developing and expanding trail system. *Mountain Bike! Atlantic Canada* will show you how easy it is to be prepared for what you expect, while reminding you that it is more important simply to be prepared to be delighted by the wonders you never imagined. So, if the idea of pulling your car off the road and setting out on your bike through a narrow gap in the woods appeals to your sense of adventure, read on . . .

Sarah L. Hale and Jodi E. Bishop

RIDE RECOMMENDATIONS FOR SPECIAL INTERESTS

Novice & Beginner

- 13 Caraquet
- 14 French Fort Cove
- 15 Kouchibouguac
- 29 Rockwood Park
- 33 French River
- 34 Homestead Trail
- 54 Dunphy's Pond
- 59 Lady Slipper Road–12-Mile Dam
- 62 Clyburn Valley
- 73 Grand-Pré Dikes
- 78 Fire Tower Trail
- 79 Mushpauk Lake
- 83 Shad Bay

Intermediate

- 1 Archer's Alley
- 4 Woolastook
- 6 Mont Farlagne
- 8 Mount Carleton Recreational Loop
- 12 Sugarloaf Mountain
- 18 Beaumont
- 22 Marven Lake
- 23 Bennett Brook
- 25 Cripps Hill
- 27 Tour of Lisson Settlement
- 31 Grand Manan/Southern Head
- 35 Anne's Land Heritage Roads
- 36 Brookvale
- 37 Charlotte's Shore Heritage Roads
- 42 Pippy Park
- 43 Torbay Coast
- 47 Petty Harbour
- 48 Shoal Bay
- 49 Kenmount Hill
- 50 La Manche Bay
- 51 Come By Chance
- 52 Sunnyside
- 53 Clarenville
- 57 Massey Drive
- 58 Pinchgut Lake
- 60 Stephenville
- 63 Lake of Islands
- 66 Pembroke Lake
- 67 Cape Mabou
- 68 River Denys Mountain
- 69 Eigg Mountain
- 70 Wentworth
- 71 Cape Chignecto
- 75 The Gorge
- 76 Black Rock
- 81 Jimmy's Roundtop
- 82 Lakes Loop
- 85 Lawrencetown Beach

Advanced

- 2 Bunker's Hill
- 7 Porter's Pacer
- 20 Hillsborough
- 24 Poley Mountain
- 26 The Mighty Salmon
- 38 Bonshaw
- 44 Pouch Cove
- 45 South Side Hills
- 46 Freshwater Bay
- 64 Money Point
- 75 The Gorge
- 84 Wrandees

Race Circuits

- 20 Hillsborough
- 24 Poley Mountain
- 36 Brookvale
- 42 Pippy Park
- 45 South Side Hills
- 49 Kenmount Hill
- 51 Come By Chance
- 60 Stephenville
- 72 Martock
- 74 Annapolis Valley Time Trial Loop
- 75 The Gorge

Single-Track

- 1 Archer's Alley
- 2 Bunker's Hill
- 4 Woolastook
- 15 Kouchibouguac (6 kilometres)
- 19 Centennial Park (options off the main trail)
- 20 Hillsborough
- 24 Poley Mountain
- 29 Rockwood Park (interior sections)
- 36 Brookvale
- 38 Bonshaw
- 42 Pippy Park
- 45 South Side Hills
- 49 Kenmount Hill
- 51 Come By Chance
- 57 Massey Drive (initial loop)
- 70 Wentworth
- 72 Martock
- 75 The Gorge
- 77 Delap's Cove
- 84 Wrandees

Coastal

- 13 Caraquet
- 15 Kouchibouguac
- 16 Bouctouche
- 21 Goose River
- 28 The Fundy Trail
- 31 Grand Manan/Southern Head
- 33 French River
- 34 Homestead Trail
- 39 Morell–St. Peter's Confederation Trail
- 43 Torbay Coast
- 44 Pouch Cove
- 46 Freshwater Bay
- 47 Petty Harbour
- 48 Shoal Bay
- 50 La Manche Bay
- 61 Trailway Provincial Park: Cape Ray
- 64 Money Point
- 67 Cape Mabou
- 77 Delap's Cove
- 80 Liverpool–Summerville Rail Trail
- 85 Lawrencetown Beach

Mountain

- 6 Mont Farlagne
- 9 Mount Carleton Summit Trail
- 24 Poley Mountain
- 53 Clarenville
- 56 Marble Mountain Summit Trail
- 64 Money Point
- 69 Eigg Mountain

Wilderness

- 7 Porter's Pacer
- 11 Restigouche River
- 26 The Mighty Salmon
- 44 Pouch Cove
- 52 Sunnyside
- 66 Pembroke Lake

Camping

- 5 Le Sentier Petit Temis
- 8 Mount Carleton Recreational Loop
- 9 Mount Carleton Summit Trail
- 11 Restigouche River
- 21 Goose River
- 22 Marven Lake
- 54 Dunphy's Pond
- 61 Trailway Provincial Park: Cape Ray
- 63 Lake of Islands
- 71 Cape Chignecto

Family

- 3 Odell Park
- 5 Le Sentier Petit Temis
- 10 Sentier NB Trails: Whites Brook–Mann Siding

Family (continued)

- 13 Caraquet
- 16 Bouctouche
- 19 Centennial Park
- 30 Sentier NB Trails: West Saint John–Musquash
- 32 Tignish–Alberton Confederation Trail
- 34 Homestead Trail
- 39 Morell–St. Peter's Confederation Trail
- 40 Souris Confederation Trail
- 41 Elmira Confederation Trail
- 54 Dunphy's Pond
- 55 Trailway Provincial Park: Gander
- 61 Trailway Provincial Park: Cape Ray
- 62 Clyburn Valley
- 65 Trous de Saumons
- 78 Fire Tower Trail
- 79 Mushpauk Lake
- 80 Liverpool–Summerville Rail Trail

Historic Sites

- 14 French Fort Cove
- 17 Sentier NB Trails: Sackville–Port Elgin
- 25 Cripps Hill
- 27 Tour of Lisson Settlement
- 33 French River
- 35 Anne's Land Heritage Roads
- 37 Charlotte's Shore Heritage Roads
- 41 Elmira Confederation Trail
- 55 Trailway Provincial Park: Gander
- 61 Trailway Provincial Park: Cape Ray
- 68 River Denys Mountain
- 73 Grand-Pré Dikes
- 79 Mushpauk Lake

Trans-Canada Trail

- 5 Le Sentier Petit Temis
- 17 Sentier NB Trails: Sackville–Port Elgin
- 30 Sentier NB Trails: West Saint John–Musquash
- 32 Tignish–Alberton Confederation Trail
- 39 Morell–St. Peter's Confederation Trail
- 40 Souris Confederation Trail
- 41 Elmira Confederation Trail
- 55 Trailway Provincial Park: Gander
- 61 Trailway Provincial Park: Cape Ray

Loops

- 4 Woolastook
- 6 Mont Farlagne
- 12 Sugarloaf Mountain
- 15 Kouchibouguac
- 18 Beaumont
- 26 The Mighty Salmon
- 31 Grand Manan/Southern Head
- 33 French River
- 35 Anne's Land Heritage Roads
- 37 Charlotte's Shore Heritage Roads
- 50 La Manche Bay
- 56 Marble Mountain Summit Trail
- 59 Lady Slipper Road–12-Mile Dam
- 67 Cape Mabou
- 68 River Denys Mountain
- 69 Eigg Mountain
- 70 Wentworth
- 76 Black Rock
- 81 Jimmy's Roundtop
- 82 Lakes Loop
- 85 Lawrencetown Beach

Out-and-Backs

- 9 Mount Carleton Summit Trail
- 10 Sentier NB Trails: Whites Brook–Mann Siding
- 11 Restigouche River
- 16 Bouctouche
- 21 Goose River
- 22 Marven Lake
- 23 Bennett Brook
- 28 The Fundy Trail
- 30 Sentier NB Trails: West Saint John–Musquash
- 38 Bonshaw
- 39 Morell–St. Peter's Confederation Trail
- 43 Torbay Coast

Out-and-Backs (continued)

46 Freshwater Bay
47 Petty Harbour
48 Shoal Bay
54 Dunphy's Pond
55 Trailway Provincial Park: Gander
58 Pinchgut Lake
61 Trailway Provincial Park: Cape Ray
62 Clyburn Valley

63 Lake of Islands
65 Trous de Saumons
66 Pembroke Lake
78 Fire Tower Trail
79 Mushpauk Lake
80 Liverpool–Summerville Rail Trail
83 Shad Bay

Point-to-Points

5 Le Sentier Petit Temis
10 Sentier NB Trails: Whites Brook–Mann Siding
17 Sentier NB Trails: Sackville–Port Elgin

32 Tignish–Alberton Confederation Trail
61 Trailway Provincial Park: Cape Ray
71 Cape Chignecto

INTRODUCTION

TRAIL DESCRIPTION OUTLINE

Each trail in this book begins with key information that includes length, configuration, aerobic and technical difficulty, trail conditions, scenery, and special comments. Additional description is contained in 11 individual categories. The following will help you to understand all of the information provided.

Trail name: Trail names are as designated on National Topographic Series (NTS) or other maps, and/or by local custom.

At a Glance Information

Length/configuration: The overall length of a trail is described in kilometres and miles, unless stated otherwise. The configuration is a description of the shape of each trail—whether the trail is a loop, out-and-back (that is, along the same route), figure eight, trapezoid, isosceles triangle, decahedron . . . (just kidding), or if it connects with another trail described in the book. See the Glossary for definitions of *point-to-point* and *combination*.

Aerobic difficulty: This provides a description of the degree of physical exertion required to complete the ride.

Technical difficulty: This provides a description of the technical skill required to pedal a ride. Trails are often described here in terms of being paved, unpaved, sandy, hard-packed, washboarded, two- or four-wheel-drive, single-track or double-track. All terms that might be unfamiliar to the first-time mountain biker are defined in the Glossary.

Note: For both the aerobic and technical difficulty categories, authors were asked to keep in mind the fact that all riders are not equal, and thus to gauge the trail in terms of how the middle-of-the-road rider—someone between the newcomer and Alison Sydor—could handle the route. Comments about the trail's length, condition, and elevation change will also assist you in determining the difficulty of any trail relative to your own abilities.

Scenery: Here you will find a general description of the natural surroundings during the seasons most riders pedal the trail and a suggestion of what is to be found at special times (like great fall foliage or cactus in bloom).

Special comments: Unique elements of the ride are mentioned.

Category Information

General location: This category describes where the trail is located in reference to a nearby town or other landmark.

Elevation change: Unless stated otherwise, the figure provided is the total gain and loss of elevation along the trail. In regions where the elevation variation is not extreme, the route is simply described as flat, rolling, or possessing short steep climbs or descents.

Season: This is the best time of year to pedal the route, taking into account trail conditions (for example, when it will not be muddy), riding comfort (when the weather is too hot, cold, or wet), and local hunting seasons.

Note: Because the exact opening and closing dates of deer, elk, and moose seasons often change from year to year, riders should check with the local fish and wildlife department or call a sporting goods store (or any place that sells hunting licenses) in a nearby town before heading out. Wear bright clothes in fall, and don't wear suede jackets while in the saddle. Hunter's-orange tape on the helmet is also a good idea.

Services: This category is of primary importance in guides for paved-road tourers but is far less crucial to most mountain bike trail descriptions because there are usually no services whatsoever to be found. Authors have noted when water is available on desert or long mountain routes and have listed the availability of food, lodging, campgrounds, and bike shops. If all these services are present, you will find only the words "All services available in . . ."

Hazards: Special hazards like steep cliffs, great amounts of deadfall, or barbed-wire fences very close to the trail are noted here.

Rescue index: Determining how far one is from help on any particular trail can be difficult due to the backcountry nature of most mountain bike rides. Authors therefore state the proximity of homes or nearby roads where one might hitch a ride, or the likelihood of other bikers being encountered on the trail. Phone numbers of local police departments or hospitals are hardly ever provided because phones are usually not available. If you are able to reach a phone, the local operator will connect you with emergency services.

Land status: This category provides information regarding whether the trail crosses land operated by the provincial or national parks or logging companies; or land owned by the Canadian government, called Crown land; or private land whose owner (at the time the author did the research) has allowed mountain bikers right of passage; and so on.

Note: Authors have been extremely careful to offer only those routes that are open to bikers and are legal to ride. However, because land ownership changes over time, and because the land-use controversy created by mountain bikes still has not completely subsided, it is the duty of each cyclist to look for and to heed signs warning against trail use. Don't expect this book to get you off the hook when you're facing some small-town judge for pedaling past a Biking Prohibited sign erected the day before you arrived. Look for these signs, read them, and heed the advice. And remember: There's always another trail.

Maps: The maps in this book have been produced with great care and, in conjunction with the trail-following suggestions, will help you stay on course. But it is strongly suggested that you obtain even more detailed maps of the area you plan to ride.

In Canada, topographic series maps provide the basic guide for route finding. Produced as part of the National Topographic Series (NTS), they are available in a variety of scales. The most useful is the 1:50,000 scale, which provides enough detail to locate most natural features and trails. With these maps, 1 km is represented as 2 cm on the map (1.25 in = 1 mile). This is not as detailed as the maps available in the United States, but for most trails this is sufficient. Unfortunately, many of the maps are badly out of date. Some are based on information from the 1970s. As a minimum, they provide a reliable guide to traditional routes and natu-ral features. They are available from local information centres and map dealers, or can be ordered directly from the Canada Map Office; see "Topographic Maps" below.

Finding the trail: Detailed information on how to reach the trailhead and where to park your car is provided here.

Sources of additional information: Here you will find the address and/or phone number of a bike shop, governmental agency, or other source from which trail information can be obtained.

Notes on the trail: This is where you are guided carefully through any portions of the trail that are particularly difficult to follow. The author also may add information about the route that does not fit easily in the other categories. This category will not be present for those rides where the route is easy to follow.

RIDE CONFIGURATIONS

Combination: This type of route may combine two or more configurations. For example, a point-to-point route may integrate a scenic loop or an out-and-back spur midway through the ride. Likewise, an out-and-back may have a loop at its farthest point (this configuration looks like a cherry with a stem attached; the stem is the out-and-back, the fruit is the terminus loop). Or a loop route may have multiple out-and-back spurs and/or loops to the side. Length given for a combination route is for the total distance to complete the ride.

Loop: This route configuration is characterized by riding from the designated trailhead to a distant point, then returning to the trailhead via a different route (or simply continuing on the same in a circle route) without doubling back. You always move forward across new terrain but return to the starting point when finished. Distance given is for the entire loop from the trailhead back to the trailhead.

Out-and-back: A ride where you will return on the same trail you pedaled out. While this might sound far more boring than a loop route, many trails look very different when pedaled in the opposite direction.

Point-to-point: A vehicle shuttle (or similar assistance) is required for this type of route, which is ridden from the designated trailhead to a distant location, or endpoint, where the route ends. Total distant is for the one-way trip from the trailhead to endpoint.

Spur: A road or trail that intersects the main trail you're following.

Ride Configurations contributed by Gregg Bromka

TOPOGRAPHIC MAPS

The maps in this book, when used in conjunction with the route directions present in each chapter, will in most instances be sufficient to get you to the trail and keep you on it. However, you will find superior detail and valuable information in the 1:50,000 scale National Topographic Series (NTS) topographic maps. Recognizing how indispensable these are to bikers and hikers alike, many bike shops and sporting goods stores now carry topos of the local area.

But if you're brand new to mountain biking you might be wondering "What's a topographic map?" In short, these differ from standard "flat" maps in that they indicate not only linear distance, but elevation as well. One glance at a topo will show you the difference, for "contour lines" are spread across the map like dozens of intricate spider webs. Each contour line represents a particular elevation, and at the base of each topo a particular "contour interval" designation is given. Yes, it sounds confusing if you're new to the lingo, but it truly is a simple and wonderfully helpful system. Keep reading.

Let's assume that the 1:50,000 series topo before us says "Contour Interval 20 metres," that the short trail we'll be pedaling is two centimetres in length on the map, and that it crosses five contour lines from its beginning to end. What do we know? Well, because the linear scale of this series is 1 kilometre to the centimetre (roughly 1 1/4 inches representing 1 mile), we know our trail is approximately 2 kilometres long (2 centimetres × 1 kilometre). But we also know we'll be climbing or descending 100 vertical metres (5 contour lines × 20 metres each) over that distance. And the elevation designations written on occasional contour lines will tell us if we're heading up or down.

The authors of this series warn their readers of upcoming terrain, but only a detailed topo gives you the information you need to pinpoint your position exactly on a map, steer yourself toward optional trails and roads nearby, plus let you know at a glance if you'll be pedaling hard to take them. It's a lot of information for a very low cost. In fact, the only drawback with topos is their size—several feet square. I've tried rolling them into tubes, folding them carefully, even cutting them into blocks and photocopying the pieces. Any of these systems is a pain, but no matter how you pack the maps you'll be happy they're along. And you'll be even happier if you pack a compass as well.

In addition to local bike shops and sporting goods stores, you'll find topos at major universities and some public libraries where you might try photocopying the ones you need to avoid the cost of buying them. But if you want your own and can't find them locally, contact:

Canada Map Office
615 Booth Street
Ottawa, ON K1A OE9
(613) 952-7000

TRAIL ETIQUETTE

Pick up almost any mountain bike magazine these days and you'll find articles and letters to the editor about trail conflict. For example, you'll find hikers' tales of being blindsided by speeding mountain bikers, complaints from mountain bikers about being blamed for trail damage that was really caused by horse or cattle traffic, and cries from bikers about those "kamikaze" riders who, through their antics, threaten to close even more trails to all of us.

The authors of this series have been very careful to guide you to only those trails that are open to mountain biking (or at least were open at the time of their research), and without exception have warned of the damage done to our sport through injudicious riding. All of us can benefit from glancing over the following International Mountain Bicycling Association (IMBA) Rules of the Trail before saddling up.

1. Ride on open trails only. Respect trail and road closures (ask if not sure), avoid possible trespass on private land, and obtain permits and authorization as may be required. Federal and state wilderness areas are closed to cycling.

2. Leave no trace. Be sensitive to the dirt beneath you. Even on open trails, you should not ride under conditions in which you will leave evidence of your passing, such as on certain soils shortly after rain. Observe the different types of soils and trail construction; practice low-impact cycling. This also means staying on the trail and not creating any new ones. Be sure to pack out at least as much as you pack in.

3. Control your bicycle! Inattention for even a second can cause disaster. Excessive speed can maim and threaten people; there is no excuse for it!

4. *Always yield the trail.* Make known your approach well in advance. A friendly greeting (or a bell) is considerate and works well; startling someone may cause loss of trail access. Show your respect when passing others by slowing to a walk or even stopping. Anticipate that other trail users may be around corners or in blind spots.

5. *Never spook animals.* All animals are startled by an unannounced approach, a sudden movement, or a loud noise. This can be dangerous for you, for others, and for the animals. Give animals extra room and time to adjust to you. In passing, use special care and follow the directions of horseback riders (ask if uncertain). Running cattle and disturbing wild animals is a serious offense. Leave gates as you found them, or as marked.

6. *Plan ahead.* Know your equipment, your ability, and the area in which you are riding—and prepare accordingly. Be self-sufficient at all times. Wear a helmet, keep your machine in good condition, and carry necessary supplies for changes in weather or other conditions. A well-executed trip is a satisfaction to you and not a burden or offense to others.

For more information, contact IMBA, P.O. Box 7578, Boulder, CO 80306, USA; (303) 545-9011.

HITTING THE TRAIL

Once again, because this is a "where-to," not a "how-to" guide, the following will be brief. If you're a veteran trail rider, these suggestions might serve to remind you of something you've forgotten to pack. If you're a newcomer, they might convince you to think twice before hitting the backcountry unprepared.

Water: I've heard the questions dozens of times: "How much is enough? One bottle? Two? Three?! But think of all that extra weight!" Well, one simple physiological fact should convince you to err on the side of excess when it comes to deciding how much water to pack: a human working hard in 32°C (90°F) temperature needs over nine litres (ten quarts) of fluids every day. Nine litres. That's two and a half gallons—12 large water bottles, or 16 small ones. And, with water weighing in at approximately one kilogram per litre, a one-day supply comes to a whopping nine kilograms (20 pounds).

In other words, pack along two or three bottles even for short rides. And make sure you can purify the water found along the trail on longer routes. When writing of those routes where this could be of critical importance, each author has provided information on where water can be found near the trail—if it can be found at all. But drink it untreated and you run the risk of disease. (See *Giardia* in the Glossary.)

One sure way to kill the protozoans, bacteria, and viruses in water is to boil it. Right. That's just how you want to spend your time on a bike ride. Besides, who wants to carry a stove or denude the countryside stoking bonfires to boil water?

Luckily, there is a better way. Many riders pack along the inexpensive and anames Potable Aqua, Globaline, and Coughlan's, among others). Some invest in portable, lightweight purifiers that filter out the crud. Unfortunately, both iodine *and* filtering are now required to be absolutely sure you've killed all the nasties you can't see. Tablets or iodine drops by themselves will knock off the well-known *Giardia*, once called "beaver fever" for its transmission to the water through the feces of infected beavers. One to four weeks after ingestion, *Giardia* will have you bloated, vomiting, shivering with chills, and living in the bathroom. (Though you won't care while you're suffering, beavers are getting a bum rap, for other animals are carriers also.)

But now there's another parasite we must worry about—*Cryptosporidium*. "Crypto" brings on symptoms very similar to *Giardia*, but unlike that fellow protozoan it's equipped with a shell sufficiently strong to protect it against the chemical killers that stop *Giardia* cold. This means we're either back to boiling or on to using a water filter to screen out both *Giardia* and crypto, plus the iodine to knock off viruses. All of which sounds like a time-consuming pain but really isn't. Some water filters come equipped with an iodine chamber, to guarantee full protection. Or you can simply add a pill or drops to the water you've just filtered (if you aren't allergic to iodine, of course). The pleasures of back-country biking—and the displeasure of getting sick—make this relatively minor effort worth every one of the few minutes involved.

Tools: Ever since my first cross-country tour in 1965, I've been kidded about the number of tools I pack on the trail. And so I will exit entirely from this discussion by providing a list compiled by two mechanic (and mountain biker) friends of mine. After all, since they make their livings fixing bikes, and get their kicks by riding them, who could be a better source?

These two suggest the following as an absolute minimum:

tire levers
spare tube and patch kit
air pump
Allen wrenches (3, 4, 5, and 6 mm)
six-inch crescent (adjustable-end) wrench
small flat-blade screwdriver
chain rivet tool
spoke wrench

But, while they're on the trail, their personal tool pouches contain these additional items:

channel locks (small)
air gauge
tire valve cap (the metal kind, with a valve-stem remover)
baling wire (ten or so inches, for temporary repairs)

duct tape (small roll for temporary repairs or tire boot)
boot material (small piece of old tire or a large tube patch)
spare chain link
rear derailleur pulley
spare nuts and bolts
paper towel and tube of waterless hand cleaner

First-aid kit: My personal kit contains the following, sealed inside double Ziploc bags:

sunscreen
aspirin
butterfly-closure bandages
Band-Aids
gauze compress pads (a half-dozen 4" × 4")
gauze (one roll)
Ace bandages or Spenco joint wraps
Benadryl (an antihistamine, in case of allergic reactions)
water purification tablets / water filter (on long rides)
moleskin / Spenco "Second Skin"
hydrogen peroxide, iodine, or Mercurochrome (some kind of antiseptic)
snakebite kit

Final considerations: The authors of this series have done a good job in suggesting that specific items be packed for certain trails—raingear in particular seasons, a hat and gloves for mountain passes, or shades for desert jaunts. Heed their warnings, and think ahead. Good luck.

Dennis Coello

AND NOW, A WORD ABOUT CELLULAR PHONES . . .

Thinking of bringing the Flip-Fone along on your next off-road ride? Before you do, ask yourself the following questions:

- Do I know where I'm going? Do I have an adequate map? Can I use a compass effectively? Do I know the shortest way to civilization if I need to bail out early and find some help?

- If I'm on the trail for longer than planned, am I ready for it? Do I have adequate water? Have I packed something to eat? Will I be warm enough if I'm still out there after dark?

- Am I prepared for possible injuries? Do I have a first-aid kit? Do I know what to do in case of a cut, fracture, snakebite, or heat exhaustion?

- Is my tool kit adequate for likely mechanical problems? Can I fix a flat? Can I untangle a chain? Am I prepared to walk out if the bike is unrideable?

If you answered "yes" to *every* question above, you may pack the phone, but consider a good whistle instead. It's lighter, cheaper, and nearly as effective.

If you answered "no" to *any* of these questions, be aware that your cellular phone does little to reduce your risks in the wilderness. Sure, being able to dial 911 in the farthest corner of the White Mountains sounds like a great idea, but this ain't downtown, friend. If disaster strikes, and your call is routed to some emergency operator in Manchester or Bangor, and it takes awhile to figure out which ranger, sheriff, or search-and-rescue crew to connect you with, and you can't tell the authorities where you are because you're really not sure, and the closest they can come to pinpointing your location is a cellular tower that serves 160 square kilometres (60 square miles) of dense woods, and they start searching for you but dusk is only two hours away, and you have no signaling device and your throat is too dry to shout, and meanwhile you can't get the bleeding stopped, you are out of luck. I mean *really* out of luck.

And when the battery goes dead, you're on your own again. Enough said.

Jeff Faust
Author of Mountain Bike! New Hampshire

NEW BRUNSWICK

The second-largest province in Atlantic Canada, New Brunswick covers 73,437 square kilometres (28,354 square miles) and borders the Bay of Fundy to the south and the Gulf of St. Lawrence to the east. Inland, Quebec meets the northern regions of New Brunswick, while to the west, the province shares a long frontier with the state of Maine. Many travelers mistakenly pass through New Brunswick expecting little more than a simple conifered landscape and some impressive coastal views as they speed along on the Trans-Canada Highway toward Prince Edward Island or Nova Scotia. As we drove, biked and thrashed about every corner of the province, we discovered regions rich with history and character, where wildlife abound and expanses of rugged and accessible wilderness still exist.

In keeping with the migrations of native peoples and the settlement patterns of the French and British immigrants, the southern portion of New Brunswick is more densely populated than the north. The rich fishing waters of the Bay of Fundy supported the economic life of many native peoples, who only moved into the mountainous northern interior when European immigrants established permanent settlements along the southern coast. Later, the Acadians (descendants of the first French arrivals) settled on the northeastern shores and areas around the Restigouche River. New Brunswick remains Canada's only bilingual province, and while you will find the majority of its citizens speak English as their primary language, a healthy portion of the population easily shifts from English to French, and a smaller portion speaks French exclusively. Geographically, French is spoken more regularly in the north, while English is more prevalent in the south.

Initially, the native peoples of New Brunswick (the Mi'kmaq, the Maliseet and the Passamquoddy) traded fish and furs for household goods and firearms, dealing with their American neighbors as well as European fishing vessels. The native tribes established amicable relations with the French, the first Europeans to settle in the province. The next several hundred years saw both an influx of European settlement and the migration of American loyalists following America's War of Independence. Fishing and farming became the mainstays of the provincial economy, whereas for later generations, lumber, paper and pulp generated most of the wealth. Manufacturing and mining also came to play a part in New Brunswick's diversifying economy. Today, there is a shift away from a natural resource- and manufacturing-based economy toward one where tourism, communications and service-based industries play larger roles.

THE TRAILS

Mountain bikers in New Brunswick enjoy a well-developed race circuit, an elaborate network of multi-use trails, and endless kilometres of logging roads and abandoned old roads, as well as areas with developed single-track trails. If you were to retrace our tracks on each of the trails included in the New Brunswick chapter of this book, you would experience the full spectrum of the province's topography and culture. Departing from the southern reaches of the province and travelling clockwise, you would head up the Saint John River Valley. On your journey, you would leave behind the highly civilized trails of Fredericton and enter the mountainous regions of Madawaska and Restigouche. Logging roads, both in use and abandoned, riddle the hillsides surrounding Edmundston and the neighboring town of Saint-Jacques. These long, rugged roads make for extended climbing and epic rides. While you're at it, travel east into Mount Carleton Provincial Park and climb the highest peak in Atlantic Canada.

If you feel confident performing roadside repairs and possess adequate map-reading skills, continue north to the Restigouche area. This wilderness of dense forests and rough terrain demands an Indiana Jones attitude and a bike and fanny pack loaded with sufficient food, water, bug repellent, maps, tools, and a compass. Better yet, find one of those Casio Pathfinder watches that feature an altimetre and a compass before heading out into the willy-wacks. Fortunately, for those less desirous of this kind of wilderness experience, the Sentier NB Trail can provide you with a taste of the northern country by way of converted rail bed. Sugarloaf Mountain's maintained trails also provide a more tame environment, while adding the challenge of frequent hills and less-groomed trail surfaces.

Continuing to the east along the Baie des Chaleurs, you will arrive in the Gloucester region, where the Acadian peninsula juts out in the Gulf of St. Lawrence. As the name suggests, people of Acadian descent make up the majority of this region's population. After suffering expulsion in 1755, Acadians were permitted to return to New Brunswick in 1764, provided that they dispersed themselves throughout the colony. Many returned and settled along the Baie des Chaleurs, where today one finds several mostly French-speaking small towns and beaches proudly displaying the Acadian flag. Flat, populous, and charming, we fondly refer to this region as the New Brunswick Riviera. Indeed, you will find no grueling single-track here, but we recommend that you try a different pace—ride leisurely along the waterfront between neighbouring villages, allowing for several stops for snacks, browsing in small shops, and swimming at any of the many beaches along the shore.

Continuing southward along the coast, you approach Miramichi, possibly the oldest place name of Mi'kmaq origin in the province. Present-day Miramichi is actually a conglomerate of small, previously independent towns that had their industrial origins in the 1900s. A sawmill established in 1899 led the economic development of the region, and since the 1920s, the spring migration of Atlantic salmon has attracted wealthy sports fishermen into the area. Fortunately, a small portion of this area's rich history can now be explored by mountain bike. Conversion of the rail bed along the Miramichi River near French Fort Cove was just beginning at the time of our research, and we expect these stretches of the Sentier NB Trail to be well traveled upon their completion.

Further south along the Northumberland Strait, the trails are mostly easy but offer some captivating scenery, including beaches, long stretches of sand dunes, and salt marshes. In Kouchibouguac National Park, you can learn about the plants and wildlife that inhabit the area while enjoying an extensive tour of the park area that includes a magnificent stretch of single-track through the woods. The Irving Eco-Centre also offers interpretive programs as well as a fascinating extended boardwalk over the dunes to compliment your ride. As you continue down the coast back into southern New Brunswick, you will find more rail bed to explore as you approach the Confederation Bridge linking Prince Edward Island to the mainland. Of particular interest is the trail between Port Elgin and Sackville, where local communities have developed links to interesting and scenic natural and historic sites.

With three-quarters of New Brunswick under your seat, it is time to head toward the most heavily trafficked region of the province. What awaited discovery between Moncton and Fredericton was more than we had imagined. There is an excellent range of riding to be found in Moncton and on either side of the Petitcodiac River. Furthermore, the trails in Fundy National Park and the Fundy Model Forest are also easily accessible from Moncton, and are popular amongst riders from Fredericton and Saint John as well. The Fundy Model Forest in particular will not disappoint. Amongst a plethora of mountain bike rides lies an oasis to which you can pedal home after a long day of climbing and cruising on the old roads and snowmobile trails: Adair's Wilderness Lodge on Creek Road. Larry and Ida Adair understand the needs of anyone venturing off into the woods, offering a haven to hunters, snowmobilers, hikers, and most recently, mountain bikers. Spend some time with Larry, learn about the lay of the land, and you too may feel inspired to tackle "The Mighty Salmon," an epic 53-km (37-mile) journey down the Big Salmon River. Your confidence will be greatly boosted by the knowledge that Larry knows this country like the back of his hand, and you will never be beyond the reach of his pick-up truck.

On your reluctant departure from Creek Road, stop at Poley Mountain and ride the race circuit. This is one of our favourite race circuits because it offers an excellent blend of single- and double-track trails on both the uphill and downhill portions of the ride. 1999 will also bring the first Canada Cup Race to this site, focusing long overdue attention on this area among riders near and far. Your next stop should be Rockwood Park, situated just minutes from downtown

Saint John. You will lose your sense of proximity to the city almost immediately upon heading out on the old road and single-track trails of this park.

West of Saint John and close to the Maine coast rises Grand Manan Island, an excellent destination at any point in the summer for a little bit of riding in a great atmosphere. The island is only 30 km (18 miles) long and 10 km (6 miles) wide, so you can exhaust the mountain biking possibilities in a weekend, or opt to take a longer look at your surroundings from a sea kayak or whale-watching boat. Ross and Cheney Islands on the seaward side of the island also provide many walks and hikes popular among birders at certain times of the year.

Although tempted to return to Adair's Wilderness Lodge or establish residency on Grand Manan Island, we were drawn back to Fredericton to have another go at the Hell 'n' Back trails at Bunker's Hill. In preparation for these travails, we tackled the immaculate single-track of Archer's Alley, a ride well suited to intermediate riders. The next day at Bunker's Hill, we encountered mildly unfavourable conditions. Greeted by a wet, foggy morning, every pedal stroke was a victory as we negotiated the tightly twisting, rocky, mossy trails. We ended our final ride exhausted, caked in mud and hungry for something other than a Cliff Bar—the sign of a good ride, and typical of many of the rides we completed in New Brunswick. We had also learned a few things

HITTING THE TRAILS

Since such a variety of trails exists in the province, you can begin riding early in the spring and continue late into the fall. Only the northern portion of the province and the rides at higher elevations will present you with a shortened season. In these areas, spring does not arrive until May, and riding should begin no earlier than June. In the southern portion of the province, riding can begin as early as late March or April; nevertheless, many of the single-track trails and the dirt roads should be left to dry until late May or June. Another caveat: while it is virtually impossible to avoid mud in any Atlantic province on account of heavy precipitation year-round, it is worth noting that August is the driest month in New Brunswick, and we enjoyed many days of riding under sunny skies in July and September.

Over and above the weather, bugs must top your list of considerations when embarking on an excursion in New Brunswick. Carry some kind of bug repellent if you are at all sensitive to mosquito or black flies, or plan to ride quickly and continuously on the trails! Since the province is characterized by extensive forest cover, the mosquito and black fly populations are significant, doubtless exceeding the human population exponentially. You will certainly encounter black flies throughout the summer in the northern reaches of the province, where Mount Carleton and the Restigouche area take the prize, in our experience, for black fly infestation. In the southern portion of the province, the black flies are less intense—but mosquitoes proliferate, even in urban areas such as Fredericton, Saint John, and Moncton.

On this topic and others you will find more detailed information within the individual rides. In many cases we will recommend topographic maps that are produced by the Survey and Mapping Branch, Department of Energy, Mines and Resources of the federal government. These are highly recommended, if not imperative to excursions into the wilderness. By and large, the trails we have explored are unmarked, and you can easily become lost by missing a turn. Another valuable resource is *The New Brunswick Atlas*, which acts as a middle resource between the provincial road map and the more detailed topographic maps. For sections of rail bed and out-and-back rides, the maps in this book will often be sufficient and will enable you to explore the entire province cost effectively. Few rides require only hand-produced maps, generally available at the trailhead, or brochures available from Visitor Information Centres throughout the province. Do not hesitate to combine resources, bringing with you every possible map and description of the area you are riding in. Maps, water, spare tubes and patches are things you can never have too many of when you are heading out on these trails.

To obtain topographic maps for any part of the province, contact one of the offices of the New Brunswick Geographic Information Corporation.

The following list of resources has been assembled to assist you further in your travels through New Brunswick:

Service Offices of the New Brunswick
  Geographic Corporation
Bathurst: (506) 547-2090
Edmunston: (506) 735-2713
Fredericton: (506) 453-3390
Moncton: (506) 856-3033
Saint John: (506) 643-6200

New Brunswick Tourism
P.O. Box 12345
Fredericton, NB E3B 5C3
(800) 561-0123

The Radical Edge
386 Queen Street
Fredericton, NB E3B 1B2
(506) 459-3478

Bungay's Bicycle & Snowboard Shop
647 Mountain Road
Moncton, NB E1C 2P2
(506) 389-2880

Adair's Wilderness Lodge
R.R. #4
Sussex, NB E0E 1P0
(506) 432-6687

RIDE 1 • Archer's Alley

AT A GLANCE

Length/configuration: 12- or 14.5-km loop (7.4 or 9 miles)

Aerobic difficulty: Moderate; many short ascents, a longer climb beneath a power line, and one steep climb on the longer loop

Technical difficulty: Intermediate to advanced; primarily single-track trails

Scenery: Fields and woodlots on the west side of the Nashwaaksis Stream

Special comments: This is a tough ride to follow, with many options; find a local rider to escort you!

Everyone has their favourite "backyard" ride, the trail or network of trails they hit after work to let off steam or to escape from the suffocating mayhem of an urban centre. Archer's Alley is the work-in-progress of an avid rider who operates according to the principal that if you want to ride, you've got to build the trails. The result is a backyard ride that resembles something close to a mountain bike park. Archer's Alley is comprised of an extensive network of trails that run between Claudie Road and the west bank of the Nashwaaksis Stream. From a foundation of woods roads and snowmobile trails, an ever-growing series of immaculate single-track trails have been cut that allow riders to stretch their legs and test their skills. The trail system, which is maintained, developed, and expanded every year, boasts a striking contrast between all the features of urban riding (mixed terrain, highway crossings, power lines, detours around contentious areas) and some of the best single-track in New Brunswick.

The ride we have described is a 12-km (7.5-mile) loop with an optional extension to a high look-off that adds a significant climb and pushes the distance to 14.5 km (9 miles). Either option follows a combination of single- and double-track trails, gravel roads, a snowmobile trail beneath a power line, and a portion of the Sentier NB Trails. All said, the riding in Archer's Alley is fairly technical and can be extremely rigourous if you move along at a fast pace. Advanced bikers will relish the course as a fun training ride, and intermediate riders will find just the right balance of trial and tribulation to keep them coming back again and again.

General location: Fredericton, on the north shore of the Saint John River.

Elevation change: Most of this ride is characterized by short climbs and descents. The longer loop option features an additional climb that adds significantly to the elevation gain for the entire ride.

… NEW BRUNSWICK

RIDE 1 • Archer's Alley

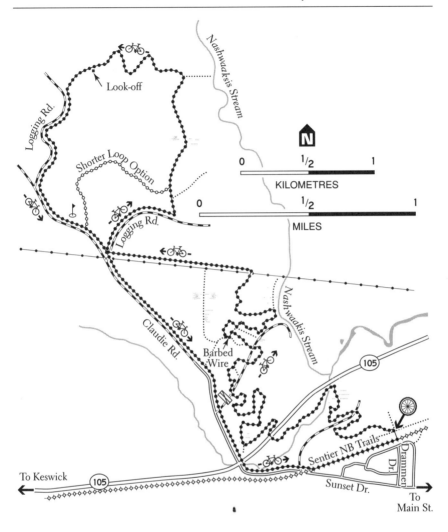

Season: Conditions are best from June through October. Certain sections of the trail network will be quite wet in the early spring and after heavy rainfall.

Services: All services are available in Fredericton.

Hazards: This ride crosses NB Highway 105 twice, and each time you will have to carefully negotiate fast-moving traffic. Additionally, the trail juts out around a tangle of barbed wire at one point. Otherwise, the only risk is getting turned around and finding yourself exploring either more or less of the trail system than you had intended.

Rescue index: Throughout this network of trails, homes or roads will be nearby and often within sight.

Land status: Primarily private land with informal access secured.

Maps: The government topographic maps for this area are Fredericton 21 G/15 and Burtts Corner 21 J/2. However, none of the trails in Archer's Alley are indicated on these maps and only a few of the surrounding roads and landmarks are visible. As of our last visit to Fredericton, a local rider had created a rough map of the trail system from GPS readings. You will probably find a copy of this map at the Radical Edge on Queen Street, where maps highlighting local rides are pinned up on the wall.

Finding the trail: From downtown Fredericton, take the Westmorland Street Bridge to Fredericton North. Stay in the right-hand lane and follow signs for Main Street. Turn left when you reach a **T** junction with Main Street. Continue straight through two sets of traffic lights. At the third light, turn left on Sunset Drive, crossing a stone bridge over the Nashwaaksis Stream. Follow Sunset Drive for approximately 2 km (1.25 miles) and then turn right on Drammen Drive. Follow Drammen Drive to its end, where there is just enough space to park a car. The ride begins over a low embankment that drops down to a section of the Sentier NB Trails.

Sources of additional information:

The Radical Edge
386 Queen Street
Fredericton, NB E3B 1B2
(506) 459-3478

Notes on the trail: Once you have popped over the embankment that separates Drammen Drive from the Sentier NB Trail, look ahead to the left for a small gap in the trees on the other side of the rail trail. Follow a short connecting trail through this gap to a **T** junction with a fairly wide, sandy trail. Turn left and then immediately veer to the right, riding away from the line of trees that you just rode through and toward a prominent white pine. At the base of the tree turn left into the woods, heading up a short, steep bank.

This early section of the ride will take you through a pine forest along a hard-packed dirt trail with few exposed rocks or roots. Keep to the widest, most obvious trail through this area until you come to a fork. Bear left onto a narrower trail that will take you out of the woods to the edge of a strawberry field. Turn right and immediately follow the first trail you see back into the woods. This trail will curve around to the left and quickly reach a **T** junction with a wider, dirt trail. Turn right and then continue straight past a trail branching off on the right. Keep to the main trail, passing a narrow path on the left before reaching a distinct fork in the trail. Bear left at this fork, onto a single-track trail that will take you through a meadowlike area that is overgrown with alders and some pines. You will emerge at the edge of a grassy clearing at a **T** junction with a double-track trail.

An exemplary stretch of immaculately maintained single-track in Archer's Alley.

Ride straight through this intersection, across the grass, to pick up a hard-packed, double-track trail with a grassy median. Pass a wide dirt trail branching off to the right and ride over an irrigation pipe that may or may not be well covered with earth. Continue straight on this main trail, which becomes a wide, hard-packed dirt road, and pass a trail branching off to the left. A short distance farther on, the main trail curves sharply around to the right at a point where another trail merges in from the left. Bear right around this curve.

As you follow the road around to the right, look for a narrow, single-track trail heading into the woods on the left. Follow this trail, which creates a short loop through the woods, until it reconnects with the dirt road at a **T** junction a short distance farther on. Turn left and continue down a slight slope, crossing a wet area before reaching the grassy bank on the south side of Highway 105. Turn left and ride parallel to the road until the metal guardrail by the side of the road ends. Turn left here, heading down the grassy bank, and look for another narrow trail heading back into the woods.

In the woods, you will ride over a series of whoop-de-doos before the trail evens out again. At a fork in the trail, choose either option; both trails reconnect a short distance farther on. You will soon emerge back at the side of Highway

105. Cross the highway and turn left. Begin looking for the entrance to a single-track trail down the bank on your right. This trail is located between two highway signs that post the speed limit as being 70 kilometres per hour, and just before a yellow sign that indicates an upcoming curve in Highway 105. Turn right and drop down the grassy embankment to the single-track trail.

The trail continues to the right but almost immediately swings to the left through a sharp hairpin turn and connects with a trail beneath a single pole line. Follow the trail beneath the pole line, heading west. After just a short distance the trail swings to the right, away from the pole line. At a fork in the trail, bear left. Ride until you come to a vague **T** junction with a narrow, single-track trail. Turn right and then, almost immediately, bear left along a less obvious single-track trail. When we rode here there was an orange metal can top nailed to a tree to mark this trail. You will follow this trail, which essentially parallels a road off to the left. After negotiating a particularly rocky and rooty section of trail you will be able to make out some homes ahead of you. The trail ahead deteriorates somewhat, and you will want to trace a tight, right-hand turn onto another single-track trail.

This next section of the ride features a technically challenging climb with some exposed rocks and small whoop-de-doos on the way up. Be aware, also, that the conditions on this stretch of trail can be rather wet in the spring. At the **T** junction at the top of the hill turn right to begin a loop that will bring you back up to this trail just a short distance to the left. The loop begins with a descent to a three-way intersection. Turn left here and climb along another fairly challenging trail, where numerous small dips and large boulders make picking the right line crucial to making it up with no dabs. Eventually you will reach a **T** junction at a large pine tree. Approximately 40 m (130 feet) to the left is the point where you began this loop. To continue the ride, turn right.

Keep to the most well-worn trail through this next section, following it down to the right and through a partially cleared area. Rocks and boulders dominate this stretch of trail, which swings around to the left and past some log piles off to the right. You will quickly meet up with a wide double-track trail at a **T** junction. This trail is the main woods road through the area, and most of the single-track trails create loops that branch off and then reconnect with it at another point. Turn right at this intersection and follow the double-track trail for only a short distance before turning left back into the woods on a narrow single-track trail marked by a large white birch tree. Although there may be some flagging tape marking this turn, you shouldn't count on it. Essentially it is the first trail that you will come to on the left. At a fork on this little loop, bear left. After a very short distance you will reconnect with the main double-track trail at a **T** junction. Turn left and, at the first opportunity, turn right onto another single-track trail, along which you will roll over a series of whoop-de-doos. Continuing a short distance on this trail will reconnect you with the main double-track trail.

This time, turn left on the main trail and then immediately right up another single-track trail back into the woods. You will climb a very short distance up this trail before bearing right at a fork. Veer up to the left past a trail option heading down to the right and find yourself at another **T** junction. Turn right and ride carefully up this next trail, which juts out to the left around some barbed wire.

Not too far from the barbed wire you will reach a **T** junction with a wide grassy trail. The ride continues to the right along this trail, but it is worth noting that you can turn left here instead and ride out to Claudie Road through a field. This route provides a quick exit from the woods should you need to shorten your ride for any reason.

Following the grassy trail to the right to continue the ride, you will descend slightly and the trail will become overgrown and less passable. At this point, look to the right for a narrow single-track trail that winds through an area of pine trees. You will come to a vague four-way intersection (the trail on the right is quite indistinct and heads up into a patch of ferns). Turn left and then left again at a **T** junction with a slightly wider trail. You will cross a little rocky causeway before reaching another **T** junction with the main double-track trail.

Turn left down the main woods road. You will descend on this trail, veering to the left and then turning left onto a trail that will take you down toward Nashwaaksis Stream. Just beyond a log jump you will come to a fork. The trail on the right goes through a large dip and continues along the bank of the stream, getting progressively more wet and overgrown. Be sure to turn left at this fork, away from the stream. You will climb along a challenging trail that includes several significant depressions. When the trail opens out at a vague grassy corridor, follow it up to the left and then back to the right, crossing over the cleared strip between the trees. Follow the trail through the trees and out to a power line. Turn left and begin climbing along a grassy double-track trail that follows alongside the power line. You will pass another grassy trail branching off to the left and continue to climb until, after a considerable distance, the trail reaches a **T** junction with a dirt road.

Looking over your right shoulder at this point you will see a logging road branching off of the dirt road. Turn right and follow this logging road, passing to the side of a cable that bars vehicular access to the road. You will ride into the clearing of an old logging yard, where a pile of harvested and never-collected logs still lies. Beyond this clearing, just as the road begins to descend, look to the left and turn left onto a grassy single-track trail. At a fork in this trail, bear left and head up a slight slope along a grassy trail that will lead you to the edge of a field.

It is at this point that you can decide to extend your ride along the longer loop option or begin the return route of the shorter loop. For the short loop, turn left at the edge of the field and look for a trail that turns back into the woods on the left. This section of the ride follows a wide, hard-packed dirt trail through a pretty stretch of woods and is by far the easiest section of the trail system. You will emerge from this trail at a **T** junction with Claudie Road, a wide dirt road. There will be a golf course on your right, and the power line you rode up earlier is just a short distance down on the left. Turn left on Claudie Road and follow it downhill, eventually continuing on pavement all the way down to a four-way intersection with Highway 105. Cross straight over this intersection onto Sunset Drive. Then cross the road and pick up the rail trail that forms part of Sentier NB Trails. Follow the rail trail back to where you began the ride, at a low embankment on the right that leads to the end of Drammen Drive.

The longer loop begins at the edge of the meadow. Ride across the meadow, heading diagonally toward the far left corner. Continue to follow the trail as it descends into the woods, and stay alert because you must cross a rocky little stream at the bottom of the hill. Beyond the stream the trail climbs a short dip and opens out at a cleared field. Once again, bear diagonally across the field to the left and begin up a subtle but steady climb through tall grass. At the far corner of this field follow a trail back into the trees. Bear right a short distance farther and descend slightly to a **T** junction with a double-track trail. Turn left, heading uphill quite steeply. The trail follows a series of switchbacks uphill and finally reaches the high point of the ride, where the view sweeps out across the landscape below. Catch your breath and then continue on the trail, following it out to a wide dirt logging road. Follow this logging road to a **T** junction with another dirt road, Claudie Road. Turn left, and head downhill. On your way down you will pass the golf course on the left as well as the trail that connects the short loop option with Claudie Road. Unless you want to head back down the power line and ride the single-track trails back to the trailhead, follow the final directions of the short loop option out to Highway 105, where you will pick up the rail trail back to Drammen Drive.

RIDE 2 • Bunker's Hill

AT A GLANCE

Length/configuration: 10-km (6.2-mile) loop

Aerobic difficulty: Rigourous; short hills, steep grades, and technical terrain make this a real workout

Technical difficulty: Advanced; rocks, exposed roots, and steep climbs on tight, twisting single-track trails

Scenery: Pines, birches, and alders line the narrow, twisting trails

Special comments: Hook up with some local riders in order to fully appreciate and explore this ride

Gnarly and single-track are words that generate two responses from mountain bikers—they love it or hate it. If you are in the former group and enjoy the kind of riding that defies logic, Bunker's Hill is a place you need to

RIDE 2 • Bunker's Hill

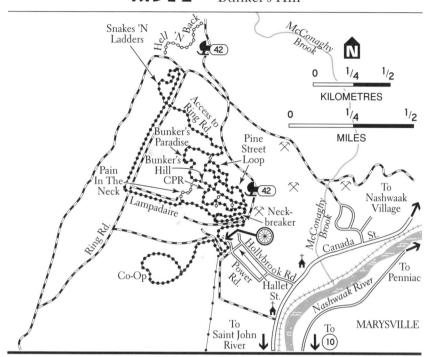

visit. It doesn't seem possible that while rattling between rocks and labouring to maintain some momentum over stretches of twisted exposed roots you can make a turn between a handlebar-width opening in the trees. Yet, despite the improbability, riders are executing these maneuvers on a regular basis on the trails of Bunker's Hill. On the 10-km (6-mile) network of trails we describe here, you will have several opportunities to do this and much more. In total, there are probably 15 km (9 miles) of trails that will offer endless hours of challenge in infinite combinations.

Bunker's Hill was created by a group of local riders who were bored with snowmobile trails and with traveling outside the city to ride some single-track; so, they began to build their own in a pocket of land that wouldn't see any further development. The result is an ever-growing network of advanced trails comprised of three main loops: a lower loop containing many smaller loops, the upper "Hell 'n' Back" loop, and the "Co-Op" loop (a new section of trails on the other side of Tower Road). All of the trails emanate from the city's water tower and are bordered by residential streets and a main snowmobile trail — making it virtually impossible to get lost. However, it is entirely possible that you will become disoriented. Not only is it wise to hook up with local riders to familiarize yourself with the trail system, but you are also likely to catch their enthusiasm for every twisted metre of these trails.

General location: On the north shore of the Saint John River in Marysville, across the Saint John River from Fredericton.

Elevation change: The riding around Bunker's Hill is characterized by many short, steep climbs, but the total elevation change is insignificant.

Season: Due to the technical nature of the terrain, avoid this trail during or after a rainfall. The driest days are likely to be found from late June to September.

Services: The trail is located just a quick jaunt over the bridge from downtown Fredericton, where all services may be found. To tap into the local network of riders or for any bike-related needs, visit the Radical Edge at 386 Queen Street (phone (506) 459-3478).

Hazards: The trails are narrow, and at times steep and very unforgiving. They should not be attempted by beginner riders not only because they can be dangerous, but also because they will likely dissuade you from ever venturing off-road again. Anyone riding these trails should be aware that you will cross a section of wire fence on the "Ring Access Road."

Rescue index: The area covered by this ride is bordered by residential streets. Assistance is never far from the trail.

Land status: Private land with permitted public access.

Maps: None of the trails on this ride will appear on any map, but for an overview of the area, see *The New Brunswick Atlas* (map 70, section E-1). It gives you an idea of just how small an area in which this network of trails covers as well as its borders. Also, as of our last visit to Fredericton, a local rider had created a rough map of the trail system from GPS readings. You will probably find a copy of this map at the Radical Edge on Queen Street, where maps highlighting local rides are pinned up on the wall.

Finding the trail: From downtown Fredericton, cross the Westmorland Street Bridge to the north side of the Saint John River. Across the bridge, continue to a four-way intersection with Union Street and turn right. You will pass through several intersections before turning left onto Gibson Street. Continue up Gibson Street, still following it once it turns into Canada Street. You will curve around a bend to the left and pass Marysville Baptist Church. Turn left onto the first street after the church, Hollybrook Road. Continue up Hollybrook to Hallet Street and turn left. Just one block over you will come to an intersection of Hallet Street and Power Road. You can park on the far side of the intersection near the wooded area.

Sources of additional information: To hook up with a club ride or for any bike-related needs, visit The Radical Edge at 386 Queen Street (phone (506) 459-3878).

Notes on the trail: From the intersection of Power Road and Hallett Street, climb the paved road heading to the water tower. At the top of the short hill turn right onto a single-track running parallel to the fence. The trail turns left, then climbs a short hill and brings you to a small open area at the base of the water tower. Turn right at the clearing, onto a single-track trail heading downhill. The trail descends and brings you to a **T** junction with a double-track trail. This is Snowmobile Trail 42, the main snowmobile trail that you will encounter frequently on the ride. At this point, you will be able to see a gravel pit down the trail to the right and a trail sign indicating a twisting trail ahead. Turn left, heading slightly uphill, and ride a very short distance before turning right onto a narrow single-track trail. This trail will bring you to a fork with the "Pain In The Neck" trail to the left and "Neck Breaker" on the right. Bear right on "Neck Breaker".

This is a short single-track trail that winds deftly through the woods, mostly descending. After a short distance, "Neck Breaker" meets at a **T** junction with the main snowmobile trail (Trail 42). Turn left, at which point you will see a sign that indicates an upcoming curve in the snowmobile trail. Almost immediately, you will want to turn back into the woods on the left, following another narrow, single-track trail. This trail is appropriately named "CPR," as it climbs steadily along very technical terrain. You will cross a trail with no name and, a short distance up the hill, "CPR" makes a hairpin turn to the left. This turn will bring you to a short, gnarly section of trail that winds tightly through the trees with plenty of exposed roots and rocks. The trail will gradually curve to the right and bring you to a **T** junction with "Bunker's Hill." This, our guide explained, is "the fun and easy" double-track that acts as the main artery for the trail system. Most of the other trails within this network branch off of and connect back to "Bunker's Hill." At this point in the ride, turning left would take you uphill toward "Bunker's Paradise," and turning right offers access to both the "Pine Street Loop" and Snowmobile Trail 42. Turn right onto "Bunker's Hill" and begin to descend. Before the trail reaches a **T** junction with the main snowmobile trail, you will come to a four-way intersection of trails. Turn left here, heading toward a stand of pines, to begin the "Pine Street Loop."

The "Pine Street Loop" is a narrow single-track that zigzags uphill through ferns and woods. It is slightly easier than the "CPR" trail, but there are areas where many exposed roots make the trail treacherously slippery when wet. At the first fork you come to, bear left to begin the loop; the right-hand trail is the one on which you will complete the loop. Just a short distance further, you will come to a second fork in the trail. Bear right here; the trail on the left is a shortcut back out to "Bunker's Hill." Along the next section of the trail, you will ride through rolling, twisting turns in the woods, still following a hard-packed surface with some sections of exposed rock. At the next trail junction, a short spur on the left heads out to the downhill section of "Bunker's Paradise." Bear right here, following the second half of the "Pine Street Loop" as it descends back to the beginning of the loop. A **T** junction marks the end of the loop, at which point you must turn right and retrace your tracks back up to the short-cut out to "Bunker's Hill."

Racing through fresh cut single-track at Bunker's Hill with the Radical Edge Rats.

The short-cut to "Bunker's Hill" will be the left-hand trail of the next fork you come to. Turn left when you reach this point and ride a short distance to a **T** junction with a wider, double-track trail. This trail is "Bunker's Hill"; turn right and begin riding uphill toward "Bunker's Paradise". You will pass the end of both the "CPR" and "Pain In The Neck" trails on your left as you climb gradually. Just when you adjust to this easy, park-like section of the ride, you will reach the beginning of "Bunker's Paradise." The area resembles a bunker, and there is plenty of evidence that a war has been fought here — a war fought between mountain bikes and ATVs — in a dark, black muddy section of trail at the bottom of a steep climb. Bikers claim that ATVs have torn up the trail in their efforts to climb the hill and continue ahead on the trail. In fact, we are told the single-track climb has been left as a narrow opening between large rocks and tree stumps for exactly one purpose: to prevent ATVs from riding through the area.

Beyond this war zone, the single-track continues to be very technical, winding through an area of small pines and large boulders. The trail will soon begin to descend, and only the most proficient of riders will be able to navigate the steep, technical terrain. As you make your way downhill, you will pass a single-track on your right; this is the short spur that connects with the "Pine Street

Loop." Eventually, you will reach a **T** junction with the main snowmobile trail (Trail 42). Turn left and ride to a **Y** intersection just a short distance ahead. At the fork, bear left onto the narrower trail, a wide ATV trail that serves as the access route to the "Ring Road."

As you head up this trail, you will have to cross over an old wire fence that now lies across the trail. Otherwise, this is a relatively harmless trail with just a few rolling whoop-de-doos. A short distance beyond the fence, you will arrive at a **T** junction with the "Ring Road" (also a wide ATV trail). Turn right and then left almost immediately onto a narrow, single-track trail. This trail needs almost no description as its twisting up and down path through the woods is summed up by its name: "Snakes and Ladders." You will follow this trail out to another **T** junction with the "Ring Road."

At the **T** junction with "Ring Road," you can turn left onto the single-track trail that leads to "Hell 'n' Back." This part of the system, which loops around and back on Snowmobile Trail 42 to reconnect with the "Ring Road" access trail, is the most technically challenging of all the trails and not recommended on wet days. To continue this ride along a more moderate route, turn right onto the "Ring Road."

As you make your way along this fairly straight stretch of trail, you will pass the entrance to "Snakes and Ladders" on your right, and then on your left, the access trail that you rode up earlier. Continue straight, following the "Ring Road" to a long, rocky downhill. Toward the bottom of the hill the trail sweeps around to the right, bypassing an open clearing of boggy ground. Continue beyond the bog and ride straight for about a kilometre (one-half mile) to a **Y** intersection with the "Lampadaire," or "Street Light" trail. Bear left onto this narrow single-track, which winds through an open forest. Conditions on this trail tend to be more overgrown than on others, and you may find yourself riding with absolutely no idea of what the trail surface looks like beneath the undergrowth. Toward the end of the "Lampadaire" trail you will pass through a swampy area and veer to the left, riding through an alley of ferns. You will then reach a **T** junction with the "Pain In The Neck" trail.

Turn right on "Pain In The Neck" and continue downhill to the intersection of this trail and "Neck Breaker." Turn right and you will find yourself, almost immediately, at a **T** junction with the main snowmobile trail (Trail 42). Turn left and continue on the snowmobile trail, past the sign indicating that the trail twists and turns ahead. When you can make out a gravel clearing ahead of you through the trees, look for a narrow trail on the right. Turn right, and pedal back up this trail to the base of the water tower. Bear left as you reach the tower and follow the fence back to the paved extension of Power Road.

If you are up for some more trails at this point, you can continue riding to the "Co-Op." This is a brand new loop that is scheduled for expansion in the years ahead. To access it, descend the paved slope in front of the water tower to the intersection of Power Road and Hallet Street. Turn right, heading into the woods on a double-track trail. Immediately after descending a short, steep slope with loose rock, turn right onto the access trail to the "Co-Op." When you reach a **Y** intersection, bear left and then, at the next opportunity, turn left onto a narrower trail. This trail is flat, and you will continue through a grassy area before reaching another ATV barricade. At this point, the trail becomes quite narrow and you will have to push your way through a series of low branches. Beyond this area, the trail curves around to the right and brings you to a **T** junction. This junction marks the beginning and end of a loop that is best ridden clockwise. Bear left, and ride for approximately 0.5 km (0.3 mile) before watching for an abrupt turn to the left. Be sure to follow the trail to the left at this point, bypassing a patch of bog. Beyond the bog, you will continue to climb for a short distance before the trail levels off briefly and then descends through a bend to the right. This is a moderate descent over rocky and grassy terrain that is best ridden at a constant, rolling speed. At the bottom of the hill, you will arrive back at the first intersection, having completed the loop. Turn left and retrace your tracks back to the trailhead.

RIDE 3 · Odell Park

AT A GLANCE

Length/configuration: 6 km (3.6 miles) of trails that form several loops through the park

Aerobic difficulty: Easy; short and flat with only one moderate climb

Technical difficulty: Basic; suitable for families and riders of all abilities

Scenery: Wooded park with botanical gardens

Special comments: Best enjoyed by families with small children

Fredericton has many kilometres of bicycle pathways throughout the city, but for a family excursion, a contained environment can make for a more enjoyable experience. Odell Park offers that and an escape from the traffic of downtown Fredericton. This short ride should satisfy curious young minds if you stop to wander around the Fredericton Botanic Garden, visit the animals in the petting zoo, and take some time to play in the spacious green park. The 6 km (3.6 miles) of bikeable trails that loop around the park touching on each of these features.

Odell Park is situated on a hillside overlooking Fredericton. The main trail through the park is a well-graded, gravel-dusted, multi-use trail that is easy to follow. All of the trails are well signed, and by following the trails along the perimeter of the park you can minimize the slope, on both the way up and down the

RIDE 3 • Odell Park

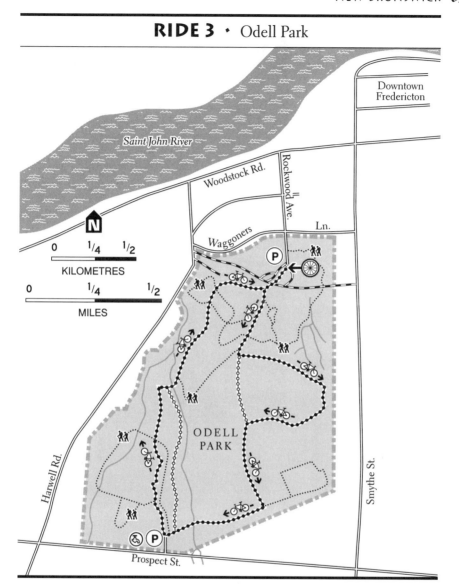

hillside. We avoided the most strenuous climb by following the "Main Woods Trail" that winds its way up the east side of the park. The rest of the ride is mostly flat, with one long descent that takes you past the botanical garden. You will end the ride on a flat woods trail that eventually emerges at the parking area.

General location: In Fredericton, on the south side of the Saint John River.

Elevation change: From top to bottom you will gain and lose 40 m (130 feet) of elevation in the park.

Under the shade of the towering pines, the trails at Odell Park offer a welcome retreat for leisurely rides in Fredericton.

Season: Due to the ease of the terrain and crushed gravel surface, it is possible to ride here from spring melt in April to the first snowfall in November.

Services: All services are available in Fredericton.

Hazards: None.

Rescue index: The park is situated in a residential and commercial area very near to downtown. It is likely that you will be able to rely on other park users for assistance. There is also a phone in the parking area near the trailhead.

Land status: Municipal park.

Maps: A map of the park with highlighted trails and distances is included as part of *The City of Fredericton Trail Guide*, distributed by the Fredericton Trails Coalition. This map can be obtained at the Visitor Information Centre at the intersection of Queen and York Streets in downtown Fredericton, or opposite Odell Park at a Visitor Information Centre off the Trans-Canada Highway.

Finding the trail: From downtown Fredericton, take King Street west, which will continue as Woodstock Road. Continue along Woodstock Road and turn left onto Rockwood Avenue. Wilmot Park is on the left at this intersection. The parking area for Odell Park is a short distance ahead, just beyond the intersection with Waggoners Lane.

Sources of additional information: To acquire a copy of the trail guide brochure, contact Fredericton tourism at (506) 460-2041. Further information on Fredericton trails can be obtained by contacting:

Fredericton Trails Coalition
P.O. Box 3715
Station B
Fredericton, NB E3A 5L7

Notes on the trail: From the parking area, begin by riding straight up toward a junction of trails near a large sign posting information on the park. You will see an animal enclosure on your left. Continue straight past the sign, and you will pass a footpath branching off to your left. Bear right, heading up trail #1, which is called the "Main Woods Trail" on the map. Continue past another footpath branching off on the right and proceed to a four-way intersection with the Aboretum Trail. Continue straight to the next main intersection. As you approach the intersection, you will pass another footpath on the right before turning left immediately to continue following the "Main Woods Trail" (ahead, the trail continues as the "Main Woods Trail Link"). From here, the "Main Woods Trail" makes a short loop around the edge of the park and will bring you past the reservoir, which is marked by two large water towers. The trail bends to the right around the water towers and then meets at a **T** junction with the "Main Woods Trail Link" to the right and the "Main Woods Trail" to the left. Turn left, continuing uphill.

At a fork in the trail, on the hilltop, bear right and descend a short hill. You will pass the "Black Forest Link" trail on the right and follow the "Main Woods Trail" toward the Prospect Street parking area. You will enter the parking area, and then turn right onto a gravel trail with a rope across the entrance. Proceed over a small wooden bridge toward a display and information board for the Fredericton Botanic Garden. Continuing past the information board, the trail progresses downhill on a slight bend to the right. You will descend quite quickly on the trail due to its moderate slope. The first trail on the left provides access to the botanical garden. (You will have to park your bike and walk around the garden, as bikes are not permitted inside.) Beyond the botanical garden the trail continues downhill to the Garden Centre. Bear right, ignoring the left spur that heads toward a paved road.

The trail wraps around the garden centre, and you will pass several varieties of compost bins before entering the woods. Upon entering the woods, there is a brief stretch of gravel before the trail returns to the standard chip rock surface of the multi-use trail. Continuing on that trail, you will pass a narrow trail on the right and then cross a small brook. At a four-way intersection with a dirt track on the left and another gravel trail on the right, continue straight. Arriving at a **T** junction, turn right. A short distance beyond the turn you will emerge at a multiple intersection near the trailhead. Ahead, there is a large, open green space and the animal enclosure to the right. To return to the parking lot, continue straight on the gravel trail.

RIDE 4 • Woolastook

AT A GLANCE

Length/configuration: 7-km (4.3-mile) loop, with many options available for an extended ride

Aerobic difficulty: Moderate; short hills on rolling terrain

Technical difficulty: Intermediate single- and double-track trails, with one advanced downhill

Scenery: Wooded slope drops to the water's edge on the arm of Mactaquac Lake

Special comments: Different race circuits are developed here every year

Driven by the enthusiasm of its owners, Woolastook Park is an exemplary recreational facility. Recently privatized, the park has been rejuvenated and redesigned to the point that it can accommodate a broad range of visitors. Woolastook hosts an annual mountain bike race that is part of the New Brunswick points series and attracts riders from all over the province. It is a prized destination by riders in Fredericton, and you can't beat these trails for uninterrupted, intermediate single- and double-track riding from start to finish.

There were about 15 km (10 miles) of completed trails at the time of our visit, but you can expect more to be added every year until the land is fully developed. The trails can be ridden in various combinations, easily creating interesting rides from 5 to 30 km (3 to 18 miles) in length. The 7-km (4-mile) loop described here traces the perimeter of the trail network and covers the full range of trails offered. It combines stretches of relatively flat terrain with a number of steep, challenging climbs and descents that make for a good workout when ridden fast. Adding to your enjoyment of riding here is the fact that water borders the trails on three sides. Not only does it offer refreshing views, but it also makes it virtually impossible to get lost or stranded. Also, you can punctuate your ride with a swim or a trip down the waterslide!

General location: Just 10 km (6 miles) west of Fredericton off the Trans-Canada Highway.

Elevation change: A total gain of 165 m (540 feet) on a series of moderate and short climbs.

Season: Spring riding will be wet and muddy, but you can begin as early as the end of May and continue through October.

Services: The park offers swimming to day visitors and an excellent campground

RIDE 4 • Woolastook

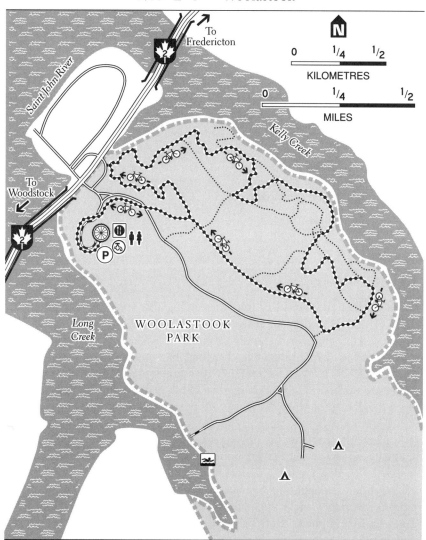

for those looking for overnight accommodations. There is a café and small store, where meals, snacks, and beverages can be purchased. The folks at the canteen will also fill up your water bottles. Access to the trails is free of charge. All bicycle-related needs should be met at any of the bike stores in Fredericton.

Hazards: You will be presented with a technically challenging, short but steep descent midway through the ride. Many riders elect to dismount and hike this section of trail to avoid collision with any number of trees or jagged, exposed rocks.

Rescue index: You will never be more than a few kilometres (a couple of miles) from the park entrance or the campground entrance, where people can usually be found.

Land status: Private park.

Maps: An excellent orienteering map showing all the developed trails may be purchased at the park office.

Finding the trail: From Fredericton, take the Trans-Canada Highway west. The park is approximately 10 km (6 miles) outside the city limits and is well signed. The exit is on the right side of the highway, just before the bridge over Long's Creek. You will loop around an underpass onto the main access road to the park. At the first fork, bear right toward the office and water park. Ample parking is available at the top of the hill near the office and canteen.

Source of additional information:

Woolastook Recreation Park
R.R. #6
5171 Route 2
Upper Kinsclear, NB   E3E 1P9
woola@nbnet.nb.ca

Notes on the trail: Departing from the parking area near the office, head back down the gravel road to the main park access road. Once you have passed a gate, you will come to a **T** junction with the main road. Turn right and continue up the road a short distance, watching for a large opening into the woods on your left. Turn left at the entrance to a double-track trail that is signed for hikers and bikers and begin on a gradual climb, passing under a power line. At the end of the climb you will come to a fork and bear left onto a smooth stretch of single-track.

A short distance along the single-track, turn left at the first opportunity onto another single-track trail that continues downhill through the woods. The trail snakes its way down, passing under a power line and across a double-track dirt trail. Continue straight, still descending through the trees, before literally dropping onto a grassy bank by the side of the main access road into the park and the Trans-Canada Highway. Bear right on the grass for a very short distance and then turn right onto a single-track trail at a narrow opening in the bushes. After passing through the opening, there is a short, steep climb back up the embankment, and then the trail continues as a slightly off-camber single-track with some exposed roots.

Arriving at a **T** junction with a grassy trail, turn right, beginning your climb up a moderate hill. As you approach the top, you will ride through a recent cut to a **T** junction with a double-track trail. Turn left and continue climbing for a short distance to a fork in the trail. At the fork, bear left on a level stretch of double-track that eventually curves around to the right. Just past the curve and after a slight downhill, you will turn left onto a narrow single-track trail branching off the main trail. This trail may be marked by flagging tape, as it is part of the race circuit. This is a short downhill that you will follow past a single-track

Gorgeous single-track trails draw both recreational riders and competitive racers to the scenic woods of Woolastook Park.

that branches off to the left through some raspberry bushes. Bearing right past this offshoot, you will swoop back uphill, almost completing a **U**.

At the end of the climb the trail will come to a **T** junction with the recently cut "Summit Loop" trail. This was a new addition to the network during our research. Due to recent cutting, the double-track was quite challenging in sections because of the large exposed roots and tree remains strewn across the trail. A single-track trail will merge in on the left, and then you will arrive, very quickly, at a fork. Bear right onto the single-track and continue to a **T** junction with a double-track trail. At the junction, turn left, following the double-track that will narrow as you advance through the woods. As the trail begins to descend, look for a single-track branching off to the left. Turn left and follow the trail as it almost backtracks in the direction you have come from. Watch closely for a fork in the trail, where the ride continues to the right. The left offshoot merely reconnects with the previous single-track you followed to the last **T** junction. Following the trail to the right will connect you with the advanced downhill.

This is a section of the ride best suited to technically proficient riders with a high tolerance for risk. The descent is relatively short but very steep. There are drop-offs over jagged patches of exposed rock and trees positioned as highly unforgiving obstacles. Even during races, many riders opt to run through this section of the ride. Toward the bottom of the hill the trail evens out and curves around to the right. This is a fast and smooth stretch of single-track that will eventually bend away from the water.

A short climb and a fork mark the end of this stretch of single-track. Bear left and continue around a bend to a small stream and boggy section. A few logs have been laid corduroy-style across the trail to help reduce erosion from this crossing. Past this section you will come to another fork in the trail where a single-track loop curves up to the right. Although it looks like it might be preferable to ride this trail in the opposite direction (downhill), continue up and your efforts will be rewarded. The climb is not terribly arduous, but it does present some small whoop-de-doos, which are always more difficult on an uphill slope. At the top the trail levels off and bends to the left, bringing you to a swift, somewhat rocky, downhill. As you approach the bottom, be prepared to make an equally swift right-hand turn back onto the double-track trail (after completing the downhill, you are just a few metres ahead of where you started the climb).

Following the double-track, you will continue along a fast stretch of trail. There is a hairpin turn to the left, and the trail begins to descend slightly. Continue downhill, toward the water, until you reach a fork. At the fork, bear right, heading back uphill. A short distance along this trail, you will reach an intersection with the "Kelly Creek Cove" trail. This is a short out-and-back trail to the water on which riders are asked to minimize their impact by sticking to the middle of the trail. From this point the ride continues uphill to the right. Continue straight, past a trail on the right and following a sign for the campground road. A short distance beyond this trail intersection, bear right. The double-track trail that continues straight ahead here merely leads out via the campground access road. The double-track trail to the right climbs gradually over the next 200 m (219 yards) before gradually descending through some muddy areas. Keep to the main trail, passing several side trails on both the left and right, until you reconnect with your starting point beneath the power line, on your left. When you reach the campground access road, turn right to exit the trail system and retrace your tracks to the parking area.

RIDE 5 · Le Sentier Petit Temis

AT A GLANCE

Length/configuration: 33-km (20.5-mile) out-and-back (16.5 km [10.25 miles] each way)

Aerobic difficulty: Easy; this trail follows an old rail bed with virtually no change in elevation

Technical difficulty: Beginner; smooth, gravel-dust trail with an even surface

Scenery: Natural habitats and communities along the Madawaska River

Special comments: You can cross the border into Quebec to extend the ride

The section of converted rail bed between Edmundston and the Quebec border marks the start of the Petit Temis Linear Inter-Provincial Park. The entire park spans 130 km (70 miles), passing rivers, lakes, and towns as it makes its way to Rivière du Loup. Along the way there are several opportunities to stop at parks and recreational facilities for swimming and other activities. There are several campgrounds and other cyclist-friendly services along the way, which makes this a popular destination for families. In particular, there are several bicycle rental companies and tour operators in the Edmundston area who can provide equipment, maps, and guided tours of the Petit Temis and surrounding area.

On this 33-km (20.5-mile) out-and-back, you will depart from the waterfront of Edmundston and wind back and forth along the Madawaska River to the community of Saint-Jacques. You will pass Les Jardins de la République Provincial Park, which has a picnic area and camping facilities as well as a botanical garden. Beyond the park you will continue along a wooded stretch of trail alongside the river and eventually arrive at the Quebec border. The ride is easy and follows a flat, gravel-dust trail that is suitable to all ages and abilities. Arriving at the border, you may choose to extend the trip to Temiscouata Lake—roughly 20 km (12 miles) farther west—for swimming and hopefully a vehicle shuttle back to Edmundston.

General location: The trailhead is located at the Pavillon de L'estacade, overlooking the Madawaska River in downtown Edmunston.

Elevation change: There is virtually no change in elevation throughout the length of this ride.

Season: This trail can be ridden from the day the snow melts in the spring to the next snowfall, late the next fall. In general, May to October are the preferred

RIDE 5 • Le Sentier Petit Temis

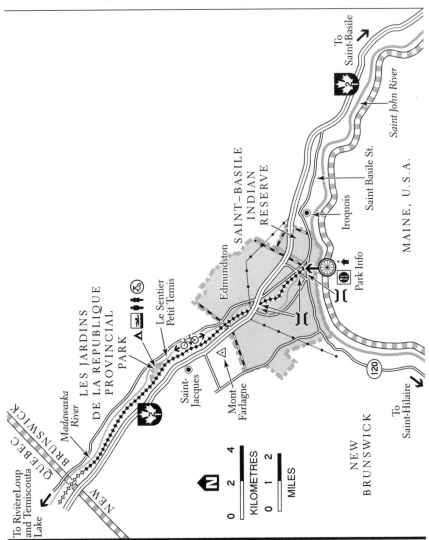

months for cycling. Fall foliage will contribute to the scenery of this ride in September and October.

Services: A café, telephone, bike store, and bike rental company are located at the trailhead. Farther along the trail, at the Jardins de la République Provincial Park, there is a water fountain, full camping services, and picnic tables. More picnic tables are located at frequent intervals along the trail. All other services are available in Edmundston.

Hazards: None.

Rescue index: The trail frequently passes through communities and recreational areas that are well populated and have several services. You are never far from assistance.

Land status: Interprovincial park.

Maps: Several brochures with detailed maps are available at the Visitor Information Centre near the New Brunswick border. The Temiscouata Bicycle Map, combined with an Edmundston city map, is an excellent resource.

Finding the trail: From the Trans-Canada Highway, follow Exit 18 into downtown Edmundston. You will enter onto boulevard Hébert and travel south, past a strip mall with a Tim Hortons, to rue Victoria. Turn left and continue on Victoria around a bend to the right and across the railway tracks. At the newly developed area along the waterfront, the start of the Petit Temis is marked by the Pavillon de L'estacade. A small parking lot is located immediately to your right, or alternative parking may be found a short distance farther down the road on a short street running parallel to the park.

Source of additional information: Le Canotier is located at the trailhead. It offers bike rentals and guided tours, and houses several informational brochures on the trail and the area. It is located at 116 rue Victoria (phone (506) 735-7173).

Notes on the trail: Departing from the Pavillon de L'estacade, you will follow the trail beyond the café and bike rental hut along the Madawaska River. Continue straight ahead, ignoring offshoots to the right that will take you into downtown Edmundston. After passing your second trail option heading into downtown, the trail will take a sharp bend to the right. The trail traverses the outer edge of the Edmundston Golf Course all the way to boulevard Acadie. Dense trees line this portion of the trail, making it highly unlikely that you will encounter any golfers or golf balls.

Cross boulevard Acadie and continue on the multi-use trail. The trail curves around to your left and crosses a bridge over the Madawaska River. Just before the bridge there is an optional trail to the right that connects with rue Victoria. It will return you to Edmundston on a paved road. Across the bridge the trail continues inland, parallel to boulevard Acadie. As you approach the Edmundston city limits and head toward Saint-Jacques, the trail nears the Madawaska River. The trail winds along the open river valley, passing by small forested and cottaged islands and marinas. Shortly after passing an abandoned rail car you will enter the town of Saint-Jacques.

A short distance beyond Saint-Jacques, Les Jardins de la République Provincial Park marks the half way point to the Quebec border. In addition to water fountains and picnic tables situated close to the trail, the park features a botanical garden and a swimming area, which make it a great place to stop for a break. Beyond the park the trail continues along the river, although farther from its banks. The trail is lined with trees on either side and continues uninterrupted to the Quebec border. There are several rest areas along the way that feature picnic tables and, occasionally, toilets. Continuing along the trail, the border will appear ahead. It is clearly signed by a large wooden archway. From here, whether you choose to continue ahead or return to Edmundston, the route is obvious along the trail.

RIDE 6 · Mont Farlagne

AT A GLANCE

Length/configuration: 23-km (13.8-mile) loop

Aerobic difficulty: Tough; long, challenging climbs on paved and dirt roads

Technical difficulty: Intermediate; lots of climbing on rocky dirt roads followed by an extended grassy descent

Scenery: A mostly wooded ride with panoramic views of the St. John and Madawaska River Valleys

Special comments: A rewarding tour with good climbs and a smokin' descent

Situated close to the Maine and Quebec borders, Edmundston is a bilingual city with a vast pulp and paper industry that trades with both the United States and Canada. Mont Farlagne is one of the highest peaks in the Edmundston area, and home of the local skill hill. A tour up and down this mountain entails departing from downtown Edmundston, following paved roads to the eastern edges of the city, and then climbing logging roads up the back side of the mountain. After descending the front side of the ski hill, you will end up near Le Sentier Petit Temis, the multi-use trail that follows along the Madawaska River. This loop touches on almost every corner of Edmundston, totalling 23 km (13.8 miles) over a variety of terrain.

Extended climbing on dirt roads and a rocketing descent down the ski hill make this ride best suited to fit intermediate riders. On your ascent of the back side of the mountain during the first half of the ride, you may appreciate the opportunity to take in the view over the Saint John River Valley into Maine. This is an excellent opportunity to refuel with some water in preparation for the final climb up the dirt road to the mountaintop; it's also a great place to finally clear your shades of the sweat that's been accumulating while labouring up the hill. From the top of the mountain, looking over the front side: you will get a view of the Madawaska River Valley that continues into Quebec. On the return

RIDE 6 • Mont Farlagne

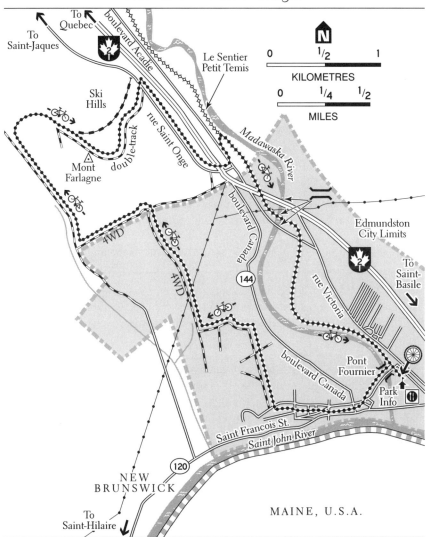

along the multi-use trail you will follow the Madawaska River most of the way back to Edmundston.

General location: The trailhead is located in Edmundston, near the New Brunswick borders of Maine and Quebec.

Elevation change: You gain 210 m (710 feet) of elevation on the climb up Mont Farlagne, reaching a maximum elevation of 490 m (1,600 feet) at the top.

Season: Expect mud in the spring, but riding may begin as early as late May and continue to October.

Services: All services are available in Edmundston, including bike accessories and service from Jessome's Source for Sports, located at 12 rue D'Amours in Edmundston (phone (506) 739-6322).

Hazards: None.

Rescue index: Throughout the ride you are never far from major roads or residential areas, where you can seek assistance from passersby.

Land status: The logging roads cut through Crown land and the final descent follows a run on a private ski hill where public access is permitted.

Maps: Although none of the logging roads appear on any map, it is still useful to refer to government topographic map Edmundston 21 N/8. Although it has fewer trail markings, *The New Brunswick Atlas* has an adequate map of the area (map 21, section B-3).

Finding the trail: Traveling west on the Trans-Canada Highway, follow Exit 18 into downtown Edmundston. You will enter onto boulevard Hébert and travel south, past a strip mall. Follow boulevard Hébert to rue Victoria and turn left. Continue along Victoria around a bend to the right and cross the railway tracks. A small parking lot is located immediately to your right, at Pavillon de L'estacade.

Sources of additional information: You may find other riders or be able to reach members of the local mountain bike club through Jessome's Source for Sports.

Notes on the trail: Departing from the pavilion, turn left onto the main paved road, rue Victoria, and climb the short hill. Continue around the bend to the left, past a branch in the road to the right. At the first four-way intersection, turn left on 34th Avenue and cross the Pont Fournier. Across the bridge the road becomes rue de L'Eglise, which you will follow to a four-way intersection with chemin Canada. Continue ahead, past a church on the right and Jessome's Source for Sports on the left. Beyond here the road narrows and you will continue on rue D'Amour's. Immediately after the road bends sharply to the right, turn left onto rue Bellevue. Here you begin a steep climb all the way to a fork in the road. At the fork, bear right onto rue Nadeau and continue to an informal **Y** intersection with a gravel road.

Looking out to your left before heading up the gravel road, you can see the sprawling St. John River Valley. Then, without further delay, bear right and continue the climb on the gravel road. At the first fork, bear right and continue past a couple of logging roads branching off to the right. At a four-way intersection, continue straight. Beyond this point, the road evens out for a short distance before heading up one last hill and then descending. As you descend, follow the main road around to the left to a **T** junction, where you will turn right onto a dirt road. You will pass a small pool through a cleared area and follow the road around to the right as it approaches a power line. Under the power line you will come to a slight rise in the trail. Look to the left at this point and branch off onto a slightly less maintained dirt road.

Paul and Sarah begin the long anticipated descent down Mont Farlagne.

This road bends around to the right, and you will pass a rejuvenating clearcut on the left that blooms with wildflowers in the early summer. When you come to a **T** junction, turn left and descend to a second **T** unction with a wide, graded dirt road. Turn right and ride on the road for nearly 2 km (1.2 miles). When you reach an old sports club marked by a sign reading "bienvenue à tous les sportifs," turn right off the main road and ride through the parking area. The old clubhouse will be on your left as you ride through the parking area and continue up a dirt road. Ignore all of the side trails on the left and right until you come to a **Y** intersection. Bear left at this fork and ride out to a meadow at the top of Mont Farlagne. Traverse the top of the mountain on the trail to the right. This will bring you to an intermediate ski run, with lights running along it. Proceed with caution! On this downhill you will gain some serious speed and have several opportunities to catch some air.

At the end of the descent, continue out to Rue Saint Onge. Turn right onto the paved road and follow it back toward downtown Edmundston. You will pass a **Y** intersection with a dirt road branching off to the right before the paved road curves around a bend to the left and passes under the Trans-Canada Highway. Continue ahead to a **T** junction with boulevard Acadie, or NB Highway 144. Cross the road and turn left, following it along the shoulder to a grassy patch under the Village de Saint-Jacques sign. Cut across the grass and turn right onto the gravel multi-use trail.

The multi-use trail is part of the Sentier NB Trail system. This particular stretch is part of Le Petit Temis, which extends between Edmundston and

44 ATLANTIC CANADA

Rivière du Loup in Quebec. Continuing to the right on the trail, you will cross the Madawaska River and arrive at an intersection with boulevard Acadie. Cross the road and continue along the trail, which enters the Edmundston Golf Course. At a vague fork where the main trail curves to the left and another trail branches off diagonally to the right, bear left, following the main trail. After rounding another bend to the right, the trail will continue straight. A short distance along, it will curve gently to the left and eventually approach the edge of the Madawaska River. As you make your way along the river, there are a few trails branching off to the left, heading into downtown. Continue straight to return to the Pavillon de L'estacade.

RIDE 7 • Porter's Pacer

AT A GLANCE

Length/configuration: 28-km (17.4-mile) combination (three loops: 12.4 km [7.7 miles], 2.7 km [1.7 miles], and 9 km [5.6 miles], connected through two short spurs, 0.5 km [0.3 miles] and 1.4 km [0.9 miles], ridden in both directions)

NB

Aerobic difficulty: Tough; there are several extended climbs in addition to many rolling hills

Technical difficulty: Intermediate to advanced; everything from paved roads to hard-packed single-track

Scenery: Along primarily forested trails you'll explore the hilly countryside around Edmundston

Special comments: Be prepared for a continuous series of hills and all kinds of terrain

This ride traces a complicated course through the hilly countryside just east of the Madawaska River in Edmundston. You will cross the Iroquois River several times along this ride, riding up and down the hills that rise above its narrow valley. The ride is ingeniously pieced together from an extensive network of ATV trails, old logging roads, and single-track trails that are connected through a few brief stretches of pavement. The route is actually a series of three loops, connected by way of two short spurs that you will ride twice, once in each direction. The lower loop is 12.4 km (7.7 miles), the middle loop a short 2.7 km (1.7 miles), and the upper loop 9 km (5.4 miles). The spur between the lower and

RIDE 7 • Porter's Pacer

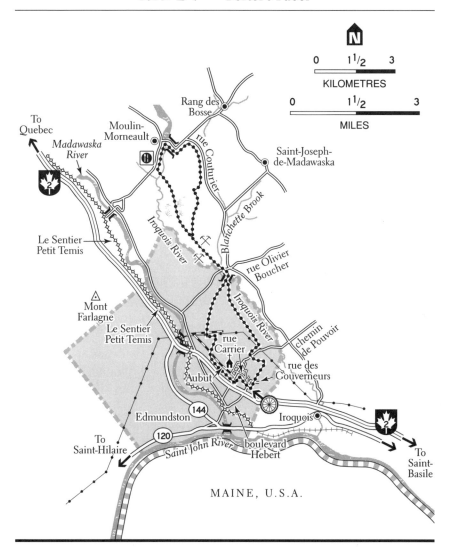

middle loops crosses a snowmobile bridge over the Iroquois River and is just half a kilometre (three-tenths of a mile) long. The second spur, connecting the middle and upper loops, extends beyond a gravel pit and covers 1.4 km (just less than 1 mile). The end result is a ride approximately 28 km (16.8 miles) in length that extends through the woods between Edmundston and the town of Moulin-Morneault.

You might, with good reason, ask who was responsible for creating such a ride. We suspect that our guide actually designed this course with the intention of staggering our minds and bodies with all of the best terrain Edmundston has to offer in just one ride. In truth, John Porter is one of the city's most well-known riders, and he knows the trails in this area as only someone who has grown up riding and racing here could. In addition to the many hills that make this an aerobically challenging ride, the length of this ride and the varied trail conditions demand both physical fitness and at least intermediate-level riding skills.

General location: East of the Madawaska River in Edmundston.

Elevation change: This ride features constant changes in elevation, for a total elevation gain of approximately 300 m (1,000 feet).

Season: You will find the best riding conditions in this area from June through September.

Services: All services are available in Edmundston. In addition, you will pass by a small convenience store about half way through the ride, in the town of Moulin-Morneault.

Hazards: Active tree harvesting operations may be under way along some sections of this ride.

Rescue index: Throughout the length of this ride you will not venture far from secondary roads and homes.

Land status: A combination of private land, logging roads, and public rights-of-way.

Maps: Although the trails that this ride follows are not indicated, the roads that encompass this ride are marked in *The New Brunswick Atlas* (map 21, sections B-1, B-2, and B-3). For additional detail, consult the government topographic map for Edmundston (21 N/8).

Finding the trail: From downtown Edmundston, drive up toward the Trans-Canada Highway on boulevard Hébert. Continue straight, passing beneath the highway. Continue straight past rue Carrier on your left, and pass the regional hospital on your right. Boulevard Hébert ends at a sharp turn in the road to the right, where the road continues as rue des Gouverneurs through a residential area. There is a small pulloff to the left at this corner, and a trail continuing straight uphill alongside a power line. Park in the gravel pulloff by the side of the road. This ride concludes with a steep descent down the trail you can see following the power line.

Sources of additional information: None.

Notes on the trail: From the parking area at the corner of boulevard Hébert and rue des Gouverneurs, ride back down boulevard Hébert. At a stop sign at a three-way intersection, turn right on rue Carrier. Follow rue Carrier through a residential area, continuing straight through several intersections. When you come to the intersection of rue Carrier and chemin du Pouvoir, turn left. Ride downhill toward the Trans-Canada Highway and turn right on Aubut, just before chemin du Pouvoir descends beneath the highway. Follow Aubut until the road turns to gravel, and then continue straight on the unpaved portion of the road.

Responding to a dare, John Porter plunges down the sheer face of a huge mound of sand and gravel in the hills around Edmundston.

Riding along the wide gravel road, you will pass a church on the right. As you continue, you will pass a very rocky trail that branches off on the right and climbs steeply uphill. After passing two more such trails on the right, you will climb a short hill. At the crest of this hill, turn off the gravel road and head uphill on a steep, rocky, double-track trail branching off on the right. Although this turnoff is not marked in any way, it is fairly easy to find if you are careful not to descend on the gravel road beyond the crest of the hill.

As you struggle uphill on this rocky trail, the combination of loose rock and a steep grade serves to create a technically and aerobically challenging ascent. Continue straight past a trail branching off on the right. When you reach a four-way intersection beneath a transmission line, turn left and follow a wide, grassy, double-track trail. You will descend slightly before reaching a **T** junction with a paved road. Turn right on this road, which is Rousseau, and follow it toward a sharp bend to the right. Instead of following the road around this bend to the right, bear left and descend a short, steep embankment to a double-track trail. This trail, essentially an old logging road, follows a power line and makes no significant turns or bends along its entire length. You will know you are on the right path when you pass a small brick building on the right.

Beyond the brick building, you will pass a logging road branching off to the right. Be sure to bear left here, keeping to the main trail, which will continue to be obvious. At a four-way intersection of dirt roads, continue straight. Then ride past a dirt road descending on the left and an open gravel pit on the right. You will begin to climb steeply beyond this point. Toward the crest of the hill you will pass a hiking trail on the right and a dirt road descending to the left. Continue straight and enjoy a rolling descent over a combination of hard-packed and loose rock conditions all the way down to the Iroquois River.

As you approach the river at the bottom of the hill, you will pass a logging road branching uphill to the right. This road is the path you will take to complete this lower loop at the end of the ride. For now, to continue the ride, descend to a small parking area at the bottom of the hill and cross the Iroquois River, using a wooden snowmobile bridge. The trail beyond the bridge will curve around to the left and connect with a paved road. This is rue Olivier Boucher. Cross the road and pick up the trail on the other side.

The trail on the other side of rue Olivier Boucher is somewhat difficult to follow, but essentially heads back toward the bank of the Iroquois River. The first section of the trail passes through a grassy area and will connect you with another paved road on which you want to bear left. Ride straight past another trail on the left, one on the right, and past two small brick buildings. Cross a small bridge marked with yellow-and-black diagonally striped lines. Beyond this bridge, bear left onto another dirt road. You may notice a fountain on the right at this point, and you will be traveling north. Bear right onto a new gravel road, from which you will see the river on your left. Beyond this point, the trail diminishes to a wide single-track trail through the woods and follows along the side of the river for a short distance.

Following the trail as it turns up to the right, away from the river, you will reach a **T** junction. Turn left here and then continue straight past a trail on the left. Continue straight again, through a four-way intersection of single-track trails. You will quickly arrive at the next portion of the ride, which traverses a large gravel pit that presents a bizarre landscape of steep gravel piles. This area is something like a huge gravel sandbox, where the most playful of mountain bikers will be able to amuse themselves, and impress others, with daredevil jumps off of steep ledges and down the sheer face of huge mounds of sand and gravel. Bear right off the trail you followed to the gravel pit, and follow a vague trail heading east-southeast across the sand.

When you reach a **Y** junction at the edge of the gravel pit, bear left. You will skirt the edge of a little patch of trees, beyond which it looks like another gravel pit on the right. You will be following a double-track dirt trail at this point. Bear right at a **Y** intersection in this trail, riding past a narrow trail on the left and heading toward a small corrugated iron shack. Keeping the shack on your right, and passing a vague dirt road on the left, continue riding on the main dirt trail, which swings slightly to the right. When you reach another **Y** intersection, bear right and begin climbing. At the next fork in the trail, bear left. The trail on the right at this junction is the path on which you will return to complete the upper loop of the ride.

The beginning of this upper loop follows a wide double-track trail. There are some areas along this trail where water and generally swampy conditions create tricky, technically challenging sections of riding. After a considerable distance through the woods, you will arrive at a **T** junction. Turn left and head downhill. After a very short distance, you will arrive at a small farm situated in a fairly large gravel clearing. Bear left through this area and, again after a very short distance, find yourself at a place called the "Aqua-Zoo." Bear right and follow the main driveway away from the zoo. You will pass a road branching off on the right before crossing the Iroquois River. Beyond the river, pass a trail branching off on the left, and continue to follow the main road out to a **T** junction with a paved road. This road is the one that runs between Saint-Jacques, to the left, and Moulin-Morneault, to the right. Turn right and ride on pavement toward Moulin-Morneault.

As you approach the village of Moulin-Morneault, the road follows a sharp bend around to the right and back over the Iroquois River. There is a small canteen, or convenience store, on the left here, where you can stop for something to eat or drink. Past the canteen, follow the main road around the bend to the right, passing another paved road heading uphill on the left. After crossing the river, the road will climb steeply. Toward the top of the hill, as the view opens out across a landscape of rolling hills, turn right on rue Couturier. This turnoff will be the first one you come to on the right.

Following rue Couturier, you will descend, still on pavement, along a few rolling hills and past homes on either side of the road. As the road begins to even out somewhat, begin to look for a grassy double-track trail on the right. When we rode here, access to this trail was directly opposite an old barn with a "skidoo" advertisement painted on the side. You can also pay attention to the house numbers on this road; the trail branches up to the right between house 424 and house 416. The trail is also visible from the road as it continues up into the hills.

After turning off of rue Couturier, you will begin a fairly extended climb upward. Continue straight through a four-way intersection of narrow trails. Beyond the crest of this hill, you will be rewarded for your efforts with a fun descent down the other side. As you descend, you will ride past a trail on the right, which is the trail you followed at the beginning of this upper loop. From this point, you will be retracing your path back to the gravel pit. Bear left at the next junction you come to, past a trail shooting off to the right. A short distance farther, you will ride past the corrugated iron shack, which will be on your left this time. Continue straight past the shack and back to the edge of the gravel pit.

At the gravel pit, instead of retracing your route back across the sand, bear left and follow the main access road out of the pit. This is a fairly obvious route, but be sure not to make any turns off the main trail. As you leave the gravel pit you will pass two fountains on the left, and then you will pass the road you followed to the riverbank on the right. Head back toward the bridge with the yellow-and-black striped sign and cross the small stream. When you reach the paved road, rue Olivier Boucher, cross back to the other side and pick up the trail that will lead you back over the snowmobile bridge across the Iroquois River.

After crossing the snowmobile bridge, head straight back in the direction of the road you followed down to this point originally. At the foot of the hill, bear left onto a logging road. This route will connect back to the trailhead another way, closing the lower loop of the ride. The logging road will climb somewhat, and you will follow it through a bend to the right. Conditions along this portion of the ride may vary according to whether any logging operations are under way. During our ride, there were many challenging sections along the trail, where deep ruts and heavy slash made the going quite tough. When you come to a four-way intersection of logging roads, turn right and head uphill toward a radio tower off in the distance. You will be traveling southward at this point, and after approximately 1 kilometre (one-half mile) you will come to a **T** junction with a paved road.

Turn right up the paved road, which is chemin de Pouvoir, and continue climbing. Just before you crest the hill (the radio tower will be visible on your right), turn left onto an unpaved road. This road will lead you to the top of a meadow, which falls away to the left, and a wooded area on the right. Follow the road to a power line and, shifting down quickly, make a sharp right turn straight uphill. Follow the trail along the power line to the crest of this steep hill, and then continue down the other side, descending steeply past a water tower and down to the trailhead and parking area at the corner of boulevard Hébert and rue des Gouverneurs.

RIDE 8 · Mount Carleton Recreational Loop

AT A GLANCE

Length/configuration: 10-km (6-mile) combination (9-km [5.6-mile] loop with out-and-back spur; spur is 0.5-km [0.3-mile] long each way)

Aerobic difficulty: Moderate; some steep climbs on dirt trails

Technical difficulty: A basic off-road ride on wide trails through the woods

Scenery: Densely forested area with some wildflowers

Special comments: Camp overnight and explore Mount Carleton Provincial Park

In the heart of northern New Brunswick, Mount Carleton rises out of the wilderness, looming at 820 m (2,700 feet) above sea level and overlooking 17,400 hectares (43,000 acres) of wild northern woods. Surrounded by pristine wilder-

RIDE 8 • Mount Carleton Recreational Loop

ness, even the mapped and marked trails in the park have a remote and uncultivated feel. The most popular trail in the park is the Mount Carleton Summit Trail (Ride 9), but there are several other options for hikers and bikers. You can ride on any of the park's dirt roads as well as the summit trail and the cross-country ski trails, which we are referring to here as the recreational trails. Surrounded by the Geologists and Missionaries Mountain Ranges, you are presented with stunning views of mountain peaks, dark green forests, and crystal clear lakes at numerous points throughout the park.

The recreational trails have been developed on rolling, grassy terrain that can be ridden in 1-, 5-, and 7-km (0.6-, 3-, and 4.2-mile) loops. This 10-km (6-mile) combination makes the most of the available terrain. Because these trails are used as cross-country ski trails in the winter, you will notice small "do not enter" signs at some trail junctions. These signs are intended to direct the flow of skiers in the winter. Our loop goes against the direction of the trails at several points, as it was our experience that the trail conditions in the summertime were more amenable to a counter-clockwise loop: you will climb the longest and steepest hills on dirt trails where the grass had been cut and descend on the more overgrown trails. The loop is short and fun and can easily be combined with some riding on dirt roads through the park. It demands strong but basic off-road skills and fitness, and some riders may find that the seeming remoteness of the trail and patches of tall grass offer an experience as close to bushwhacking as they will ever want to get.

General location: Mount Carleton Provincial Park in north-central New Brunswick.

Elevation change: Over one long climb and several rolling hills you will gain a total of 175 m (575 feet) in elevation.

Season: Snow can arrive at Mount Carleton as early as October and linger well into May. The best months for riding are June to September. Throughout the summer season, black flies thrive here, and while they are not bothersome on the trail, you are likely to find them waiting hungrily for you upon your return to the campground and in other flat, open areas in the park.

Services: Apart from basic camping services, there are no facilities in the park. It is recommended that you even bring your own water, as you must purify the water available at the park before drinking it. The nearest bike stores are located in Edmundston, Campbellton, and Bathurst, a minimum of 70 km (42 miles) away.

Hazards: None.

Rescue index: You will never be more than 5 km (3 miles) from the regularly trafficked main access road in the park. It is recommended that all visitors register at the Visitor Reception Centre before setting out on any excursion in the park.

Land status: Provincial park; there is an entry fee for all park visitors.

Maps: Maps of the cross-country ski trails are available at the Visitor Reception Centre.

Finding the trail: From the Visitor Reception Centre at the park gates, ride or drive along the unpaved main park access road. At a three-way intersection with the road out to Armstrong Brook Campground, continue straight. You will be following signs for Nictau, Mount Carleton, and the group camping area. Continue ahead to a gravel road branching off to the right and signed to the office/bureau and cross-country ski trails. Turn right and follow the road around a bend to the right. You will arrive at an area with several

Mountain bikers put the cross country ski trails at Mount Carleton to good use in the summer.

maintenance buildings. Immediately to the left there is a log cabin and an outhouse. The sign for the cross-country ski trailhead is farther to the left, at the edge of the woods.

Sources of additional information: Contact New Brunswick Tourism with any general questions at (800) 561-0123. Or you can reach Mount Carleton Provincial Park directly at (506) 235-0793.

Notes on the trail: Begin riding along the double-track trail just beyond the log cabin. The trail will curve to the right, and you will pass the first offshoot on the right, signed "do not enter." Continue straight and ride up a short but very steep hill that marks the beginning of a long and gradual climb. On a more gradual section of the climb you will pass a trail on the left, also marked with a "do not enter" sign. This is the trail you will come out of at the end of the ride. Continuing ahead, you will pass another trail to the right heading downhill; this trail will swiftly return you to the trailhead, forming a short 1-km (0.6-mile) loop.

Past the trail on the right and still climbing on the double-track, you may find raspberry bushes along the side of the trail (we find these are well worth looking out for, particularly when they ripen in August). At the end of the climb you will arrive at a four-way intersection with a gravel track. To the left is a communication tower, and to the right the trail has a log across it. Continue straight. A short distance farther you will come to the "Link Trail" on the left. This is the crossover trail that divides and intersects the two loops. For a short 5-km (3-mile) loop you can turn left and return to the trailhead. Alternatively, bear right and continue around the second loop. Ahead, the trail will take a slight bend to the right and then curve gently to the left. The trail evens off at this point, and you will follow a more winding course up and down only short slopes and hills.

The outer section of the ride is likely to be more overgrown, despite the fact that the park does mow the trails in the summer. Beyond the outermost point, the trail continues to curve around to the left and begins to descend. The conditions improve considerably on the downhill. About half way along the descent you will arrive at the intersection with the cross-over trail. Continue ahead, or turn left to repeat the outer loop. The trail straight ahead winds through a section of tall grass before curving to the right and continuing to descend. From this point back to the spur, the trail becomes more technically challenging. There are some rutted areas and a few steep slopes with loose rock. You will pass two trails branching off to the left before reconnecting with the spur that leads back to the trailhead. Continue straight through this intersection and you will soon arrive back at the cabin.

RIDE 9 • Mount Carleton Summit Trail

AT A GLANCE

Length/configuration: 8.8-km (5.5-mile) out-and-back (4.4 km [2.75 miles] each way)

Aerobic difficulty: Strenuous; constant but gradual climbing for most of the ride

Technical difficulty: Intermediate to advanced; rocky and sometimes eroded conditions

Scenery: Expansive views across a wilderness landscape that extends as far as the eye can see

Special comments: Mount Carleton is the highest peak in the Maritimes

The summit of Mount Carleton has all the rugged, windswept character that you would expect of the highest peak in the Maritimes. At 820 m (2,690 feet) above sea level, the summit is one of the few places in New Brunswick where a rigourous climb will reward you with the exhilarating feeling of being on top of

RIDE 9 • Mount Carleton Summit Trail

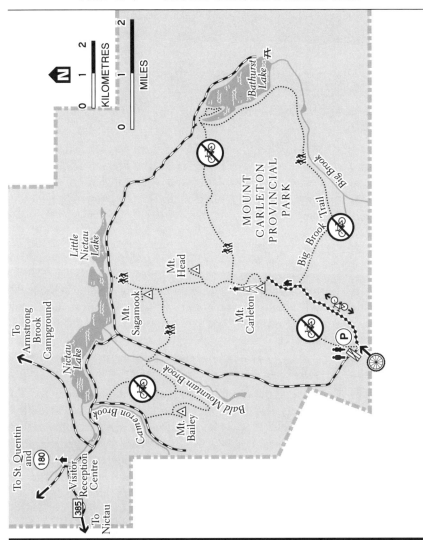

the world. This ride begins at the base of Mount Carleton, in the middle of the wooded wilderness of Mount Carleton Provincial Park. The trail climbs 4.4 km (2.75 miles) to the summit, creating an 8.8-km (5.5-mile) out-and-back excursion.

The ride to the summit of Mount Carleton follows an old road, which was once used to bring supplies to the ranger's cabin part way up the mountain. The road is now quite narrow, and you will encounter some stretches where exposed rock and roots present a considerable technical challenge. Conditions become more difficult and feature a tough, rocky ascent beyond an intersection with the

Big Brook Trail. From this point on, the ride requires excellent technical skills and strong cardiovascular fitness. Toward the end of the climb, all riders will have to dismount and scramble up the last 122 m (400 feet) to the summit. This footpath threads its way between huge boulders and finally emerges at the dramatic, exposed summit of Mount Carleton. An old fire tower at the top of the mountain offers some shelter from the wind and makes an excellent vantage point from which to take in the 360° view.

General location: Mount Carleton Provincial Park is located in north-central New Brunswick.

Elevation change: You will begin riding at 366 m (1,200 feet) and climb gradually to 427 m (1,400 feet) at the intersection of the Big Brook Trail. From this intersection, the trail climbs more steeply and ends with a final 122-m (400-foot) scramble to the summit that must be tackled on foot. Total elevation gain for the trip is 454 m (1,490 feet).

Season: June through September offer the best conditions for riding. Snow can arrive at Mount Carleton Provincial Park as early as October and may linger well into May.

Services: Besides camping facilities, there are no services available at the park. Because of the relatively isolated location of the park, it makes sense to plan on camping for at least one or two nights. Be sure to bring enough food and water for the duration of your visit. Water, though available at the park, must be purified before drinking. Other than an outhouse, there are no services available at the trailhead.

Hazards: The conditions at the summit of Mount Carleton can be fierce. Be sure to carry extra clothing—even on a fine summer's day, the wind at the top of the mountain can be cold. If possible, wear or pack in shoes that you feel comfortable hiking in, as the last 400 m (1,312 feet) of this trail require scrambling up a steep footpath over rocks and huge boulders. A suggestion for any activities in the park: wear light-coloured clothing and bring insect repellent. Apparently black fly season begins as the last snow melts and lasts until the first snow flies.

Rescue index: The park requests that all trail users register at the Visitor Reception Centre before setting out on a hike or a ride. At the summit of Mount Carleton you will be only 4.4 km (2.75 miles) from the trailhead but a considerable distance from the main park road. Be sure to allow plenty of time for your ride, at least three hours if you plan on making it to the summit and back. Park policy also warns that an injury or accident could leave you waiting for assistance for a long time and that no attempts to rescue lost or injured people will be made after dark.

Land status: Provincial park; there is an entry fee for all visitors to the park.

Maps: A very basic map of the roads and trails at the park is available at the Visitor Reception Centre. For a more detailed view of Mount Carleton and the

You will have to hike the final 400 metres up Mount Carleton to reach the highest point in the Maritimes, but it is well worth the view.

surrounding area, consult the government topographic map, which is Nepisiguit Lakes 21-O/7.

Finding the trail: From the Visitor Reception Centre, drive down the unpaved main park access road. You will pass a turnoff on the left for Armstrong Brook Campground, and then a turnoff on the right for the park headquarters and recreational trails. Continue straight on the access road until you come to a road on the right signed to Mount Bailey. Turn right and follow the road all the way to its end at the base of Mount Carleton, where you will find a large parking area. The ride begins up the gated continuation of the access road.

Sources of additional information: Contact New Brunswick Tourism with any general inquiries at (800) 561-0123. Alternatively, you can reach the park directly at (506) 235-0793.

Notes on the trail: From the parking area, begin riding up along the continuation of the dirt access road, past a gate barring vehicular traffic. Beyond the gate, you will pass the trailhead to the western route up Mount Carleton on the left. There is a wooden archway marking the beginning of this trail, which is closed to bikers.

Continue straight, following the old road that forms the eastern route up to the summit. You will pass a large sign for Mount Carleton to the right of the trail. Beyond this sign, the trail curves around to the left, crosses a rough patch of rocks and boulders, and begins following an obvious path along the old road.

The first few kilometres (a mile or so) of the ride are moderately challenging, climbing steadily but gradually along a hard-packed, grassy trail that is studded with exposed and loose rocks. The trail is obvious and easy to follow all the way to an intersection with the Big Brook Trail. At this point, turn left and head up a steep, rocky gully. All but the most accomplished of riders will find it necessary to walk this section, before resuming on less difficult terrain a short distance farther up. Generally speaking, this second half of the ride is more technically challenging than the first.

A short distance beyond the rocky gully, you will pass the ranger's cabin to the right of the trail. There is an interpretive station at this site, which provides information about the people who once worked at the fire tower on the top of the mountain. Although the trail flattens out somewhat beyond the cabin, conditions gradually deteriorate and become increasingly rocky. You will not have to travel far over this terrain, however, as the trail soon leads into a small clearing. At this point the trail turns left and narrows to a hiking trail. This last 122-m (400-foot) stretch of the trail is impossible to ride. Leave your bike and scramble up the rocks to the summit of Mount Carleton. There is an old fire tower at the top, and the rugged summit offers panoramic views of the wooded wilderness and lakes that characterize the interior of the province.

The return trip begins back down the hiking trail, to the clearing where you left your bike. From there, retrace your route to the parking area. Although the descent is a first-class bone rattler, the sharp and keen-eyed will be able to pick a fast path through the rocks and cruise back to the trailhead in no time at all.

RIDE 10 • Sentier NB Trails: Whites Brook–Mann Siding

AT A GLANCE

Length/configuration: 22.5-km (14-mile) out-and-back (11.25 km [7 miles] each way)

Aerobic difficulty: This ride is suitable for all fitness levels

Technical difficulty: Easy; wide, graded recreational trail with crushed rock surface

Scenery: Forested wilderness of the Appalachian Mountain region

Special comments: Excellent opportunities for spotting wildlife, particularly moose, deer, and fox

Highway 17 runs through the northwest corner of New Brunswick, connecting the border town of Saint-Leonard with Tide Head at the tip of the Chaleur Bay and passing through the towns of Saint-Quentin and Kedgwick, among others. The route has been described as one of the most spectacular journeys through the province's forested wilderness. Luckily for riders, a multi-use trail is being developed between these communities, along the corridor of an abandoned railroad. This trail, the Appalachian Range Trail, is an initiative being headed up by the New Brunswick Trail Council. Part of the Sentier NB Trails network, it will allow riders, hikers, and horseback riders to wander, off-road, through the heart of New Brunswick's Appalachian region. When this trail is completed, it will be possible to create any number of single- or multi-day trips through the region. Particularly exciting will be the connection between the Appalachian Range Trail and the Restigouche Trail, which will extend northeast from Upsalquitch to Campbellton. When this portion of the trail is complete, riders will be able to tour through the forested hills and river valleys of northern New Brunswick, all the way to the coastal scenery of the Baie des Chaleurs.

This ride begins east of the town of Kedgwick, where the rail trail crosses Highway 17 at Whites Brook. The ride follows the rail trail through the forested wilderness on the south side of the highway, covering 11.25 km (7 miles) before reconnecting with the highway at Mann Siding. It is also possible to pick up the trail in both Kedgwick and Saint-Jean-Baptiste-de-Restigouche, extending the ride in either direction, or, if you can arrange for transportation, turning it into a point-to-point excursion. Of particular interest may be the Kedgwick Forestry Museum and Park, where the history and significance of the logging industry in this area is exhibited. Without any side trips, the total

RIDE 10 • Sentier NB Trails: Whites Brook–Mann Siding

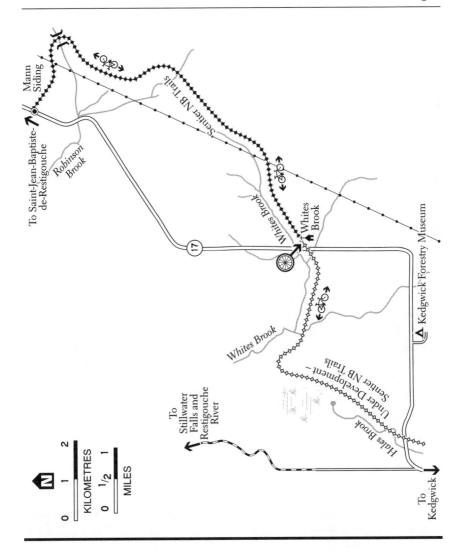

out-and-back trip from Whites Brook to Mann Siding is 22.5 km (14 miles). The entire ride follows the smooth gravel surface of the railroad bed–turned–recreational trail and features no significant hills. Combine these conditions with the many opportunities to spot wildlife, and you've got a great family excursion!

General location: Northeast of the town of Kedgwick, off of Highway 17.

Elevation change: Following the route of the old railroad, this trail is characterized by very slight grades, with no appreciable gain in elevation.

Season: The best time to ride this trail is in the autumn, when the foliage turns the landscape into a tableau of vivid colours. Conditions on the trail should be good from June through October.

Services: All services are available in Kedgwick. Camping is available at the Kedgwick Forestry Museum and Park, located on Highway 17 just east of downtown. For additional information, contact the park in writing at:

> Kedgwick Forestry Museum
> P.O. Box 224
> Kedgwick, NB E0K 1C0
> (506) 284-3138

Hazards: None.

Rescue index: You will not travel more than 5.5 km (3.5 miles) from Highway 17.

Land status: The Sentier NB Trail is a multi-purpose, all-season recreational trail.

Maps: At any tourist information centre in New Brunswick it is possible to pick up information on the status and development of the Sentier NB Trail. While we discovered this information to be inconsistent and sometimes unreliable, the basic maps of the trail system are useful and do outline the route of existing and proposed sections of the trail. Should you choose to lengthen this ride, it would be wise to obtain the most updated information about the status of the trail. Additionally, the route of the abandoned railroad is indicated in *The New Brunswick Atlas* (map 13, section C-2 and C-1; map 5, section C-5).

Finding the trail: From Saint-Leonard or Campbellton, follow NB Highway 17 toward the town of Kedgwick. If you are traveling northeast from Saint-Leonard, Whites Brook will be a short distance beyond Kedgwick. If you are traveling southwest from Campbellton, you will come to Whites Brook just before entering the town of Kedgwick. A sign for Sentier NB Trails marks the point at which the rail trail crosses the highway. There is an old white church by the side of the trail, where plenty of parking is available.

Source of additional information: The New Brunswick Trails Council is involved with several trail initiatives in the province, including the Sentier NB Trail. For additional information or to obtain an update on trail development, contact the council at the following address:

> New Brunswick Trails Council, Inc.
> 320 Maple Street, Suite 103
> Fredericton, NB E3A 3R4
> (506) 459-5639 or (800) 526-7070
> nbtrails@nbnet.nb.ca

Notes on the trail: From the old white church building at Whites Brook, begin riding along the portion of the rail trail heading northeast in the direction of Saint-Jean-Baptiste-de-Restigouche, and away from the town of Kedgwick. The trail is wide, graded, and surfaced with crushed rock. Although there are trails and cart tracks branching off the trail on both sides, the route remains obvious and easy to follow along the length of the ride. In the spring, wildflowers create an ever-changing bouquet along the side of the trail, and in the autumn, the trees paint the woods with red, yellow, and orange. At any time of year the trail surface will be patterned with the tracks of deer and moose. Along with these animals, you may catch a glimpse of foxes, as we did on an evening ride in the middle of the summer.

Your approach to Mann Siding will be announced by a long wooden bridge, located just 2 km (1.2 miles) from Highway 17. When you reach the highway, turn around and retrace your tracks back to Whites Brook. Alternatively, to extend the ride, cross the highway and follow the rail trail for a short distance farther, to the small town of Saint-Jean-Baptiste-de-Restigouche. Return to Whites Brook by way of a shuttle, if you have arranged for it, or ride back along the same route. Although the connection into town had not been completed when we rode here, it should also be possible to continue riding on the trail from Whites Brook, all the way into the town of Kedgwick.

RIDE 11 • Restigouche River

AT A GLANCE

Length/configuration: 43.5-km (27-mile) out-and-back (21.75 km [13.5 miles] each way)

Aerobic difficulty: Intermediate to advanced; the length of the trip requires good conditioning

Technical difficulty: Modest; the final descent to the river requires intermediate-level riding skills

Scenery: Logging roads drop to the smooth waters of the Restigouche River; side trip to Stillwater Falls

Special comments: Camp at the river and make this a multi-day adventure

This ride follows a logging road from downtown Kedgwick all the way to the east bank of the Restigouche River. The ride is long, 43.5 km (27 miles) out to the river and back, but requires no advanced technical skills. In fact, the relatively easy terrain makes this ride a good choice for an overnight camping trip. Most of the ride follows well-maintained logging roads, along which it is no disadvantage to be riding with racks and panniers. As you near the river, leaving

RIDE 11 • Restigouche River

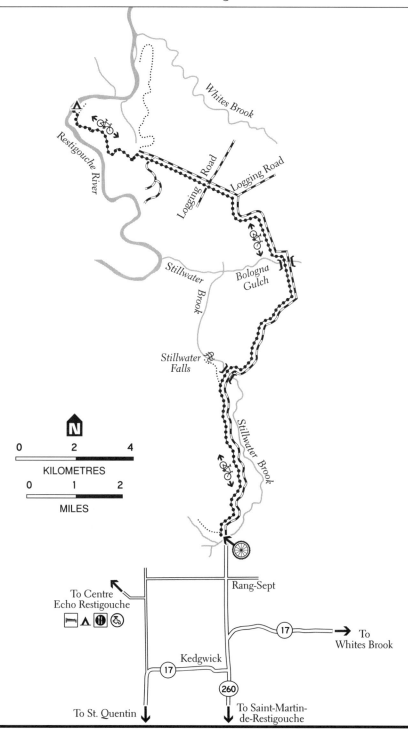

behind the cleared areas of recent cutting, the trail closes in and becomes more difficult to navigate. Nevertheless, this short stretch of the trail can still be handled with a loaded bike, and the rewards are many: you will reach the Restigouche River, which meanders through a deep forested valley, and a beautiful site ideal for camping.

Another scenic feature of this ride is a possible side trip to the falls on Stillwater Brook. The turnoff for this trip is just 5.6 km (3.5 miles) from the trailhead and makes an excellent adventure and side trip on either the way down or the trip back up from the Restigouche River. For those looking for just a short ride, Stillwater Brook can stand as a destination in its own right. However you choose to explore it, it is best to ride the double-track access trail branching off of the main logging road to a small grassy clearing. From here, the trails are best explored on foot and require at least intermediate hiking skills, strength, and agility. At the time we visited this area the trails had only recently been developed. Had we not encountered a group of students and a New Brunswick warden on their own trek out to the falls, we would never have found them and might, to this day, be wandering through the woods of this vast New Brunswick wilderness. With the directions we have included in the following trail description, you will certainly make it to the falls. Furthermore, it is likely that the site has been developed further since we were there.

General location: Kedgwick, in northern New Brunswick.

Elevation change: Between the point at which you begin this ride, 313 m (1,025 feet), and the Restigouche River, 107 m (350 feet), you will gain 190 m (625 feet). The ride back up from the river features a gain of 366 m (1,200 feet), for a total elevation gain of 556 m (1,825 feet) for the out-and-back trip.

Season: Conditions should be suitable from June through September. Plan your trip according to your tolerance of black flies and midges, which tend to be at their worst earlier in the summer.

Services: All services are available in Kedgwick. Of particular note is the Centre Echo Restigouche, located a short distance from downtown on the bank of the Kedgwick River. While the centre is primarily a source of services for guided canoe trips, the staff have a tremendous knowledge of the area and can point you in the direction of some good mountain biking opportunities nearby. Centre Echo Restigouche is also a great place to camp or rent a cottage, and there is a restaurant in their beautiful new lodge. For riders planning to camp at the river, it is imperative to bring enough water and supplies for the two-day journey. No services are available at the campsite on the river, and any water you collect should be filtered and treated.

Hazards: The first portion of this ride follows logging roads that are heavily used during the week. Keep a lookout for trucks, and remember that they have the right of way. The side trip to Stillwater Falls is a challenging hike in an area that has only recently been developed. The trip involves descending and then climbing back up a steep cliff by way of a rope attached to a tree at the top.

The final approach to the Restigouche River follows an old road through a lush forest of ferns and spruce trees.

Anyone attempting this climb should use extreme caution, as any loose rocks that are dislodged while hikers climb up or down the cliff are sent tumbling down to the stream below. Be sure, when you are waiting below for your turn, to stand to the side so as to avoid any falling rock. The hike continues up the rocky bed of Stillwater Brook. For this portion of the excursion, hiking boots (rather than cleated cycling shoes) are the best way to enjoy this epic adventure.

Rescue index: At the Restigouche River you will be a long 21.75 km (13.5 miles) from the trailhead, where there are a few seasonal camps. Downtown Kedgwick is an additional 5 km (3 miles) from the trailhead.

Land status: Crown land.

Maps: It is imperative that you ride with the government topographic maps for this area. There are two: Kedgwick 21-O/11 and Menneval 21-O/14. The trail is also outlined in *The New Brunswick Atlas* (map 13, section B-2 and B-1; map 5, section B-5).

Finding the trail: From NB Highway 17 in Kedgwick, follow the road through a sharp turn to the left after passing the local IGA and following signs to Campbellton. Route 260 heads off to the right at this junction. Follow Highway 17 for a short distance, to where it curves sharply to the right. At this point, continue straight, heading north on a paved, single-lane country road called Rang Sept. Continue straight through a four-way intersection and then follow the road over a small brook. Park at the side of the road where the pavement turns to gravel.

Source of additional information: We benefited greatly from the helpful advice and warm hospitality of the folks at Centre Echo Restigouche during our explorations in this corner of New Brunswick. If you are planning a trip to this area, we highly recommend that you do the same:

Centre Echo Restigouche
P.O. Box 362
Kedgwick, NB E0K 1C0
(506) 284-2022

Notes on the trail: From where you have parked, continue riding north up the unpaved portion of the road. Bear right up the first rise, passing a less maintained logging road branching off on the left and riding up past several seasonal camps. After approximately 5.6 km (3.5 miles), you will reach a grassy double-track trail branching off on the left. Just beyond this fork, the main logging road crosses Stillwater Brook by way of a bridge and swings sharply to the right. The grassy double-track trail is the access route to the trails that lead to Stillwater Falls. If you plan to visit the falls, turn left here and refer to the second-to-last paragraph of this trail description for further directions. Otherwise, continue on the main logging road.

Beyond the turnoff for Stillwater Falls, the logging road crosses Stillwater Brook and swings around to the right. Ride past a grassy double-track trail on the left, and then simply continue to follow the obvious path of the road. You will climb slightly over the next few kilometres (a mile or so) before descending into Bologna Gulch, where you will cross a second bridge. On our own up until this point in the ride, we were as surprised to see a large doe bounding off into the woods here as she was to see us rapidly descending toward the gulch!

Past the bridge, the road curves around to the left and begins climbing up to the highest point on the ride. Recent logging activity in this area has opened up the woods considerably, and you will pass numerous side roads to both the left and the right. At the highest point you will pass a significant logging road branching off on the right. Continue straight here, and a short distance farther, continue straight through a four-way intersection of logging roads. You will be descending along the main road at this point.

As you continue to descend, you will pass two smaller logging roads on the left, and then another, more significant road, also on the left. Beyond this junction, the main logging road deteriorates and large puddles fill ruts in the trail. You may be surprised, as we were, to encounter loggers working with horses and selectively clearing the woods.

At a split in the trail, bear right and follow what looks like an older road. This road quickly narrows to a grassy double-track trail that winds downhill through much denser woods. You may encounter fallen trees along this section of the trail, which also harbours loose and exposed rocks. Just after the trail swings around to the right, there is a side trail on the left that descends to the water. Continuing straight for a short distance will also take you down to the river, to the site of a fire pit and picnic benches. Make yourself at home! Whether you set up camp or turn around to finish the ride in the same day, the return trip follows the same route back to the trailhead.

To explore the trails around Stillwater Brook and to visit the falls, head down the access road that branches off the main logging road just 5.6 km (3.5 miles) from the trailhead. This will be a left turn as you ride out from the trailhead, or a right-hand turn if you are riding back up from the Restigouche River. Ride along the double-track access trail, which has a grassy median, to a small clearing that serves as a parking area for four-wheel-drive vehicles. To the right of this opening begins one of the footpaths to the falls. Although the entrance to this trail might be overgrown, the path is clear once you locate it. (At the time we explored this area, the trail was marked by a mere whisp of orange flagging tape.)

This trail is the most obvious route to the falls and follows a narrow footpath to the top of the steep cliffs dropping down to the brook below. To facilitate your journey down to the brook, a rope has been secured to a tree at the top of the cliff. Use as much caution on this descent as you would if you were on your bike, and make sure you keep enough space between yourself and the next person: loose rocks tumbling down the slope can make the trip rather hazardous.

When you reach the brook, turn right and begin walking upstream. Be sure you can identify the spot you came down before heading up the stream, as you will need to use the rope to scale back up the cliff on your return. The so-called hike to the falls actually entails walking up the brook, scrambling over rocks, and avoiding the deepest pools. Your feet will be just the first things to get wet! The brook runs through a narrow ravine, which creates a moist, hazy, and almost tropical atmosphere, where mosses and tiny ferns flourish on the rock faces rising up steeply above the water. Perhaps because of the epic journey required to reach them, the falls are quite spectacular, and there are plenty of large boulders nearby on which to enjoy a picnic.

To return to the trailhead, make your way back down the stream and keep your eyes peeled for the dangling rope up the left side of the ravine. Again, use caution on your ascent, as any rocks you send tumbling will head straight down to the brook and to anyone waiting below. Follow the footpath back out to the clearing, and then ride back on the access road to its junction with the main logging road. Turn right on the logging road to return to the trailhead.

RIDE 12 • Sugarloaf Mountain

AT A GLANCE

Length/configuration: 10.5-km (6.5-mile) combination (8.5-km (5.3-mile) loop with a 1-km (0.6-mile) spur ridden twice)

Aerobic difficulty: Moderate; several rolling hills on grassy trails

Technical difficulty: Beginner to intermediate riding on loose dirt and rock

Scenery: A woods ride with several views of Pritchard Lake

Special comments: Host of the annual Maritime Mountain Bike Festival

In its brochures, Sugarloaf Provincial Park boasts 25 km (15.5 miles) of mountain bike trails. The bulk of the trails follow the cross-country ski trails, except during the Maritime Mountain Bike Festival, when some hiking trails are made available for racing purposes. Our preference is for the 10.5-km (6.5-mile) combination around Pritchard Lake. It is an aerobically stimulating ride with several moderate hills, and the trail alternates between grassy dirt trails and gravel roads. The ride is technically easy, with the exception of some hills that require a willingness to climb and descend on loose dirt and rock. While the expert cross-country ski trails may offer steeper hills and more adventurous terrain, they are not maintained in the summer and are characterized by overgrowth that does little to enhance a rider's experience.

That said, Sugarloaf Provincial Park is a destination to keep your eye on. It is one of the few parks in Atlantic Canada promoting its mountain bike trails, and it hosts the annual Maritime Mountain Bike Festival. This is a three-day festival in early July, coordinated by the mountain bike club in Campbellton. The event is chock-full of activities for people with little or lots of mountain biking experience. It includes a race that is part of the New Brunswick points series, and the course includes some single-track trails from which mountain bikers are prohibited at other times. While the ride described here does not feature any single-track, it is rumoured that there is a network of single-track trails at the back of the mountain. However, you will have to pry that information from a local rider, if you can.

General location: Sugarloaf Mountain Provincial Park, near Campbellton.

Elevation change: You will gain a total 185 m (610 feet) of elevation on several moderate hills.

RIDE 12 • Sugarloaf Mountain

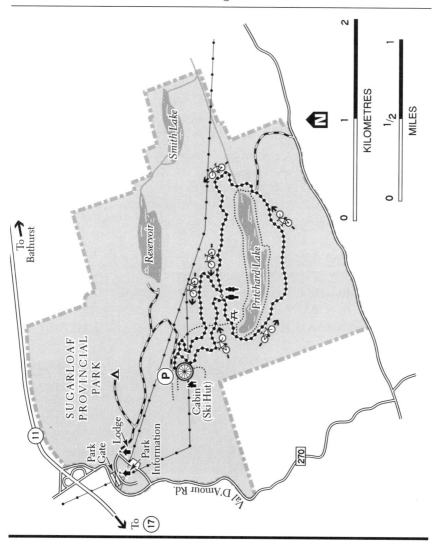

Season: Because the park is situated quite far north in New Brunswick, expect the season to start in late June and continue to the end of September. Also, black flies and mosquitoes are of minimal concern while riding but can be a problem during rest stops or if you are camping overnight throughout the summer season.

Services: The park offers camping and a variety of recreational activities. All other services are available in Campbellton. Your biking needs can be met at Le Vélo à l'Èxtrême Bike Shop, where you may also find local club riders and inquire about weekly club rides. It is located at 74 Roseberry Street in Campbellton (phone (506)-753-3554).

Hazards: Poor traction on loose dirt and rock inhibits steering in some areas and should be approached with caution.

Rescue index: There is a campground office a short distance from the trailhead, and you are likely to encounter people at various points on the trail.

Land status: Provincial park; there is an entry fee for all visitors.

Maps: A map of the cross-country ski trails is available from the Visitor Information Centre as you enter the park.

Finding the trail: From Campbellton, follow NB Highway 11 west to Route 270. The entrance to the park is clearly signed off of Route 270. Once in the park, bear left past the kiosk at the park entrance and follow signs to the Ski Lodge/Pavillon de Ski. Continue past the lodge on the right, as well as the entrance to the campground on the left. Continue to follow the main road, which will turn to gravel after you round a bend to the right, all the way up to a gravel parking area at the top of the hill. The entrance to the trails is an opening in the trees on the left side of the road, just before the parking area.

Sources of additional information: You can reach Sugarloaf Provincial Park by calling (506) 789-2366. Mountain bike tours and rentals are available by contacting Velo Restigouche at (506) 753-6194.

Notes on the trail: Beginning from the parking area, ride back to the opening in the trees on the right and head into the woods. There is a map of the trails straight ahead, and the ski lodge is to the right. From here, begin riding on the middle trail, following the yellow dots on the trees.

Entering the cross-country ski trail network, the trail is wide and the surface is a combination of dirt, loose rock, and grassy patches. A short distance along the trail, there is a less distinct trail branching off on the left. Bear right to continue on the main trail. A short descent brings you to an intersection under a set of power lines. Cross beneath the lines and continue straight, back into the woods, following signs for Pritchard Lake. At a **Y** intersection not far from the transmission line, bear right, still following the yellow dots. You will climb gradually on this wide dirt trail for a moderate distance. After the trail levels off, you will arrive at a **T** junction. The right option returns you to the trailhead. To continue this ride, turn left, following the yellow dots toward Pritchard Lake.

The trail swings to the left, and you will pass a footpath heading into the woods on the right. A short distance farther, you will pass a picnic area before reaching a fork in the trail. At the fork, bear right and begin climbing. The trail climbs steadily and is punctuated by a short, steep section before it levels out and curves to the right. Arriving at a four-way intersection with a major dirt road, continue straight ahead, onto a trail posted with both a cross-country ski figure and a sign prohibiting snowmobiles from using the trail in the winter.

Continuing ahead, you will pass through another four-way intersection, following the yellow sign that reads "7.2 km."

By continuing straight ahead, you are avoiding the steep, rocky climb to the right that will also take you to Pritchard Lake. On this grassy trail you will pass another footpath on the right and eventually arrive at a **Y** intersection. Bear right (uphill) past an outhouse and a picnic table on the left, following the yellow sign that reads "6.6 km." As you crest the hill, you will join a more maintained, double-track gravel road. Continuing on the road, you will arrive at an open grassy field with some wild rose bushes and a picnic table. To the left there is a narrow, grassy walking trail that approaches the shoreline at one end of Pritchard Lake. This is a pleasant side trip, giving you an opportunity to pause and take in the view over the lake. The ride continues to the left along the trail that is farther up from the water's edge as you begin to make your way around Pritchard Lake.

At the first **Y** intersection bear left, following a gravel road to continue on your circuit around the lake. A short distance farther, there is another viewpoint out to the lake before the road continues in the woods to the end of the lake. The road descends to the other end of the lake and ends at an intersection with the major park road (this appears as a black line on the park map). Continue across this gravel road to a four-way intersection with a gravel road. Straight ahead there is a dirt trail heading into the woods that will return you to the trailhead. For an open view onto Pritchard Lake, turn left and follow the gravel road a short distance to the water's edge. When you are ready to return to the trailhead, retrace your track and turn left at the first opportunity, onto the dirt trail heading up through the woods.

Following the dirt trail, you will have to tackle two short but monstrous climbs. The climbs are followed by a descent to a three-way intersection, with a sign pointing to the right for the ski hut and a familiar looking outhouse and picnic table to the left. Turn right following the signs to the lodge. You will have a bone-rattling descent to a **T** junction, where you will turn right onto a dirt trail. The trailhead is just a short distance from here. Continue straight at the stop sign under the power lines and complete one final rocky climb to return to the ski lodge.

RIDE 13 · Caraquet

AT A GLANCE

Length/configuration: 25-km (15.5-mile) combination (5.6-km [3.5-mile] loop with out-and-back spur; spur is 9.7 km [6 miles] each way)

Aerobic difficulty: Easy; only one short grade at the beginning of the ride

Technical difficulty: Easy; wide, graded recreational trail with a surface of crushed stone

Scenery: Sweeping coastal views across the brilliant waters of Baie des Chaleurs

Special comments: Excellent family or group ride; plan for a swim and picnic at the beach

There is a festivity surrounding the town of Caraquet in the summertime, one that comes from the bustling activity of a small strip of shops, the salt wind blowing in off the Baie des Chaleurs, and all the evidence of a distinctly Acadian culture. This spirit is at its peak at the beginning of August, when the colours of the Acadian flag—the French tricolour with a yellow star rising in the blue—grace every shop and home as part of the Acadian Festival. In this vibrant and energetic community it is easy, in fact, to imagine the sound of blowing whistles announcing the approach of incoming trains. However, all that remains of the old railroad is its scenic path into Caraquet along the Baie des Chaleurs, only recently converted into a recreational trail. For riders, this trail makes a perfect introduction to the Acadian Peninsula.

Beginning from Carrefour de la Mer (Crossroads of the Sea), a busy little port located at the edge of town, this ride picks up a short spur of the multi-use recreational trail before connecting to the old railroad bed. You will ride through Caraquet, traversing the high bank overlooking the Baie des Chaleurs, before the trail turns inland and toward the communities of Bertrand, Burnsville, Saint-Leolin, and Grande Anse. The route we have described is a 25-km (15.5-mile) combination ride, a short 5.6-km (3.5-mile) loop connecting to a 9.7-km (6-mile) spur that is ridden twice, once in each direction. The ride nears its end at an access point to a beach and lighthouse, where covered picnic tables provide the perfect place for a post-ride swim and picnic. Throughout the ride the trail conditions are good, traversing the classic, wide, graded crushed-stone pathways that characterize most sections of the Sentier NB Trail. There is also a very short section on pavement at the beginning of the ride. Riders of all skill and fitness levels will enjoy this ride. In addition to a scenic tour through Caraquet, the trail

RIDE 13 • Caraquet

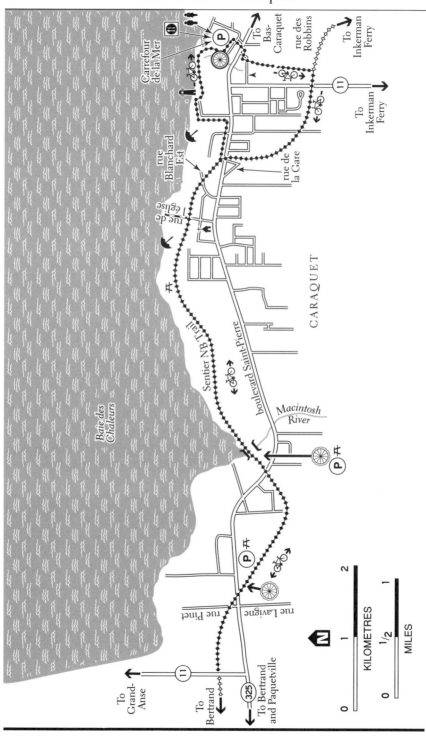

offers access to several beaches, and, for riders looking for a longer tour, the ride can be extended for a considerable distance in either direction. Indeed, for anyone seeking a multi-day tour, this portion of the recreational trail can be ridden as part of a 58-km (36-mile) point-to-point tour between Inkerman Ferry and Grande Anse. When completed, this trail will extend past Shippagan, across Ile Lameque, and all the way out to Ile Miscou.

General location: Caraquet, on the Acadian Peninsula in northeast New Brunswick.

Elevation change: There is no significant change in elevation along the entire length of this ride. A short climb from Carrefour de la Mer to the beginning of the recreational trail is the only noticeable grade.

Season: Conditions on this rail trail should be good from early spring all the way into October. August is a glorious time to ride, when the breeze coming off of the Baie des Chaleurs feels warm and the revelry of the Acadian Festival fills the air.

Services: All services are available in Caraquet. Additionally, there are rest rooms, a snack bar, and a restaurant at the trailhead at Carrefour de la Mer. For riders considering an extended tour, basic services are also available in both Grande Anse and Inkerman Ferry. From June through August, guided bicycle tours depart from Carrefour de la Mer. These tours make use of the recreational trail and last approximately two-and-a-half hours. Bikes, helmets, and snacks are part of the package, and seats are available for anyone traveling with small children. For further information on these tours, contact "Caraquet à Velo" at (506) 727-2811.

Hazards: There are several road crossings along the length of this ride.

Rescue index: This ride never ventures far from busy NB Highway 11, the main road through Caraquet. The extensions of this ride to Grande Anse and Inkerman Ferry do pass through slightly more isolated areas, but frequently cross secondary roads and pass through small communities where assistance should be readily available.

Land status: Provincial recreational trail.

Maps: The best maps available are those delineating the route of the Sentier NB Trail. You should be able to pick up the most recent brochure on this portion of the trail, the Sentiers Peninsule Acadienne, at the Information Centre located at the trailhead. Be aware that some of these brochures incorrectly indicate that certain portions of the trail have been completed, when in fact no trail actually exists and development is still under way. Be sure to make careful inquiries if you plan to ride any other portions of the Sentier NB Trails network.

Finding the trail: Driving into Caraquet on NB Highway 11, follow signs for the Information Centre and Carrefour de la Mer. If you are driving north from Miramichi, turn right when you reach a **T** junction with boulevard Saint-Pierre est (east) in Caraquet. Carrefour de la Mer will be just a short distance down the road on the left. If you are driving in from Bathurst, continue straight on the main street when Highway 11 turns right. You will soon see the port and large parking area of Carrefour de la Mer on the left.

Sources of additional information: For general information about the area, contact the Information Centre at (506) 727-1705. For further details and up-to-the-minute information about the recreational trail and its continued development, call Sentiers Peninsule Acadienne at (506) 727-4199.

Notes on the trail: From the parking area at Carrefour de la Mer, ride back out to boulevard Saint-Pierre est (east) and turn right. Ride uphill on pavement for a short distance. When you see the regional office for New Brunswick Fisheries and Aquaculture, turn left up rue des Robins. The road will curve to the right almost immediately. Instead of following it around the bend, bear left onto an unpaved path that marks the beginning of the recreational trail.

You will climb gradually up this first stretch of the recreational trail, passing through a wooded, parklike area where benches have been placed along the sides of the crushed gravel trail. After a short distance, you will reach a **T** junction with the main section of the multi-use trail. Turn right here; the trail to the left continues all the way to the community of Inkerman Ferry. As you follow the trail to the right, you will be riding along one side of a power line. After another short distance, you will come to Highway 11. Cross the road carefully and pick up the continuation of the recreational trail on the other side.

Continue along the recreational trail, which remains obvious and easy to follow, across another road. Beyond this intersection you will quickly approach downtown Caraquet, where the trail joins the main street near rue de la Gare. Simply cross the main street, which is boulevard Saint-Pierre, and pick up the trail on the other side. There is a small park at the beginning of this portion of the trail, which is signed as place de la Gare. As you follow the trail out of town, you will cross a grassy clearing and another paved road, rue Blanchard est (east). The trail continues straight beyond the road and toward the edge of the Baie des Chaleurs, along what is indisputably the most beautiful section of the ride.

As you leave town, the trail moves quite close to the Baie des Chaleurs. The water will be on your right, at the foot of a gentle slope that falls away from the trail. The first dirt road you cross is rue de l'Eglise. This road drops down to one of the main beaches in Caraquet, la plage de Caraquet, which is also called la plage de l'Eglise. This is another wonderful beach worth returning to at the end of the ride.

Beyond rue de l'Eglise, you will pass a cemetery and Eglise Saint-Pierre-aux-Liens not far from the trail on the left. Wildflowers grow in a profusion of colours along this section of the trail, which quickly reaches a pavilion and rest area overlooking the Baie des Chaleurs. From this point, the trail continues along the edge of the shore before crossing a bridge over Macintosh River and turning inland. A short distance beyond the bridge you will reach another rest area with a shelter and picnic tables. This rest area is located at the junction of the trail with Highway 11 and provides parking for anyone looking for an alternative place to begin the ride.

Cross Highway 11 carefully, and follow the trail through a more wooded area on the other side of the road. At another rest area, also equipped with a shelter and picnic tables, the trail crosses Highway 11 again. This site, near the city limits of Caraquet, makes another good place from which to begin the ride. Beyond this road crossing, the trail continues for just a short distance before intersecting with Highway 11, just below the junction of Highway 11 and Route 325. Unless you wish to continue on the trail toward Bertrand, turn around here.

The ride follows the same route all the way back to place de la Gare, where the trail intersects with the main street through downtown Caraquet. Instead of crossing the road and picking up the trail on the other side near rue de la Gare, turn left on the main road. Ride on pavement until you see rue Foley on the left side of the street. There is a large Irving service station on this corner. Turn left down rue Foley and pick up a gravel trail that follows the edge of a parking area. At the end of the parking area you will see a staircase on your left descending to a beach, a lighthouse, and a number of covered picnic tables. This is an excellent place to stop for lunch or a swim before you complete your ride.

From the beach, the ride follows a gravel trail that continues straight past the wooden staircase. You will descend a short hill toward Carrefour de la Mer. Turn right at the base of this hill, as the trail that continues straight ahead leads out to a pier and is closed to cyclists. You will ride along a grassy trail that leads toward a small wooden bridge. Follow the trail over the bridge and out to the parking area at Carrefour de la Mer.

RIDE 14 • French Fort Cove

AT A GLANCE

Length/configuration: 10 km (6.2 miles) out-and-back (5 km [3.1 miles] each way)

Aerobic difficulty: Moderate; a short ride with some climbing on dirt trails

Technical difficulty: Suitable for beginning and intermediate riders

Scenery: Bird's-eye view of the cove and out to the Miramichi River

Special comments: More single-track to explore in the woods around the cove

RIDE 14 • French Fort Cove

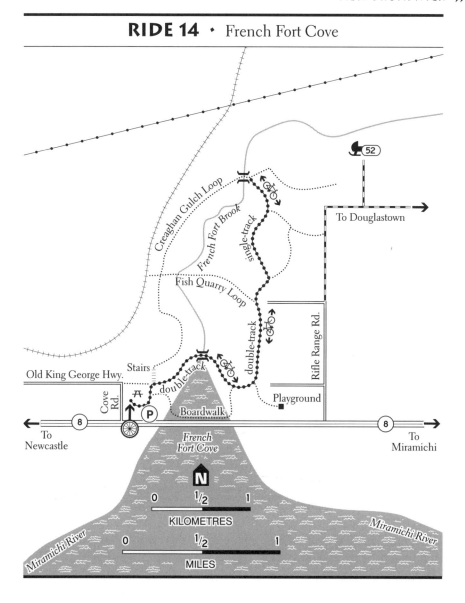

Local legend has it that pirates came up the Miramichi River and buried boxes of gold and other treasures under the rocks at the mouth of French Fort Cove. A more widely known fact about the Mirimachi River is the quality of the salmon that swim in its pools. Few people travel here without a fishing rod. Hiking and biking trails had only recently been developed here at the time of our research, and we suspect they may have been inspired by the provincial multi-use trail system that passes through the area. A section of trail at French

Fort Cove is part of the Sentier NB Trail system. Eventually it will extend well beyond the cove, ultimately creating a link to east Miramichi.

In the meantime, there is a 10-km (6.2-mile) out-and-back route that offers several views of a dramatic gulch that plunges down to the French Fort River feeding into the cove and the Miramichi River. Climbing on loose dirt and sections of tightly winding single-track requires intermediate skills, but we highly recommend this ride to beginners wanting to develop their skills. The brevity of the difficult sections and easier riding on the double-track and multi-use trails make this an ideal place to improve your conditioning and your skills. Your efforts climbing the side of the gulch and negotiating the single-track will be rewarded with views down the cove and out to the Miramichi River. This ride combines great scenery and a good variety of trails, which we hope will remain accessible to mountain bikers as the park develops.

General location: French Fort Cove is located just off of the King George Highway in Miramichi West.

Elevation change: A total 100 m (330 feet) of elevation is gained on short hills in both directions.

Season: Most of the trails will dry quickly with some sunshine in the spring. Riding can begin as early as May and continue through October.

Services: All services are available in Miramichi. For basic bike repairs, contact Jim Hondas of Triple "R" Bicycles (phone (506) 778-8706).

Hazards: The trail becomes hazardous if you try to complete the Creaghan Gulch Loop. The vertical descents and brook crossing become considerably more challenging and dangerous when you are hiking your bike on steep dirt slopes.

Rescue index: The trail is bordered by residential streets on both sides. You are never more than 5 km (3 miles) from the trailhead.

Land status: A municipal park developed and maintained by the city of Miramichi.

Maps: The City of Miramichi Trail Guide, available at the Visitor Information Centre, is the most detailed map you will find. The area is so confined that a topographic map is not required.

Finding the trail: From Miramichi, follow NB Highway 8 (King George Highway) out of town. You will pass French Fort Cove on the right. Just beyond the cove, turn right up Cove Road. There is a large billboard at the intersection, and a large parking area is a short distance up on the right-hand side.

Sources of additional information: Contact the Miramichi City Community Recreation Department at (506) 623-2300.

Notes on the trail: From the parking lot, begin on a short, gravel spur that starts from an opening in a wooden fence. After a very short distance, the spur ends at a **T** junction with the main trail (at the site of a picnic pavilion). Turn left to follow the gravel trail through the park. The trail climbs gradually for a short

In and around French Fort Cove, there are excellent stretches of single-track to explore.

distance, and then descends around a bend to the right. You will pass a set of stairs that lead to a set of hiking trails on the left. Continue straight down the hill on the gravel trail, following the Sentier NB Trail sign. At the bottom of the hill you will cross a small bridge at the end of the cove and follow the trail as it curves to the right.

The trail will begin to climb. You will pass another gravel trail branching down to the right before arriving at a fork in the trail. The right branch descends to a wooden boardwalk that follows the edge of the cove, while the left branch leads up to another trail that continues around the gulch. Turn left, uphill, to a **T** junction, then turn left again, continuing on the gravel trail. To the right is a short spur connecting to a children's play area. A short distance along, you will pass through a set of wooden posts and emerge at a sandy opening at the end of a paved road. Turn left onto a dirt trail and then, almost immediately, turn right onto a double-track trail. This trail has a sign at the entrance identifying it as the Fish Quarry Trail. This trail follows the edge of the gulch and provides some views out to the forested valley below. Soon you will reach the **Y** intersection of the Fish Quarry and Creaghan Gulch Trails. The Fish

Quarry Trail descends steeply to the left, down to the gulch. Bear right, entering onto the Creaghan Gulch Trail.

The Creaghan Gulch Trail begins with a moderate climb on loose dirt. At the end of the climb, a single-track trail branches off to the left, toward the edge of the gulch. You can turn left to follow this intermediate stretch of single-track, which features some exposed rocks, roots, and stumps, as well as some dips and turns. Scrubby trees, blueberry bushes, and ferns line the trail, and you will catch occasional glimpses of the cove. To avoid the single-track, continue ahead on the dirt trail. You will pass over some rocky sections and then come to a bend in the road to the right. Just before the bend there is a narrow single-track on the left that connects back to the Creaghan Gulch Trail. At the junction of the short single-track and the Creaghan Gulch Trail, the continuation of the Creaghan Gulch Trail was under construction when we rode. Approaching from the left on the narrow single-track, the trail suddenly widened to a recently bull-dozed double-track trail. Continuing on this wider stretch of trail, you will soon reach the top of the loop. This is the turnaround point for the out-and-back ride. At this point, most riders will want to simply turn around and retrace their tracks to French Fort Cove and the parking area.

If you continue beyond this point, expect to hike your bike a considerable distance. Not only does the trail climb and descend the gulch twice on extremely vertical angles, but at the bottom of the first descent there is a brook crossing that has been bridged with a narrow log and a rope suspended overhead. Beyond the bridge, there is a climb that follows the most direct route to the top of the gulch: straight uphill! After climbing back up the other side, you can resume riding on the narrow and somewhat overgrown single-track. This stretch is very technical and made more difficult by the fact that you cannot see through the overgrown bushes to the rocks and roots you are riding over.

Eventually, the trail widens slightly on a more used stretch of trail. This stretch of single-track, although short, is very enjoyable, as you can see far enough in advance to pick a path between the obstacles. This final stretch of single-track brings you to the wooden stairs you spotted at the beginning of the ride. Dismount as you approach the stairs, and walk your bike to the main gravel trail. Bearing right on the main trail will return you to the parking area.

RIDE 15 • Kouchibouguac

AT A GLANCE

Length/configuration: 28.6-km (17-mile) loop

Aerobic difficulty: Modest; a lengthy ride on mostly flat, easy terrain

Technical difficulty: Novice- and beginner-level riding on the gravel bike paths and single-track

Scenery: Coniferous forests, salt marshes, and lagoons on the Gulf of St. Lawrence

Special comments: Go prepared to take a variety of side trips and enjoy other recreational opportunities

Kouchibouguac National Park has been designed for families and recreational enthusiasts. It has successfully transformed areas of salt marsh, lagoon, and sand dunes into popular areas for canoeing, picnicking, and swimming, and it has an expansive network of bike trails. While there are over 20 km (12.5 miles) of standard, 1.5 m-wide (4.5-feet), gravel-dusted bike trails, the park has gained respect among mountain bikers for its 6 km (4.2 miles) of single-track. By the same token, the trail has also helped mountain bikers gain respect from the hordes of uninitiated riders who embark on their first off-road ride here.

On this 28.6-km (17-mile) loop, you will travel through most of the park, enjoying both inland and coastal scenery. A good portion of the multi-use trail traces the edge of the Kouchibouguac River and the shores of the Gulf of St. Lawrence. Just as these shores have been turned into recreational areas, the 6-km (4.2-mile) single-track trail has turned a picturesque stretch of woods and marshlands into a mountain biker's playland designed to be accessible to all riders. We saw families and groups of beginner and advanced riders enthusiastically ploughing through the mud and negotiating roots and rocks along this stretch of trail. The entire ride can be completed by beginners with a basic level of fitness. In fact, for a playful ride with friends or family, Kouchibouguac cannot be beat.

General location: Located on the eastern coast of New Brunswick, about an hour south of Miramichi.

Elevation change: With the exception of a few rolling hills, the terrain at Kouchibouguac is relatively flat.

Season: The park offers full services from mid-May to mid-October, which coincides with ideal months for cycling.

RIDE 15 • Kouchibouguac

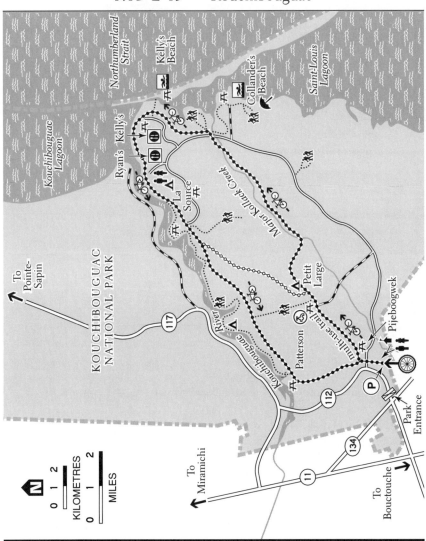

Services: Most services can be found in the park. There are several campgrounds, various cafés with assorted menus, and water pumps at most of the picnic areas. The staff at Ryan's bike rental kiosk may even be able to tackle small bike repairs. To arrange for bike rentals, contact the rental centre at (506) 876-2571.

Hazards: Travel on the single-track is permitted in only one direction (west to east); going against the flow is hazardous to you and other riders.

Rescue index: The frequency of serviced rest stops and the volume of park visitors on any given day makes assistance easy to find at any point on the trail.

Land status: National park; there is a park entry fee for all visitors.

Maps: The park map available at the Information Centre is sufficient for this ride.

Finding the trail: The park is located an hour north of Moncton, off of NB Highway 134 between Kouchibouguac and Saint-Louis-de-Kent. The park entrance is a well signed, right-hand turn off of this secondary highway. There is ample parking in the main lot, near the Information Centre, just past the park gates.

Sources of additional information: You can reach Kouchibouguac National Park's Visitor Information Centre at (506) 876-2443.

Notes on the trail: Exit the parking area at the Information Centre and turn right onto the main park road. A short distance ahead, you will see a sign for Pijeboogwek, with a small bike insignia. Following the sign, turn left into the parking area and continue along the trail to the first junction, where there is a park map. Bear right, following the gravel cycling path through the woods toward Petit Large. As you approach Petit Large you will pass a park access road on the right and see a sheltered area replete with a park map, bike racks, a water pump, picnic tables, and toilets. Ride past the first trail branching off to the left toward Middle Kouchibouguac and continue to a fork. A warning sign is posted here regarding the Major Kollock Trail, a single-track trail that follows to the right. You are also presented with the option of turning left and following a gravel-dust trail to a point near South Kouchibouguac on the opposite side of the trail system. Bear right and follow the single-track; you will find that it isn't as threatening as the sign might lead you to believe.

Beginning at the west end of the Major Kollack Trail, you will ride through heavy ferns and an area of low-lying vegetation that resembles the sea floor. A boardwalk has been constructed over the boggy sections, but it is easily wide enough to ride on. As you advance farther into the woods, you can expect a few depressions and some twists and turns in the trail that will test your basic bike-handling skills. At the completion of the single-track, you will emerge at a graveled opening, resembling a small parking area, off the main park road. Turn right onto the paved road, and follow it a short distance to a dirt access road to Collander's Beach on the left-hand side. Turn left and follow the road to the picnic area and rejoin the main cycling path that enters the woods on your left.

Back on the main cycling path you will curve to the left, heading inland away from the salt marsh. You will pass a footpath on the left that you can hike along to reach the marshes. Continuing ahead, you will reach the highly developed area surrounding Kelly's Beach. There are several services here, including a parking area, café, and puppet theatre. Just beyond this strip you will arrive at a fork in the trail where you can access a boardwalk that crosses a lagoon and sand dunes on its way to Kelly's Beach. If the very idea of sand dunes and a beach hasn't already tempted you toward this excursion, then perhaps the strategically placed bike racks will act as the final motivation. Trust us, it is well worth the walk to see the jellyfish in the lagoon and to walk on the beach.

Back at your bike, you will continue along the coastline, passing several inter-

A sacred stretch of single-track in Kouchibouguac National Park.

pretive signs that describe the waterfowl and ocean food chain. The trail will curve around to the left, beginning up the mouth of the Kouchibouguac River, and you will pass a rental area and restaurant at Ryan's. The trail continues to follow the edge of the river, and hiking trails branch off to the right to picnic areas and interpretive signs. Arriving at another full service picnic area at La Source, the trail continues farther inland toward Middle Kouchibouguac. The trail continues to be fairly flat through this next wooded section. Continue past the cycling trail that cuts diagonally through the woods to Petit Large to the next junction at Middle Kouchibouguac. This is another full-service picnic area, and there is another trail branching to the left that also connects to Petit Large. Continue straight and begin climbing the moderate slope. There may be sections of loose gravel, but it is still a technically easy, although somewhat prolonged, climb. At the top the trail rolls gently and will bend sharply to the left away from the Patterson shelter area. This is the final stretch of trail that leads to the Pijeboogwek parking area. From the parking area, turn right on the main road to return to the Information Centre.

RIDE 16 • Bouctouche

AT A GLANCE

Length/configuration: 24-km (15-mile) out-and-back (12 km [7.5 miles] each way)

Aerobic difficulty: Easy; gravel trail with minimum elevation change

Technical difficulty: Basic; wide, flat gravel surface suitable to all riders

Scenery: Woodlands, marshes, and sand dunes

Special comments: Combine the ride with a hike along the dunes

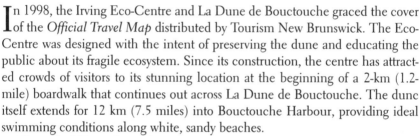

In 1998, the Irving Eco-Centre and La Dune de Bouctouche graced the cover of the *Official Travel Map* distributed by Tourism New Brunswick. The Eco-Centre was designed with the intent of preserving the dune and educating the public about its fragile ecosystem. Since its construction, the centre has attracted crowds of visitors to its stunning location at the beginning of a 2-km (1.2-mile) boardwalk that continues out across La Dune de Bouctouche. The dune itself extends for 12 km (7.5 miles) into Bouctouche Harbour, providing ideal swimming conditions along white, sandy beaches.

This ride follows the 12-km (7.5-mile) Forest Trail, a recreational trail that links downtown Bouctouche with the Eco-Centre and La Dune de Bouctouche. The journey is a 24-km (15-mile) out-and-back, and is an excellent way to begin a day's excursion exploring the area and its interesting ecology. From Bouctouche, the Forest Trail winds through an Acadian forest, along a salt marsh, and across two rivers before emerging at a parking area directly across from the Eco-Centre. The trail is wide, hard-packed, and surfaced with gravel-dust, which makes this an easy ride on a smooth surface with very few climbs or descents. Along the trail there are several benches, scenic rest areas, and interpretive signs identifying the varieties of trees, animals, plants, and wildflowers that inhabit the area. From the parking area at the end of the trail, a short ride across Highway 475 will take you to the entrance of the Eco-Centre at the edge of La Dune de Bouctouche. The centre, which offers wonderful interpretive programs, rises impressively against the backdrop of the dune, along which the boardwalk extends beyond where the eyes can see.

General location: About 45 minutes northeast of Moncton on the east coast of New Brunswick.

RIDE 16 • Bouctouche

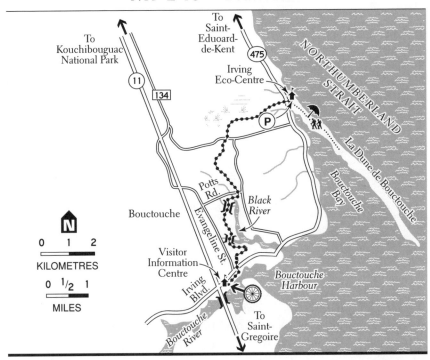

Elevation change: There is no appreciable elevation gain on this ride which features only a few small rolling hills.

Season: Ideal riding conditions can begin as early as April and continue through November in years with minimal rainfall.

Services: With the exception of bicycle-related needs, all services are available in Bouctouche. For bike service or accessories, visit Bungay's Bicycle & Snowboard, located at 647 Mountain Street in Moncton.

Hazards: The trail crosses some busy paved roads. Exercise caution at these intersections.

Rescue index: Assistance is readily available at both ends of the trail, either from services downtown or at the Irving Eco-Centre interpretive building.

Land status: The Forest Trail is a public right-of-way through private land.

Maps: Maps of the trail are available from the Visitor Information Centre in Bouctouche.

Finding the trail: From Moncton, you can either follow NB Highway 134 all the way to Bouctouche, or take the main NB Highway 11 and exit onto NB Highway 134 just outside Bouctouche. Following Highway 134 into the town, you will follow the signs to the Visitor Information Centre, which is located at the corner of chemin du Couvenant and Irving Boulevard.

Source of additional information: For information on the Irving Eco-Centre, La Dune de Bouctouche, or the Forest Trail, contact:

Irving Eco-Centre Manager,
R.R. #1, Site 3, Box 5
Bouctouche, NB E0A 1G0
(506) 743-2600
ladune@nbnet.nb.ca

Notes on the trail: From the parking area at the Visitor Information Centre, turn right onto Irving Boulevard. At the next block, turn left onto Evangeline Street and continue up the road a short distance. The trailhead for the Irving Forest Trail will appear on the right, just beyond a dirt road. Turn right onto the dirt road, and then bear left to begin riding along the crushed-gravel multi-use trail. The trail follows alongside the road a short distance and then veers right into the woods.

Entering the woods, the trail will begin to climb, gradually winding its way along the river. At the crest of the hill the trail drops down to the left and crosses a wooden bridge over Black River. Across the bridge the trail curves to the right and continues through the forest. Further along the crushed gravel trail, you will descend to another wooden bridge and then climb gradually up the other side. After a short distance, the trail levels off and you will arrive at a **T** junction with Potts Road. Turn right onto the paved road; the continuation of the trail will be signed on the left-hand side after a short distance (there was a portable toilet at the trail entrance at the time of our research).

Embarking on this section of trail from the road, you will be met by blossoming wildflowers in the early summer. Continue riding, passing a dirt trail on your left, to a boardwalk over the marshes. At the end of the boardwalk and after a short climb, you will reach a **T** junction with another paved road. Turn right on the paved road and continue a short distance to the trail entrance on the left-hand side. An opening in the bushes marks the start of the trail, and once again, there will also be several road signs helping to direct you. The first portion of this section of the trail is lined with alders, and then you will emerge at a marshy area. Beyond the marsh, the trail winds through the woods on a slight uphill slope. Eventually, you will reach the end of the trail (marked by a trail map and interpretive sign) at the edge of a parking area. Ride through the parking area and out to Highway 475. The Eco-Centre is just a short distance across the road, and bike racks at the entrance will allow you to easily hop off your bike and explore the dunes. To return to the trailhead, simply backtrack along the Forest Trail.

RIDE 17 • Sentier NB Trails: Sackville–Port Elgin

AT A GLANCE

Length/configuration: 67.2 km (42 mile) combination (30.4-km [19-mile] out-and-back spur ridden twice; 6.4-km [4-mile] loop)

Aerobic difficulty: Lengthy, but the ride demands only a basic level of fitness

Technical difficulty: Beginner riding on the flat multi-use trail and dirt roads, and some intermediate riding on single- and double-track trails

Scenery: Lots to view; woods, salt marshes, and farmlands, and a historic site at the mouth of the Gaspereau River

Special comments: May be shortened to a 31.4-km (19.6-mile) point-to-point with a vehicle shuttle

The trail systems that make up the Sackville–Port Elgin ride demonstrate the synergy that can exist between local and provincial trails. The ride, which is a 67.2-km (42-mile) combination, makes use of the original right-of-way of the New Brunswick and Prince Edward Island Railway. The trail, now part of the Sentier NB Trail system, follows the converted railroad bed from Sackville to Port Elgin, where it connects with a local trail system that follows the Gaspereau River out to Fort Gaspereau National Historic Site. The multi-use trail provides a direct, easy-to-follow route between the two towns, and its link to the local Gaspereau Trail will give you the chance to discover more about the local community, the natural environment, and the history of the area.

On the multi-use trail between Sackville and Port Elgin, you will pass through an ever-changing landscape of salt marshes, mixed farmlands, and woodlands. In Port Elgin, following the Gaspereau Trail along the Gaspereau River, you will learn about the history of trade and settlement in the area through a series of interpretive signs, historic sites, and a visit to Fort Gaspereau National Historic Site overlooking Baie Verte. While the ride is lengthy, it is technically easy, and the distance will be manageable for most beginner riders with a moderate level of fitness. On the outbound spur along the Sentier NB Trail, you will enjoy a gradual decline over some sections of the trail. Of course, the return route features the same grade in reverse and, although the trail appears to be flat, you may have to gear down and work a little harder to return to the trailhead. The loop that begins on the Gaspereau Trail in Port Elgin presents some brief stretches of single- and double-track trail that require intermediate skills. However, these trails are very short and easy enough to walk through, even with a bike.

RIDE 17 • Sentier NB Trails: Sackville–Port Elgin

General location: The trailhead is in Sackville, roughly 53 km (32 miles) south of Moncton.

Elevation change: There is no significant change in elevation along the length of this ride.

Season: You can begin riding on the multi-use trail in early spring and continue until the snow falls in November. Spring rains should deter riders from heading out on the Gaspereau Trail until late May or June, as it will be very muddy and become more eroded in wet conditions.

Services: All services can be found in Sackville, with the exception of a bike store. Port Elgin has a Visitor Information Centre off of the highway and a few restaurants and town services. The nearest bike store is in Moncton.

Hazards: There were two bridges under construction at the time of our research. One was passable, but the other required a detour. Inquire about the trail's status at the Sackville Visitor Information Centre or with Sentier NB Trail by calling (800) 526-7070.

Rescue index: For most of the ride you will be near main roads and houses where you can seek assistance. The longest stretch between intersections is 10 km (6 miles) on the multi-use trail.

Land status: All of the land is owned by the province and designated for recreational purposes.

Maps: The multi-use trail appears as a rail bed in *The New Brunswick Atlas* (map 66, section E-5; map 75, section B-3). Additionally, maps of the Sentier NB Trail are available at Visitor Information Centres throughout New Brunswick, including the centres in Port Elgin and Sackville.

Finding the trail: From the Trans-Canada Highway, take Exit 541 into downtown Sackville. At the end of the off-ramp, at a **T** junction with Main Street, turn right if you are approaching from the west and left if you are approaching from the east. The trailhead is located at the Tantramar Regional High School, which is the first right off of Main Street on the north side of the Trans-Canada Highway. There is a large parking area at the bottom of a short paved hill. A shelter with a trail map and other information at the southwest end of the parking lot marks the start of the trail.

For vehicle shuttles heading to the other end of the trail, take Highway 2 to Aulac and then follow Highway 16 toward Port Elgin. At the intersection of Highways 16 and 15, turn off a major rotary and follow the signs for Port Elgin. Follow the road to a T [style Gothic] junction with Main Street. Access to the trail is down a lane directly ahead of you and to the right of the Scotia Bank.

Source of additional information:

> The New Brunswick Trails Council, Inc.
> 235 Main Street
> Fredericton, NB E3A 1E1
> (800) 526-7070

Notes on the trail: Departing from the parking lot at the Tantramar Regional High School, head out on the multi-use trail that runs parallel to the highway, which will be on your right. Continue until you reach a large wooden sign at an intersection with a multi-use trail that runs perpendicular to the one you are on. Turn left, and after a short distance bear right on the main trail, passing an offshoot on the left that leads toward a wooden bridge. The trail continues straight, lined by grassy fields all the way to Middle Sackville. As you approach a four-way intersection with a paved road, you will see Silver Lake to the left and the

In Port Elgin, the Gaspereau Trail offers scenic riding along the river to the shores of Baie Verte.

Middle Sackville United Baptist Church across the road on the right. Cross the road (Church Street) and continue along the multi-use trail.

Leaving Middle Sackville, you will ride through farm fields and cross a series of intersections with paved secondary roads. The land surrounding this stretch of the trail is populated with houses. After passing beneath a power line, you will cross a dirt road and continue through a stretch of farm fields and pastures. Here, the farmhouses are spaced farther apart and you begin to lose your sense of proximity to Sackville, or any other town. Surrounded by flat, open fields, you will make your way fairly quickly through this area of farmland, eventually arriving at a four-way intersection with a paved road. Again the trail continues directly across the road, heading into the woods after a short distance.

Continuing across the road, you will be commencing the longest stretch of uninterrupted trail between Sackville and Port Elgin. The ride continues straight, lined with trees on both sides, for the next 10 km (6 miles). There is a very slight decline for a considerable distance on this section of the ride, which will help you close the gap on the next intersection more quickly. Approximately two-thirds of the way along the trail you will cross the Brooklyn Bridge. (We anticipate that its construction will be complete upon publication of this guidebook. The bridge was incomplete but passable at the time of our research.) Beyond the bridge, a short distance farther on the trail, you will cross a dirt road which may also be signed as Snowmobile Trail 52. Continue straight on the rail trail to an intersection with a paved highway. Cross this road with caution and resume riding on the multi-use trail on the opposite side of the road.

The next stretch of trail is wooded, but it soon opens up on an area of salt marshes as you approach Highway 970 and Baie Verte. When you reach the intersection with Highway 970, you should be able to follow the trail on the other side of the highway. However, at the time we rode here, a missing bridge over a wide channel of water forced us to create a detour. You will be able to see whether the bridge has since been reconstructed by traveling a very short distance to the left along the highway. Once you find out, you can either continue to follow the detour along the highway, or backtrack to the intersection and rejoin the trail to ride across the new bridge. If you continue along the highway, turn right onto the next paved road and then take an immediate left back onto the trail. Whether you bypass or are able to ride across the bridge, continue straight on the trail the rest of the way to Port Elgin. A short distance outside the town, you will ride through an intersection with chemin Fort Moncton Road (Fort Road). This is the road on which you will return after visiting Fort Gaspereau National Historic Site, just over 2 km (1.25 miles) down the road on the right. The intersection marks the beginning of the loop portion of this ride, which starts by continuing straight along the rail trail.

Arriving in Port Elgin, the rail trail ends and you will see an old building on your left that once housed the Copp Woolen Mill. To your right, the Gaspereau Trail begins along a short stretch of wooden boardwalk. At this point, the ride continues along the Gaspereau Trail to the right. However, this is an easy place from which to ride into Port Elgin and meet up with your vehicle shuttle (if you have arranged for one). Should you choose to shorten your ride at this point, turn left up Spring Street and then continue straight across the Port Elgin footbridge. The meeting point we have recommended is at the far end of the bridge, in a small lane that runs beside the Scotia Bank.

Continuing the ride along the Gaspereau Trail, you will come to an information board that includes a map of the trail and details about the route. Beyond this point, the boardwalk ends and you will continue riding along a grassy trail that traces the perimeter of a small lagoon and then follows along the edge of the Gaspereau River. You will pass through a wooden gateway before emerging on a dirt road, Riverside Drive. Turn left and follow a series of arrows back onto a grassy double-track trail immediately to the left. A short distance along this trail you will arrive at Shady Beach, where there is a sheltered stand with a map, as well as a bench and a picnic table near the river's edge. Shady Beach was one of the beach areas used by the Mi'kmaq as a summer encampment.

From Shady Beach, you will follow the trail back to Riverside Drive. Cross the dirt road and re-enter the trail on the other side, passing through a wooden gate. You will ride through a meadow of wildflowers and raspberries before following the trail around to the left to ride up a grassy, double-track trail called Fish Road. As you enter Fish Road, you will pass a gate barring access along the old road to the right. Consider, as you make your way up this narrow, shaded trail, that fish processing plants and smoke houses once lined the road. Continue straight, past a trail branching off to the right, toward Gaspereau Point. The trail narrows as it approaches the river and winds through the woods. This is a more challenging stretch of trail, presenting some exposed roots and tight turns. Just before the trail turns right away from the river, there is an opening and a wooden deck built at Gaspereau Point. There is an open view of the Gaspereau River feeding into Baie Verte.

From here, the trail continues to wind tightly inland toward another marshy area. The trail is a combination of hard-packed dirt, some exposed roots, and marshy patches where narrow wooden planks have been laid. You will pass a trail on the right that connects back to Fish Road, then pass through some short boggy sections. Once you reach the marsh, you will ride across another planked boardwalk that begins with some turns but straightens when it reaches and continues parallel to Fort Road. Toward the end of the boardwalk there is a raised section with a couple of stairs on either end. You will have to walk your bike over the bridge and resume riding on the other side, out to the dirt road. Turn left when you reach the dirt road and ride just a short distance to the entrance to Fort Gaspereau National Historic Site, which is a gravel road on the left that leads out to a lighthouse, cemetery, and rock cairn.

Upon arriving at Fort Gaspereau National Historic Site, you will learn that the fort was built by French troops in 1751 to prevent the British from invading the Chignecto Isthmus. You will also learn that the fort was determined to be "of little strategic importance" and was ultimately burned down by the British in 1756, just five years after its construction. Regardless, the fort was situated at a beautiful site overlooking the waters of Baie Verte, and there are picnic tables from which to enjoy the view.

Departing from the historic site, turn left on Fort Road. You will pass Indian Road branching off on the left before Fort Road turns to pavement. A short distance further, you will approach a **T** junction with Highway 970. Just before this junction, the Sentier NB Trail crosses Fort Road. Turn left on the trail to return to Sackville, or, if you have arranged for a vehicle shuttle, turn right to return to Port Elgin.

If you are returning to Port Elgin to meet a vehicle shuttle, the parking area behind the Scotia Bank in Port Elgin is an excellent place to meet. Ride back along the multi-use trail to Port Elgin. Arriving at the start of the Gaspereau Trail, turn left and ride along the paved road, Spring Street. This road will bring you to a wooden footbridge that crosses over the Gaspereau River. Cross the bridge, and you will arrive at the parking area behind the bank, which is located on Port Elgin's Main Street.

RIDE 18 • Beaumont

AT A GLANCE

Length/configuration: 24-km (15-mile) combination (two overlapping loops; a 9-km [5.6-mile] loop within a 15-km [9.4-mile] loop)

Aerobic difficulty: Lots of moderate hills; a great workout when ridden fast

Technical difficulty: Intermediate; rocky, hilly terrain on double-track trails with some stretches on dirt roads

Scenery: Spectacular views of Hopewell Cape across the Petitcodiac River

Special comments: Good cruising on the downhills and many trail options

Spectacular views, challenging terrain, and exuberant riders combined to make this one of our most memorable rides. Heading out with a group of bikers sporting more colourful combinations of Lycra than we had ever encountered was initially daunting. However, once the group assembled and we began to ride, we soon discovered that we were amidst people who had mastered the art of combining fun and fitness. Most of these riders emanated from Bungay's Bicycle & Snowboard Shop in Moncton. There you can obtain information about the Moncton Mountain Bike Club and probably get the name and phone number of the person leading the week's group ride. It is our experience that exploring new trails is often best done with at least one guide, if not a group of knowledgeable riders.

Our ride at Beaumont began on a 9-km (5.6-mile) warm-up loop and concluded on a longer, 15-km (9.4-mile) loop. The combination creates a loop-within-a-loop that includes only a short overlap. Both loops begin and end at the parking area, and will give you a thorough introduction to the network of trails within the area. The ride distance comes to a total of 24 km (15 miles), and the undulating, rocky terrain is best for fit riders with intermediate to advanced skills. The first loop is a short but rigorous ride that will get your blood flowing. It features climbs and descents on rocky, hard-packed, double-track trails and touches only briefly on dirt roads. On the second loop you will cross to the east bank of the peninsula and complete a circuit around its perimeter, riding along the Memramcook River to Fort Folly Point, and then returning to the trailhead along the shore of the Petitcodiac River. This part of the ride expands upon the first loop and follows a combination of double-track trails and dirt roads. The view from the tip of the peninsula is the scenic highlight of the entire ride, and

RIDE 18 • Beaumont

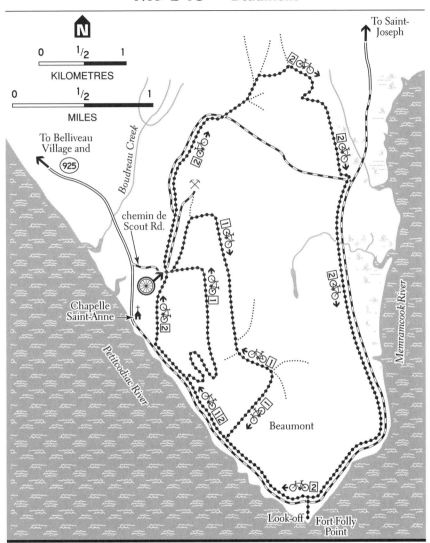

encompasses the irregular, rocky shores of Hopewell Cape across the Petitcodiac River and the expansive waters of Shepody Bay.

General location: The trailhead is located in Beaumont, a half-hour southeast of Moncton on the Petitcodiac River.

Elevation change: Over two moderate hills and several short climbs you will gain a total 250 m (820 feet) in elevation.

Season: Most riders will want to wait until June to head out on these trails, to allow even the most shaded areas to dry. Good riding conditions continue through September but peak in August, New Brunswick's driest month.

Services: All services are available in Moncton.

Hazards: Approach all descents with caution. Visibility may be reduced due to alder growth, and the terrain may be challenging due to steep grades and loose rock.

Rescue index: The closest source of assistance is several kilometres (a few miles) back down the highway.

Land status: A former scout camp on Crown land.

Maps: With the exception of the dirt road, the trails described here do not appear on any map. With the trail description, guidebook map, and government topographic map Hillsborough 21 H/15, you will greatly reduce your chances of getting lost. Also, because of frequent multiple intersections, you may find it useful to bring a compass or sport your Casio Pathfinder, the jazzy combination altimetre, compass, and timepiece, to ensure you are heading in the right direction of the trails.

Finding the trail: From Moncton, take NB Highway 106 east toward Saint-Joseph. Once outside the city, you will bear right onto Highway 925, which follows closely along the Petitcodiac River. Continue on Highway 925 through Gautreau Village, to Pre-d'en-Haut. In Pre-d'en-Haut, Highway 925 continues around a sharp curve to the left. Continue straight at this point, following signs for Beaumont. Still following the Petitcodiac River, you will drive through Belliveau Village and Boudreau Village before seeing signs for Beaumont Road and Camp Beaumont. Turn left, following an arrow, when you reach chemin de Scout Road. This is a well-maintained dirt road that curves to the left before reaching the parking area, a clearing on the left-hand side of the road that is situated directly across from a grassy field.

Source of additional information: You can reach members of the Moncton Mountain Bike Club through Bungay's Bicycle & Snowboard Shop, located at 647 Mountain Road (phone (506) 389-2880).

Notes on the trail: From the parking area, turn right onto chemin de Scout Road and then turn left at the first intersection. You will climb a short hill before passing a narrow trail branching off on the right. At just over 0.5 km (0.3 mile), turn right onto a snowmobile trail and up a steep, loose, rocky grade. At the top, the trail becomes grassy and you will follow it around a curve to the right. Around the bend, you will come to a split in the trail and bear left, heading up a grassy double-track. This is a challenging climb that brings you to another fork. A snowmobile trail continues to the left, and the ride continues to the right, heading south.

The next portion of the ride will initiate you into the downhill terrain that characterizes the peninsula. Riders catching the most air claimed to apply very little pressure to their brakes. For a roller-coaster descent, keeping regular contact

Patrick slows for a photo before beginning another rocketing descent at Beaumont.

between the ground and your tires, apply moderate pressure and maintain a consistent speed as you make your way down. Either way, the overgrown alder bushes will prevent you from anticipating any of the bumps, so you might as well relax and enjoy the ride. Emerging from the alders at the bottom of the hill, continue straight past a trail branching off to the left. Continuing ahead, the trail widens, becoming almost roadlike, and bends sharply to the right. After the bend, watch for an opening in the trees and turn left, uphill, on a narrow dirt trail. At the crest of this hill you will come to a grassy clearing and a three-way intersection. Turn right and descend to a **T** junction with a dirt road.

At the **T** junction, turn right and continue along the dirt road. You will continue to ride parallel to the Petitcodiac River a short distance before turning right at the first opportunity. You will follow a grassy, double-track trail up a series of switchbacks that represent the toughest climb of the ride. At the crest of the hill continue straight, following signs for Snowmobile Trail 51. You will pass a sign for La Pointe to the right and continue to follow the trail as it curves around to the left, descending a steep hill. On the descent you will pass through a **T** junction with a trail heading up to the left. Continue straight, following the trail back to the parking area and completing the first loop of the ride.

To begin the second loop, pass the parking area on your left and continue riding along chemin de Scout Road. As you pass a clear-cut on the right, you will also pass an indistinct grassy trail on the left, and then arrive at a fork. Choose the double-track trail to the left, which will bear left for a short distance and then jog in slightly to the right. The trail will straighten for a short distance and then curve to the right. Slow down through this gentle curve, so as not to miss the narrow dirt trail branching off to the left just around the bend. Following this trail, you will soon arrive at a three-way intersection. The left is signed for snowmobiles, and you will bear right, heading east-northeast. You will climb a short distance, and then arrive at a **T** junction with a double-track trail and turn right. The trail begins to descend, and then takes a sharp turn to the right and continues up a steep hill. Beyond the crest of the hill, the trail bends to the right and then continues straight (past a few rough trails off to both the left and right) to a **T** junction with a dirt road.

At the end of the climb the trail descends immediately down the other side. There is a bend to the right, and then you continue straight to a **T** junction with a dirt road. Across the road is a blueberry barren, and to the left you can see the Memramcook River. Turn left at the dirt road, continuing down a short hill, and bear right at the next **T** junction with a dirt road.

After the right-hand turn onto the dirt road, you will continue inland toward the southern tip of the peninsula. As you approach the tip, the road will follow more closely along the shore. It will curve to the right, then straighten and continue a short distance inland across the tip. A trail branches off to the left and drops down to Fort Folly Point, where there was once a lighthouse. You can perch on the edge of a cliff here and take in the surrounding scenery. To the right you are looking out over Shepody Bay to Hopewell Cape and Hillsborough. Across the Memramcook River to the left you can see the town of Dorchester. From here, return up the hill and continue on the main trail to the left.

Still following the main road, you will pass a logging road on the right. You may recognize this road from earlier in the ride, when you descended to this point on the first loop. Continue straight on the dirt road, and on your right-hand side you will also pass the switchback trail you turned up on the first loop. Continue along the road a short distance further, to a point where an old "ski-doo" trail turns off the road to the right near a few old apple trees. The ride concludes along this trail to the right, but you can also continue straight on the dirt road for a short but interesting side trip. On the right-hand side of the road, just beyond a small knoll, you will reach the site of an old church and cemetery. This site, Le Village Indienne and Chapelle Saint-Anne, dates back to the mid-1800s. An interpretive sign highlights some of the history of the area, and describes the building of the stone church as well as cabins and a wooden chapel that no longer exist. Once you have satisfied your curiosity, turn back down the dirt road and then turn left on the "ski-doo" to return to the trailhead and complete the second loop.

RIDE 19 • Centennial Park

AT A GLANCE

Length/configuration: 15 km (9.4 miles) of trails comprised of three loops that are 4 km (2.5 miles), 5 km (3.1 miles), and 6 km (3.8 miles) in length

Aerobic difficulty: Basic; mostly flat with a very few short hills

Technical difficulty: Beginner; wide dirt and gravel-dusted trails

Scenery: Mostly forested urban park with a look-off over the swimming area

Special comments: Maze of single-track trails branching off the main trails

The trails in Moncton's Centennial Park are spread over 450 acres of park land. The 6-km (3.8-mile) loop described here is an easy-going ride that may be extended by exploring the single-track trails in the park. Mountain bikes have taken to the area for evening rides and use it as a local training area. From the main multi-use trail that loops through the park, you can branch off onto stretches of single-track that wind their way through the woods along the hillsides surrounding the main trails. By familiarizing yourself with the main multi-use trail system, you will be well prepared to venture into the woods, creating endless circuits by combining these trails with the single-track.

The loop described here traces the longest route around the perimeter of the park. It follows a mostly flat, dirt-and-gravel trail that is suitable to all ages and abilities. You will ride through the woods, arriving at picnic areas and recreational spots throughout the park. Given the number of regular visitors to the park and the variety of recreational activities the area accommodates, you will frequently encounter other bikers, hikers, and park users, which makes this an ideal place to develop your off-road skills.

General location: Within a few minutes' drive of downtown Moncton.

Elevation change: There is no significant change in elevation.

Season: The park is usually clear of snow by April, and riding conditions are good beginning in May and continuing through October.

Services: There are washrooms and picnic areas within the park, as well as a beach and water park. All other services are available in Moncton.

Hazards: None.

RIDE 19 · Centennial Park

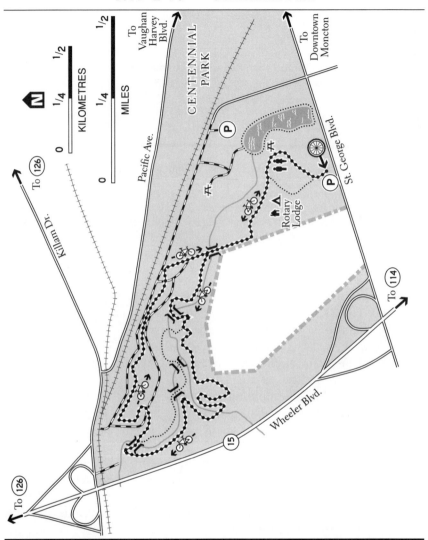

Rescue index: You can probably rely on other park users for assistance, or make your way to the Kiwanis Camp near the entrance to the park. It is staffed year-round and will provide assistance.

Land status: Municipal park with recreational areas managed by local community service groups.

Maps: There is a map at the start of the trail, and all of the main trails have been blazed.

Finding the trail: From the Trans-Canada Highway, take Exit 496 and begin travelling south on Highway 115 (Promenade Elmwood). Turn right when you reach Morton Avenue and continue straight across Highway 15, at which point the road becomes Connaught Avenue. From Connaught, turn left at a lighted intersection onto Mountain Road. Continuing on Mountain Road, you will turn right at the first lighted intersection onto Vaughan Harvey Boulevard. A short distance along, you will turn right again at the first lighted intersection onto St. George Street. The entrance to the park is on the right-hand side of the road, signed with a "Rotary Lodge" billboard. Plenty of parking is available here.

Source of additional information: It is best to hook up with a local cycling club to explore the single-track trails in the park. Weekly club rides leave from Bungay's Bicycle & Snowboard Shop, located at 647 Mountain Road (phone (506) 389-2880).

Notes on the trail: There is a large billboard at the edge of the parking area that outlines all the main trails in the park. Begin the ride by following the main trail that extends straight from the parking lot. At the first opportunity, you will turn right onto a wide dirt trail heading into a sparsely treed area. Continue ahead and follow the trail as it curves around to the left. Ignore the trails branching off to your right and stay on the main trail, bearing left. Ignore the trail branching of to your right and stay on the main trail, bearing left. As you approach an observation point at a shelter with picnic tables, the ride continues along a trail on the left that heads into the woods. You may want to first ride up to the observation point, where you can look out on the water park area below. Continuing the ride along the trail in the woods, you will be heading toward the main park area where you can follow any of the three loops.

Continuing on this wide dirt trail, it will curve gently to the right and then cross a small bridge. Turn left across the bridge, following the trail parallel to the river. This stretch of the trail snakes its way toward the first intersection. It will bend to the right as it approaches a second bridge, and then curve around to the left on the other side. Finally, it will bend to the right as you near the first fork in the trail. At the fork, bear left to follow the longest, orange loop that takes you around the perimeter of the park. If you bear right instead, the trail cuts across the middle of the park, resulting in a 4-km (2.5-mile) loop following the green blazes, and a 5-km (3.1-mile) loop following the yellow blazes, back to the parking area.

Following the orange blazes, the trail continues parallel to the river and takes a sharp bend to the left. Around the bend it begins to curve gently back to the right. The trail will again begin to snake its way toward a bridge that crosses back over the brook. Across this bridge, the trail swoops down toward the middle of the park. As you curve down to the right, you will pass a trail on the left that is part of the yellow loop. Continue past this trail and complete the short **U** in the orange trail. As the trail swings back up to the left, you will pass the other end of the yellow trail on your left. Continue to follow the orange trail as it begins to curve to the right.

Around the bend to the right, you will arrive at a fork. Once again, the trail on the right cuts across the middle of the park, and would return you to the first intersection beyond the second bridge at the start of the ride. Bear left here to continue to follow the outer edge of the park Continue through a four-way intersection with a wide dirt-and-gravel trail, which may be signed as the sled trail, and follow it around a curve to the right. It will soon straighten out and continue parallel to the rail bed for a considerable distance. Eventually the trail will bend sharply to the right, returning you to the first bridge. Continue straight over the bridge to return to the parking area, or bear right to repeat the loop. On the return to the parking area, bear left on the trail to avoid crossing through the Kiwanis Camp. You will loop back around through the wooded opening, bearing right as you pass the observation point. Follow the dirt road from the observation point back to the main access trail, and bear left to return to the parking area.

RIDE 20 • Hillsborough

AT A GLANCE

Length/configuration: 8-km (5.6-mile) loop

Aerobic difficulty: Moderate; constant, rolling climbs

Technical difficulty: Intermediate to advanced; single- and double-track trails

Scenery: Stunning terrain through an old gypsum quarry and wooded area

Special comments: Home to the annual White Rock Fat Tire Festival

No discussion about mountain biking in New Brunswick, let alone the Moncton area, is complete without mention of the racecourse at Hillsborough. The course is set in a former gypsum mining area and is renowned for its treacherous, brilliant-white surface and random sinkholes. The 8-km (5.6-mile) course outlined here basically follows the outer limits of the quarry and represents about half of the bikable trails here. It begins at the typical starting point of the race, in the "pit area," and continues on double- and single-track trails that wind up and down short hills, around and through the main mining area. These trails demand excellent bike handling skills, as the gypsum offers little in the way of traction and is very unforgiving in a wipeout situation—just think-

RIDE 20 • Hillsborough

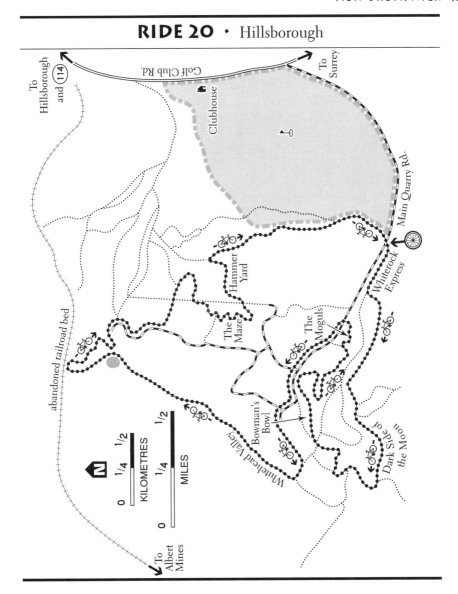

ing about it is discomforting. Nonetheless, local riders love to train here because they get an excellent workout.

General location: Hillsborough is situated on the west bank of the Petitcodiac River, approximately 22 km (14 miles) south of downtown Moncton.

Elevation change: This race circuit is characterized by only short, steep climbs and descents.

A smooth double-track trail leads to an old gypsum mine at Hillsborough.

Season: Good conditions on this course should exist from late June through October.

Services: All services are available in Moncton, a relatively short drive away.

Hazards: This course wends and weaves through an old gypsum mine. Along some portions of the ride, the trail features an unusually slick surface that closely resembles shards of white ceramic plates in both consistency and sharpness. A fall on this surface is bound to be painful. Of additional note is the vast and potentially confusing network of trails in this area. It is wise to travel with a copy of the Hillsborough orienteering map, or (even better) with a local rider familiar with the trail system.

Rescue index: Though the network of trails in this area is vast, you will not wander far from a busy golf course near the trailhead.

Land status: This trail follows roads and trails through a former mining area that now serves as a recreational site for many outdoor enthusiasts. It is owned by the Provincial Department of Education. In addition to a golf course and developing recreation centre, the area is used commonly by hikers, bikers, and orienteering buffs.

Maps: The only useful map for this ride is the Hillsborough orienteering map. To purchase a copy of this map, contact the president(s) of the local Falcon Orienteering Club:

Ed and Luella Smith
R.R. #2
Albert, NB E0A 1A0
(506) 887-2030

Finding the trail: From Moncton, drive approximately 16 km (10 miles) south on Route 114 to the town of Hillsborough. A short distance into the town, turn right on Golf Club Road, which heads toward the Hillsborough Outdoor Recreation Area. Continue down the road, past the entrance to the outdoor club, and on toward a golf course. Just past the golf course clubhouse, bear right at a fork in the road. At the intersection go straight, keeping the golf course on your right. The road narrows beyond this point, and just after passing a small quarry, you can simply pull over and park to the side of what is referred to as the "pit area."

Source of additional information: For more information about this ride or to arrange for guided mountain bike tours (and even caving) in the area, contact Richard and Kathy Faulkner at:

Baymount Outdoor Adventures
17 Elwin Jay Drive
Hillsborough, NB E0A 1X0
(506) 734-2660

Notes on the trail: From the "pit area," begin the ride by continuing west on the Main Quarry road. Just 300 m (383 yards) up the road, bear left at the Y intersection and begin the short (but steep) three-hill climb known as the "Whiterock Express." After leveling out for 200 meters (120 yards), you come to a four-way intersection. Turn left, find the granny gears, and grunt your way uphill to the next intersection just beyond the end of this climb.

At the intersection, follow the single-track trail to the right and begin the interesting descent around the section of the quarry referred to as "The Dark Side of the Moon." At the end of this run, turn right on the double-track road and head once again for the main quarry. Continue to the rear of the main quarry to a main intersection with two dirt roads; both head east toward the starting point and a single-track trail leading into the quarry. This marks the start of the most interesting and technically challenging section of the course: 1.5 km (0.9 mile) of single-track through rough, open gypsum terrain that culminates in a long, sweeping descent and short steep climb out of "Bowman's Bowl."

Having successfully passed through this treacherous stretch of terrain, turn left as you climb out of the bowl onto the "Lower Quarry Road." The stretch of easy riding on this dirt road is short-lived as you will turn right at the first opportunity into "the Moguls," a series of small gypsum tailing piles dumped over 50 years ago, creating a roller coaster effect. Once through the Moguls, turn right (back on Lower Quarry Road) and head west. Continue past one road branching off to the right, and turn right at the second opportunity. This trail should feel washboarded like an old railroad bed. In fact, this is an old mining railroad route that will end in roughly 400 m (437 yards) at the Milton Quarry. Just beyond the end of this rough road, turn right toward a steel gate to begin the thrilling descent through "Whitehead Valley."

At the bottom of the hill, continue to the end of the valley, past a pond, then turn left and climb a short hill to the abandoned railroad bed (scheduled to become part of the Sentier NB Trails initiative by the year 2000). Turn right onto the railroad bed and travel only 15 m (16 yards) before turning right again onto a challenging downhill single-track. The single-track will return you to the pond at an intersection, where you will turn left onto a double-track trail. Continue on this double-track to the next significant **Y** intersection, where you will bear right and follow the woods road as it winds gradually uphill. Near the end of this climb, you will be faced with yet another climb, at the end of which you will turn left.

Continue a short distance on this road straight through a **T** junction to a single-track trail that twists and turns like a snake until it reaches the main road. Cross the road and enjoy a crazy ride through "the Maze," a single-track trail that winds its way through several narrow ravines. Exiting the Maze, turn left and then immediately right into a low-lying area known as the "Hamm Yard." At the end of this open area, you must make a 160° turn to the right. The trail straight ahead leads you back to the golf course clubhouse, while the sharp turn to the right leads you back to the parking area. As you head toward the parking area, you will pass the tee-off area of the golf course's seventh fairway—fore!

The trail description for the Hillsborough ride was generously provided by Sean Ritchie, our guide and mountain bike rider extraordinaire.

RIDE 21 • Goose River

AT A GLANCE

Length/configuration: 15.8-km (9.8-mile) out-and-back (7.9 km [4.9 mile] each way)

Aerobic difficulty: Strenuous; continuous climbing and descending on both steep and moderate hills

Technical difficulty: Beginner to intermediate; primarily grassy, double-track trail with some areas of loose rock

Scenery: This forested trail reaches a glorious look-off over the Bay of Fundy

Special comments: Plan this ride as a multi-day tour, camping at the mouth of Goose River

RIDE 21 • Goose River

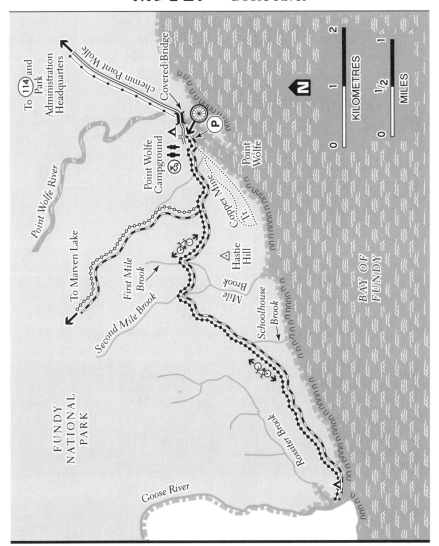

Of the handful of trails open to mountain bikers in Fundy National Park, the Goose River trail is the only one that provides access to the edge of the rugged cliffs overlooking the Bay of Fundy. The trailhead is located at Point Wolfe, where one of the two covered bridges in the park spans Point Wolfe River. From Point Wolfe, the ride traces a hilly, inland route to the mouth of the Goose River. This point is truly the highlight of the trip: the trail suddenly opens up to breathtaking vistas across the Bay of Fundy and toward Martin Head, farther down the coast. Primitive campsites perch atop the high cliffs rising up from the mouth of the river, where a sheltered, rocky beach and sandbar provide opportunities for further exploration.

This ride follows an old cart track through heavily wooded terrain, rolling across a series of hills and valleys created by fast-flowing streams. It is a 15.8-km (9.8-mile) out-and-back excursion that is well signed and easy to follow. The trail is hard-packed and includes sections of grassy double-track as well as gravel and loose rock. Although the ride requires only basic bike handling skills, its grueling hills demand cardiovascular fitness and endurance. That said, this ride makes an excellent overnight trip for hardy riders equipped with racks and panniers. The mouth of the Goose River is a peaceful place to linger, and the primitive campsites available are possibly the most beautiful in the park. To use these sites you must register in advance at the Visitor Centre, or by calling the park at the number listed below. For riders looking for an extended, backcountry adventure, the Goose River Trail can be ridden in conjunction with the Marven Lake Trail (see Ride 22). By camping at the mouth of the Goose River one night, and at Marven Lake for another, a full three-days' worth of riding and exploring offers unlimited possibilities for adventurous riders visiting the park.

General location: Fundy National Park.

Elevation change: You will begin this ride at an elevation of roughly 46 m (150 feet) above sea level. The trail immediately climbs to 213 m (700 feet), and then rolls through several steep gullies before descending to the mouth of the Goose River at sea level. Total elevation gain for the ride is a substantial 488 m (1,600 feet).

Season: Summer activities begin in the park in late May and continue through October.

Services: The park offers full-service, primitive, and wilderness campsites. With the exception of firewood (which may be purchased at the park), visitors are responsible for bringing their own supplies. There are rest room facilities located at the trailhead for this ride. All bike-related needs are best met in either Sussex or Moncton.

Hazards: Expect to encounter rough, eroded conditions over the steepest sections of this trail. After heavy rainfall, narrow gullies may develop and make riding more difficult. Remember to always yield to hikers.

Rescue index: At the farthest point on this trail, at the mouth of the Goose River, you will be 7.9 km (5 miles) from the trailhead, where assistance can be sought at the Point Wolfe Campground. The park is staffed year-round, and there are first-aid stations and telephones at the Visitor Centre, Wolfe Lake Information Centre, and all campground kiosks. If you are concerned about heading out on the trail, register with park staff at the Information Centre and be sure to check out with them at the end of your day.

Land status: National park; from mid-May to mid-October there is an entry fee for all visitors to the park.

Maps: Basic trail maps are included in *Salt & Fir*, the visitor guide available at the Visitor Centre. For more detailed information, refer to the government topographic map Waterford 21 H/11.

Finding the trail: You can enter the park on NB Highway 114 from Sussex through the west entrance, or from Moncton through the Alma entrance. From either direction, make your way to the Park Administration Headquarters, located near the coast on Highway 114, at the junction with chemin Point Wolfe. Turn off of Highway 114 in front of the headquarters building, and drive down chemin Point Wolfe all the way to its end. You will drive through a covered bridge over Point Wolfe River and continue uphill to a large parking area at the end of the road, passing the entrance to Point Wolfe Campground on the right. The trailhead is located at the far end of the parking lot, near a collection of trail signs.

Source of additional information:

> Fundy National Park
> P.O. Box 40
> Alma, NB E0A 1B0
> (506) 887-6000
> Fundy_info@pch.gc.ca

Notes on the trail: At the far end of the parking lot, you will find some trail signs and the trailheads for the Copper Mine trail and Rat Tail, Goose River, Marven Lake, and Bennett Lake trails. Begin riding up the narrow trail signed for Goose River. You will very quickly come to a **T** junction with a wide gravel road. Turn left and begin climbing.

You will not be eased into this ride along the Goose River Trail, but will face the most difficult climbing at the very start. The trail surface along this first portion of the ride is also the most rocky, and may feature narrow, eroded gullies created by heavy rain. On this initial climb you will pass a little waterfall to your left as the trail crosses Hastie Brook. After the first rigorous kilometre (0.6 mile), a fork in the trail signals that the worst of the climbing is over. A sign at this intersection will direct you to follow the path to the left, signed to Goose River, which is 6.9 km (4.2 miles) farther along the trail.

Beyond the fork, the ride continues over rolling terrain along the old cart track. As you follow the trail around the north side of Hastie Hill, the trees on either side stand tall and limit views beyond the immediate corridor created by the trail. Before too long the terrain changes dramatically, and you will descend and then climb steeply through the narrow valleys created by First Mile Brook and Second Mile Brook. The cart trail has suffered some damage due to erosion on these steep sections of the ride, and the loose rocks and gravel make the already strenuous climbs still more challenging.

Beyond Second Mile Brook, the trail evens out somewhat and rolls more gently toward the coast. After dipping slightly through the small valley created by Schoolhouse Brook, your approach to the mouth of the Goose River will be announced by a view overlooking the Bay of Fundy and Martin Head. This view comes just before the trail begins a long descent toward the water. As you proceed gradually downhill, you will reach the #4 camping area on the left side of the trail. Here, a stunning view of the Bay of Fundy, steep coastal cliffs, and Martin Head provides ample reward for the hilly, cloistered ride. Farther on, you will reach another camping area. Beyond this point it is recommended that you leave your bike and follow, on foot, a narrow trail that drops down steeply to the mouth of the Goose River. Among the charms of this sheltered area is a rocky beach that literally dazzles the eye with the countless variations in the colour of the smooth stones and pebbles that sweep down to the water in a series of small ridges.

The return trip from the Goose River follows the same hilly path back out toward Point Wolfe. If you have planned an extended tour and aim to follow the Marven Lake trail to the campsites located at Chamber Lake or Marven Lake, simply ride back to the signed fork in the trail and turn left, heading uphill and following signs for Marven Lake. Otherwise, continue straight and enjoy the descent from the fork back to the parking area at Point Wolfe.

RIDE 22 · Marven Lake

AT A GLANCE

Length/configuration: 16-km (10-mile) out-and-back [8 km [5 miles] each way)

Aerobic difficulty: Strenuous; continuous climbing and descending over modest hills

Technical difficulty: Beginner to intermediate; hard-packed cart track with some sections of loose rock

Scenery: This wooded corridor leads to the banks of Marven Lake and Chambers Lake

Special comments: Camping opportunities available at Marven and Chambers Lakes

This ride is a 16-km (10-mile) out-and-back trip along an old road leading out past Chambers Lake to Marven Lake. For most of the ride, conditions are easy and require no advanced technical skills. There are, however, a few hills with rougher, more eroded terrain, and a number of sections of the trail where flooding might occur. Good cardiovascular fitness is recommended, since the

RIDE 22 • Marven Lake

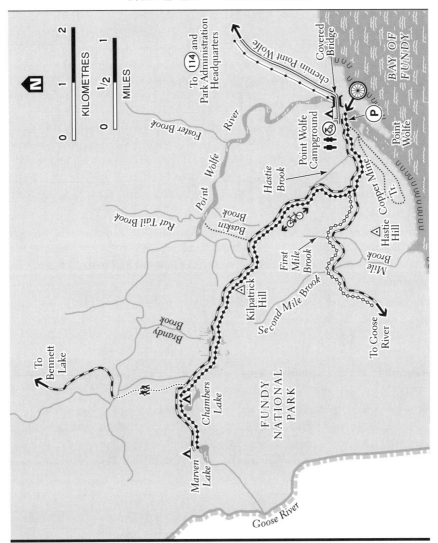

trail rolls over a series of seemingly endless hills through pleasant, coastal forests of spruce and fir.

The technically easy terrain on the Marven Lake Trail makes the ride a good choice for those looking for an overnight tour. Even with panniers full of camping equipment and food, you will find that the trail presents no significant obstacles and can easily be completed in a morning or afternoon. There are primitive campsites located near the shores of both Chambers Lake and Marven Lake. These sites offer riders and hikers alike the opportunity to experience the beauty and quiet of the park's inner wilderness. To use these sites, you must register in advance at the Visitor Centre, or by calling the park at the number listed below. Refer to Ride 21, the Goose River Trail, for suggestions on linking the two rides to create a three-day, two-night, mountain biking tour. Furthermore, although the trail is closed to mountain bikers, the Bennett Brook Trail to Point Wolfe River is a worthwhile side trip along a narrow footpath that descends to the steep bank of the river.

General location: Fundy National Park.

Elevation change: This ride begins near Point Wolfe at an elevation of roughly 46 m (150 feet). The trail climbs steadily to 259 m (850 feet), before rolling through two small valleys and peaking at 290 m (950 feet) atop Kilpatrick Hill. From Kilpatrick Hill, the trail continues over rolling terrain to Marven Lake at 244 m (800 feet). Total elevation gain for the out-and-back ride is approximately 656 m (2,150 feet).

Season: Summer activities begin in the park in late May and continue through October. Portions of the Marven Lake Trail are susceptible to flooding, so inquire about recent and upcoming weather conditions before you head out on the trail.

Services: The park offers full-service, primitive, and wilderness campsites. With the exception of firewood (which may be purchased at the park), visitors are responsible for bringing their own supplies. All bike-related needs are best met in Sussex or Moncton. Rest rooms are located at the trailhead.

Hazards: After heavy rainfall, some sections of this trail may disappear beneath water. As with all rides in Fundy National Park, remember to yield to hikers.

Rescue index: At Marven Lake, the farthest point on this trail, you will be 8 km (5 miles) from the trailhead and the kiosk for the Point Wolfe Campground. If you are concerned about heading out on the trail, register with park staff at the Information Centre and be sure to check out with them at the end of your day.

Land status: National park; from mid-May to mid-October there is an entry fee for all visitors to the park.

Maps: The park visitor guide, *Salt & Fir*, includes a basic map of all the trails in the park. For more detailed information, refer to the government topographic map Waterford 21 H/11.

Finding the trail: You can enter the park on NB Highway 114 from Sussex through the west entrance, or from Moncton through the Alma entrance. From either direction, make your way to the Park Administration Headquarters, located on Highway 114 at its junction with chemin Point Wolfe. Turn off of Highway 114 in front of the headquarters building and drive down chemin Point Wolfe all the way to its end. You will drive through a covered bridge over Point Wolfe River and continue uphill, passing the entrance to Point Wolfe Campground on the right, before reaching a large parking area at the end of the road. The trailhead is located at the far end of the parking lot.

Source of additional information:

Fundy National Park
P.O. Box 40
Alma, NB E0A 1B0
(506) 887-6000
Fundy_info@pch.gc.ca

Notes on the trail: At the far end of the parking lot you will find the signs and trailheads for the Copper Mine trail and Rat Tail, Goose River, Marven Lake, and Bennett Lake Trails. Begin riding up the narrow trail signed for Marven Lake. You will very quickly come to a **T** junction with a wide gravel road. Turn left and begin climbing. This first section of the trail features the steepest, most eroded terrain of the entire ride. Although conditions are technically quite easy, the extended climb requires cardiovascular fitness and serves as a rigourous initiation to the ride.

You will pass a little waterfall as the trail crosses Hastie Brook, and just 1 km (0.6 mile) into the ride, you will reach a fork in the trail. Turn right and continue uphill, following the sign for Marven Lake, 7 km (4.3 miles) from this point. The first incline on this trail has quite a bit of loose rock, but the trail soon levels out and descends somewhat, continuing as a wide gravel road with a grassy median. The trees on either side of the road rise up dramatically, overshadowing the trail and turning it into a long wooded corridor. You will cross over a culvert before the trail curves to the left slightly and heads uphill. After a short distance on even ground, the trail descends gently and bends around to the right. Throughout the length of the trail you will catch glimpses into the forest undergrowth of lush ferns and carpets of moss.

After a gradual descent, the trail will actually begin to drop more steeply. You will cross a little brook and then traverse a low-lying stretch of trail that may be covered in water. After crossing another small brook that runs through a culvert, you will climb gradually to a sign and trail for Point Wolfe River and Foster Brook on the right. This trail is closed to cyclists, so continue straight on the main trail. You are almost at the half way point here, with Marven Lake 4.4 km (2.7 miles) farther down the trail.

Past the sign for Point Wolfe River and Foster Brook, you will begin up a slightly steeper climb before traversing another even stretch. The trail continues in much the same way as it began, but as you gain some elevation, the path ahead will seem to open up as though there were light at the end of this tunnel between the hills. This climb takes you to the top of Kilpatrick Hill, and although the trail continues downhill from this point, a sea of ferns at the crest of the hill brightens the trailside.

Beyond the ferns, you will descend gradually to another low spot before climbing a gradual rise. Descending again, you will ride through another low-lying area where water may cross the trail. When we rode here after a night of heavy rain, we startled a pair of ducks contentedly swimming across the trail. From this point, you will once again climb gradually, reaching the junction with the Bennett Brook Trail, which branches off to the right along a narrow trail on which bikes are prohibited. Bear left here, following the main trail. Marven Lake is just eight-tenths of a kilometre (one-half mile) farther along the trail.

Beyond the intersection, you will come to a turnoff on the left for Chambers Lake, where there are a few campsites. Farther along the trail you will come to a picnic area. Beyond this site the trail narrows considerably and descends to Marven Lake. A small wooden boardwalk heading out to the lake provides a good vantage point for observing moose and beaver, both animals that favour the boggy edges of shallow lakes such as this.

The return trip is simply the same trail in reverse: turn around and retrace your tracks back to Point Wolfe.

RIDE 23 · Bennett Brook

AT A GLANCE

Length/configuration: 10-km (6-mile) out-and-back (5 km [3 miles] each way)

Aerobic difficulty: Moderate; long gradual climbs in both directions

Technical difficulty: Mostly beginner, with some intermediate riding on double-track trails

Scenery: A forested ride that descends to a tributary of the Point Wolfe River

Special comments: A hike-a-bike excursion

The main attractions at Fundy National Park are the dramatic cliffs that plunge into the ocean and a shoreline of colourful, rocky beaches. These sights are stunning by sea kayak or a walk on the beach; however, turning inland on a mountain bike, there is thickly forested, rolling wilderness terrain to discover. The Bennett Brook Trail offers an exemplary 10-km (6-mile) out-and-back ride on a rolling old road. Following the natural curves of the landscape, you will eventually arrive at the shores of Bennett Brook and find yourself surrounded by tall, forested hillsides.

Because of a short stretch of intermediate trail near the beginning of the ride and the rolling hills, this trail is best suited to advanced beginners with a good level of fitness. The more difficult stretch of trail is characterized by exposed roots and rocks and involves crossing a rocky streambed. Beyond this stretch the trail

RIDE 23 • Bennett Brook

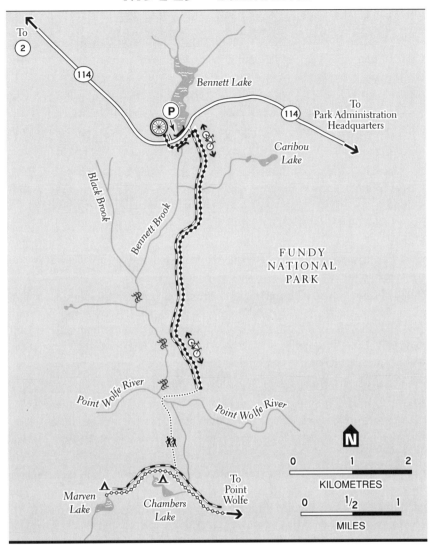

continues as a grassy double-track that eventually narrows to a footpath on the final approach to Bennett Brook. Bikes are not permitted on the footpath, so you should lock your bike or hide it in the trees before heading off on the final stretch of trail.

The footpath descends steeply and rapidly to the shores of Bennett Brook. Here you will fully appreciate the difference between a main river and its tributary. The brook gives way to the large rocks and juts of land, meandering its way along before being swallowed up and carried away by the wider, rushing Point Wolfe River. By fording the brook you can scramble up the opposite bluff for another view of the area, or to continue to Marven Lake. Mountain biking is also permitted on the Marven Lake Trail. If you are willing to hike your bike for 2 or 3 km (1 or 2 miles), it is possible to do a point-to-point excursion (with a vehicle shuttle) from the Bennett Brook trailhead to the Marven Lake trailhead (see Ride 22).

General location: Fundy National Park, near the Wolfe Lake or west entrance of the park.

Elevation change: Gain 105 m (345 feet) of elevation on several rolling hills on the outbound trip. The return trip presents a rolling descent over which you will climb a few moderate hills for a total gain of 165 m (540 feet) on the return trip.

Season: Summer activities begin in the park in late May and continue to October.

Services: The park has full-service, primitive, and wilderness campsites. With the exception of firewood (which may be purchased at the park), you are responsible for bringing your own supplies. The nearest bike stores will be found in Sussex or Moncton.

Hazards: The trail presents a technically challenging section of exposed roots and rocks that is particularly hazardous when wet. There is also a rocky streambed crossing that riders should approach with caution.

Rescue index: The park is staffed year-round, and there are first-aid stations and telephones at the Visitor Centre, Wolfe Lake Information Centre, and all campground kiosks. If you are concerned about heading out on the trail, register with park staff at the Information Centre and be sure to check out with them at the end of your excursion.

Land status: National park; there is an entry fee for all park visitors.

Maps: Government topographic map Waterford 21 H/11 features the trails on the west side of the park, or you can acquire a park map with trails indicated on it from either the main Visitor Centre at the park entrance or the one located at Wolfe Lake.

Finding the trail: You can enter the park on NB Highway 114 from Sussex through the west entrance, or from Moncton through the Alma entrance. The parking area for the Bennett Brook trail is located at Bennett Lake, off of NB Highway 114, near the west entrance to the park. Bennett Lake is clearly signed for swimming, picnics, and paddling, and is located at the bottom of the dip in the road as you approach from either direction. At the bottom of the dip, turn onto the paved driveway that parallels Bennett Lake on the north side of the road. You will pass a canoe rental building on the right as you make your way to the parking area.

Source of additional information:

Fundy National Park
P.O. Box 40
Alma, NB E0A 1B0
(506) 887-6000
Fundy_info@pch.gc.ca

Notes on the trail: The Bennett Brook Trail begins on the south side of the highway, across from Bennett Lake. To access the trail, backtrack to the main road past the lake and canoe rental shop. Ignore the trail sign for Bennett Brook on the left as you approach the main road, and continue to the stop sign. Turn left, crossing the highway, and follow the shoulder of the road around the bend and partway up the hill. At the end of the guardrail, on the right-hand side of the road, there is an opening in the trees, which is the unsigned beginning of the Bennett Brook Trail.

Begin the trail by descending the embankment. At the bottom of the hill there is a sign, for Bennett Brook and Marven Lake directing you ahead. Passing the sign, you will cross a wooden bridge and begin riding on an ATV-width, grassy trail with some exposed rocks. After a brief rocky section, the trail climbs a moderate grade for a short distance, bringing you to another flat, rocky section at the top. Walled by trees on both sides, the trail continues without deviation to a deteriorating corduroy-logged bridge, beyond which the trail begins to climb gradually. The climb is interrupted by a dip for a narrow brook crossing. A steep climb up the opposite embankment brings you to the more technical section of trail, with its sprawling roots and randomly scattered rocks. This section of trail continues gradually uphill.

At the end of the climb, the trail merges onto an old road, which continues to the right. A short distance farther, the trail bends to the left. Following the wider, grassy trail, you will begin a gradual, slightly rolling descent. You will eventually arrive at an opening which marks the half way point of the outbound ride. Beyond the opening, the trail continues to descend a gravel hill into another forested area. Finding yourself again surrounded by trees on both sides, you will have no option but to continue ahead and climb the grassy hill. This hill presents a moderate grade up to a longer hill that curves slightly to the left, preventing you from actually seeing the end of it until just before arriving at the top.

The trail will level out briefly and curve to the right. From here, the trail continues to roll constantly, presenting short climbs and descents for nearly a kilometre (a little over half a mile). The final descent sneaks up on you; what you expect to be just another rolling hill continues downhill, allowing you to gather considerable speed. You will be relieved to discover an area at the bottom of the hill just long enough to give you adequate time to brake and avoid launching into the wall of trees at the end of the trail.

This point marks the end of the ride. To the right, a sign prohibiting mountain bikes stands at the entrance to a narrow, descending hiking trail. This trail leads to Bennett Brook and onward to Marven Lake. Without damaging the undergrowth, stash your bike in the woods and continue to walk to Bennett Brook. You will discover that the trail does become impractical for cyclists, as it narrows significantly, it drops quite steeply, and the surface becomes jaggedly rocky with many exposed roots. Arriving at the bottom of the trail, the hillsides loom dramatically overhead, and you will watch the gradual flow of Bennett Brook get carried away by the rushing waters of the Point Wolfe River. On the return trip you will backtrack on the trail to the paved road and then return to the parking area.

RIDE 24 • Poley Mountain

AT A GLANCE

Length/configuration: 5-km (3-mile) loop

Aerobic difficulty: Strenuous; this is one of the most grueling race circuits in the province

Technical difficulty: Intermediate to advanced; combination of double- and single-track trails

Scenery: Breathtaking views of the surrounding area from the top of Poley Mountain

Special comments: Poley Mountain will host the first 1999 Canada Cup Mountain Bike Championship race

---

The mountain bike race circuit at Poley Mountain is a 5-km (3-mile) loop that features a significant amount of climbing. In fact, the first half of the loop is relentless, as it strings together a series of steep climbs that do not end until you reach the summit of the mountain. It is well worth keeping in mind the fact that, on race day, riders complete up to five circuits of this course! The trails are fantastic: challenging single-track sections linked together along fun double-track trails and some logging roads. The end of the ride also features some grassy trails that traverse the side of the mountain and a few steep downhill sections that weave tight turns in between narrow strips of forest. All in all this ride is best suited to intermediate and advanced riders in good physical condition. The highlight of the ride is the summit, where you will most likely be able to cool off and enjoy the breeze as you gaze out over the rolling hills of the Dutch Valley and the Fundy Model Forest.

The race circuit at Poley Mountain is short, and if you find yourself feeling restless once you reach the base lodge at the end of the ride, you can head back out for as many more loops as you can survive. Additionally, there are a number of logging roads and snowmobile trails extending off the mountain. Equipped with a topographic map and a snowmobile trail map of the area, you can explore any number of trails around Poley Mountain. The area is confined to distinct boundaries: Parlee Brook to the west, Trout Creek to the north and east, and the Walker Settlement Road to the south. Snowmobile Trail 39 extends from the base of Poley Mountain to the Walker Settlement Road, which can be ridden in conjunction with the Parlee Brook Road for a long tour around the mountain. Recent timber harvesting and the development of the mountain's trail system have also resulted in several new logging roads that offer infinite possibilities for off-road exploration.

RIDE 24 • Poley Mountain

General location: Poley Mountain is located approximately 16 km (10 miles) southeast of the town of Sussex.

Elevation change: You will begin this ride from the access road at 107 m (350 feet). The race circuit climbs to the summit of the mountain at 274 m (900 feet), for an approximate elevation gain of 167 m (550 feet).

Season: The riding season at Poley usually begins in June and continues through the end of September.

Services: All services are available in nearby Sussex. There are no services at the trailhead.

Hazards: Although the race circuit at Poley Mountain is well laid-out, be aware of the potential hazards common in any ski area. These include lift equipment and snow-making equipment. Also, the race circuit at Poley may change slightly from year to year. Chances are good that you will be able to follow the course we have described anyway, but you may notice tracks and wear patterns that suggest alternate routes.

Rescue index: Though the distance is not far, dropping down the summit of Poley Mountain to reach assistance along chemin Waterford Road involves a challenging ride.

Land status: Private resort.

Maps: The map we have included for this ride is the only one we know of that outlines the race circuit. The government topographic map for the area, Waterford 21/H11, is useful for additional information about the general area and imperative if you are thinking of extending your ride to include some exploring along the roads and trails off the mountain.

Finding the trail: From Sussex, drive out toward Sussex Corner on NB Highway 121. You will see signs for Poley Mountain. At a junction with NB Highway 111, turn right on Needle Street. Bear left at the next fork, and continue driving on chemin Waterford Road, passing an elementary school on the left. Continue straight on this road, following signs for Poley Mountain all the way to the access road to the resort, which you will see on your right. Because the gate across the access road is likely to be closed in the summer, park along the side of the access road and ride up to the parking area at the base lodge to reach the trailhead.

Sources of additional information:

Poley Mountain Resorts Ltd.
P.O. Box 1097
Sussex, NB E0E 1P0
(506) 433-7653

Notes on the trail: As you ride up the access road to the base lodge, head toward the far-right corner of the parking lot, where a fence separates the parking area from the grassy slope that serves as the ski resort's learning centre in the winter. The lodge will be just a short distance ahead on your left. Turn right out of the parking lot and begin riding the beginner ski hill, parallel to the fence. You will be descending down the edge of a field that slopes away from a small wooden structure that bears the sign: "Welcome to Kids Camp." At the bottom of the slope, bear right at a fork, following a vague, double-track path along the farthest trail heading up on the left.

You will climb on this trail, which curves around to the left and ascends steeply. At the first opportunity, turn right off of the main ski trail and follow a double-track dirt trail into the woods. Almost immediately upon entering the double-track trail, you will arrive at a fork. Bear left, avoiding the narrow trail to the right that descends along another ski run. A brief wet stretch may follow after this turn as you continue uphill. The climb quickly levels off beyond this point, and the trail curves to the left through a stand of pine trees.

Beyond the bend in the trail, you will emerge from the woods and come into view of a recently cleared hillside across a small valley to the right. You will come to a fork in the trail here. Bear right and descend into the valley along a rocky gravel track. At the bottom of the hill you will ride through a small stream. Beyond the stream, at a three-way intersection, turn off of the main trail (which continues on to the right) and head uphill to the left. You will cross another little stream across a dip in the trail before climbing more steeply again, up a hard-

Single- and double-track trails wind their way up, down, and around Poley Mountain.

packed dirt and gravel road. Keep to the main trail at the top of this road, following it around a bend to the right and passing a narrow ski trail heading downhill on the left.

The trail levels out for a short distance beyond this bend, entering a clearing and following a hard-packed dirt trail. Having traversed the clearing, you will approach a strip of trees and begin climbing again. At this point the trail begins to deteriorate, and the climb becomes more technical due to the number of exposed roots and loose rocks. Wind your way uphill, picking your way through some eroded areas on the trail. You will continue to climb, before traversing a slightly more level stretch of trail and following the trail as it bends to the left, heading in toward Poley Mountain.

At a fork in the trail, ignore the tempting path that follows a hairpin turn around to the right and descends a short distance before climbing along a wide dirt road. Instead, continue straight through an area overshadowed by blue spruce. A short distance beyond this intersection, you will pass a vague, grassy trail branching off to the left, heading downhill. Continue straight on the main trail, continuing up the final lip of the climb. When you reach a high point in an evergreen forest, where the road continues straight ahead of you and begins to descend, look for a single-track trail on the left. Turn left here and begin a glorious stretch of downhill.

You will zigzag down, descending over rolling terrain along a narrow trail that may be quite soft. You will emerge from the woods over a drop-off, popping back out onto one of the ski runs. Traverse the ski run, dropping down the slope a short distance to the left and looking for the continuation of the single-track trail into the woods on the right. You will ride through another strip of trees before coming out on another ski run. Traverse this run by following a trail that heads slightly up the slope to the right before entering the woods again. After generally traversing the mountainside along a trail through the trees, you will emerge once more on a grassy ski slope near the top of the mountain. Turn right here, heading uphill for the final climb to the summit of Poley Mountain.

The trail climbs to the top of the quad, which is a blue chairlift. A bench is poised at the side of the trail here, welcome relief from the seemingly endless climbing involved to reach this point. It is well worth pausing to appreciate the view before continuing straight to ride up to the true summit of the mountain. Pass a small shelter on the left, where the downhill races begin, and follow the trail heading straight up and over the summit. You will pass a gravel trail that descends the side of the mountain on the right.

Bear left over the crest of the hill, heading along a single-track trail down the backside of the mountain. This trail descends steeply over soft ground for a short distance, before connecting with a wide ski run named "Carousel." Turn right on this trail and go down the slope, looking for another single-track trail that heads into the woods on the right. This section of single-track weaves tightly through the woods before emerging on the same ski slope, a short distance farther down the slope. At this point, turn left and head back up the slope toward a sign for the glades.

You will climb for a short distance, heading back in the direction you came down, before bearing right into the glades. A new single-track trail zigzags downhill through this area. Tight turns and several whoop-de-doos make the descent quite challenging, as does the very soft ground. As you descend, you will approach a logging road. Keep to the single-track trail that parallels this road slightly higher up on the slope. This section of trail features some off-camber riding and some large dips before dropping down to the right onto the logging road.

Bear left on the logging road. You will be descending slightly, passing a wide ski run over to the right. The bike trail swings up to the left and then bends around to the right before traversing a gravel ski run. There may be logs placed on the downslope of this hill, supporting a narrow little trail along the width of the ski slope. You will enter the woods again and negotiate some more rolling terrain with deep depressions. This trail then emerges on a grassy slope with a surprising little dip in the middle. Traverse this slope and then cross through another wooded section. You will come out onto another grassy ski run that can be distinguished by the lighting equipment along its edge.

Head under the lights and toward the quad. You will cross beneath the chairlift before heading across two abrupt drops that will connect you with another ski trail. You will be able to see the base lodge down the hill to the right. Traverse the next ski trail and ride back into the woods along a path that quickly veers rather steeply to the right and sends you down a kamikaze-downhill that drops steeply along an impossibly narrow trail. You will emerge, at last, onto the ski run where the course traces an **S**-turn down the grassy slope to end up at the lodge. This is the final stretch of the course, where racers will go for speed and stun the spectators below with their swift, zigzag descent of the hill. Enjoy!

RIDE 25 · Cripps Hill

AT A GLANCE

Length/configuration: 16.4-km (10-mile) combination (two short spurs, ridden twice, connected to a 6-km [3.75-mile] loop); or 26-km (16-mile) loop

Aerobic difficulty: Intermediate to advanced; considerable climbing on mostly gradual hills

Technical difficulty: Intermediate; double-track riding along active and abandoned logging roads

Scenery: You will ride to an old cemetery and tour through the woods of the Fundy Model Forest

Special comments: Before your ride, pick up a packed lunch from Adair's Wilderness Lodge

Located at the heart of the Fundy Model Forest are the churches, cemeteries, and many other reminders of the first communities to settle and develop along the southern coast of New Brunswick. At the crest of Cripps Hill is one such reminder: a small 100-year-old cemetery nestled against a hillside in a grassy meadow. With recent interest in preserving such historic places, local groups have worked to clear and restore this cemetery. It is now a place where worn and weathered headstones punctuate a mowed, grassy slope that has been opened up to the surrounding landscape of rolling hills. The Catholic community that settled in this area established the cemetery at Cripps Hill. Chambers Settlement, located a short distance farther up the road, was also part of this community. On the other side of Creek Road was the Protestant settlement. There, Londonderry Church and the adjoining cemetery still stand as reminders of the largely Irish population that emigrated here around the time of the potato famine. For a complete tour of this area,

RIDE 25 • Cripps Hill

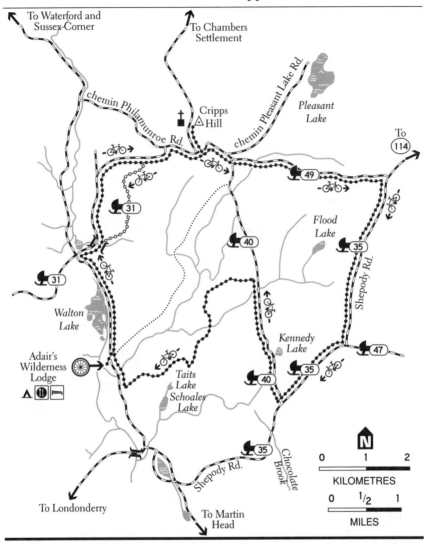

consider riding the Tour of Lisson Settlement (Ride 27), which includes a trip up to Londonderry Church.

This ride begins from Adair's Wilderness Lodge on Creek Road and follows a series of old and new logging roads to the small cemetery atop Cripps Hill. From the cemetery you can choose to return immediately to Adair's, or embark on a longer excursion. The shorter of the two options is a 16.4-km (10-mile) combination ride: a 6-km (3.75-mile) loop with a spur at either end—the first a 3.7-km (2.25-mile) spur, ridden twice, that connects to Adair's, and the second a short 1.5-km (1-mile) spur, also ridden twice, to the cemetery and back. Alternatively, the longer ride is a 26-km (16-mile) loop, which includes a short side trip to the cemetery. This option provides a longer tour through the wilderness area bounded by Creek Road to the west and by Shepody Road to the south and east. Both rides feature mostly double-track riding on old logging roads and some distance on active forestry roads that are wider, graded, and gravel surfaced. Beginning- and intermediate-level riders will enjoy the shorter ride, which requires a moderate level of fitness and makes a perfect morning or afternoon ride. The longer ride demands more endurance and requires sound map-reading skills, but still only requires an intermediate level of skill. Because of its length, this option should be considered a full-day excursion.

General location: Fundy Model Forest is located in southern New Brunswick, on the coast between Sussex and Martin Head.

Elevation change: Both options for this ride begin from Adair's Wilderness Lodge, at an elevation of approximately 229 m (750 feet). From there, both options climb to an elevation of 335 m (1,100 feet) atop Cripps Hill. The short option then descends back to Adair's over several very short climbs, for an overall elevation gain of approximately 137 m (450 feet). The longer loop option covers more varied terrain and concludes back at the lodge after a total gain of approximately 213 m (700 feet).

Season: Favourable conditions can be found between May and October.

Services: All services are available in Sussex. Closer to the trailhead, Adair's Wilderness Lodge includes lodging, guide service, and a fine restaurant, where you can even arrange for a packed lunch. Adair's is a perfect place at which to stay and to use as a base camp for exploring the many riding opportunities in the Fundy Model Forest.

Hazards: Throughout the Fundy Model Forest, active tree harvesting operations may be encountered at certain times. Although this ride was not in the vicinity of any such operations during the time we rode it, be aware of the potential for fast-moving logging trucks on these roads.

Rescue index: Although you will never venture more than 6 km (3.75 miles) from a major logging road, assistance may be as far as 8 km (5 miles) away. Adair's Wilderness Lodge is open year-round and provides the most reliable source of assistance in this area.

Land status: This ride tours an area known as the Fundy Model Forest. The forest is actually a partnership of many groups and organizations working together with the shared goal of ensuring the environmental sustainability of land used for social and economic gains.

Maps: Although not all the roads and trails used on this ride are indicated, the most useful map to carry with you in conjunction with the map we have provided is the government topographic map Waterford 21 H/11. Snowmobile trail maps, available at Adair's Wilderness Lodge, can also be helpful, as many of the trails are signed with snowmobile trail numbers throughout the year.

Finding the trail: The trailhead for this ride is Adair's Wilderness Lodge, located approximately 23 km (14 miles) from Sussex Corner. From Sussex, drive out toward Sussex Corner on NB Highway 121. At the junction with NB Highway 111, turn right on Needle Street. Bear left at the next fork and continue driving on chemin Waterford Road, passing an elementary school on the left. Approximately 16 km (10 miles) out of Sussex, you will pass the entrance to Poley Mountain on the right and drive through the small community of Waterford. Beyond Waterford, keep to the main road, passing a turnoff on the right that leads to Walker Settlement and bearing left across a bridge over Trout Creek. Continue straight past another road branching up to the left toward Chambers Settlement. The road becomes unpaved beyond this point. Continue straight all the way to Adair's Wilderness Lodge, which will be on your right.

Source of additional information: Larry and Ida Adair have created an oasis in the forest with the recent building and development of their wilderness lodge. Whether you are looking for lodging, guide service, or an excellent meal, any ride in the Fundy Model Forest would be incomplete without a stop at Adair's.

> Adair's Wilderness Lodge
> 900 Creek Road
> Shepody, NB E4E 5R9
> (506) 432-6687

> Fundy Model Forest
> R.R. #4, Aiton Road
> Sussex, NB E0E 1P0
> (506) 432-2806

Notes on the trail: From the driveway of Adair's Wilderness Lodge, turn left and begin riding up Creek Road, a wide, graded dirt road. You will pass Walton Lake on the left and several trails branching off to the right before reaching a distinct four-way intersection. Turn right up a double-track trail with a grassy median that may be signed as Snowmobile Trail 31. Continue on this trail over a bridge. Pass another double-track trail branching off to the left and then a small camp, also on the left. You will be climbing along a wide gravel road. When you come to a trail branching off to the left at a small clearing, turn left. Snowmobile Trail 31 continues straight ahead at this point and will be the trail on which you return if you opt for the shorter ride to Cripps Hill and back.

You will climb gradually along this next section of the ride, which traverses a low ridge parallel to Creek Road below on the left. You will pass through an area that has recently been cut before the road swings around to the right. After following the road through this curve and then through another curve to the left, you will come to a three-way intersection. Turn right here; the trail continuing straight merely dead-ends a short distance farther. This portion of the trail is more overgrown, and the gravel double-track road you were following becomes grassier. Continue straight until you reach a small grassy clearing. At this point, be sure to bear left. The trail to the right is the other end of Snowmobile Trail 31—the route by which you will return for the shorter ride.

Beyond the junction with Snowmobile Trail 31, you will begin to climb. Keep to the main trail, passing several gravel openings off the trail to the left before climbing steeply along a rocky, eroded section of trail. You will pass through another gravel clearing before the trail gradually evens out. Along this next portion of the ride, the trees by the side of the trail have grown inward, creating a tunnel-like arbour across the trail. You will descend a short slope, crossing a wood culvert. Veer left beyond this culvert and ride out to a **T** junction with a wide gravel road. This is chemin Philamunroe Road; turn right.

Follow chemin Philamunroe Road as it snakes through the woods, rolling over undulating terrain. After a short distance you will come to a three-way intersection. Turn left to ride up Cripps Hill. At the top of the hill you will find a cemetery in a cleared, grassy field on the left. This is a great place to stop and explore or just take in the quietness and beauty of the surrounding hills. This spot also marks the half way point for the shorter ride, or approximately one-third of the journey for the longer option.

From the cemetery, both rides require that you descend back to chemin Philamunroe Road. Then, for the shorter ride, turn right and follow the main road for little more than half a km (three-tenths of a mile), before turning left back into the woods on the trail you rode up on. There will probably be signs for Snowmobile Trail 31 at this turnoff. A short distance along this trail, bear right, continuing to retrace the route you followed in. You will cross back over the wooden culvert, ascend a slope, and ride back through the trees that create an arbour over the trail. Beyond a gravel clearing, you will descend steeply. Pass a few more gravel openings to the right of the trail before descending again. When you reach a **T** junction, turn left, and follow signs for Snowmobile Trail 31. This is where you diverge from the route you followed in, which follows the trail down to the right. This portion of the loop follows Snowmobile Trail 31 down to the four-way intersection at Creek Road. Turn left when you reach Creek Road, following it all the way back to Adair's.

Should you choose the longer loop—a tour that will take you out to Shepody Road, up Snowmobile Trail 40, and along an old woods road back to Adair's lodge—descend back down Cripps Hill to chemin Philamunroe Road and turn left. You will ride past a less maintained road on the left before the main road curves around to the right. Continue past a newer road on the right, and keep to the main road until you come to a distinct fork. The road on the left, chemin Pleasant Lake Road, branches up to Pleasant Lake. Bear right here, heading down a short slope and following signs for Snowmobile Trail 40. A short distance from this fork, you will come to an intersection with a double-track trail branching off to the left. Turn left here, leaving Snowmobile Trail 40 and continuing along the path of an old logging road that may be signed as Snowmobile Trail 49.

This next portion of the ride follows an old woods road that gradually deteriorates to a rough grassy track through the woods. You will be following this trail, essentially straight, all the way to where it intersects with Shepody Road at a **T** junction. There are good wildlife viewing opportunities along this trail, which is traveled by few people and frequented often by moose, deer, and bear. Be sure to keep to the main trail, passing any logging roads branching off to the left or right. Just a short distance along the trail, you will come to a meadowlike area and a small brook, where you might see trout swimming in the shady, shallow water. Farther on, you will be riding past a plantation of spruce trees planted sometime in the late 1970s. You will begin to climb gradually through this plantation, up a slope that becomes quite rocky in places. At a rough, wet area, the trail diverges, where a new, drier route has been created to the right. The two trails reconnect almost immediately, so choose either one. Beyond this spot you will ride into a more open, cleared area, before heading back up another gradual slope to traverse a plateau distinguished by a dense undergrowth of ferns. From here, you will descend past another meadowlike area on the left. This is a crossing point on the trail for deer. Continue to stay straight, passing any old logging roads branching off the main trail.

Gradually, you will ascend another slope to where the trail becomes rockier and then begins to descend slightly. You will ride past a boggy swale on the left, before coming to an intersection with a driveway on the left. Continue straight here. After a short distance you will come out at a **T** junction with a wide, graded dirt road. This is Shepody Road, which may also be signed as Snowmobile Trail 35. Turn right.

Ride along Shepody Road for approximately 5 km (3 miles). You will first ride past an area on the left that has been recently harvested. On the right, you will pass Flood Lake Road and then several driveways that lead up to private camps. Continue on Shepody Road, past a trail on the left that will most likely have been recently widened. This is Snowmobile Trail 47 and is shown as being a significant road on both the topographic map and the snowmobile trail map. A short distance beyond this junction, you will pass a trail on the left that descends to Little Salmon River. A short distance farther, you will come to the junction of Snowmobile Trail 40, the next distinct road on the right. Turn right at this junction, heading up toward Kennedy Lake.

Snowmobile Trail 40 follows a fairly wide, established logging road. You will pass Kennedy Lake on the right after a short distance. Less than 2 km (1.25 miles) beyond the lake, look for an unmarked trail on the left and turn onto it. You will ride through an area that has been cut, before crossing a bridge over a brook that originates from Flood Lake. Beyond the bridge bear right, following a double-track trail. Ten years ago, before it was cut, this area was a deer yard in the winter. Despite the tree harvesting that has occurred here, the area still offers plenty of wildlife-viewing opportunities.

Through a small gravel clearing, pass a trail branching off to the left. Continue to follow the main trail as it curves around to the left, passing a grassy offshoot over your right shoulder. You will then descend gradually along a twisty section of the road, down a partially eroded stretch of the trail. Continue straight through a four-way intersection. The trail you pass to your right leads out toward a rifle range, and the trail on the left leads down toward Taits Lake. Continue to follow this double-track through the woods for a short distance, following it out to a **T** junction with a wide, graded dirt road, which is Creek Road. To the right, before you actually reach Creek Road, turn right on another snowmobile trail. Follow this snowmobile trail up to another junction a short distance ahead. Turn left here and cross Creek Road, back into the parking area for Adair's Wilderness Lodge.

This ride was presented to us by Larry Adair—the knowledgeable woodsman and entrepreneur who generously guided us through the trails in this area.

RIDE 26 · The Mighty Salmon

AT A GLANCE

Length/configuration: A 53-km (33-mile) combination (37-km [23-mile] loop, with two spurs of 2.5 km [1.5 miles] and 5 km [3 miles], each ridden twice)

Aerobic difficulty: A lengthy ride that requires good conditioning

Technical difficulty: Intermediate riding on rocky old roads with some easy stretches on graded gravel roads

Scenery: Vast open landscapes and new growth forests on the way to the mouth of the Big Salmon River

Special comments: Arrange for transportation for a shorter point-to-point excursion

The Mighty Salmon is an epic 53-km (32-mile) combination ride that travels through the Fundy Model Forest and virtually parallels the Big Salmon River. The ride begins from the comfort of Adair's Wilderness Lodge, then ventures into the wild heart of Southern New Brunswick. The outbound destination, the Salmon River Park at the mouth of Big Salmon River on the Bay of Fundy, is reached by following a rough and rugged trail of mostly abandoned logging roads and snowmobile trails that are popular among ATV riders in the summer. On the return trip, the ride follows well-graded logging roads.

The juxtaposition of interests in the Fundy Model Forest is unabashedly revealed on these back roads. A tenuous balance is being struck between the

RIDE 26 · The Mighty Salmon

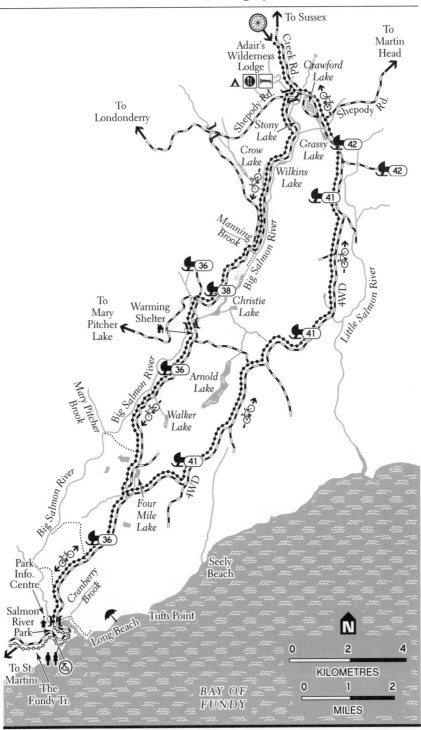

economic, environmental, and social needs of the forest's users. As a result of the clear-cutting, there are endless kilometres (or miles, for our American cousins) of trails for snowmobilers, ATV users, and mountain bikers. Due to regular use, the trails are clearly marked and in excellent condition. However, following the rocky, hard-packed dirt roads in this wilderness area, you will pass through forests of various ages and stages of cutting and regeneration. The views of fresh clear-cuts can be startling in contrast to the surrounding landscape, where new forests reach ambitiously toward the sky and virgin forests stand in defiance.

To complete the loop and take in the scenic stops along the way, plan for a full-day trip. All riders should head out on this ride prepared for an extended and demanding trip. Be sure to carry plenty of water, food (we attribute our successful completion of this ride to the substantial chocolate macaroon cookies from Adair's contained in our lunch), and spare tubes or a patch kit and pump. Extra clothing, topographic maps, and a compass are also essential on this trip. Because unexpected things can happen on a ride of any length—and the risk becomes greater on a ride of considerable length—this is an excellent opportunity to share our new axiom: It is sometimes not enough to be perfectly prepared for what you expect.

General location: The Fundy Model Forest is located on the southern coast of New Brunswick, between Sussex and Martin Head.

Elevation change: On several moderate hills throughout the ride, and one extended climb back up from the mouth of the Big Salmon River, you will gain a total of 425 m (1,400 feet) in elevation.

Season: Allow for enough time for snow to melt and the runoff to subside before hitting the trails. Although sections of the trail will still be muddy, the season can begin as early as May and continue through October.

Services: The trailhead for this ride is at Adair's Wilderness Lodge, where you can arrange for camping or cabin accommodations, as well as transportation from the Salmon River Park or the neighbouring town of St. Martin's. You can also purchase packed lunches that will sufficiently nourish you on this trail. All other services, including biking needs, can be obtained in Sussex.

Hazards: As you will be riding on several logging roads, there may be trucks on the road—even with reduced logging in the area. Stay alert and give way to all approaching vehicles.

Rescue index: Riders are advised to carry first-aid and bike repair kits, as there are no sources of assistance between Adair's and the Salmon River Park. With the exception of the few ATV riders you may encounter on the trail, you will have to rely on people at Adair's or the Salmon River Park for assistance.

Land status: This ride passes through Crown land, on logging roads and old roads that are signed as snowmobile trails and maintained by the Fundy Trail Riders Snowmobile Club.

Maps: It is strongly advised that you carry government topographic maps 21

H/11 (Waterford) and 21 H/6 (Salmon River) on this ride to avoid getting lost in the maze of trails and logging roads in the area.

Finding the trail: The trailhead for this ride is Adair's Wilderness Lodge, located approximately 23 km (14 miles) from Sussex Corner. From Sussex, drive out toward Sussex Corner on NB Highway 121. At the junction with NB Highway 111, turn right on Needle Street. Bear left at the next fork, and continue driving on chemin Waterford Road, passing an elementary school on the left. Approximately 16 km (10 miles) out of Sussex, you will pass the entrance to Poley Mountain on the right and drive through the small community of Waterford. Beyond Waterford, keep to the main road, passing a turnoff on the right that leads to Walker Settlement and bearing left across a bridge over Trout Creek. Continue straight past another road branching up to the left toward Chambers Settlement. The road becomes unpaved beyond this point. Continue straight, all the way to Adair's Wilderness Lodge, which will be on your right.

Sources of additional information: The Fundy Model Forest Network produces the *Mountain Bike Tour Map and Guide* brochure, which features a shorter loop on the Big Salmon River. This brochure is available at Visitor Information Centres throughout the province, as well as at the Sussex Source for Sports, on Broad Street. You can also obtain them through the Fundy Model Forest Network at (800) 546-4838 or fundyfor@nbnet.nb.ca.

Notes on the trail: From Adair's Wilderness Lodge, turn right and begin riding along Creek Road. Follow Creek Road to a junction with Shepody Road. There is a brown house with green trim on the left-hand side of the road and a single-lane dirt road branching off to the right. Turn right, following the narrower dirt road down to a small bridge over the Big Salmon River. Just beyond the bridge, turn left at the first opportunity, onto a double-track trail heading south, parallel to the river. Ahead, there is a Fundy Model Forest mountain bike trail sign (a circle with a bike) in the trees, a trail you can follow to complete the shorter loop described in their brochure.

This hard-packed, double-track dirt trail continues on a slight decline. You will lose sight of the Big Salmon River and then come to a branch in the trail to the left. Following this branch, you will very shortly arrive at an outlet overlooking Wilkins Lake. Returning to the main trail, you will continue on a gradual descent to a grassy clearing. Continue straight through the clearing on the rocky double-track, ignoring a grassy offshoot to the right. Past the clearing, the trail forks again, offering two options for crossing Crow Brook. To the left you will ford the brook, and to the right there is a bridge that has been built for snowmobiles in the winter. The bridge is made up of four logs and some randomly placed wooden planks more suitable for a snow-covered winter crossing than a summer crossing on a bike. Dismount to cross the bridge. Soon after crossing the brook, the two trails will merge and you will continue down a narrow grassy trail lined with alders.

At the end of the slope you will cross a rusting culvert that is somewhat buried under some rocks. Beyond the culvert the road climbs gradually on a loose, rocky incline and then makes an obvious bend to the right. Continue around the bend a short distance to a **T** junction with a wider, graded gravel road. Turn left onto the gravel road, traveling south. Heading through a previously logged area, you will pass recently cleared and replanted blocks. As you continue along the road, there will be two sections that have been seriously eroded, the first over Manning Brook and the second a short distance farther on another downhill slope. On a long descent you will come to a four-way intersection with Old Big Salmon River Road, now Snowmobile Trail 36. Turn left, following a sign for Salmon River Park, now 15 km (9.3 miles) away. Turning left, you will begin a long descent on a rocky gully. Near the bottom, you will cross a wooden bridge over a brook and then continue to the main bridge over the Big Salmon River. The view is impressive from either side of the bridge, but even more so just beyond the bridge, from the warming shelter on the right-hand side.

The main trail beyond the shelter climbs steadily along terrain that is still very rocky. Keep to the main trail, and ride to a **T** junction with a wider road at the site of a recent clear-cut. Bear right here, following the sign for Snowmobile Trail 36. Riding on this trail in late summer, watch for ripened blackberries, since you may welcome the opportunity for a rest and a snack at this point in the ride. The trail continues on this road along the high ridge of the Big Salmon River, which is down to your right. Climbing a slight hill along this section of the ride, we saw a moose grazing on the trees. At the sight of us he darted farther into the trees, avoiding having his picture taken, and we continued ahead. You will begin a rolling descent past a couple of small clear-cuts. Then the trail climbs, and you will enter a much larger clear-cut area. There are several logging roads branching off the main trail that should be ignored as you make your way through this vast, barren landscape.

At the end of the rocky descent through the clear-cut block, the road widens and begins to climb gradually. At the crest of the hill you will catch a glimpse of the Bay of Fundy in the distance, and to the right is a signed hiking trail to Mary Pitcher Falls. This is a short side trip to a popular scenic spot. The only downside to the expedition is the climb back from the falls to return to your bike! Continuing toward the Big Salmon River, you will descend another rocky slope. You will pass a pond on the left, and the road will level out, although it will still be quite rocky. This long middle section of the ride ends with a short drop down a hill as the trail bends to the right. At a three-way intersection with Four Mile Lake in view, bear right, still following Snowmobile Trail 36. You will pass Four Mile Lake on the left and continue to a **T** junction with another wide gravel road. This point marks the beginning of the out-and-back spur to the river. Turn right to continue to the Salmon River Park. To the left, Snowmobile Trail 41 is the road on which you will return.

Turning right, you are faced with a short hill. At the top you may feel a slight head wind coming in from the coast—a sign that you must be getting close! You will snake across the plateau for a couple of km (just over 1 mile), passing several logging roads to your left and right. There is a brief rolling section, and then you will begin the final descent. Entering into the trees, the descent begins gradually but becomes much steeper. As the grade becomes even more steep, you will appreciate the bends in the road that help to slow you down as you descend this steep, rocky hill. Finally, the trail just drops off, and you will arrive swiftly at the mouth of the Big Salmon River. The little stream you crossed at the beginning of the ride has grown into a formidable river on its way to the Bay of Fundy.

At this point, you can follow a dirt road to the left to Long Beach, or cross the suspension bridge that spans the Big Salmon River. The suspension bridge will take you to an interpretive centre and picnic area across the river. Here you can connect with the Fundy Trail (see Ride 28) and continue to St. Martin's for a 40-km (24-mile) point-to-point, if you have arranged for transportation back to Adair's. To complete the loop back to Adair's Wilderness Lodge, you will have to climb back up the hill to the three-way intersection with Snowmobile Trail 41. On the return trip, you will climb steeply for the first kilometre (one-half mile), then face a rolling climb for the next 1.5 km (about 1 mile). A short ride along a flat stretch of trail brings you to the short hill, just before the three-way intersection where you began the out-and-back trip to the park. To complete the loop portion of the ride, continue straight, following Snowmobile Trail 41.

Continuing on the snowmobile trail, there will be two short climbs before you reach a **T** junction with another wide gravel road. At the junction, turn left and descend. You will cruise past a main logging road on the left and then arrive at a fork. At the fork, bear right, following a flat stretch of road. On this stretch of road, you will pass several logging roads branching off to the left and right at regular intervals. There are also several clear-cuts in varying stages of logging and regeneration. After passing a gravel pit, the road gradually descends and becomes slightly wider. After the descent, you will pass a wide logging road and then begin a short climb. Arriving at a fork with a double-track trail to the right, follow the left branch, sticking to the main road. You will pass a clear-cut and then cruise down another hill. There are drainage ditches at the top and bottom of this hill to be aware of as you pick up some speed. There is a small wooden bridge over a brook at the bottom, and then the road curves to the right. After a brief flat section there is a moderate climb, and you will pass another major clearing area on the right with an extensive logging road cutting across to the horizon. Still following the main road, you will continue past a couple of small clear-cuts and several logging roads just before swooping downhill.

At this point, you are approaching the final stretch of the ride. The downhill is followed by two short climbs, and as you continue ahead, you approach a bend in the road that passes Snowmobile Trail 42 on the right. Around this bend is the homeward stretch. At the next three-way intersection, there is a yellow sign for the Fundy Footpath to the right. Bear left here and pass Grassy Lake on the left; then come to a **T** junction with Shepody Road. Turn left, and descend past Crawford Lake and the rod and gun club. At the bottom of the hill you will arrive at the intersection of Shepody and Creek Roads, with the brown house with green trim on your right. From here, there are just a few rolling hills to climb back to Adair's, which will appear on your left.

RIDE 27 • Tour of Lisson Settlement

AT A GLANCE

Length/configuration: 14.8-km (9.3-mile) combination (4.6-km [2.9-mile] loop with two spurs; spurs are 3.2 km [2 miles] and 2.4 km [1.2 miles], each ridden twice)

Aerobic difficulty: Tough; an extended climb and several rolling hills on rough, dirt roads

Technical difficulty: Beginner to intermediate riding on dirt roads and ATV-width trails through the woods

Scenery: Forested hills and an historic church and cemetery

Special comments: May be combined with other trails departing from Adair's Wilderness Lodge

On this 14.8-km (9.3-mile) combination, you will see the remains of the Protestant Lisson Settlement in environs that closely resemble the land's pre-settlement state. Indeed, because of a national forestry program in this area, much of the land has been reclaimed by wilderness and protected as part of the Fundy Model Forest. Today, the dramatic hills and old roads are best experienced on a mountain bike, where long climbs are rewarded with swift descents. Further, you are able to venture into the woods on narrow double-track trails that emerge at surprising openings. The ride follows well-marked, hard-packed dirt roads, grassy ATV-width trails, and rocky old roads that also serve as snowmobile trails in the winter. The variety of the terrain, the undulating landscape, and the remoteness of the area make this an excursion best suited to reasonably fit intermediate riders who are also capable of handling their own trailside repairs.

General location: Situated in the Fundy Model Forest, southwest of Sussex Corner.

Elevation change: A significant elevation gain of 105 m (345 feet) is achieved on the first hill. As the ride progresses, you will have several climbs and descents of up to 50 m (165 feet), for a total elevation gain of 325 m (1,065 feet).

Season: The dirt roads will be muddy in the spring and after a heavy rainfall. The

RIDE 27 • Tour of Lisson Settlement

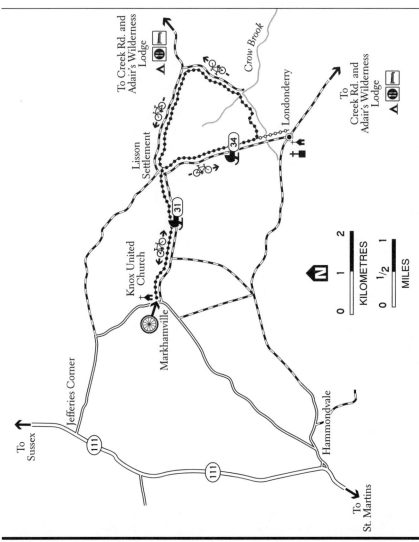

best months for riding are June to October. In the fall, colourful foliage adds to the enjoyment of this ride.

Services: Sussex is a thriving community, complete with large grocery stores, markets, an excellent café, and Sussex Sports Experts for basic biking needs. There are no services at the trailhead.

Hazards: Exercise caution descending the overgrown double-track trail that descends to Crow Brook midway through the ride. Visibility is reduced, and the trail is pitted and rutted.

Rescue index: Assistance is accessible within a reasonable proximity to the trail. There are several homes near the start of the ride, and although at the farthest point you will be 8 km (5 miles) from the trailhead, you may encounter ATV riders along the trail.

Land status: This ride follows dirt roads and old roads that are public rights-of-way on Crown land.

Maps: Government topographic map Waterford 21 H/11 is an excellent resource for this and many other rides in the area. Good maps of the area are also featured in *The New Brunswick Atlas* (map 81, section A-3, A-4), as well as in the brochure distributed through bike stores and Visitor Information Centres by the Fundy Model Forest Network.

Finding the trail: From Sussex, follow NB Highway 121 to Sussex Corner. As the road curves to the left, you will bear right onto Needle Street, following signs for Route 111 South and St. Martins. At the first fork in the road bear right, following signs for Markhamville. You will continue along the road for a good distance, past Jeffries Corner. You will come to a white building, and directly across from it, turn left onto a paved road. Continue up a slight rise to a **T** junction and turn left. Still following the paved road, bear left at the first fork and continue through a small cluster of houses. Pass a dirt road branching uphill to the right, beyond which Knox United Methodist Church is visible a short distance ahead. Just beyond the dirt road, which marks the start of the trail, pull over and park in front of the church.

Source of additional information: Contact Adair's Wilderness Lodge for information on other rides in the area and alternate directions departing from Creek Road.

>Adair's Wilderness Lodge
>R.R. #4
>Sussex, NB E0E 1P0
>(506) 432-6687

Notes on the trail: From the parking area at Knox United Methodist Church, backtrack to the southern edge of the church property and turn left onto the wide dirt road, heading uphill. The first break in this long, steady climb comes after you have gained 90 m (295 feet) of elevation and reached an intersection with a road branching off to the right. Continue straight, following this road east (also marked as Snowmobile Trail 31). You will resume climbing for a short distance past blueberry barrens on the right. At the top you will reach a clearing and then pass through a moderate dip in the road that brings you to a **T** junction. At the junction turn right, following signs for Londonderry Church and Snowmobile Trail 34. This road is narrower and less maintained than the dirt road on which you were previously riding. Around a slight bend it begins to climb. You will continue to climb until you reach a dirt road branching off to the left, just before a driveway leading to a house. At this point you can either turn left onto the dirt road to complete the Lisson Settlement loop, or continue ahead to Londonderry Church.

The short side trip to Londonderry is a worthwhile out-and-back excursion. Not only does it offer a glimpse into the history of Irish settlement in New Brunswick in the 1800s, but it also features an excellent downhill on the way. There is a dramatic swoop through a significant dip in the road that drops almost 50 m (165 feet) in elevation. All of this height is gained back immediately on the other side, but with a racing descent you will scoot up the other side with minimal exertion. Once you have passed through the big dipper, the road levels out, and the church and cemetery will soon appear on the right.

To continue your ride from the Londonderry Church and adjacent cemetery, retrace your tracks to the dirt road just beyond the driveway leading to the house. Approaching the turn from this direction, the road will appear on your right. The road quickly narrows to a double-track trail and begins to descend to Crow Brook almost immediately. As you progress the trail becomes more overgrown, so you will be riding through lush vegetation of low-lying bushes, tall grasses, and trees. At times your visibility is greatly reduced by alder branches, and the trail is less predictable, as it is rutted and pitted in patches. At the bottom the trail opens up, and you will cross a very narrow section of the brook. On the other side, bear left up a short, albeit challenging, rocky knoll. Continue, bearing left, to follow another double-track trail with a grassy median. Pass a dirt trail branching off to the right and descend along a wooded corridor. Here the trail begins to deteriorate slightly, presenting more bumps and dips.

This trail drops down to an intersection with a wider, more maintained dirt road. To the right the road continues to Vinegar Hill and out to Adair's Wilderness Lodge. Turn left to complete the loop back to the Markhamville trailhead. After a short distance you will arrive at an opening on the right with blueberry barrens up on the hillside and an open meadow by the side of the road. Beyond this opening, the road continues ahead to a well-marked three-way intersection. Turn left, heading downhill and following signs for Snowmobile Trail 31 west. A few rolling hills and one final climb will complete the loop, returning you to the first **T** junction at the start of the ride. Turn right and enjoy the cruise back to Knox United Methodist Church.

RIDE 28 • The Fundy Trail

AT A GLANCE

Length/configuration: 21-km (12.6-mile) out-and-back (10.5 km [6.3 miles] each way)

Aerobic difficulty: Strenuous; constantly rolling terrain and two significant climbs

Technical difficulty: Beginner; smooth, fine gravel surface with some paved sections along the steepest grades

Scenery: Stunning coastal scenery

Special comments: Swimming at the Big Salmon!

The Fundy Trail was constructed along previously untouched wilderness on the shores of the Bay of Fundy. With the construction of the Fundy Trail and Parkway (which essentially parallels the Fundy Trail), pristine beaches and spectacular coastal scenery are now accessible to everyone. Having borne witness to the early stages of the area's development, it is our hope that the glimpse at untouched wilderness that the parkway and trail afford will remain intact, subjected to minimal further development. Although you need only a couple of hours to follow this 21-km (12.6-mile) trail out to the Salmon River and back again, it is well worth putting aside the time to linger. There are fantastic views of the Bay of Fundy, several ideal beaches for swimming, and a suspension bridge to cross at the Salmon River Park at the end of the trail. For a more extended trip, this trail may also be combined with the Mighty Salmon (Ride 26) for a point-to-point ride with a vehicle shuttle.

As part of the Sentier NB Trails initiative, the Fundy Trail is the standard 2-m-wide (8-feet), fine gravel surface that characterizes this multi-use trail network. Though similar to many sections of the Sentier NB Trail in that regard, the Fundy Trail differs in one very important way: elevation. The trail hugs the Fundy coastline and plunges in and out of several river valleys on its way to the Big Salmon River. Alternating between the coast and inland forests, the trail winds and rolls its way to the mouth of the Big Salmon River. To assist users of the trail, steep sections have been paved, providing a solid surface on which to negotiate switchback turns and reduce the resistance on the climbs between the surface and your tires . Also, speed limits have been posted to protect all users. Still, the steep hills and winding trail make for an alarmingly strenuous and technical rides, despite the highly civilized terrain.

RIDE 28 · The Fundy Trail

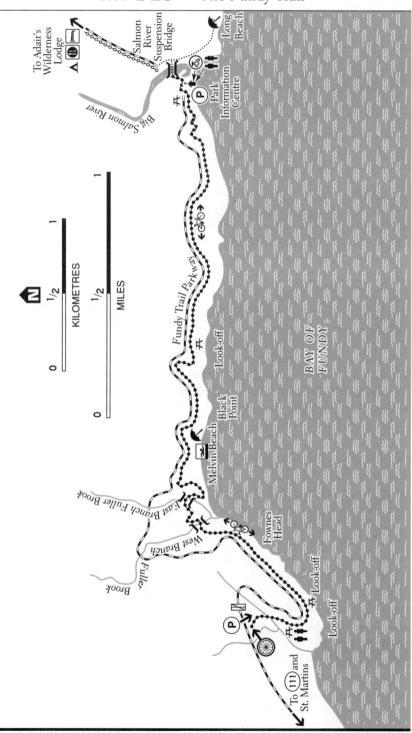

General location: This ride traces the coast of the Bay of Fundy, departing from St. Martins and continuing to the Big Salmon River.

Elevation change: Nearly 600 m (1,900 feet) gained on steep, paved switchbacks and many rolling hills.

Season: The trail can be ridden from spring to fall (June to September), but to enjoy the views, avoid cloudy days, as well as rain and fog.

Services: Currently there are no services along the trail, with the exception of a few outhouses. Most services are available in St. Martins, but the closest bike shop is in Sussex, approximately 55 km (34 miles) north of St. Martins.

Hazards: Although this is a wide, smooth, multi-use trail, there are sections of loose gravel and some very steep grades that require good bike handling skills. Due to the number of trail users, bikes are restricted to 15 and 20 km (10 and 15 miles) per hour along the trail.

Rescue index: Frequent traffic on the trail and the nearby parkway means you will never be far from assistance.

Land status: Provincial multi-use trail.

Maps: There are maps of the trail available at the St. Martins Visitor Information Centre, located in the lighthouse as you approach the trailhead. The trail is also featured in *The New Brunswick Multi-Use Trail System Trail Guide*, available at Visitor Information Centres or by calling (800) 526-7070.

Finding the trail: Take Route 111 South from Sussex Corner to St. Martins. When you reach the community of St. Martins, turn left, following Main Street through town to a small harbour and the site of the Visitor Information Centre. Bear right and drive through a covered bridge, continuing on the main road past a beach and some caves on the right. At the next fork, bear right, continuing on Little Beach Road to its junction with Melvin Beach Road. Continue straight to the trailhead, which is 8 km (5 miles) from the tourist information lighthouse. You will see the start of the trail on the right, just before the tollgate for the Fundy Parkway.

Source of additional information: The Fundy Trails Council is producing up-to-date information on the New Brunswick Multi-Use Trail System. They can be reached at (800) 526-7070.

Notes on the trail: Departing from the trailhead at the Fundy Trail sign, you will descend a gravel slope that bends to the right at the bottom. A short distance along the trail, you will reach the first parking area by the side of the road, with outhouses, a telephone, and a garbage can. Continue ahead, following the gravel trail, which will curve to the left and head uphill. The next section of trail is by far the most civilized, with the most viewpoints and picnic areas.

At the top of the hill, the trail rolls gently and veers toward the edge of the cliffs. At 1 km (0.6 mile), you get your first view out to the Bay of Fundy. If you continue beyond the shelters and picnic tables, you will come to a look-off point from which a panoramic view of the Fundy coast extends to the horizon. Beyond the look-off point, the trail continues a little farther inland in prepara-

The Fundy Trail hugs the edge of the cliffs, offering stunning views over the Bay of Fundy.

tion for a significant descent and climb through the gorge of the west branch of Fuller Brook. As the trail begins to descend, the gravel turns to pavement, drops off steeply, and switchbacks down one side of the gorge. At the bottom you will cross a wooden bridge and immediately begin the arduous climb up the other side. On the climb, you will pass an outhouse and a set of stairs descending to a small beach on the right.

At the end of the climb, the trail swings around to the right, past an offshoot to the left. Following the red arrow and continuing around the bend, the pavement turns to gravel as you enter the woods. Farther along, you will cross another wooden bridge over the east branch of Fuller Brook, following signs to Black Point. A short distance beyond this bridge, there is a scenic view overlooking a waterfall and Melvin Beach. The trail continues through a primarily wooded landscape, with frequent look-offs to the Bay of Fundy.

The final descent to the mouth of the Big Salmon River is paved and switchbacks along the hillside. As you near the end, you will pass a parking area and continue on the edge of the cliff to the interpretive centre. The view here is spectacular, as the river pours between the forested and rocky hillsides, out to the Bay of Fundy. Beyond this point, the trail continues up past the interpretive centre. There is a flight of stairs, and then the path brings you to a suspension footbridge across the Big Salmon River. On the other side, a double-track trail continues to the right to Long Beach, and the riverbanks provide excellent spots for swimming and snacks. Regardless of your intentions, the side trip to the bridge is well worth a visit. To return, simply retrace your tracks to the St. Martins trailhead.

RIDE 29 • Rockwood Park

AT A GLANCE

Length/configuration: 11.2-km (7-mile) loop

Aerobic difficulty: Moderate; rolling terrain with some steep climbs on a gravel road

Technical difficulty: Beginner riding on the gravel road; intermediate to advanced skills required on the single-track

Scenery: Wooded area with many ponds, lakes, streams, and wetlands

Special comments: Good variety of trails suitable to all abilities

---

Rockwood Park is situated within minutes of downtown Saint John but appears unaffected by its urban proximity. In the park you will ride on trails that wind through low-lying woods and wetland areas, and periodically arrive at openings overlooking small lakes. You will discover trails blossoming with wildflowers and grassy fields of colour in the early summer. Equipped with the detailed orienteering map of the park, you can explore several loops, using the main gravel road through the park as the starting point to lead into the network of single-track trails.

The 11.2-km (7-mile) ride described here heads out on the main gravel trail and creates a loop on the return trip, utilizing a combination of single- and double-track trails. The main trail offers a scenic ride over rolling hills and just two short, steep climbs. The single-track trails head into the woods and through marshy areas, on challenging terrain that requires intermediate to advanced skill and, in some areas, a hankering for mud. On all of these trails you will enjoy the natural features of the park, and there are opportunities to swim and fish at several of the small lakes, including one near the end of the ride, with a beach, changing facilities, and a swimming area.

General location: Rockwood Park is located just 5 minutes from downtown Saint John.

Elevation change: The hills throughout this ride range from small to moderate, with no significant change in elevation.

Season: Riding on the main trail can begin as early as May, but single-track trails should be avoided until early summer. Ideal months for riding are mid-June to October.

Services: Rockwood Park has camping, swimming, and other recreational facilities, but all other needs should be met in St. John. For bicycle service

RIDE 29 · Rockwood Park

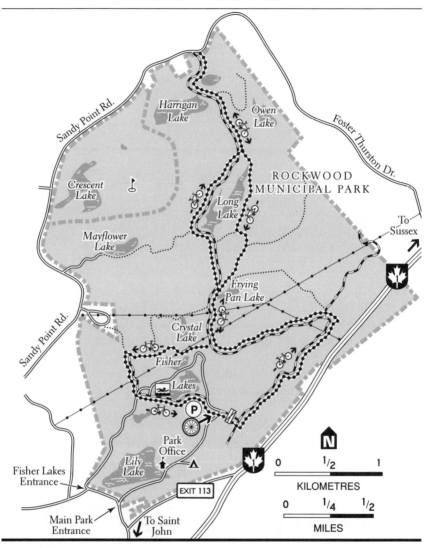

and accessories, visit the Bike Works, located at 22 Water Street (phone (506) 652-BIKE).

Hazards: Equestrians use the trails regularly; give way to horseback riders at all times.

Rescue index: You are never far from help, as you are likely to encounter other visitors or park staff on the trails. You will also find assistance at the park's Information Centre or other recreational areas situated near the trailhead.

Pausing to take in the view at the handle of Frying Pan Lake.

Land status: City of Saint John Municipal Park.

Maps: A detailed orienteering map of the park may be purchased from the Information Centre at the entrance.

Finding the trail: The main entrance to the park is on Mount Pleasant Avenue, which can be reached from Highway 1 west, off of Exit 113. The park is immediately to the right at the end of the off-ramp. Coming from the east, take city centre Exit 111 and turn right on Union Street, following it to Route 100 (City Road). Continue up the overpass at Haymarket Square, which will bring you to the main entrance of the park. Once in the park, continue up the paved road, bearing to the left to the first parking area. It is on the left-hand side near the stables and children's farm.

Source of additional information: For further information on the park, contact the City of Saint John Parks Department at (506) 658-2829.

Notes on the trail: Begin on a wide gravel path leaving the parking area in a southerly direction. At the entrance you will pass through an open green gate, and after a very short distance along the gravel path, you will arrive at a **T** junction. Turn left at the junction onto a wide gravel trail. Continue straight along this trail, and bear left past a trail continuing up to the right into a grassy meadow. A short distance farther along, you will cross under a power line and continue to follow the trail around a bend to the left. You will pass a steep, eroded, rocky trail heading uphill on the right, and then cross under the power lines again. At this point the trail begins to climb, steeply at times, up two moderate hills and over a final lip. The gravel surface softens as you advance up the hill, increasing the difficulty for short periods during the climb.

Before a final rise into a clearing, turn right onto another wide gravel trail that descends under another power line. Climbing up the other side of this short dip, you are at a high point, surrounded by the magenta flowers of Rhodora, daisies, and wild strawberry plants. From here you can also see Crystal Lake to the left. Continuing ahead, you will pass Frying Pan Lake before coming to a grassy clearing overlooking Long Lake on the right. The trail continues as a wide gravel road, with only a few washed-out or eroded sections of loose rock. You will follow this main trail, ignoring all the single-track options to the left and right, all the way to Harrigan Lake. Beyond the lake the trail continues just a short distance to the main, paved park road. At this point, turn around to begin the return trip.

Returning from Harrigan Lake, you can retrace your tracks on the main trail or explore some single-track options. The first single-track trails on the left and right are dead ends, so turn into the second trail on the left, just past the lake. There may be some vegetation obscuring the opening to this narrow single-track, and you will know you have overshot the entrance if you curve around a fairly sharp bend to the right on the main trail. Turning left onto the single-track, you will wind through the woods a short distance before crossing a bog. Beyond the bog, the trail descends steeply to a stream that feeds Long Lake. You will pedal over a small bridge and then climb steeply up the other side. The trail continues to roll through some wet areas to a **T** junction at a rough opening with some trees. Bearing right will return you to the main trail almost immediately, or you can bear left and continue on the single-track. Bearing left, the trail continues through a rough, wooded area on a slight climb. Equestrians use this trail, and some sections are more challenging since they have been eroded and pitted with hoof ruts. You will pass a trail branching off to the left that will take you on a long loop into some very wet areas and then back to the main trail near the parking area. In June and July this area is sure to be swarming with mosquitoes (and therefore we suggest bearing right here instead). A short distance past this intersection, you will arrive at a **T** junction overlooking Frying Pan Lake. Turn left and return to the main trail.

You will reach the main trail at the clearing under the power lines. Cross under the power lines, and at the next **T** junction, turn right. (Turning left returns you to the parking area, the way you came.) Following the trail to the right, you will pass a trail branching off to the left and then arrive at another **T** junction. Turn left, and follow this trail to a large parking area. Bear left as you make your way across the Fisher Lakes parking area. Continue on the paved trail that extends from the end of the parking area and traces along the lakes' edge. Continuing straight on this trail, you will arrive at a paved road that curves to the left and right. Turn right, and continue to bear right once it merges with the main park road. A short distance farther on this road, you will arrive back at the parking area.

RIDE 30 • Sentier NB Trails: West Saint John–Musquash

AT A GLANCE

Length/configuration: 30-km (18-mile) out-and-back (15 km [9 miles] each way)

Aerobic difficulty: Easy; a mostly flat ride on a gravel-dusted surface

Technical difficulty: Beginner; suitable for riders of all ages and abilities

Scenery: Observe waterfowl in a natural setting

Special comments: Completion of the multi-use trail to Saint John is scheduled for 1999

Development of a provincewide multi-use recreational trail is well under way in New Brunswick. Currently, Sentier NB Trails has converted several hundred kilometres of rail bed that will one day be connected, end to end. The section of trail from West Saint John to the Ducks Unlimited Musquash Marshland is an example of the scope of the project and its ongoing development. This 30-km (18-mile) out-and-back trail will soon be connected with downtown Saint John and currently offers riders a sample of what multi-use trails can offer recreational riders of all levels.

Beautiful scenery and opportunities to view waterfowl in a natural setting are the highlights of this ride. The passage through inland woods and shoreline areas of woods, bog, and waterfront is representative of the variety of landscape to be experienced throughout the Sentier NB Trails system. As evidenced by this ride, rail trails are easy to navigate, and information is readily available through the New Brunswick Trails Council and Visitor Information Centres throughout the province. These trails make outdoor recreation accessible to everyone and help nurture appreciation and increase awareness of our natural surroundings. So get out and explore, and enjoy these trails with your friends and family!

General location: The trailhead is situated just west of Saint John, off of the Trans-Canada Highway.

Elevation change: This ride follows the route of an abandoned railroad bed, with virtually no change in elevation.

Season: The trail may be ridden from the end of the spring thaw until there is snow on the ground. To avoid the rain and other inclement weather, hit the trails between June and September. In the prime riding season, mosquitoes,

RIDE 30 • Sentier NB Trails: West Saint John–Musquash

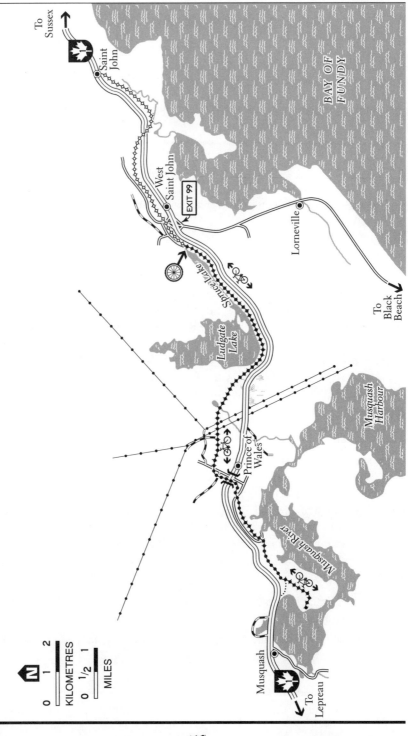

black flies, and other water-loving, relentless, biting insects await in the marshlands. Bring bug repellent if you plan to watch the waterfowl.

Services: There are no services at the trailhead, but all services are available in nearby Saint John.

Hazards: Apart from the biting insects that can drive you to distraction, there are no hazards on this trail.

Rescue index: You are always close to the Trans-Canada Highway, where there is regular traffic flow, making it possible to flag down cars for assistance. Also, you will pass through a small community near the marsh.

Land status: Public rights-of-way on a provincially owned trail system.

Maps: The trail is featured in *The New Brunswick Multi-Use Trail System Trail Guide*, available at Visitor Information Centres or by calling (800) 526-7070.

Finding the trail: Departing from Saint John on the Trans-Canada Highway, travel west to West Saint John. Take Exit 99, and turn right at the **T** junction at the end of the off-ramp. Follow the road to the flashing yield light, and turn left at the first opportunity onto Old St. Stephen Highway (unsigned). Follow it to its end at the City of Saint John Spruce Lake Water Treatment Facility. The trailhead is on your left, marked by a Sentier NB Trail sign. A small gravel opening acts as a parking area at the trailhead.

Source of additional information: The New Brunswick Trails Council publishes trail guides that can be acquired at most Visitor Information Centres or by contacting them at:

New Brunswick Trails Council
235 Main Street
Fredericton, NB E3A 1E1
(800) 526-7070

Notes on the trail: Begin by traveling west on the trail, passing through the gate facing Spruce Lake, across from the water treatment facility. The trail hugs the shores of the lake and closely parallels the Trans-Canada Highway for the initial stretch of the ride. You will reach the end of Spruce Lake after traveling for 2 km (1.2 miles) and continue along the shores of the considerably narrower Ludgate Lake. At the end of the lake, the trail veers away from the highway and a double-track ATV trail branches off to the left. Continue going straight on the rail bed, as the ATV trail is merely a detour that rejoins the trail just a short distance along.

Farther along the trail, you will pass through a gate with a Sentier NB Trail sign. Beyond the gate, you will enter a wooded area with a few patches of bog that are visible alongside the trail. Continuing on the trail, you will come to an opening and cross an isthmus between a pond and a river. The Trans-Canada Highway will be in view again on the left as you approach the end of this crossing. Once you have reconnected with the main land, you will see a single-track trail on the right branching off into the woods. Continue straight ahead, following the trail

Departing from West Saint John, the trail meanders beside Spruce Lake.

inland through wet forested areas scattered with ponds and marshy areas. On this section, the trail becomes harder packed, so you will find yourself traveling faster, suddenly emerging at an opening under a telephone line and then a series of power lines. At this point, you are half way to the marsh.

Just beyond the power lines, you will pass a logging road on the right and see signs of clearing. Farther along, the trail bends to the left, passes a Saint John Water Treatment Facility sign, and brings you to a four-way intersection with Menzie's Stream Road. Continue straight on the road ahead, which turns into pavement. You will continue onto an overpass crossing the Trans-Canada Highway on the paved shoulder. Follow the sign for Prince of Wales to a **T** junction with a stop sign. Turn right onto Prince of Wales Road, and continue on the road, around to the left and across a bridge. At the top of the short hill at the end of the bridge, you may descend the dirt trail that is heading toward the woods on your left. This trail leads to a dirt track that closely traces a path behind a series of houses and then continues as the multi-use trail.

Beyond the houses, the trail continues straight through the woods. You will emerge at an opening with some more houses to your left. Continue going straight, following the road as it curves to the right. Heading toward the highway, bear left, off the main gravel road, onto another unpaved road of coarse gravel. The gravel becomes quite deep and chunky, making for a lengthy slog over the next kilometre (one-half mile) to the trail that connects with the Musquash River and marshlands. At the end of the climb the trail resumes as a double-track dirt road that descends to the marsh area. (At the time of our research the trail had only recently been dug up, and it may be scheduled for resurfacing.) Entering the marsh area, the trail ends abruptly at an incomplete bridge in the middle of the marshlands. From this point, you can watch for waterfowl and birds nesting in the area. To return, retrace your tracks along the multi-use trail to the parking area.

RIDE 31 • Grand Manan/Southern Head

AT A GLANCE

Length/configuration: 9-km (5.5-mile) loop

Aerobic difficulty: Easy; a short and mostly flat ride

Technical difficulty: Intermediate; rough, rocky stretches of single- and double-track trail

Scenery: Dramatic cliffs on the west shores of Grand Manan Island

Special comments: You may spot seals and whales from the viewpoints along the shore

Grand Manan Island is a small piece of New Brunswick paradise. With only one main road and 2,500 residents, a lot is packed in and available on this island. It is a popular destination from which to sea kayak, whale watch, or venture on a puffin trip, and we are about to add mountain biking to the island's repertoire of outdoor adventures you can pack into a weekend. The island is small enough, we discovered, that you can arrive on the ferry at North Head at 6:30 p.m., set up your tent at the southern end of the island, and return to the community centre at the middle of the island in time for a concert at 8:00 p.m. With respect to the mountain biking opportunities on the island, the loop we have described here is short enough that you can satisfy your fat tire cravings and still have the time, and the energy, to go sea kayaking.

Despite its small size and popularity, Grand Manan does not feel crowded at all. On the 9-km (5.5-mile) loop around Southern Head you will be filled with a sense of grandeur, looking out over the endless expanse of salt water and traveling inland through the woods and past a large pond and marshy area. The island is predominantly flat but sits high above the salt waters of the Bay of Fundy and Grand Manan Channel. The trail follows single-track paths and ATV tracks around the lower end of the island with minimal elevation change,

RIDE 31 • Grand Manan/Southern Head

[Map showing the Grand Manan/Southern Head ride route, including Grand Manan Island, Grand Manan Channel, Bradford Cove, Bradford Cove Pond, Spring Rocks (Look-off), Millan's Brook, Southwest Head Light, Southern Head Beach, Bay of Fundy, Deep Cove, Seal Cove, Route 776, and directions to Hay Point and Seal Cove.]

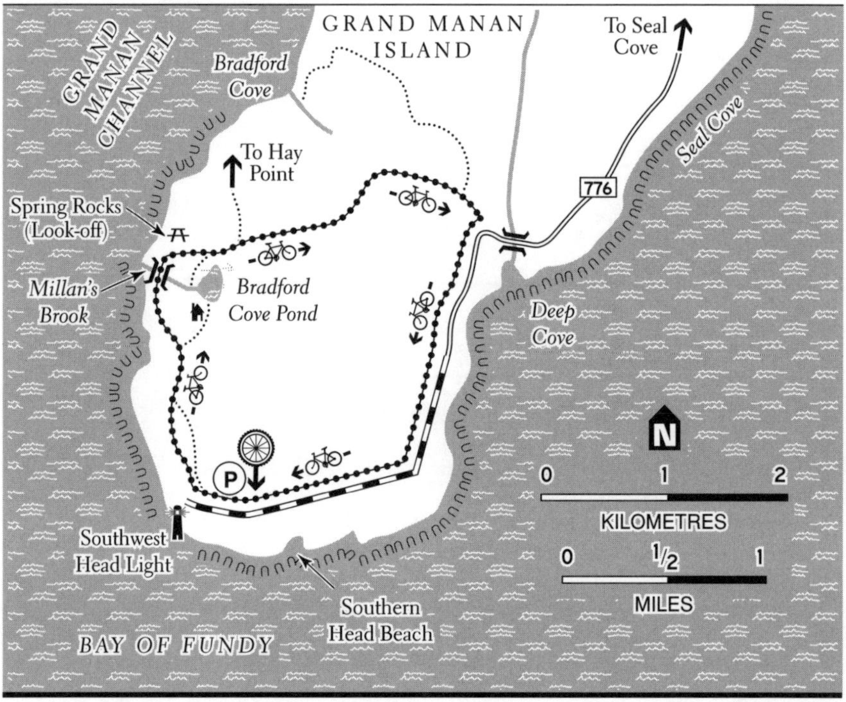

but it offers great views over dramatic cliffs that plunge several stories to the ocean. The ride, though not difficult, does require good bike handling skills on the single-track paths that head out to the edge of the cliffs and on the rocky sections of double-track trail. If this has just whet your appetite, there are other parts of the island to explore by mountain bike, including Ross Island, as well as a network of old roads and dirt trails in the middle section of the island, but we think you might be tempted by other activities.

General location: Off of the southern coast of New Brunswick, on Grand Manan Island.

Elevation change: Minimal; there are just two short, gradual climbs.

Season: To avoid the rain and fog, July and August are ideal months for cycling; however, the summer season begins in June and continues on through September.

Services: All services are available on Grand Manan, but very few are open on Sundays throughout the year. Bicycle service can be obtained from Adventure High, located at the northern head of the island (phone (506) 662-3563).

Hazards: The primitive bridge over Millan's Brook requires you to dismount. Approach the descent to the brook with caution.

Rescue index: The trail traces the outer perimeter of Southern Head, but you are never more than a few kilometres (a mile or so) from the trailhead or the main paved road. Help should be close at hand.

Land status: All trails are public rights-of-way on Crown land.

Maps: A single government topographic map, Grand Manan 21 B/10, covers the lower two-thirds of the island and this trail. A laminated topographic map of the island is also available at Adventure High in North Head.

Finding the trail: To reach the trailhead at Southern Head on Grand Manan, you must first take a ferry to the island. Ferry service is provided by Coastal Transport from a ferry terminal located at Black's Harbour in the southwest corner of New Brunswick. The journey is two hours long, the car ferry makes five or six trips a day, and it is advisable to arrive an hour in advance of the ferry's departure. For information on fares and the ferry schedule, contact Coastal Transport at (506) 662-3724.

Once on Grand Manan you will follow the only main road on the island. It is a continuation of Highway 776, which you took to Black's Harbour. The road resumes at the ferry docks in Castalia. From the ferry docks, turn left at the first intersection and follow this road all the way to Southern Head. As you approach Southern Head, the road will curve and dip to the left over a small bridge. Shortly beyond this point, the pavement turns to gravel and continues straight to the parking area at the lighthouse for Southern Head Beach. Bear right, toward the lighthouse, and park in the grassy opening.

Source of additional information: Cycling tours of the island, sea kayaking excursions, and information are available through:

Adventure High
P.O. Box 40, North Head
Grand Manan, NB E0G 2M0
(506) 662-3563

Notes on the trail: From the parking area at Southern Head, begin riding up the gravel road toward the lighthouse. Continue through the opening between the lighthouse and a white building with red doors, onto a grassy double-track trail at the edge of the cliff. At the first **Y** intersection with a double-track that cuts across the grassy field to the right, you may also bear left, following the sandy footpath along the cliffs. As the trail veers inland, you will pass a small white sign for Brutus Cove, the site of a shipwreck in 1842. This is the first of several signs you will see along the trail that identify points where boats have smashed into the rocks and survivors have scrambled to safety.

As you advance along this inland trail, the terrain becomes more challenging. ATVs have rutted sections of the trail, and there are some exposed roots and rocks to negotiate. Follow the coastal trail almost all the way to Bradford Cove Pond. As you approach the pond, you will see a small building in a clearing ahead. At this point, look on the left for a single-track trail that is signed to Spring

Riding along the edge of the cliffs at Southern Head, the waves crash on into shore 160 metres below.

Rocks and Hay Point. Turn left on the trail, and descend through a grassy meadow to Millan's Brook. Riding on this narrow footpath is quite technical, with quick twists and turns over exposed roots and rocks. There is a slight descent to a primitive log bridge over the brook, where you will, by necessity, dismount and hike your bike to the other side. The trail climbs up the other side of the embankment and continues to a grassy opening. At the entrance to this opening, Spring Rocks is signed to the left and Hay Point and Bradford Cove to the right. Stopping for a view at Spring Rocks, you may see whales in the distance in the channel and seals on the rocks along the shore.

The ride continues up to the right. Climb up the grassy slope to a **T** junction with a double-track trail. You will drop over a short lip to the trail and turn left, following signs for Hay Point and Bradford Cove. A short distance along the doubletrack, you will reach a fork with a single-track heading toward Hay Point. This is an optional side trip to another scenic viewpoint on the Grand Manan Channel. Continue straight, following the right fork toward Deep Cove. This next section of trail will bend to the right and take you down over a short bank, into a rough and rutted area quite close to Bradford Cove Pond. Follow the trail around the tip of the pond, and after passing through a soggy, potentially very wet section, watch for a path that leads away from the pond and back into the woods. There was a yellow bucket top nailed to a tree and more yellow dots on the trees at the entrance when we passed through.

Bearing left onto the double-track trail, the ride is initially quite rocky and rutted with ATV tracks. You will ride past a small cottage on the left and come to a three-way intersection. Continue straight, and beyond here you will descend a slightly smoother old road. At a **T** junction with a double-track trail that is signed for Deep Cove, bear right. The trail continues in much the same combination of dirt and rock, and is signed Deep Cove Road. The trail descends gradually, and you will arrive at a **Y** intersection and continue to follow the wide sandy trail to the right. Ride past the Lambert Camp Ridge Trail on the right, and follow the trail as it bends around to the left and soon brings you to a **T** junction with a paved road.

You will emerge under a power line and bear right on the paved road to return to Southern Head. A short climb lies ahead on the pavement, and then the road turns to gravel. As you descend the gravel road, it becomes quite rough. The washboard effect will cause you to lose some valuable speed for the final climb, but from here it is just a short distance to Southern Head. At the top of the hill the road levels off, and the parking area is within view.

PRINCE EDWARD ISLAND

Bounded on its seaward side by the Gulf of St. Lawrence and by the Northumberland Strait on the other, tiny Prince Edward Island has much to offer the itinerant mountain biker. Canada's smallest, most densely populated province rests on a great plain of sedimentary rock that found itself separated from the New Brunswick mainland by rising waters some five thousand years ago. The primary highway across Prince Edward Island spans almost 280 kilometres (175 miles) from North Cape to East Point, and the distance between the north and south shores can vary from as few as 6 kilometres (4 miles) to as many as 64 kilometres (40 miles). As a result, it is virtually impossible to travel any distance on the island without chancing upon a breathtaking view of the shore.

Despite its captivating beauty, Prince Edward Island did not attract European settlers until after the Treaty of Utrecht in 1713, at which time the French handed over their colonies in New Brunswick, Nova Scotia and Newfoundland. Taking stock of their options, the French decided to develop Ile Royal (Cape Breton Island) and Ile Saint-Jean (Prince Edward Island), and the first French settlers arrived on Prince Edward Island's shores in the spring of 1720. They established good relations with the native Mi'kmaq people, the sole inhabitants of the island until that time. When the deportation of Acadians from neighboring New Brunswick and Nova Scotia began in 1755, nearly 1,500 of them sought refuge on the island. The Acadians enjoyed only a brief reprieve from conflict with the British, however, and 1758 brought another round of deportations. Many Acadians were sent back to France while others escaped to the region around the Baie des Chaleurs and Quebec.

A complete survey of the island followed British acquisition of the colony and resulted in its division into 67 parcels of roughly 8,100 hectares (20,000 acres) each. Awarded by lottery, many of the recipients of these parcels became absentee landlords. New settlers, this time from Scotland, Ireland, and England, arrived on the island over the next hundred years and lived as tenants. The resulting landlord/tenant system created much unrest and discontent on the island and began a long history of land controversy that still affects mountain biking today. With no assurance as to the longevity of their leases, settlers had little incentive to improve their land. Indeed, improvements would only result in higher taxes. With no land up for sale, settlers found it impossible to become property owners.

Fortunately, the Land Purchase Act of 1875 succeeded in buying out the original landowners and facilitating resale of the land to the island's inhabitants. Today, the government still regulates land ownership and, as mountain bikers have discovered, landowners remain protective of their land and its uses.

Since the arrival of the first settlers, agriculture and the fisheries have comprised the primary industries of the island. Golden fields of hay and lush green potato fields will become familiar sights as you tour. Today, Prince Edward Island produces roughly 30 percent of all potatoes grown in Canada, and remains the largest supplier of seed potatoes in North America. Talk to farmers, and they will attribute their success to the island's unique red soil—a surprisingly thin layer of organic material, high in oxidized iron, lying atop the bedrock. Along the shores you will see exposed red rock, or red beds, that are shaped into long, smooth shelves and other unusual formations. Evidence of the fishing industry will also attract your eyes: mussel cultures, lobster traps, and scores of fishing boats. While lobster provides the bulk of the fisheries' revenue, the trademarked Malpeque Oysters and Island Blue Mussels also play a significant role in the fishing economy and enjoy international acclaim.

Today, Prince Edward Island attracts both domestic and international visitors with its charming combination of sand, sea, and rolling hills, so it won't surprise you that tourism has become an engine of economic development—second only to farming. Tourism began on the island in the nineteenth century when word of the striking coastal scenery and pastoral landscape first reached Britain and the United States. The rumours brought many visitors to the still-popular Cavendish Beach on the north shore. More recently, the Confederation Bridge linking Prince Edward Island and mainland New Brunswick has created a tourism boom, bringing new seekers of outdoor recreation to the island and its two major cities, Charlottetown and Summerside.

With its countless, little-trafficked roads, resident islanders and vacationers alike have long deemed the island an ideal place to cycle. More recently, multi-day adventure holidays that combine cycling with activities like golf, sea kayaking, and deep-sea fishing have become popular. Outside Expeditions in Charlottetown can service mountain bikers with single- and multi-day adventures that may combine dirt-road cycling tours with kayaking. As the popularity of mountain biking increases, we expect to see a subgroup of tourists who escape even the lightly-traveled dirt roads to experience all that Prince Edward Island has to offer.

THE TRAILS

The provincial capital of Charlottetown has grown into the mountain biking hub of Prince Edward Island. Situated near the middle of the island, Charlottetown lies midway between the arrival and departure points of the Confederation Bridge and the Marine Atlantic Ferry terminal. Macqueen's and Smooth Cycle, two of the best full-service bike shops in the province, are both located downtown, making Charlottetown an excellent base for rides at either end of the island or any point in between. A single trip to Smooth Cycle can furnish you with many important things. Whether you need major service or just a small part, the staff at Smooth Cycle will get you back in the saddle as quickly as possible. Furthermore, you will be able to chat with members of the local mountain bike club and competitors from the growing racing community. From the gregarious owner, you can gain up-to-the-minute information on trail openings or closures, as well as relevant news on the latest landowner disputes, be they emerging or recently resolved. The legacy of the island's land development means riders here, more than in any other province in Atlantic Canada, face a nearly insurmountable challenge when searching for land to develop for off-road mountain biking.

Fortunately, the strong dedication of both individuals and government organizations to the development of the sport of mountain biking has resulted in an ever-expanding network of trails. Furthermore, while mountain biking terrain may be difficult to come by on Prince Edward Island, the available terrain provides both the scenery and the challenge that riders of all levels expect of any mountain biking excursion. Forming the foundation of the opportunities available to mountain bikers on the island is the Confederation Trail, a multi-use recreational trail that has been developed by the Canadian government along the former railroad bed. This trail will one day span the entire island, traversing 350 kilometres (218 miles) and touching on provincial highlights from Tignish to Elmira. Its completion may mark the first province-wide stretch of the grand Trans-Canada Trail—a project that will ultimately see the country linked coast-to-coast by a recreational trail. Other government initiatives that have benefited mountain bikers on the island include the opening of the Homestead Trail in Prince Edward Island National Park, and the preservation of Scenic Heritage Roads.

Unique to Prince Edward Island, heritage roads are narrow, red clay lanes bounded at times by thick foliage. They date back to the early European settlement and traverse certain portions of the island, protected by Provincial Government regulations that have spared them from burial beneath cement or asphalt. Following the undulating contours of the landscape, the roads we have included here offer some of the most captivating island scenery and have intriguing stories to tell. Similarly, the Homestead Trail in Prince Edward Island National Park preserves a unique cross-section of inland and shoreline terrain ripe for exploration by mountain bike.

If you're seeking more advanced riding, give a hearty thanks for the efforts of dedicated riders who have obtained permission to build and use woods trails suitable for mountain biking. Although there are relatively few trails to chose from, the two single-track rides on Prince Edward Island are among the most challenging in Atlantic Canada. The Nordic Centre at Brookvale Provincial Park northwest of Charlottetown provides the province's most elaborate network of single-track trails. Several races in the "Red Mud Cup"—the provincial race circuit—find a home here, and 1998 saw the Nordic Centre host the Atlantic Mountain Bike Championships to rave reviews from participants.

From the young riders who hang out in the service end of Smooth Cycle, you can obtain descriptive anecdotes about the latest trails developed at the Brookvale course. If you compare their names to the trail names you find on maps for the race circuit, you are likely to discover that you are talking to mountain biking trailblazers. Their anecdotes and impressions of the single-track trails at the park will add useful information to the maps on display or those circulating around Smooth Cycle.

Bonshaw Hills, located just southeast of Brookvale, offers the other single-track trail on the island. Originally a prized single-track loop, an incident between a mountain biker and a landowner has reduced the ride to a short out-and-back. The story serves as a reminder of the precarious "tire-hold" mountain biking has on the limited single-track terrain of Prince Edward Island, and forces us to remember how our individual actions contribute to the whole. By acting responsibly on the trail you may help enhance the image of mountain bikers and further the cause of local riders.

HITTING THE TRAILS

Apart from following the golden rules of good mountain biker etiquette, there remain a few other things to remember before heading out on these trails. Prince Edward Island's temperate climate allows for riding most of the year, although, as in every Atlantic province, substantial precipitation may inhibit your plans. An average rainfall of 87 centimetres (roughly 40 inches) and 340 centimetres (roughly 120 inches) of snow can make for some extremely wet spring and fall seasons that limit access to the single-track trails and dirt roads. July and August claim honors for the driest and most popular months for cycling on the island, although the season may begin as early as April and continue through November.

Riding on an island this size makes it virtually impossible for you to get lost. Inevitably you will emerge from the easily navigable trails at a road crossing or intersection that will appear on any highway map. In fact, for the rides described here, you need only equip yourself with the highway map available from any tourist information centre. Any additional information by way of trail notes and perhaps some words of advice from a local rider will ensure you easily complete all the trails. While we would not call any of the rides described in this chapter "remote" in the traditional, backcountry sense, we do advise all riders to carry their own tools, replacement inner-tubes, and repair kits. Once you reach a trailhead you are unlikely to find any nearby services, let alone a bike store. Remarkably, with adequate, yet simple preparation, you are likely to discover that the absence of services outside the urban centres will actually enhance your experience exploring this island paradise north of the 49th parallel.

Please contact the following resources with any further questions about cycling or visiting Prince Edward Island:

Island Trails
P.O. Box 265
Charlottetown, PEI C1A 7K4
(902) 894-7535

Tourism PEI
P.O. Box 2000
Charlottetown, PEI C1A 7N8
(800) 463-4PEI

Smooth Cycle
172 Prince Street
Charlottetown, PEI C1A 4R6
(902) 566-5530

MacQueen's Bike Shop & Travel
430 Queen Street
Charlottetown, PEI C1A 4E8
(902) 368-2453

Outside Expeditions
Box 2336
Charolottetown, PEI C1A 8C1
(902) 892-5425
info@getoutside.com

PEI Cycling Association
(902) 368-4548

RIDE 32 • Tignish–Alberton Confederation Trail

AT A GLANCE

Length/configuration: 21.5-km (13.3-mile) point-to-point (21.5 km [13.3 miles] one way, then vehicle shuttle), or 43-km (26.7-mile) out-and-back

Aerobic difficulty: Suitable for all fitness levels; the out-and-back option requires some endurance

Technical difficulty: The crushed stone surface requires little or no technical skill

Scenery: Mixed woods, which provide a habitat for a wide variety of bird life

Special comments: Tignish marks the very beginning of the proposed 350 km (217.5 mile) Confederation Trail

North Cape forms the northwest tip of Prince Edward Island. Among all the attractions on the island, this site is one of the most isolated. Unlike the rolling agricultural interior of the island, North Cape is rugged and windswept and enchants visitors with the drama of the ever-changing realm between land and sea. Just a few kilometres (a couple of miles) south of North Cape, Tignish is the starting point for Prince Edward Island's section of the Trans-Canada Trail: the Confederation Trail. This ride follows the first 21.5 km (13.3 miles) of the trail, which will one day span the entire island, along 350 km (217.5 miles) of the railroad corridor abandoned in 1989. The ride can be enjoyed as a 43-km

RIDE 32 • Tignish–Alberton Confederation Trail

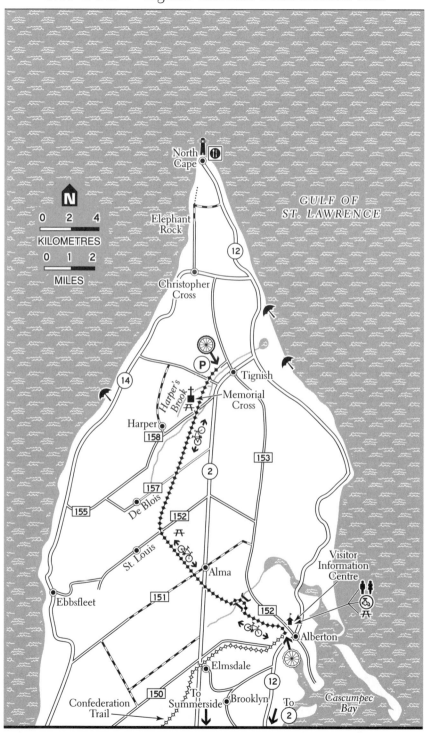

(26.7-mile) out-and-back excursion, with a rest stop in Alberton; or, if you can arrange for transportation, as a 21.5-km (13.3-mile) point-to-point between Tignish and Alberton. Either way, riders of all ability levels will enjoy the wide, smooth trail surface that features no demanding hill climbs or technical terrain. There are picnic tables and shelters along the length of the route.

Just over 1 km (0.6 mile) outside Tignish, the trail passes a memorial cross. This small monument was erected in memory of four railroad workers, who were killed near this site in a train crash on February 21, 1932. A poem on display here tells the story of the accident, which occurred when one train slammed into the back of another one caught on the tracks in heavy snow. This monument is the first of a series of points along the Confederation Trail that document the history of the railroad on the island. Beyond this site, the trail passes through an ever-changing landscape of fields and meadows, mixed hardwood and softwood forests, and occasional wet areas where rushes and cattails line the trail. In Alberton, the trail reaches the site of the old train station, which has been restored. There are picnic benches and shelters in a small green park around the station, making it a great place to stop and enjoy a picnic before setting out on the return trip. For riders wishing to ride farther along the Confederation Trail, there is a map in Alberton that illustrates the route of the trail as it continues south toward Bloomfield.

General location: Western Prince Edward Island, just over 80 km (50 miles) northwest of Summerside.

Elevation change: This abandoned railroad bed features only slight inclines. The maximum slope is less than 2 percent.

Season: The riding season on the Confederation Trail extends from the time the snow clears in the spring to the first snowfall of winter. The best months to ride are June through September, with July and August being the driest months.

Services: Most services are available in both Tignish and Alberton. Furthermore, there is quick access from the trail to a service station on Route 152, approximately half way along the ride. For bike service and repair, however, this corner of the island offers only basic services. The best resource for bike-related needs is Smooth Cycle, a shop in Charlottetown that offers service, repair, and bicycle rentals.

Hazards: There are several road crossings along this route, where caution must be used. In particular, the trail crosses busy Highway 2 about 6 km (3.75 miles) outside of Alberton. Wooden barricades will alert you to this and all other crossings.

Rescue index: Due to the number of road crossings throughout this ride, you will never be far from primary or secondary roads where assistance can easily be sought.

Land status: The Confederation Trail is part of the Trans-Canada Trail and follows a former railroad bed along a multi-use recreational trail on public land.

Maps: A map of the entire length of the Confederation Trail is available through most community and provincial Visitor Information Centres. In addition, the trail is clearly indicated on the Provincial Highway Map.

Finding the trail: PEI Highway 2 is the main highway through the western part of the island. Drive on this road into Tignish, and then turn left at a **T** junction with Route 153. Just beyond an Irving service station on the left side of the street, turn left onto Spring Lane. Drive just a short distance down Spring Lane, to its junction with School Street. At this point, you will see a gravel parking area on the right. The Confederation Trail begins here.

Sources of additional information: The Visitor Information Centres on the island distribute maps of the Confederation Trail, as well as any number of catalogues and brochures for information on accommodations and other services. To obtain such information prior to arriving on Prince Edward Island, call (800) 463-4734. For additional information on the Confederation Trail, you may also want to pick up a copy of J. Dan McAskill and Kate MacQuarrie's *Nature Trails of Prince Edward Island*, a 1996 publication in the Island Pathways series.

Notes on the trail: A large sign at the trailhead is clearly visible from the parking area. In addition to general information about the trail, you will notice that this is kilometre 0 of the Confederation Trail. The trail itself is easily recognizable: a wide, graded, multi-use pathway surfaced with stone dust. The route from Tignish to Alberton is clear and easy to follow for its entire length, and is posted at regular intervals with small signs that mark the passing kilometres.

A short distance from Tignish, you will cross a paved road. Beyond this road the trail curves around to the left, and you will cross a bridge over a tributary of Harper's Brook. Farther on, you will come to a picnic table and the memorial cross erected to mark the site of the Tignish train wreck of February 21, 1932. Beyond this site and just past the 4-km (2.5-mile) point, you will ride across another bridge, this one over Route 158. There is a view of Harper's Brook from this site.

In the community of DeBlois, you will cross a red dirt road before riding along a stretch of trail that is coloured with a profusion of wildflowers in the spring and early summer. After passing a large farm building on the left of the trail, you will reach St. Louis, which is approximately half way between Tignish and Alberton. The trail crosses Route 152 at this point, and you will be able to see a service station down the road on the right. Cross the pavement and pick up the rail trail on the other side. There is a grassy picnic area by the side of the trail here that includes a trail shelter.

After crossing another paved road, you will ride past another farm building and very quickly reach a junction with Highway 2. Beyond the highway, a red dirt road parallels the trail on the left for a short distance. Not far from the highway, a high bridge spans the Huntley River. Beyond the bridge you will pass a large gravel pit on the left, before crossing another paved road just 3 km (1.8 miles) from Alberton. This next stretch of trail includes amusing little interpretive signs that were designed to help you identify various bird species. Unfortunately, at the time that we rode here, all the pictures had been removed and all that remained were the descriptions. Continue riding the final few kilometres (a mile or so) to Alberton, where an old station still stands in a now grassy area filled with picnic tables and shelters.

RIDE 33 • French River

AT A GLANCE

Length/configuration: 19.5-km (12-mile) combination (12.9-km (8-mile) loop with two out-and-back spurs; the first spur is 1.1 km (7 miles) each way, the second spur is 2.3 km (1.4 miles) each way)

Aerobic difficulty: Intermediate; several long climbs present some physical challenge

Technical difficulty: Modest; easy riding along wide dirt roads and some pavement

Scenery: A ride out to Cape Tryon on the coast along roads that pass through rolling hills and farmland

Special comments: Take some time to explore two pioneer cemeteries near New London Bay

No ride on Prince Edward Island captures the contrast of the community's two primary industries as well as French River. This ride curls inland through the rolling hills and picturesque farmland that describe the province's interior landscape. Then, jutting back out toward the ocean, the ride parallels the high cliffs near Cape Tryon and drops down to a fishing village on New London Bay. For riders, this loop offers gorgeous views out to the ocean and a startling yet beautiful juxtaposition of green or golden hillsides and blue, blue water. Following a combination of primarily unpaved roads and some short connecting links on pavement, this ride demands no advanced technical skills, but it does present some challenge in the way of a good workout. Although Prince Edward Island features no monumental changes in elevation, the old unpaved roads drop steeply through dips and small stream valleys.

The main portion of this ride traces a 12.9-km (8-mile) loop from French River, through the farming communities of Long River and Park Corner, and around Cape Tryon to New London Bay. There are two worthwhile side trips along the way, however—both short out-and-back spurs that turn this ride into a 19.5-km (12-mile) combination. The first is a short 2.2-km (1.4-mile) out-and-back trip to the lighthouse at Cape Tryon. Although this site is likely to be windy, the meadow atop the high cliffs overlooking the Gulf of St. Lawrence makes a wonderful place to stop and enjoy a picnic. Beyond this point and closer to the end of the ride, it is possible to follow a dirt road to the lighthouse overlooking New London Bay. This trip involves a 4.3-km (2.7-mile) out-and-back ride to a point from which you will be able to look out toward the sand dunes at Cavendish Beach in Prince

RIDE 33 • French River

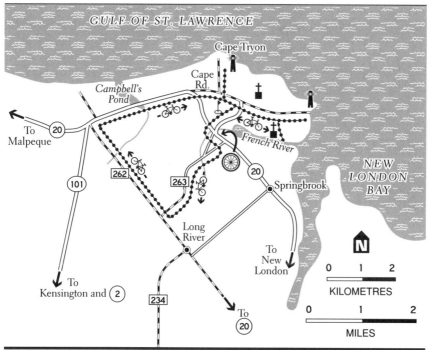

Edward Island National Park. There are also two old cemeteries to explore here, which stand as reminders to the arrival of early settlers in this area 200 years ago.

General location: French River is located on the north shore of the island, overlooking New London Bay, less than 20 km (roughly 12 miles) northeast of Kensington and roughly the same distance west of Cavendish.

Elevation change: From where you begin this ride near the shore of New London Bay, you will ride inland and follow a route over rolling hills. Although the elevation gained on this ride is not overwhelming, you will climb and descend throughout the length of the ride.

Season: As this ride follows well-established dirt roads, conditions can be good from late May through October. Keep in mind, though, that July and August are the driest months on the island.

Services: There is a convenience store at the trailhead, and most services are available in nearby Cavendish. All bike-related needs are best met in Charlottetown.

Hazards: Be aware that you will be sharing these roads with occasional traffic.

Rescue index: Riding along these secondary and dirt roads, you will never be far from assistance.

Land status: Public through-roads

Maps: Consult the Provincial Highway Map, section D-7.

Finding the trail: From Cavendish, follow PEI Highway 6 heading west to New London. In New London, turn right onto Highway 20, and cross Southwest River toward French River and Springbrook. Continue straight through Springbrook, and drive to a four-way intersection, where a Shell station and Jollimore's Grocery and Canteen will be on the right. Turn left here, onto Route 263, and pull over and park by the side of the road.

Source of additional information: Outside Expeditions offers guided biking tours and bicycle rentals.

>Outside Expeditions
>North Rustico Harbour
>P.O. Box 2336
>Charlottetown, PEI C1A 8C1
>(902) 892-5425 or (800) 207-3899

Notes on the trail: Begin riding up Route 263, heading away from New London Bay and the gas station and convenience store. You will pass a small pond down below and to the right of the road before the pavement ends. Continue straight along the unpaved portion of Route 263. You will ascend a gentle slope as the road curves around to the left and then bears right, passing another unpaved road on the left. Follow the road as it winds through a wooded area before descending a small hill with fields on either side. You will reach a **T** junction with a paved road, Route 262.

Turn right up Route 262—also known as Long River Road—passing a farm on the right and beginning up the first extended climb of the ride. As you approach the top of the climb, the view across the Gulf of St. Lawrence presents a striking contrast to the rolling hills of the surrounding countryside. Just beyond the crest of this hill the pavement ends, and you will continue straight along the red unpaved portion of the road. From this point, the road descends quite steeply, dropping down to cross a small stream that runs into Campbell's Pond. The descent to this stream is somewhat eroded, so be wary of sections of loose rock and gravel. From the stream, the road rises uphill on the other side.

You will climb to a **T** junction with a paved road at Park Corner. There will be a farm straight ahead of you. Turn right and ride on pavement down a short hill and past Campbell's Pond on the left. You will climb on pavement beyond the pond, approaching a sharp bend in the road to the right. Before this bend, turn left onto the unpaved Cape Road.

Follow Cape Road fairly close to the shore, heading toward New London Bay. When the road descends a short hill, look on the left for a dirt country lane. This narrow road leads straight toward the ocean and a lighthouse at Cape Tryon. The side trip is well worthwhile, leading up to a grassy area at the top of steep cliffs dropping down to the ocean below. Cormorants favour this stretch of coast-

PRINCE EDWARD ISLAND 167

The lighthouse beckons at the end of the red dirt road at Cape Tyron.

line, and you will see plenty perched within the nooks and ledges of the cliff face. From the lighthouse, turn around and follow the trail back to a **T** junction with Cape Road. Turn left to continue the ride.

After turning out of the road to Cape Tryon, you will climb, passing part of the French River Public Golf Course, which borders the road on the right. Shortly beyond this point you will come to a junction with a paved road on the right. The ride can be completed at this point by following the paved road down to the right. However, there is a lot to explore down the gravel road that continues straight ahead.

If you choose to include this second side trip in your ride, you will descend gradually along the gravel road, passing potato fields and, in the spring and early summer, colourful lupine by the side of the road. The road drops toward New London Bay. Near the bottom of the hill, bear right at a fork, heading toward a small lighthouse. Just a short distance farther, you will see a mowed, grassy trail on the right. Leaving your bike at this trailhead, follow the path on foot. A short walk will lead you to Yankee Hill Pioneer Cemetery. The cemetery takes its name from the tragedy of a storm remembered as the Yankee Gale. In 1851, between the 3rd and 5th of October, this storm caused many New England ships to capsize offshore near this site.

Leaving the cemetery, you can ride back to the main dirt road and turn right, continuing down toward the water. As the road follows a bend around to the left, bear right instead, and follow a grassy trail toward the lighthouse. No longer used, this lighthouse is apparently leased for a dollar a year to a couple who looks after and maintains it. Nestled on the grassy slopes overlooking New London Bay, the view from this site is as peaceful and relaxing as they come. Turn around and make your way back up the main dirt road.

On your way out, look to the right as you ride back up the road, and turn right onto a narrow path that leads to a stone monument. Set in the middle of a sea of potato fields, this monument stands to commemorate the arrival of early settlers in this area 200 years ago. A plaque on the monument will provide you with some details about the various settlements that were established. Beyond the stone monument is Simsfield Pioneer Cemetery. When you finish exploring, ride back out to the dirt road and turn right. At the crest of the hill, turn left on the paved road and descend past the French River Public Golf Course. You will pass a small fishing village and pier on the left before returning to the four-way intersection where you began the ride.

RIDE 34 • Homestead Trail

AT A GLANCE

Length/configuration: 10.2-km (6.3-mile) combination (a 4.6-km [2.8-mile] loop, and a 5.6-km [3.5-mile] loop ridden as an 8.7-km [5.4-mile] figure-eight)

Aerobic difficulty: Easy; mostly flat trails with just two short hills

Technical difficulty: Beginner; the trails are wide and grassy, requiring no technical skill

Scenery: Outstanding views out to the sandy shores of New London Bay

Special comments: An excellent outing with the kids

Prince Edward Island National Park is the perfect destination to combine a fun cycling excursion with swimming, sea kayaking, or hiking with the family. The Homestead Trail is the only trail open to bikers in the park, and it offers

RIDE 34 • Homestead Trail

a satisfying combination of woodland and shoreline scenery. The trail is well maintained, surfaced with a combination of hard-packed dirt and gravel, with a few grassy sections that accommodate riders of all ages and abilities. Along the shoreline there are captivating views of sand dunes and red stone cliffs that are characteristic of the north shore of Prince Edward Island. Inland, the trail winds through salt marshes, woodlands, and farmlands.

Generations of Mi'kmaq, Acadians, and British utilized these shore and inland areas for fishing and farming. However, the cliffs and sand dunes became a great attraction for travelers from all over the world, and the north shore became a fashionable vacation destination in the late nineteenth century. On this 8.7-km (5.4-mile) combination, you will experience the full range of terrain and come to fully appreciate the valuable role of the national park in preserving and protecting the diversity of this area. The Homestead Trail is a great destination for families and small groups in search of a scenic location for a refreshing bike jaunt.

General location: Prince Edward Island National Park, near Cavendish, on the north shore of the island.

Elevation change: Minimal; the trail is mostly flat, with a couple of short hills.

Season: The park is open daily throughout the year, with the ideal cycling sea-

The coastal stretch of the Homestead Trail in PEI National Park traces the salt marshes and sand dunes of New London Bay.

son nestled between late May and early October. The driest months on Prince Edward Island are July and August.

Services: There are a variety of attractions and services, including food and accommodations, in the vicinity of the park. However, you are in an area with no bike services, so any biking needs should be attended to at bike stores in Charlottetown.

Hazards: There are no hazards on this ride, since the trail is well maintained.

Rescue index: In case of an emergency, you can obtain help at the campground entrance near the trailhead. You may contact a park warden by phone at (902) 963-3052, or the RCMP at (902) 566-7111.

Land status: National park; there is an entry fee for all park visitors.

Maps: The trail is clearly marked in the guide to Prince Edward Island National Park, and there is a large-scale detailed map posted at the trailhead. It is also signed at major junctions.

Finding the trail: From PEI Highway 2, turn onto Highway 13 and travel north toward Cavendish. You will approach the park through the Cavendish entrance and purchase your permit. Follow signs for Cavendish Beach West. The trail is adjacent to the entrance to the Cavendish Campground and is signed with hiking symbols that indicate the trailhead for the Homestead Trail.

Sources of additional information: The park will respond to all inquiries at:

Parks Canada
2 Palmer's Lane
Charlottetown, PEI C1A 5V6
(902) 672-6350

Notes on the trail: The trailhead is located at the northern end of the parking lot and is marked by a large sign with a map of the trail and an introduction to the area. Begin up the wide, graded, red dirt road to a multiple intersection. Turn onto the gravel trail on the left (do not follow the sign directing you straight ahead). This trail opens into a farmer's field and curves gently to the right. Across the field, you will enter the woods and descend a short hill on a loose gravel surface. At the bottom of the dip, you will climb another short hill before the trail finally levels off. Continue straight for a short distance to a junction easily identified by a picnic area with some tables, a water pump, and an outhouse. Just before the picnic area, a trail branches off to the right. This is the joiner trail—the section of the ride where the short and extended loops intersect. Turn right onto this grassy double-track and head toward the water. The trail will narrow and become gravelly just before your view is filled with the shores of New London Bay. At a **T** junction, you can turn right to return to the parking area, or continue the ride on the extended loop to the left.

Following the continuation of the ride to the left, the trail is flat and follows the shoreline of New London Bay. You will dart back and forth, in and out of the woods, enjoying the salty breezes as you near the shoreline. The trail eventually veers left, away from the water, and follows along the edge of a farm field. The trail is clearly marked by wooden posts at regular intervals, so you won't wind up on one of the many cart-trails branching off to the right. Continue to follow the trail as it bends around to the left again and takes you between two farm fields. This stretch returns you to the junction with the picnic area at the joiner trail. Turn left, and traverse the joiner trail back to the water.

This time, turn right when you reach the **T** junction and begin the ride back to the parking area. You will cross a bridge and pass through an area of salt marsh, all the while taking in the view out to the sand dunes on New London Bay. After crossing another small bridge, you will pass through another salt marsh. The trail curves to the right, offering a last view across the water before entering the woods for the final stretch of the ride. Bear right when you reach the wide, red dirt trail, and follow it back to the parking area.

RIDE 35 • Anne's Land Heritage Roads

AT A GLANCE

Length/configuration: 13-km (7.8-mile) loop

Aerobic difficulty: Tough; high hills and frequent climbing make this an aerobically challenging ride

Technical difficulty: Novice riding on clay roads, and a brief stretch of pavement with some challenging descents on rocky hills

Scenery: Lush vegetation ranging from delicate flora to dense woodlands

Special comments: Popular among locals as an early season training ride

PE

Looking for a workout? The Princetown-Warburton and Perry Heritage Roads in the Anne's Land region of Prince Edward Island will provide just that. On this ride you will have to work hard on every metre of its 13 kilometres and sweat over every foot of its 7.8 miles. You will climb and descend several moderate hills of hard-packed dirt with patches of loose rock and chunky gravel. The ride is well suited to all levels of riders with good conditioning, or to those striving to achieve a higher level of fitness. Beginners will find some descents on loose rock challenging, and riders with intermediate to advanced skills should find sufficient challenge in the topography and the few rough patches to feel satisfied at the end of the ride.

The Princetown Road was one of the first roads on the island, dating back to 1771. At the time, it acted as a main road into the former capital of Prince County (now Prince Edward Island), Princetown. This road is being preserved in its original state by provincial government regulations under the Planning Act. Since the road has been designated a heritage road due to its age and historical significance, the regulations prohibit alteration of it in any way. Further, local landowners have voluntarily agreed to protect the woodlands and hedge-rows that line the roads. This makes for a unique riding experience on hilly roads that are lush with vegetation.

General location: Located off of PEI Highway 2, approximately 20 minutes west of Charlottetown in Fredericton.

Elevation change: You will gain approximately 250 m (820 feet) over rolling terrain, with two long climbs accounting for about 150 m (490 feet).

Season: Clay roads are muddy in the early spring after the first thaw but should

RIDE 35 • Anne's Land Heritage Roads

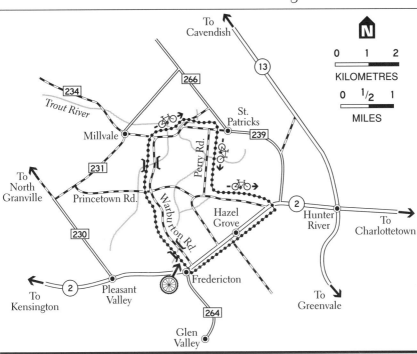

be in good condition for riding by mid-June. The driest months are July and August, and the cycling season can continue through October.

Services: With the exception of the occasional service station along Highway 2, there are few services outside Charlottetown. Any biking needs can be met at either of Charlottetown's bike stores: Smooth Cycle, located at 172 Prince Street (phone (902) 566-5530), or MacQueens, at 430 Queen Street (phone (902) 368-2453).

Hazards: None.

Rescue index: There are many houses en route, and the roads intersect with paved roads at either end, so you are never more than a few kilometres (a couple of miles) from a frequently trafficked road.

Land status: A combination of protected and paved provincial roads.

Maps: All roads appear on the Prince Edward Island Highway Map, available at all Visitor Information Centres.

Finding the trail: From Charlottetown, take PEI Highway 2 west, and continue beyond the city limits. You will pass through the towns of Milton, Brookfield, Hunter River, and finally, Hazel Grove. The Warburton Road is the second road on the right-hand side, past Hazel Grove. You will turn right just before the road bends to the right, prior to reaching the junction with Route 264 to Glen Valley on the left. Park at the side of the road near the intersection.

Source of additional information: A brochure titled *Scenic Heritage Roads of Prince Edward Island* is produced jointly by the Department of Environmental Affairs, the Department of Provincial Affairs, and the Attorney General, and is available at local and provincial Visitor Information Centres.

Notes on the trail: The ride begins on Warburton Road in a northerly direction. On this hard-packed red dirt road, you will begin to descend immediately. At the bottom of the dip you will cross over a stream and then begin a moderate climb that brings you to a fork. Bear right past the double-track trail on the left (a farmer's road), and continue on the red clay. Surrounded by maple trees and softwoods, you will begin a gradual descent after the first bend. The downhill continues after the next bend to the left and follows the road as it closely parallels a stream.

Arriving at a four-way intersection with Princetown Road, continue straight (bearing slightly to the right and descending in a northeasterly direction). The road passes over the stream that has been on the left, and continues to descend to a **T** junction with Millvale Road. Turn right on this paved road and begin a short uphill climb. You will crest the hill and descend, crossing a couple of streams. Continue past a road branching off to the left (leading up to Route 266), and then prepare for a climb as the road you are pedaling along changes from pavement to gravel. The road bends to the left, beyond which you will continue straight for a short distance. At the first opportunity, turn right onto another unpaved, red dirt heritage road. This is the Perry Road, which signals the beginning of your return trip.

The Perry Road is narrower and graveled, and has a grassy median. It is heavily forested with hardwood and softwood trees, and thick with ground vegetation of ferns and bushes. If you explore a section by foot, you may be able to find the provincial flower, the pink lady's slipper. The road continues downhill, and the surface gradually deteriorates. The lower sections of the hill have been most affected by erosion, presenting sections of accumulated loose rock and dirt. At the bottom you will enjoy a brief flat stretch before heading up the final climb. You will climb steadily for about half a kilometre (quarter of a mile), and just when you think you have reached the top, you will be faced with a final lip. From the top, cruise down the other side, striving to gain sufficient momentum to carry you up the gradual uphill that follows.

Arriving at a **T** junction, turn left onto a much wider red clay road. This is the continuation of the Perry Road that was built after a demonstration of political protest. The owner of the property on which the road began halted construction of the road when a new government was elected. Another property owner offered up his land to the newly elected government to enable the road's completion. This has resulted in the dog-leg to Highway 2. En route to Highway 2 the road rolls briefly before arriving at the paved road. Turn right on Highway 2, and ride along the shoulder to the second road on the right, Warburton Road, just 3 km (1.8 miles) away!

RIDE 36 • Brookvale

AT A GLANCE

Length/configuration: 6.5-km (4-mile) loop

Aerobic difficulty: Moderate; only short, steep climbs

Technical difficulty: Intermediate to advanced; some highly technical sections of single-track

Scenery: This is a beautiful course through wooded terrain in the highest area on the island

Special comments: This circuit serves as the racecourse for the annual "Red Mud Mountain Mayhem"

The Nordic Centre at Brookvale Provincial Park has recently become the site of several mountain bike races and events, including the Atlantic Canada mountain bike championship, "Red Mud Mountain Mayhem." In addition to the cross-country ski trails, the course at Brookvale features some excellent single-track trails. These trails have been developed and maintained by very dedicated riders on the island. In fact, some of the trails here bear names that reflect the work and riding of certain individuals. "Cory's Climb," for example, and "Luke's Lunge" are named after the first riders to lay tracks on these specific sections of the course. The hard work that these few riders have contributed to all of us looking for good riding is a tremendous example of how a ski area can be turned into a multi-season park.

This ride follows a 6.5-km (4-mile) race circuit that traces a rather erratic loop through the park. The terrain is quite hilly, and the single-track trails have been cut to take full advantage of all possible gains in elevation! In addition to these narrow hard-packed trails, you will ride along portions of the cross-country ski trails over double-track trails and logging roads. The course is well balanced and will challenge intermediate-level riders, while giving more advanced cyclists plenty to enjoy. Though short, this course will provide all riders with a good workout, and demands at least moderate cardiovascular conditioning.

General location: The Nordic Centre at Brookvale Provincial Park is located in central Prince Edward Island, almost exactly half way between Summerside and Charlottetown.

Elevation change: You will climb and descend along only short, steep hills.

Season: The best riding conditions at Brookvale are from June through September, with July and August being the driest months.

RIDE 36 · Brookvale

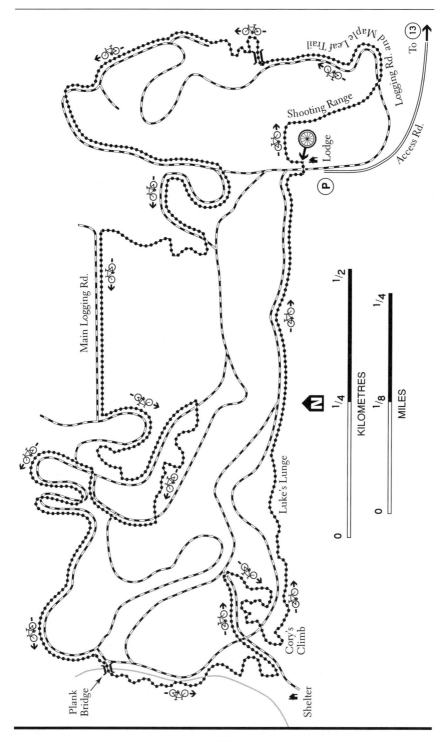

Services: There are no services at the trailhead. Basic needs for food or water can be met along Highway 2, to the north, or along the Trans-Canada Highway, to the south. All bike-related services or supplies are most easily accessed in Charlottetown.

Hazards: There may be times when active tree harvesting operations are under way at the park. Keep your ears pricked for sounds of heavy machinery, and always grant such vehicles the right-of-way.

Rescue index: During the summer there are not likely to be many visitors to the park, apart from mountain bikers and possibly some hikers. While this ride never ventures far from Route 13, assistance may not always be close at hand.

Land status: Provincial park.

Maps: At the trailhead, there is a large sign highlighting the cross-country ski trails at the park. Though this map will help you orient yourself in relation to the ski trails, it does not include the single-track trails used by mountain bikers. The map we have included is the best we could find; the only other potential source of information would be the local riders involved in developing the trail system.

Finding the trail: Brookvale Provincial Park is located on Route 13, which runs between PEI Highway 2 and the Trans-Canada Highway. From Charlottetown, drive west on Highway 2 to the community of Hunter River. Turn left here onto Highway 13, heading south. Follow Highway 13 all the way to the entrance to the park, which will be on your left. Continue straight past the Alpine Centre and continue for approximately 1 km (0.6 mile), up to the entrance to the Nordic Centre, which will also be on your left. Drive in on an unpaved access road to reach the trailhead at a huge Canada Games Cross Country Ski Trail System Map, located to the left of a small lodge.

Source of additional information: The staff at Smooth Cycle in Charlottetown may be able to give you some tips and suggestions about riding at Brookvale, among other places on the island. Smooth Cycle is located at 172 Prince Street, or you can contact the store at (902) 566-5530.

Notes on the trail: Begin this ride by facing the cross-country trail system map and turning right, to drop down a grassy slope, heading toward the shooting range. At the base of the hill, turn right and ride along the back side of the shooting range, traversing the base of a hill before turning left and heading uphill along a wide, old logging road that serves as one of the main cross-country ski trails. Follow this trail as it continues to swing around to the left and quickly descends. Look to your right almost immediately, and turn right over a hump and a small bridge to connect with a short stretch of single-track trail through the woods. Bear left when this trail connects back with the main ski trail and head uphill.

Continue to follow the main ski trail as it descends, curling around to the right, and then climbs, curving to the left. Descend once more, and as the main trail bends to the right, you will see a black arrow ahead of you on the trail. Duck into the woods on the right here, turning onto a single-track trail through the

Narrow single-track trails wind through the densely treed hills of Brookvale Provincial Park.

woods. This turnoff may be marked with flagging tape. This single-track trail follows a winding path in the woods and through several sharp turns. When you emerge on another wide logging road, turn left.

You will ride straight for some distance along this dirt road. When you reach a **T** junction with another logging road, turn left again. You will be riding on a hard-packed double-track trail with a grassy median. Pass another logging road branching off on the right before you crest a slight hill and begin to descend. As the main trail curves gradually to the right, continue straight onto a newly cut single-track trail through the woods. This trail is a shortcut to another wide ski trail, or logging road. When you emerge from the woods, turn left.

You will ascend gradually along this wide trail, climbing two small knolls. Keep your eyes peeled for another narrow single-track trail ducking into the woods on the right. You will have to make a hard right turn onto this trail, which may be marked with flagging tape. Traversing through the woods again, you will follow a pine needle–carpeted trail with some areas of exposed roots. When you come to a grassy logging trail, turn right. A short distance farther, you will come to a **T** junction, where you must turn left.

From this point, you will continue on the main logging trail, passing several secondary trails off to the right and left. Your course will follow a series of bends before you pass two more logging roads in quick succession, the first on the left and the second on the right. Beyond the second turnoff the main trail begins up a slight rise. Turn right immediately, onto a single-track trail that begins over a plank bridge. This next stretch of single-track is one of the highlights of the ride, as it meanders along a beautiful path through the woods alongside a small stream. The terrain is fairly technical, and you will encounter some roller-coaster–like hills and whoop-de-doos.

When you emerge from the woods, you will find yourself at a **T** junction with another logging road. To the right you will see a little shack with a sign that points to the "Hardwoods Loop" continuing straight, and another that directs you to the Nordic Lodge, 1 km (0.6 mile) to the left. Turn left here, descending, and at the first opportunity turn right onto a logging trail that is signed as a shortcut to the "Hardwoods Loop." This trail is a 1-km (0.6-mile) spur known to mountain bikers as "V.P." At the junction of another logging trail, where there is a "you are here" sign, turn right onto a single-track trail that is called "The Body." This trail covers some more technical terrain and includes a climb over a peculiar mound that resembles a body. After crossing "The Body," you will ride up to a point where you can continue straight to merge with a logging road. Bear right here instead, continuing on the single-track trail. This section of the trail is called "Taco Hell" and features a series of wheel-threatening whoop-de-doos.

If you make it safely out of "Taco Hell," you will reach a four-way intersection with a wide logging road going to the left and right. Continue straight across this logging road, and then begin up a section of single-track trail called "Cory's Climb." You will come to an intersection where you can follow a short loop around to the right before following the main trail as it bears left and continues straight up toward the edge of a field. Follow the trail, which runs along the edge of the woods at the perimeter of the field, and descend on a hill that is named "Luke's Lunge." Turn right when you come to a **T** junction with another logging road. Then, at a four-way trail junction at the crest of a little hill, bear right and duck through a narrow strip of trees back down to the ski lodge where you began the ride.

RIDE 37 • Charlotte's Shore Heritage Roads

AT A GLANCE

Length/configuration: 16-km (10-mile) loop

Aerobic difficulty: Challenging; the frequent climbs throughout the ride require good physical condition

Technical difficulty: Minimal; the clay roads are in very good condition and suitable to all levels of riders

Scenery: A changing landscape of hard- and softwood forests, farmland, and spruce stands

Special comments: Popular early season ride

The heritage roads of Prince Edward Island are red dirt roads characterized by high hills and many twists and turns. They were among the first roads built in the province and tend to follow an "as the crow flies" route between points, with little regard for the often dramatic contours of the landscape. Due to their historical significance, these roads are preserved in their original state and are protected against paving or other alterations by the Provincial Government. The McKenna and Currie-Farrar Heritage Roads on this ride date back to 1862 and 1904 respectively, and were named after original property owners in the area. The Appin Road is undated, but believed to be derived from Appin communities in Scotland. Each of these are part of a historic network of clay lanes in southwestern Queens County.

Charlotte's Shore is a hilly, 16-km (10-mile) loop utilizing these historic old roads and short, connecting stretches of pavement. The riding is aerobically stimulating but technically easy—suitable for fit riders of all levels. The trail passes through farmsteads and forested areas following, for the most part, a hard-packed, usually smooth clay surface. At the crest of the hills you can overlook the picturesque landscape of farmlands and spruce stands, and you will appreciate the shade of canopied lanes after riding through the areas of open farming fields. Rarely frequented by automobiles, these roads seem designed to accommodate the needs and interests of a mountain biker.

General location: This ride is located west of Charlottetown, near Brookvale Provincial Park.

Elevation change: Over one extended climb and several rolling hills, you will gain a total of 225 m (740 feet) of elevation.

RIDE 37 • Charlotte's Shore Heritage Roads

Season: The roads will be muddy in early spring as the ground thaws; riding should begin by mid-June and continue through October.

Services: All services are available in Charlottetown, including full bike sales, service, and rental at Smooth Cycle, located at 172 Prince Street (phone (902) 566-5530), or service and touring information at MacQueen's, located at 430 Queen Street (phone (902) 368-2453), in downtown Charlottetown.

Hazards: None.

Rescue index: The area is sporadically populated with farmhouses and situated near two popular provincial parks. Help should be close at hand.

Land status: Protected provincial roads.

Maps: All the roads referred to on this trail are reasonably well marked on the provincial highway map available at all Visitor Information Centres.

Finding the trail: From Charlottetown, take the Trans-Canada Highway heading west. Continue to a junction with Route 235 in North River and bear right, heading toward East Wiltshire and Kingston. Continue on Route 235 through Kingston and then Emyvale. Past Emyvale you will come to a junction where

Route 235 bears right and heads up to Highway 13. Bear left at this junction, turning onto Route 237. Follow Route 237 for approximately 1.6 km (1 mile) until you reach the unpaved portion of the road. Parking is suggested at the side of the road where the pavement turns to gravel.

Source of additional information: A brochure titled *Scenic Heritage Roads of Prince Edward Island* is produced jointly by the Department of Environmental Affairs, the Department of Provincial Affairs, and the Attorney General, and it is available at local and provincial Visitor Information Centres.

Notes on the trail: Departing from where the pavement turns to gravel, continue straight ahead. The ride begins with a moderate climb, bears right, and then levels off as you pass a farm road on the left. Past this point, the road will level off for a short distance. You will then continue through a dip in the road, ignoring all the other roads branching off to your left and right. At the other side of the dip, you will enjoy a swift descent on a moderate slope.

At the bottom of the hill the road curves to the left and levels off—briefly. Another good climb awaits but proves not to be as grueling as you may have expected. When you reach a **T** junction with a cart track that continues straight, turn right onto a red clay road. This is the McKenna Road, which narrows as you enter a canopy of trees on a rolling descent. As you make your way downhill, the road will curve around to the right and flatten for a short distance. It will then drop off and flatten again, descending past some dirt roads to the left and right, bringing you to a **T** junction with Route 246.

At the junction, turn left onto the paved road, following the sign toward DeSable. Continue along the pavement for two short climbs. At the crest of the second hill the road winds around a bend to the right, almost creating a **U**. You will begin to descend, and after passing an orchard you will turn left onto the Currie-Farrar Road (this road is not signed). This turn sets you off on another climb, marking the beginning of a stretch of rolling terrain that continues to the next intersection. The final climb snakes uphill, and then you descend to a staggered four-way intersection with Route 237 at the community of Appin Road. Turn left onto the paved road, and then, at the "Matheson" mailbox and before the road turns to gravel, turn right to continue up the clay heritage road.

The first climb on this road is short and immediately drops off when you reach the crest of the hill. Shortly after that descent, you will begin a long, gradual climb. Over the course of this hill you will gain almost 75 m (250 feet) of elevation over a kilometre (one-half mile) of climbing. Having reached the highest point, you are rewarded with views of the surrounding countryside. After taking in the view, enjoy the extended cruise down the other side. At the end of the descent, as the road levels off, it winds through the woods, emerging at an opening amidst a number of farmer's fields. A gradual climb follows, as does a descent to a stop sign.

At this **T** junction, turn left onto the dirt road (Route 249). At this point, you are homeward bound. Route 249 is mostly flat with a couple of slight bends, and ends with a gradual climb back to Route 237. Bear right when you reach a yield sign at the junction of Route 249 and Route 237, and then return to your car just a short distance down the road.

RIDE 38 · Bonshaw

AT A GLANCE

Length/configuration: 10-km (6-mile) out-and-back (5 km [3 miles] each way)

Aerobic difficulty: Rigourous; short steep climbs on challenging technical terrain

Technical difficulty: Advanced; exposed roots and rocks on a winding single-track trail

Scenery: Dense woodlands

Special comments: Look for tire-grabbing gremlins in the whoop-de-doos

Bikers covet this 10-km (6-mile) out-and-back ride because it is all that remains of two elaborate single-track trails that were once available to mountain bikers in the Bonshaw Hills. The trail offers the most challenging terrain on the island and is the only single-track available outside the racecourse at Brookvale. Despite being an advanced trail, there are enough sections manageable by intermediate riders to make this an excellent ride for anyone willing to work at sharpening his or her skills and enjoy the workout.

The ride follows a single-track trail through a heavily wooded hillside, along constantly rolling terrain. You will climb up steep embankments and drop down abrupt banks on a winding narrow trail. A stretch of rolling whoop-de-doos tops anything we experienced elsewhere in the province, or in the whole of Atlantic Canada. We attribute our difficulties with this stretch to families of tire-grabbing gremlins that we are certain inhabit the dramatic **V** ditches. With all these challenges, this ride is certain to exhaust most of its riders, regardless of whether they can bike the full course.

General location: West of Charlottetown, near Bonshaw Provincial Park.

Elevation change: The ride begins at the base of a valley and climbs steadily for 5 km (3 miles) to a turnaround, partway up one of the Bonshaw Hills.

Season: It is best to postpone riding here until the dry months on the island: July and August. Thick mud would prevent riding here in the early spring, but the season could extend from June to September in years with minimal rainfall.

Services: All services are available in Charlottetown.

Hazards: This area is highly contentious, and both landowners and trail users (hikers and bikers) have been involved in sensitive land-use debates. Be sure to follow the trail closely and respect all postings to avoid generating any conflict with property owners on either side of the trail.

RIDE 38 • Bonshaw

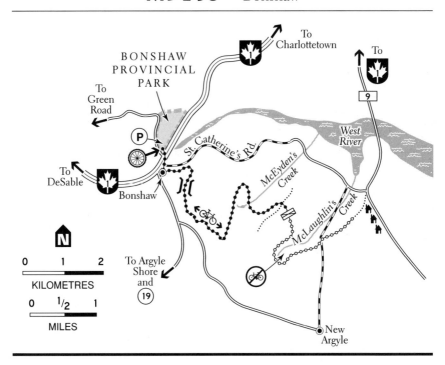

Rescue index: Although the trail is short, the nature of the terrain on this ride makes it feel like a much greater undertaking. You are unlikely to encounter anyone along the trail and it is advisable not to ride alone.

Land status: The trail follows a public right-of-way between sections of private land.

Maps: The trail does not appear on any map, but it may be possible to obtain a sketch of the ride from Smooth Cycle, located at 172 Prince Street (phone (902) 566-5530), in downtown Charlottetown. Furthermore, at the time we rode here, the trail had been marked with blue flagging tape and collars on some trees.

Finding the trail: From Charlottetown, follow the Trans-Canada Highway west. You will pass a golf course and the Bonshaw 500, and begin to descend toward Green Road. Just after the sign for Green Road, turn right into a grassy parking area at Bonshaw Provincial Park.

Source of additional information: To keep up-to-date as to what parts of this ride are still open to bikers, stop into Smooth Cycle in Charlottetown.

Notes on the trail: From the parking area at Bonshaw Provincial Park, ride back out to the highway and turn right, continuing downhill for a short distance. After crossing a bridge, turn left on the unpaved St. Catherine's Road. You will climb

Larry leads the pack through the challenging single-track trails in the Bonshaw Hills.

along this wide, graded dirt road for less than 1 km (about 0.5 mile). At the crest of a slight rise, look into the woods on the right side of the road for a small log ramp. This ramp marks the beginning of the trail and spans a ditch at the side of the road. Turn right to cross the ramp, gearing down as you do so in preparation for a difficult climb up a steep, single-track trail that forges a path through the woods over exposed roots and rocks.

As you make your way up the trail, you will cross a small bridge. Beyond the bridge, continue straight on the single-track trail, crossing a wider, grassy trail. When you come to a **T** junction with a second grassy trail, turn right and then immediately turn left back onto a narrow, easy-to-follow trail through the woods. After just a short distance you will reach the edge of a narrow field. Heading toward the far left corner of the field, follow a narrow, single-track trail beaten down through the grass. You will cross a grassy, double-track cart trail before reentering the woods along a hard-packed dirt trail over roots and exposed rocks.

As you continue along this trail, bear right past a narrow trail on the left. The main trail is well-marked at this point in the ride, identified by a series of blue collars wrapped around trees at the side of the trail. The next fork is marked by a tree tagged with a one-of-a-kind red collar, and you will see a narrow but well-traveled trail branching off to the left and a vague, overgrown trail continuing around to the right. Bear left here, onto the narrower trail. A short distance ahead, you will cross a wider trail, beyond which you will continue straight over fairly difficult terrain all the way to a primitive fence and a red dirt road at the edge of the woods.

Once you reach the edge of the woods, follow the trail around a sharp turn to the right (guided by the primitive fence) and avoid descending to the road, which traverses private property. You will follow a flagged trail through the woods over increasingly difficult terrain. Only the experts among the group with whom we rode weren't dismounting periodically to hike their bikes up steep climbs and over treacherous sections of exposed roots and rocks.

After passing through a muddy section, you will zigzag your way up a short hill, crossing yet another vague but wider trail. Continue straight and prepare yourself for a rolling section of terrain punctuated by wheel-grabbing whoop-de-doos. The dips along this section of the trail are up to a couple of feet deep, requiring considerable strength and skill if you are to keep your bike in motion. Continue until you reach a tree by the side of the trail that is identified by a small sign as a beech. Turn left at this tree and follow a steep, gnarly single-track trail down what locals affectionately refer to as "Face-Plant Hill." At the bottom of the hill, bear right and begin to climb, passing a tree that bears a sign identifying it as a striped maple.

As you continue to climb, you will cross another wide dirt trail. The next landmark is an obvious intersection of trails, marked by an island of trees in the center. A wide trail will be continuing to your left and right at this point and the single-track trail continues straight ahead. Proceed up the single-track trail to a gate. Do not proceed any further. Turn around and retrace your tracks to the park.

RIDE 39 • Morell–St. Peter's Confederation Trail

AT A GLANCE

Length/configuration: 23-km (14.3-mile) out-and-back (11.5 km [7.1 miles] each way)

Aerobic difficulty: Easy; suitable for all fitness levels

Technical difficulty: Crushed stone surface requires little or no technical skill

Scenery: An abundance of wildflowers in the spring and gorgeous views over St. Peter's Bay

Special comments: This ride follows one of the most scenic sections of the Confederation Trail

RIDE 39 • Morell–St. Peters Confederation Trail

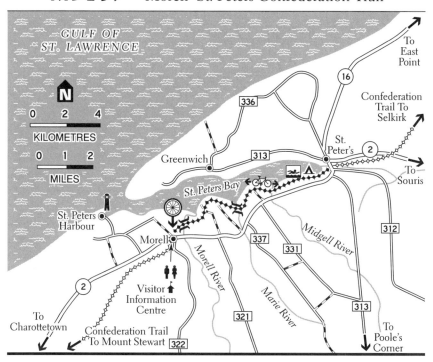

Offering a classic Prince Edward Island blend of meadows fringed with wildflowers and breathtaking coastal views, this section of the Confederation Trail extends between Morell and St. Peter's on the eastern part of the island. St. Peter's was the site of the first French settlement on Prince Edward Island (then known as Ile Saint-Jean). The ride is an easy 23-km (14.3-mile) out-and-back that makes an excellent easy excursion for novice riders or groups of mixed ability levels. The ride simply follows the wide, well-graded surface of the former railroad bed that has been converted to a multi-use trail. The trip is one of the most beautiful and interesting along the Confederation Trail, highlighted by glorious views over St. Peter's Bay. Dotted throughout the bay are the nets for one of the island's most well-known industries: commercial mussel farming.

General location: Eastern Prince Edward Island, 45 km (28 miles) northeast of Charlottetown.

Elevation change: The elevation change along the length of this ride is minimal, since it follows an abandoned railroad bed.

Season: The riding season on the Confederation Trail extends from the time the snow clears in the spring to the first snowfall of winter. The best months to ride are June through September, with July and August typically showcasing the driest conditions.

Sea, sand and sky surround you on the Confederation Trail between Morell and St. Peter's.

Services: There is a Visitor Information Centre at the trailhead in Morell. However, apart from maps and trail information, this location offers no other services. A Co-op store on a corner across from the trailhead should offer enough in the way of food and water. The closest source for bike-related items is Smooth Cycle, a shop in Charlottetown that offers service, repair, and bicycle rentals.

Hazards: Exercise caution at road crossings, and expect to meet other trail users on your ride.

Rescue index: This section of the Confederation Trail never strays far from PEI Highway 2.

Land status: The Confederation Trail is part of the Trans-Canada Trail and follows a former railroad bed along a multi-use recreational trail on public land.

Maps: A map of the entire length of the Confederation Trail is available through most community and provincial Visitor Information Centres. In addition, the trail is clearly indicated on the Provincial Highway Map.

Finding the trail: From Charlottetown, head east on PEI Highway 2 toward Mount Stewart and Morell. The trailhead is located directly off of the highway in Morell, at a point where the Confederation Trail crosses the road. There is plenty of space to park off the road, just outside a Visitor Information Centre operated by the Heritage Bays and Dunes Association and located opposite the post office.

Sources of additional information: The Visitor Information Centres on the island, including the one at the trailhead in Morell, distribute maps of the Confederation Trail, as well as any number of brochures with information on accommodations and other services. To obtain such information prior to arriving on Prince Edward Island, call (800) 463-4734. For additional information on the Confederation Trail, you may also want to pick up a copy of J. Dan McAskill and Kate MacQuarrie's *Nature Trails of Prince Edward Island*, a 1996 publication in the Island Pathways series.

Notes on the trail: Begin riding north on the Confederation Trail toward St. Peter's. Along the first portion of the ride, you will cross two bridges, passing fields of potatoes and wheat. In the spring and early summer there are wildflowers galore along this portion of the trail.

Gradually, the trail curves toward the water and nears St. Peter's Bay, which will be on your left. At this point, the views extend out toward the ocean, and you will be able to see the precise pattern of buoys that mark the position of mussel nets in the bay. Continue to follow the wide gravel trail into St. Peter's. The bay will be directly on your left, and the highway parallels the trail on the right. Turn around when you reach a junction with the paved highway, or extend your trip along the portion of the Confederation Trail that extends on the other side of the highway.

RIDE 40 • Souris Confederation Trail

AT A GLANCE

Length/configuration: 19.5-km (11.7-mile) loop

Aerobic difficulty: Easy; only a few short hills

Technical difficulty: Basic; the ride follows a gravel-dusted multi-use trail, hard-packed dirt roads, and some pavement

Scenery: Rolling farmlands and mixed forests

Special comments: Souris is a recreational hub that features a beach and provincial park

This ride is an easy 19.5-km (11.7-mile) loop that follows the relatively wide, graded surfaces of both the Confederation Trail and the New Harmony Heritage Road. You will trace the route of the old Prince Edward Island railway and then ride over rolling hills on the heritage road, as you

RIDE 40 • Souris Confederation Trail

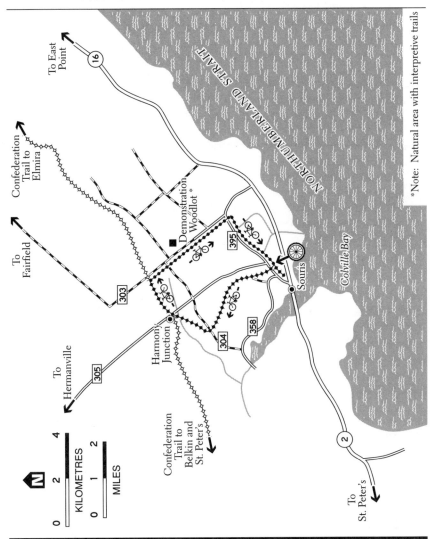

experience the landscape that was first cultivated by early settlers in this region. The recent development of the Confederation Trail and the continued maintenance of this heritage road in its original state have ensured preservation of different aspects of the island's history (see also Ride 35 and Ride 37).

From Souris, the ride is mostly flat. The grade on the Confederation Trail never exceeds 2 percent, which makes for almost effortless riding. Turning off the rail bed onto the New Harmony Heritage Road, there will be a few short hills. You will pass a Demonstration Woodlot, with a short nature trail that you can hike around while learning about the process of rejuvenating the forests and returning the land to its original state. As you return on the final, paved portion of the ride, you will climb a more extended hill and be rewarded with a view of the Souris River Valley. The scenery, few rolling hills, and moderate distance of this ride make it a short, refreshing jaunt, ideal to beginner riders with a basic level of fitness.

General location: Southeastern Prince Edward Island, off Highway 2.

Elevation change: Minimal; mostly flat with some brief sections of small, rolling hills.

Season: The best months to ride on the island are June through September, with July and August being the driest months.

Services: Most services are available in Souris, but be cautioned that there are no facilities at the trailhead. Contact Cycle East in Souris for rentals or minor bike service at (902) 687-4087.

Hazards: There are several crossings over secondary highways throughout the ride. Exercise caution at all intersections.

Rescue index: You are never far from help, due to frequent road crossings and your proximity to Souris.

Land status: The Confederation Trail is part of the Trans-Canada Trail and follows a former railroad bed along a multi-use recreational trail on public land.

Maps: The Confederation Trail appears on the Prince Edward Island Highway Map and has its own brochure. Both maps are available at Visitor Information Centres throughout the island.

Finding the trail: The trailhead is located near the junction of PEI Highway 2 and Union Avenue in Souris. At this intersection there is a gravel lot on the northeast corner, across from the fire station, where parking is available.

Source of additional information: For information on Prince Edward Island, call (800) 463-4PEI.

Notes on the trail: The ride starts at a sign for the Souris Confederation Trail, west of (and within sight of) the parking area. Traveling north, the trail begins as a fine gravel path that quickly becomes very overgrown and hardly discernible. Continue past several large storage-type buildings, and cross a paved road. The trail continues more conspicuously on the other side, and you will come to a small park with a sheltered picnic table and a sign for the "Hearts in Motion" walking path.

You will cross another paved road (Route 358) as you leave the park, beyond which the trail is very well maintained and marked at every kilometre for the next 6 km (4 miles) to Harmony Junction. As you begin this portion of the ride, you will pass a view of the Souris River on the left. The trail then gently curves around to the right and you will pass through a wooded area that is interrupted by small clearings and fields. When you reach an intersection with a red dirt road, simply continue straight along the Confederation Trail. Beyond the red dirt road, the trail takes on the appearance of a double-track with a grassy median, and it opens up on a farmer's field to the left before reentering the woods. When you reach an intersection with another red dirt road, continue straight once again and continue on the trail all the way to Harmony Junction.

As you approach Harmony Junction, you will pass a double-track trail veering to the left. This connects with the Confederation Trail coming from St. Peter's. Bear right, heading toward the paved road, and cross carefully over Route 305 to the other side. Continue on the gravel-dusted trail, which is a continuation of the Confederation Trail headed toward Elmira (for an extended trip, see Ride 41 to continue onto the Elmira Loop). When you reach a four-way intersection with a red dirt road, turn right off the Confederation Trail and begin riding along Route 303, the New Harmony Heritage Road. This is a Scenic Heritage Road that once served as the main link between the north and south shore for the early farmers in the area. The Prohibition years added a bit of infamy to the reputation of the New Harmony Road, as rumrunners favoured its scenic expanses for hiding their illegal cargo.

As you travel down the first stretch of the New Harmony Heritage Road, you will find yourself shaded by a leafy canopy above you. Continue through the first intersection you come to, crossing an unpaved gravel road (Route 304). A short distance beyond this intersection, you will arrive at a sign for a nature trail; this trail will take you into the Demonstration Woodlot, which is complete with interpretive signs.

Beyond the woodlot, the road continues up two short hills to a **T** junction with Route 335. Turn right on the paved road, following signs for Souris. When you come to a **T** junction with another paved road, turn left and continue to follow signs for Souris. A short distance along, you will reach a point at which the Confederation Trail intersects the road. Turn left onto the Confederation Trail to return to the trailhead a short distance away.

RIDE 41 · Elmira Confederation Trail

AT A GLANCE

Length/configuration: 34-km (20.4-mile) combination (16-km [10-mile] loop with an out-and-back spur; the spur is 9-km [5.4-miles] long each way)

Aerobic difficulty: Easy; requires only a minimum fitness level

Technical difficulty: Beginner; combination of gravel-dusted multi-use trail and a hard-packed dirt road

Scenery: Passes through woodlands and farmlands with a magical history

Special comments: Appeals to children of all ages

The eastern tip of Prince Edward Island juts precariously into the Gulf of St. Lawrence. This narrow strip of land often bears the brunt of storms that blow in from the Gulf, striking here in full fury and then tempering as they continue across the island. Given these volatile weather patterns, this end of the island is not densely populated. However, it brims with the life and colour of local legends. The stories and the history of this part of the island begin to unfold on this ride, which begins at the Railway Museum in Elmira and advances into the surrounding woodlands and farm fields on heritage roads. The ride is sure to delight anyone willing to take a moment to exercise their imagination as well as their limbs.

From the Railway Museum in Elmira, the ride begins with a 9-km (5.4-mile) spur along the Confederation Trail to Baltic. From Baltic, the ride turns off the multi-use trail and begins a 16-km (10-mile) loop, starting along a short stretch of paved road and continuing on one of the province's preserved and protected heritage roads, the Glen Road. You will follow the Confederation Trail back to Baltic to complete the loop and then continue, retracing your tracks back to Elmira. The total distance pedaled along this combination ride is 34 km (20.4 miles). The gravel-dusted trails and hard-packed, red dirt roads that make up this ride provide an excellent surface for bikes, including those equipped to pull or carry young passengers. To top off your enjoyment of this excursion, the enchanting woodlands and open fields will provide a perfect blend of amusement, sun, and shade for a half-day excursion.

General location: Elmira is situated on the far eastern tip of Prince Edward Island.

Elevation change: The Confederation Trail reaches a maximum grade of 2% on Prince Edward Island. There is no appreciable gain in elevation on the multi-use trail and the few rolling hills on the heritage road, and the paved portion of the ride amounts to very little in the way of climbing.

Season: The best months to ride on the island are June through September, with July and August being the driest months.

Services: Elmira is a small town centre offering only basic services and no bicycle service and repair. At the trailhead there is a Railway Museum, with washroom facilities and an ice cream counter. Some bike services are available in nearby Souris from Cycle East, which is primarily a rental store.

Hazards: Exercise caution at road crossings, and expect to meet other trail users on your ride.

Rescue index: Both the Confederation Trail and the heritage roads are well-trafficked routes, so help should always be nearby. Also, the Railway Museum has a telephone that may be used for emergency purposes.

Land status: The ride utilizes sections of the Confederation Trail, a multi-use recreational trail on public land, and provincially protected heritage roads.

Maps: This ride is easily navigated using the Prince Edward Island Highway Map, available at all Visitor Information Centres.

RIDE 41 • Elmira Confederation Trail

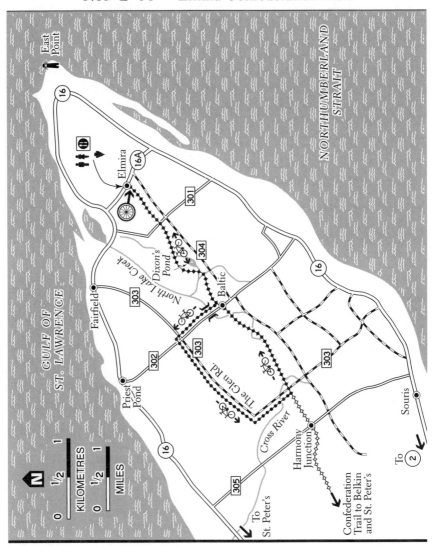

Finding the trail: The trailhead is located at the Railway Museum in Elmira, in the Bays and Dunes region of Prince Edward Island. From the Charlottetown area, travel east on Highway 2 and then pick up Highway 16 in either St. Peter's or Souris. Travel on Highway 16, along either the north or the south shore, toward East Point. A short distance from East Point, turn onto Highway 16A, which runs vertically between North and South Lake. From the south shore, you will turn left on Highway 16A and pass through the town of Elmira. The Confederation Trail will be signed on the left a short distance beyond down-

PRINCE EDWARD ISLAND 195

Off-road riding from the Glen Road near Elmira.

town. From the north shore, you will turn right on Highway 16A and travel approximately 3 km (1.8 miles) to the trailhead, easily identified on the right side of the road.

Source of additional information: A brochure titled *Scenic Heritage Roads of Prince Edward Island* is produced jointly by the Department of Environmental Affairs, the Department of Provincial Affairs, and the Attorney General, and is available at local and provincial Visitor Information Centres.

Notes on the trail: Begin by traveling west on the Confederation Trail from the parking area at the Railway Museum. The trail is flat and travels through a mostly wooded corridor, opening out at intervals to views of potato fields to the left and right. Continue through the first intersection with a paved road (Route 301). Beyond this intersection, you will pedal along a relatively long, uninterrupted stretch of the trail toward Baltic. As you draw near to Baltic, you will pass Dixon's Pond, which, after a dry summer, may bear a greater resemblance to a grassy bog! A short distance beyond the pond you will arrive in Baltic, at a four-way intersection with another paved road (Route 302). This point in the ride marks the beginning of the 16-km (10-mile) loop. Ahead you can see the stretch of the Confederation Trail that you will return on, but first, turn right onto the paved road (Route 302).

After turning right on Route 302, descend the hill and cross the bridge over North Lake Creek. Beyond the bridge, continue ahead a short distance, and turn left at the first opportunity onto a gravel road. This is the beginning of the Glen Road, a provincially designated Scenic Heritage Road. "Glens" are magical spots. They are characteristically green and bright, pass through woodland and farmland, and are believed to be filled with intriguing sights and characters. This glen is a popular destination to watch for sprites, and it is well remembered for being the lifelong home of the island's most acclaimed fortune teller. You can begin your journey into the glen in search of a giant elm. It is said that this tree is the biggest on the island, and that two people will be unable to reach each other's hands around its base. It is situated near the beginning of the gravel road, at the eastern extremity of the glen.

Continuing on the Glen Road, you will pass a gravel road branching off to the right, just before a descent to the hay fields. You will continue on a flat stretch of road amidst fields to your left and right. The fields end abruptly as you enter the woods. The forest is thick on either side—likely an ideal place to watch for sprites who are said to inhabit the woods here. As the road opens up, you will arrive at a **T** intersection. Turn left, following the wider red dirt road and ignoring the narrow, single-lane dirt road through the woods on the right. This is a wide stretch of road lined with trees on either side. Approximately 2.5 km (1.5 miles) from the **T** junction, you will come to an unsigned four-way intersection with the Confederation Trail. If you were to continue straight at this point, you would be picking up the latter portion of the Souris loop (Ride 40). Although these two rides can be linked, doing so turns this ride into a 54-km (32.4-mile) round-trip.

Turn left at the intersection with the Confederation Trail. Heading east to return to Elmira on the multi-use trail, you will be on a slightly uphill grade. On Prince Edward Island the grade of the railroad bed is never more than 2 percent, but you will notice yourself traveling more slowly and working a little harder. This section of the trail is fairly long, approximately 7 km (4.2 miles) to the next intersection and there are no opportunities to branch off. As you approach the next intersection, the trail will assume an ever-so-slight downhill slant, and you can cruise to the four-way intersection with the paved road. You are now near the start of the ride, at the point where you first branched off the Confederation Trail to begin the loop. Cross the road and continue straight on the spur back to Elmira.

This ride is dedicated to Bea Murphy and family—thank you for the fine meals, good company, and the "Murphy Magic" you shared with us during our research.

NEWFOUNDLAND

If Prince Edward Island is the most understated of the Atlantic Provinces, Newfoundland is arguably the most extraordinary. The island is the last point of land in the New World, and it is as big and bold and dramatic as Prince Edward Island is small, quaint, and pastoral. Indeed, among all the Atlantic Provinces, Newfoundland offers the most impressive landscape and some of the wildest, most backcountry adventures. Not only is the island the largest of the four Atlantic Provinces—a sprawling combination of peninsulas and forested wilderness—but it is geographically isolated from the rest of Canada. Unless you choose to fly, access to the island involves a long journey by ferry from Sidney, Nova Scotia, to either St. John's or Channel-Port-aux-Basques.

The easternmost province of Canada actually consists of two areas separated by the Strait of Belle Isle: the Island of Newfoundland, and Labrador on the mainland. Our research and travels did not take us to Labrador, which not only enjoys the reputation of being one of the world's truly wild places, but also remains far less accessible than the island of Newfoundland. However, it is nearly impossible to travel through Atlantic Canada without being wooed by fantastic tales of Labrador's beauty and appeal. As one of the largest unspoiled natural areas remaining in the world, Labrador will certainly attract mountain bikers along with the growing number of adventurers eager to explore its vast landscape and rich history and culture.

The Province of Newfoundland and Labrador was the last to join the Confederation and did not become part of Canada until 1949. However, the island was one of the earliest places in the New World to be explored and settled, and St. John's calls itself North America's oldest European-founded city. Archeological evidence supports the theory that the Norse occupied a settlement at the tip of the island's Northern Peninsula by A.D. 1000. However, the first fully documented arrival was in 1497, when John Cabot (Giovanni Caboto) led an English expedition in search of a northern spice route. Cabot did not succeed in his mission, but he did find land and seas literally teeming with cod. He claimed the land for England and called it New Found Land. It is likely that the island and surrounding seas were already known to Basque fishermen before Cabot ever entered on the scene. However, with the intent of keeping their source of cod a secret, the Basques never made claim to any of the land.

When Jacques Cartier "discovered" the mouth of the St. Lawrence for France some 37 years after Cabot's first voyage, Newfoundland became an area that would be contested between the French and the English as it developed into a major fishing port. In 1763, at the end of a battle between England and France, the British denied France of all its North American possessions. To this day, the tiny islands of St. Pierre and Miquelon are all that remain of French holdings in Newfoundland.

Whereas the development of most of New England featured a gradual decrease in dependence on fishing, Newfoundland (along with Nova Scotia) remained almost entirely dependent on fishing. Although the island covers a total of 110,681 square kilometres (68,789 square miles), the land is almost entirely unfit for farming. The English actually prohibited settlement on the island until the beginning of the nineteenth century, simply using the island as a fishing station. In a tragic story of the fragile balance of nature in the light of technology, the waters around the island of Newfoundland were eventually overfished. In 1992 the waters around Newfoundland, the Grand Banks, and most of the Gulf of St. Lawrence were closed by the Canadian government. Today, small "outports" still dot the rocky coast, lingering as evidence of how fishing was not just an economic mainstay but also a way of life. Before there were any roads in Newfoundland, these small settlements were connected via water or along cart tracks that followed the shoreline or turned inland to woodlots and summer meadow gardens. Although roads and the railroad opened up the interior of the province, many of the rides we have included follow these old paths between communities nestled in coves along the shore. The trails are exhilarating, steeped in history, wild, and are great vantage points for spectacular views and vistas.

THE TRAILS

On our first day in Newfoundland we made the first of what would prove to be numerous invaluable contacts. We were directed to a community just north of St. John's, where we found and rode along the old cart tracks overlooking Tor Bay. We were immediately awed by the high, rugged cliffs, the views out to the ocean, and the excellent conditions for mountain biking. Imagine our delight when what to us was unfamiliar movement in the cove proved to be a whale. Returning to our lodging, we told our story to our host, who simply smiled with the wisdom of one who has always lived in Newfoundland and said: "But of course you saw a whale!"

Riding in Newfoundland will reward both local riders and visitors to the island with many such chance encounters, with magnificent views, wildlife, and extraordinary people. The life of the sport is anchored in the cities of St. John's (on the east coast) and Corner Brook (on the west coast). Both cities are home to active mountain biking communities that have grown to support several excellent bikes stores, organized group rides, a decent race series, and lots of trail development. Local riders have not only worked to develop and maintain trail systems but have also begun documenting and mapping various areas. In particular, Doug Miller in Corner Brook has produced an excellent resource for mountain bikers: *Mountain Biking in and around Corner Brook* is a spiral-bound booklet available for sale at local bike stores, including Skates and Blades Sports and T&T Bicycles.

Though St. John's and Corner Brook share the distinction of being at the core of mountain biking in Newfoundland, the character of the riding in each area is unique. The trails in and around St. John's find their foundation in the extensive network of former cart tracks and footpaths that were once the only connection between communities and "outports" on the coast. The trails we explored with a number of local riders make up the best collection of coastal rides in all of Atlantic Canada. The terrain is quite rough through this part of the province, and you will come to appreciate Newfoundland's other name, "The Rock," as you negotiate trails strewn with rocks and boulders the size of babies' heads. The rewards for persevering with this terrain are great, however: trails like Freshwater Bay, Petty Harbour, and Shoal Bay all drop to exquisite coves where whales and even icebergs can be observed in summer months. Just outside the city, rides around Tor Bay and Pouch Cove, one of the island's earliest settlements, will also provide you with spectacular views and lead to dramatic cliffs overlooking the ocean. All in all, St. John's has something to offer everyone. After sampling the intricacies of the race circuits, the breathtaking coastal scenery, and the adventures offered up by rides in areas like Pouch Cove and Petty Harbour, we predict that visitors to this surprising mountain biking mecca will be as sorry to leave as we were.

Riding in Corner Brook is inextricably tied to the city's identity as a mill town. Through the cooperation of Corner Brook Pulp and Paper Ltd. and the development of organizations such as the Newfoundland Model Forest Group, much of the riding in the area is based along a vast network of active and abandoned logging roads. Marble Mountain, boasting a vertical drop of over 550 metres (1,800 feet), features a ride that allows ambitious climbers to survey the wooded landscape of the area, including grand views of the Humber Valley. Generally speaking, the trail conditions on this side of the island are less rocky than their counterparts in and around St. John's. The trails are also oriented toward the forested interior of the province, rather than the coast.

Between St. John's and Corner Brook, the vast interior of the island has seen less specific mountain bike trail development. However, the Newfoundland section of the Trans-Canada Trail (Trailway Provincial Park) will one day link these two hubs of activity. Riders can already enjoy long completed sections of the trail in and around Gander, as well as numerous rides that make use of small sections of the trail. The Come By Chance race circuit, La Manche Bay, and Clarenville rides all utilize sections of the abandoned railway bed. Also, toward the centre of the province is Terra Nova National Park, where two trails offer riders the opportunity to explore some of the province's most beautiful wilderness.

At the time of our research, Newfoundland's most well-known park, Gros Morne National Park, had no trails open to mountain bikers. However, from Corner Brook there is apparently a route that leads up to the southern perimeter of the park, through an area managed by the Newfoundland Model Forest Group. This ride is one we have heard several riders speak of, and would be well worth investigating for riders eager to reach the ancient tablelands and dramatic fjords that characterize the area in and around Gros Morne. Farther up the Northern Peninsula, dirt roads and informal trails exist, but as yet no trails have been established for use by off-road riders.

South of Corner Brook, Stephenville features a good race circuit and access to some tremendous riding along the southern shore of the Port au Port Peninsula, overlooking St. George's Bay. Be sure to try to hook up with some local riders, who will be more than willing to guide you to some short but superb sections of coastal riding. Continuing down to Channel-Port-aux-Basques, another section of the Trailway Provincial Park offers splendid coastal riding up to Cape Ray.

HITTING THE TRAILS

The vast expanse of terrain, dramatic scenery, and exhilarating wilderness of Newfoundland demands more from riders than a simple willingness to venture outward. Landmarks are few, the weather is changeable, and it is very easy to get lost. Being prepared will make your riding experience safer and more enjoyable. Many of the areas we explored by mountain bike are crisscrossed by numerous trails, footpaths, cart tracks, and game trails. None of these trails are signed, and many do not appear on any maps.

Although we have taken extreme care to provide precise and detailed trail descriptions for every ride, it is still possible that you will become lost. For most of the trails we have described for this province, it is highly recommended that you obtain and carry with you the appropriate topographic maps for the area. A compass is also important, as are the skills to use it. We also discovered that aerial maps depict paths and trails not indicated on many of the topographic maps. We have referred to these maps on trails where there is no such thing as having too many resources at your fingertips. As with any outdoor activity, it is also important to remain alert to the conditions of the trail, and especially to changes in the weather. Along with plenty of water and food, carrying extra clothing and raingear is a good idea, especially for longer rides.

The best conditions for riding in Newfoundland usually occur in July and August. Although we did not have the opportunity to experience it ourselves, winter riding is also very popular. In the St. John's area especially it is not uncommon for large groups of riders to hit their favourite trails in the winter. Trails that are known for their rocky and rough conditions can actually be ridden with greater ease in the winter, when snow cover creates smooth surfaces and less technically demanding terrain.

Although there are about 30 tourist information centres scattered across Newfoundland, resources for riders in the province are scarce once you leave the cities of St. John's and Corner Brook. Even in these cities you may not be able to find specialized parts for your bike. Much of the terrain is rough, so it is very important to ride with a good collection of tools and spare tubes. Despite the distances involved in traveling through Newfoundland, and the extra precautions necessary for exploring its trails, the province (to our surprise and delight) was our favourite in Atlantic Canada. Instead of being overwhelmed by the rugged terrain and vast wilderness, we were most struck by the welcome we received from everyone we met. Perhaps it is because the mountain biking community is so small that it is also so friendly. And, despite the relatively small community, you will find riders always willing to join you for a ride and people eager to share their favourite trails. In Newfoundland we are certain that you will encounter the same spirit that we did: a captivating enthusiasm that values mountain biking as an opportunity to experience the outdoors, the wild, the beautiful, the unexpected, and the undiscovered.

The following list of resources will help you plan a trip to Newfoundland and connect you to some of the most useful stores and services:

Department of Environment
& Lands, Lands Branch
Howley Building
P.O. Box 8700
St. John's, NF A1B 4J6
(Topographic and aerial maps)

Destination Newfoundland
and Labrador
P.O. Box 215
St. John's, NF A1C 5J2
(800) 563-6353

Canary Cycles
294 Water Street
St. John's, NF A1C 5J2
(709) 579-5972

Earle Industries Ltd.
51 Old Pennywell Road
St. John's, NF A1C 5L7
(709) 576-1951

Play It Again Sports
Corner Brook CO-OP Building,
Box 553
Corner Brook, NF A2H 6E6
(709) 639-PLAY

RIDE 42 · Pippy Park

AT A GLANCE

Length/configuration: 8-km (5-mile) loop

Aerobic difficulty: Moderate; this ride is characterized by low hills with only short climbs

Technical difficulty: Intermediate to advanced; single- and double-track trails over extremely rocky terrain

Scenery: Splendid views of downtown St. John's, St. John's Harbour, and Signal Hill

Special comments: Bring your swimming gear!

Pippy Park is as fine an example of an urban playground as you can find anywhere. Located on the northwestern edge of downtown St. John's, the park is easy to find and offers everything from a golf course and campground to many kilometres of excellent mountain bike trails. For riders, one of the best ways to tour the park is along the race circuit, an 8-km (5-mile) loop that follows both single- and double-track trails over the technically challenging, rocky terrain characteristic of many trails in the vicinity of St. John's. In fact, we considered Pippy Park to be the best sales pitch for fully suspended mountain bikes in town. Don't be alarmed, however: we are also living proof that even riders with rigid frames can master the art of riding through gullies scattered with baby head–sized boulders! Due to its relatively short distance, this provides beginning-level riders interested in improving their skills with an excellent introduction to riding rocky and eroded trail conditions. Intermediate and advanced riders will enjoy the challenge of negotiating the varied terrain with as few dabs as possible.

Pippy Park extends across an area known as Three Pond Barrens and has lots to offer riders more intent on recreation than feats of technical expertise or competitive race times. The race circuit that we describe is just one option for riding at the park, and provides a useful tour along single- and double-track trails over rugged, open terrain, as well as paths that lead into woods and meadows. Once you have familiarized yourself with the major landmarks in the park, consider exploring alternative routes. Particularly useful as orienting landmarks are the three ponds that are situated at the centre of the race circuit: Left Pond, Middle Pond, and Big Pond. Be sure to carry your swimming gear with you, for these ponds are the best swimming holes in town!

General location: The city of St. John's, on the Avalon Peninsula.

RIDE 42 • Pippy Park

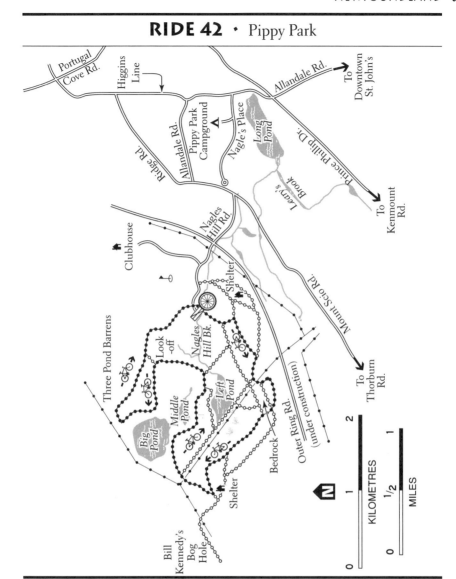

Elevation change: This ride features only modest changes in elevation.

Season: Riding conditions anywhere on the Avalon Peninsula are affected more by the weather than the time of year. The months from June through September generally offer the best conditions, with July and August offering the warmest days and the most ideal temperatures for swimming partway through the ride.

Services: All services are available in St. John's.

Hazards: Hikers and walkers also use the trails at Pippy Park, so ride with caution and with respect for other trail users.

Rescue index: Although the trails in the park can be confusing (there are many!), you will never be far from assistance.

Land status: City park. At the time of our research, the uses of the trails through Pippy Park were being re-evaluated. It is possible that certain trails may be designated for uses other than mountain biking or that more trails will be made available to riders. Respect all signs and keep off any trails that clearly prohibit bikes.

Maps: Pippy Park trail maps are available at the park headquarters, located in the registration office at the entrance to the campground and trailer park. The entrance to the camping area is well signed and is located off Allandale Road on Nagles Place. Alternatively, you can obtain a copy of the map by contacting Pippy Park at the following address:

Mt. Scio House
P.O. Box 8861
St. John's, NF A1B 3T2
(709) 737-3655

Finding the trail: Pippy Park is located quite close to downtown, so you can probably ride to the trailhead. Although there is parking available for vehicles, should you choose to drive, space can be limited. Either way, follow Torbay Road out of town, and turn left when you reach Newfoundland Drive. Continue straight through the intersection with Portugal Cove Road, following Higgins Line. After just a short distance, turn right up Ridge Road. Follow the road around to the left (it becomes Mount Scio Road), and then turn right up Nagles Hill Road and make your way to the top. You will pass the golf course on your right and a lounge called the 19th Hole before Nagles Hill Road curves quite sharply to the left. Shortly beyond this bend in the road, the paved road turns to gravel and a gate prevents vehicular access up the trail. Parking for vehicles is on the side of the road.

Source of additional information: Earle Industries is one of the bike shops in St. John's, and if you are unfamiliar with area, it is well worth stopping by the shop to talk with the folks there. Any of the staff will be able to provide you with directions to Pippy Park, and will probably offer you some good tips on riding the racecourse there.

Earle Industries Ltd.
51 Old Pennywell Road
St. John's, NF A1C 5L7
(709) 576-1951

Notes on the trail: Begin riding straight along the wide gravel access road that continues beyond the gate at the end of Nagles Hill Road. Ride past the first rocky trail branching off on the right. Shortly after that intersection, turn left onto a narrow single-track trail. You will get a great view of St. John's Harbour and Signal Hill before you descend into a wooded area along a rocky trail with both loose and exposed rock. At a **T** junction with a slightly wider trail, turn right (turning left here will take you back out to Nagles Hill Road). Following the trail to the right, you will continue to enjoy a view overlooking the city. Also on your left will be a transmission line and the Outer Ring Road which, though under construction at the time we rode, is due to open in the near future.

Keeping to the main trail, you will veer around to the right and find yourself following a route marked with yellow cross-country ski trail arrows. Farther up the trail, although there is an arrow pointing down and to the left, continue straight on the more distinct trail. At the crest of a very small, gravelly hill, there is a trail branching off on the right and you can see the transmission line on the left. Bear left and ride to a **T** junction at the transmission line. Turn left and follow the trail as it swings around to the right. At a four-way intersection, turn right up one of the main trails through the park. This trail will split at a **Y** intersection immediately before reaching an area of exposed bedrock. Bear left, and continue to bear left past the strip of bedrock on your right.

Beyond the bedrock, you will ride across an open, exposed area of barrens toward some woods. Follow the trail into the woods, and continue straight past a trail branching downhill to the left and marked by a fire pit. At a distinct **Y** in the trail, bear right along a trail posted with a red arrow. The trail along this stretch is crossed by a tangle of roots and then passes through an area of stubby little trees. When the trail intersects with the transmission line, continue straight and pick up the continuation of the single-track trail on the other side. The trail you continue on is best described as a rock garden, and contains some of the most technical riding on the circuit.

The rock garden trail will take you up to the edge of Middle Pond. Keep to the main trail, avoiding the trails on the left that just drop down closer to the water. At a significant **Y** in the trail, bear left, following an odd little sign made out of the bottom of a can that reads "Better Way!" At a **T** junction with a wide gravel path, turn left. You will climb steadily, negotiating rocks and loose gravel until you crest the hill and reach a four-way intersection. The ride continues along a trail that branches off on the left. However, you may want to follow the trail to the right for a short side trip. This trail will lead you to a scenic look-off atop a small grassy knoll, not far from the four-way intersection. The view from this spot is impressive and encompasses much of downtown St. John's, including the harbour and Signal Hill.

From the look-off, retrace your tracks back to the four-way intersection and follow the trail (now on your right) that branched off to the left. You will descend on a gravel path that swings to the right and then opens out at a meadow. There is a water pump here, and the remains of some old buildings. Follow the trail through a larger meadow, passing some more stone remains. The trail descends as it swings to the far corner of the meadow and heads toward the woods, where it narrows to a really tight single-track between the trees. After riding just a short distance on that trail, you will come to a five-way intersection; take the trail immediately on your right, heading north. You will reach Big Pond, which will be on your left, where you may find a lot of people swimming. Continue straight on the trail until you reach a **T** junction with another wide double-track trail.

From this **T** junction, another branch of the transmission line can be seen to the left; the ride continues to the right. After two tough, rocky sections of the trail, you will pass a trail branching off on the right into a meadow. Continue straight, and then continue straight again as you pass a second trail branching off on the right. You will ride up to the top of a windy, barren area that overlooks the city and the harbour. There is a three-way intersection at this spot. The ride continues straight (the trail on the right connects back to the look-off you made a short side trip to earlier in the ride). Follow the trail to the edge of Captain's Hill Golf Course. The trail traverses a ridge at the edge of the golf course and then turns down a rather treacherous-looking chute. Before you know it, you'll be pedaling out onto Nagles Road, at the curve in the road just before the trailhead.

RIDE 43 • Torbay Coast

AT A GLANCE

Length/configuration: 10-km (6-mile) out-and-back (5 km [3 miles] each way)

Aerobic difficulty: Modest; mostly flat with a few short, steep climbs

Technical difficulty: Intermediate narrow single-track along the coast, as well as rocky, inland double-track

Scenery: A popular destination for whale watching from the high cliffs overlooking the ocean

Special comments: Several side trips to the edge of the cliffs may be biked, and also present opportunities to explore on foot

The coastal paths and old roads featured in this ride from Torbay to Flat Rock are part of the East Coast Trail. This trail will be made up of many local paths linked together to form one continuous path that will traverse 340 km (204 miles) of the eastern Newfoundland coastline. For three years preceding our research, volunteers at the East Coast Trail Association have taken on the formidable task of flagging and developing the trails that follow old roads and hunting paths that once formed primary links between communities. Although the project is expected to be near completion by the summer of 1999, at the time of our research there was no sign of flagging or trail work along this particular section. However, the trails that comprise this ride were in good condition and

RIDE 43 • Torbay Coast

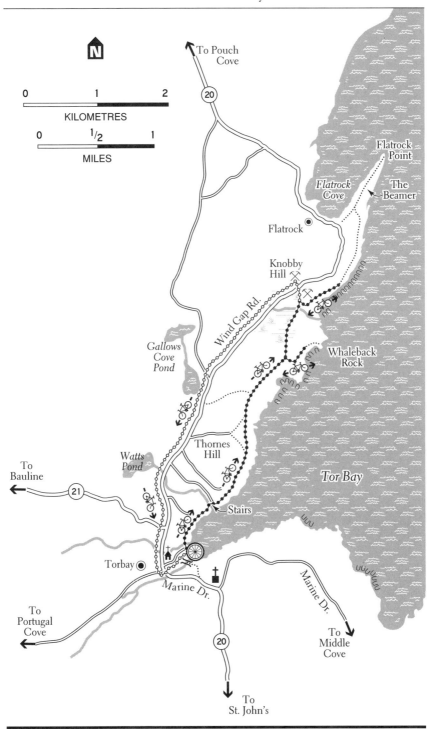

Perched atop the bluffs of Tor Bay, it appears we have reached the edge of the world.

characterized by hard-packed dirt with a few loose, rocky sections. With the expectation that the trails will remain in their original condition, we anticipate that attention to the potential erosion from increased use and a judicious distribution of trail blazes by the East Coast Trail Association will enhance all riders' and hikers' experience of this stunningly beautiful stretch of coastline.

The ride to Flatrock from Torbay is a 10-km (6-mile) out-and-back trip with the option to form a loop by returning on the pavement. The trail weaves toward and then out from the coast, following footpaths and old roads through woods, farm fields and along the edge of the cliffs that plunge into Tor Bay. It offers an easy-paced, intermediate ride along primarily hard-packed dirt trails over rolling terrain. You will find that the favoured look-off points on the coast have well-trodden paths, but that even these most-visited sites feature views that have remained unchanged over time. We returned exuberant from the ride, proclaiming we had spotted a whale in the cove. We were informed by our local host that we had seen a minke whale and that our sighting, while remarkable for us, would not be recorded in the local annals! Still, we maintain that the possibility of watching whales in the bay is an unusual and compelling feature of this ride.

General location: On the Avalon Peninsula, a half-hour northwest of St. John's.

Elevation change: Following the edge of the coast, the few short climbs on this ride amount to very little overall change in elevation.

Season: To help preserve these trails and keep mountain bikers welcome on this primarily hiking network, allow sufficient time for the trail to dry in the spring, and avoid riding soon after or during a rain. Ideal riding conditions begin in mid-June and may continue to September, but July and August are the driest months.

Services: There are convenience stores and a few restaurants on the way to Torbay, where you can buy water and other basics. All other needs, including bicycle-related ones, can be met in St. John's.

Hazards: Sections of the trail trace the edge of the cliffs and should be ridden with caution. Give way to hikers at all times.

Rescue index: As you are unlikely to encounter a lot of hiker or biker traffic on the trail, you can rely on the nearby paved roads to flag down assistance.

Land status: The trail is on public land that has been developed and maintained by the East Coast Trail Association.

Maps: Although the trails do not appear on the government topographic map for the area, the St. John's 1N/10 map is useful in navigating your way along the coast. Although not available at the time of publication, the East Coast Trail Association may have maps of the trail. They may be contacted at (709) 570-7509, or by writing to:

East Coast Trail Association
General Delivery
Bay Bulls, NF A0A 1C0

Finding the trail: From St. John's, take Route 20 (Torbay Road) north toward Torbay. As you enter Torbay, you will pass Marine Drive on the right and descend a long hill. Cross the bridge at the bottom of the hill and immediately turn right onto Lower Street. At the end of the road you will come to an area called "the Battery," where you will find a parking area close to the beach.

Source of additional information: The staff at The Outfitters, located at 220 Water Street in St. John's, are well informed about the east coast trails and will also sell you maps. You can reach the store by phone at (709) 579-4453.

Notes on the trail: Departing from the parking area at "The Battery," bear left and pick up the trail just past the beach. The gravel road will become a rocky double-track trail that leads uphill, following the shoreline of the bay. At the first **Y** intersection bear right, following the more distinct path that continues alongside a fence at the edge of the cliff. A short distance further, the trail begins to descend gradually and approaches the top of a steep gully. At the top of the gully, the trail continues down steep wooden steps to the Torbay community wharf at Tapper's Cove. Dismount and hike your bike down the steps.

Cross the paved area of the wharf and ascend the far side of the gully by way of another flight of steps.

At the top of the steps, continue on the grassy double-track, tracing a path along the edge of the cliffs. The combination of ocean air, dramatic cliffs, and the occasional whale appearing suddenly in the cove make this a unique and captivating stretch of trail. As you continue along the trail, you will appreciate the frequent outline of a wooden rail fence to keep you from plunging into the ocean! After passing a field of cows and horses, you will come to a three-way intersection with a gravel road, a grassy trail, and a double-track into a farmer's field. Continue straight, following the grassy trail in the middle.

The grassy trail is littered with rocks and continues inland to a four-way junction of dirt roads. Begin to descend to the right on a wide gravel road. Continuing on the gravel road, you will pass another road on the right and then arrive at a grassy opening. Beyond a picnic table and a camper, the trail continues to the right and ascends a hill into the woods. This short climb is on a grassy double-track with some loose rocks. At the top the trail returns to a hard-packed dirt-and-grass cart track continuing straight ahead. Following this trail, you will come to a Y intersection and bear right. Beyond the intersection, you will cross a rocky brook bed and follow the trail between two fields separated by an open-mesh wire fence. The fence is lined with pink wild roses, bluebells, irises, raspberries, and blueberries; an assortment of wildflowers and bushes that bloom in each month of summer. To the right you can look out over the bay.

Just past a grassy trail branching off to the left into the fields, you will arrive at a vague intersection with five trail options. The trail continues most obviously ahead, but turning right offers a short side trip. Following the right-hand trail leads to a spectacular view from atop the cliffs, looking out over the ocean. There is a narrow footpath that descends the sloped portion of this high bluff. Descending a short distance will give you a terrific view of the cliff face. From here, backtrack to the intersection and continue on the well-beaten path.

Back on the main trail there is a short, challenging, rocky descent that is followed by a rockier continuation of the trail at the bottom. You will then cross some wet areas, where ladders have been constructed over the puddles for hikers. Continue to an opening, where trails lead out of a gravel pit to the left and the right. Taking the option to the right, you will climb a short hill and follow a grassy single-track out to the edge of the cliffs. Here you are rewarded with another dramatic view over the edge of cliffs which plunge straight down to the ocean. A narrow footpath branches off to the left of the single-track. At this point, it is worthwhile to abandon your bike and hike a short distance up the hill for a view of the nearby community of Flatrock and out to the end of "The Beamer" — an appropriate name for this rocky peninsula.

Returning to your bike, follow your path back to the gravel pit area. From the gravel pit you can choose to simply retrace your tracks back along the coast to the trailhead, or to exit onto Wind Gap Road and follow the pavement back to Torbay. To return on the pavement, ride straight across the gravel pit and continue on a wide double-track trail on the other side of the pit. This trail covers the short distance to the paved road. Turn left and return to Torbay, where you began the ride.

RIDE 44 • Pouch Cove

AT A GLANCE

Length/configuration: 22-km (13.7-mile) combination (12-km [7.5-mile] loop with out-and-back spur; spur is 5 km [3 miles] each way)

Aerobic difficulty: Strenuous; many hills of varying difficulty, and an extended climb back from Cape St. Francis

Technical difficulty: Moderate; primarily double-track trails and dirt roads with some areas of loose rock

Scenery: Stunning coastal and inland scenery

Special comments: Allow a day for this epic tour through a beautiful corner of Newfoundland

This ride through the starkly beautiful landscape surrounding the community of Pouch Cove is a rewarding exploration of stunning coastal scenery, long-traveled pathways, and a lighthouse on the remote tip of Cape St. Francis. The ride utilizes a combination of old cart tracks and footpaths that once linked the communities along this shoreline. In this way it offers a fascinating glimpse into the history of the bonds between neighbouring communities and the lifestyles of people who once used these trails to access winter woodlots and summer meadow gardens on the outskirts of town. Our guide through this area had been walking the land and the trails of this portion of the Avalon Peninsula all his life. Thanks to his willingness to share this small corner of paradise, we were able to develop a ride that we think will appeal to the most adventurous riders. So, if you're seeking to experience the wilderness of Newfoundland; the unexpected delights of berry picking; the history of old, established pathways; and the splendour of coastal scenery, read on . . .

This ride covers a total of 22 km (13.7 miles), beginning with a 12-km (7.5-mile) loop around the community of Pouch Cove and ending with a dramatic 10-km (6.2-mile) out-and-back trip to Cape St. Francis. The initial loop begins

RIDE 44 • Pouch Cove

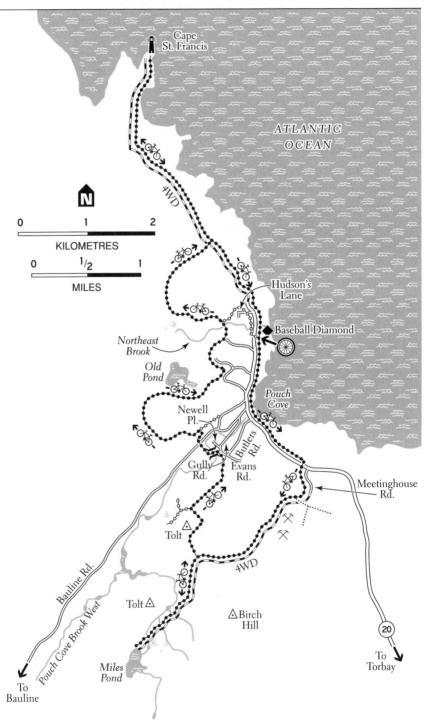

NEWFOUNDLAND 213

Following the rocky remains of an old road toward the Tolt, which rises up to the right, from Pouch Cove.

on pavement and then follows a rough double-track road up to a rocky ridge and prominent, rocky outcropping called the Tolt. From here, a short out-and-back side trip leads inland to Miles Pond, where opportunities for spotting wildlife abound. The ride continues from the Tolt as a meandering tour along a series of old pathways through and behind the town of Pouch Cove. The out-and-back excursion to Cape St. Francis caps off the ride and follows a rough, unpaved road out to a lighthouse. Throughout all sections of this ride, the terrain is not so much technically difficult as it is unpredictable. The route, in its entirety, does involve some significant elevation change. We recommend that you put aside a whole day for this ride, taking the time to enjoy the views, the unexpected opportunities to watch moose or whales, and the sweet treats offered up by the many raspberry and blueberry bushes along the way. Cape St. Francis is an excellent place to linger before turning around and returning to Pouch Cove. Whether it is the pounding surf, the determined passage of fishing boats, or the winding footpaths along the bluffs, there is much here to be explored and enjoyed.

General location: Pouch Cove is less than one hour north of St. John's, on the Avalon Peninsula.

Elevation change: You will climb and descend continuously on this ride for a total elevation gain of approximately 389 m (1,275 feet).

Season: July and August are the best months to explore this ride. Depending on the year and the amount of rainfall, the weather may oblige by providing good riding conditions in June and September as well. If possible, save this ride for a clear day, for the views will be spectacular.

Services: Pouch Cove, though small, is home to both a convenience store and a café that will satisfy any needs for food and water. All other needs, including bike-related services, must be met in St. John's.

Hazards: As with many rides in Newfoundland, losing the trail is the biggest danger on this ride. The middle portion of the ride can be particularly confusing, as the route we have outlined exists amid a maze of other trails. Aerial maps are extremely useful when used in conjunction with the topographic maps for the area, particularly for riders unfamiliar with the land. During the two days we spent researching this ride, we were also extremely grateful for the directional assistance of our Casio Pathfinders! This ride is situated in an area where sudden changes in the weather are likely. Be aware of any changes, and turn back if conditions turn for the worse. High winds, rain, and fog can turn this landscape into an unforgiving environment.

Rescue index: If you stick to the main trail, you will never be more than 5 km (3 miles) from assistance. In fact, the trail frequently emerges in the busy neighbourhoods that extend from the centre of Pouch Cove. However, it is easy to lose the trail, and assistance is not something you will be likely to come by unless you can make your way back into the community of Pouch Cove.

Land status: Crown land.

Maps: The government topographic maps for this area are Pouch Cove 1 N/15 and St. John's 1 N/10. We found the aerial maps of the area to be tremendously helpful as well, particularly maps 95028-55 and 95028-6.

Finding the trail: From St. John's, travel north on NF Highway 20 toward Pouch Cove. As you drive into town, pass the convenience store on your left and continue straight past the road to Bauline, also on the left. A short distance from the centre of town, you will come to a small park with a baseball diamond on the right. There is plenty of room here to park.

Sources of additional information: There are no official sources of information on this ride, as it is made up of largely informal trails that pass through public land. Any local residents you encounter on or near the trail are likely to be quite knowledgeable about the area.

Notes on the trail: From the baseball diamond, turn left and ride back down the road you drove up on. You will continue on Highway 20 past the road to Bauline, now on your right. You will pass the convenience store, also on the right, before crossing a small bridge and passing Butlers Road on the right. Highway 20 begins to climb from this point, but you do not have to continue for too long before turning right on Meetinghouse Road. Follow Meetinghouse Road to a vague four-way intersection, where the main road curves to the right and rocky cart tracks continue straight and to the left.

Follow the main road around to the right. From this point, you can see the continuation of the road as it climbs up through a saddle between Birch Hill and a rocky mound called the Tolt. After a short descent, you will pass the site of

Hudson's excavating and two large gravel pits. Bear right past the second gravel pit, passing a gravel road that branches off to the left and enters the pit. Beyond the gravel pit, you will continue up the main road, gradually climbing up into the saddle. The road is wide and four-wheel-drive accessible, and the climb, though steady, is not too steep. The landscape around you is fairly typical of Newfoundland: a beautiful yet barren tableau of weathered trees, colourful splashes of fireweed, and scattered boulders and rocky ridges that attest to the glacial activity of the past. In August, when we rode here, there were raspberries and blueberries along the side of the trail.

When you reach the high point in the saddle, the Tolt will be on your right and, looking back over your shoulder, you will see the small town of Pouch Cove overlooking the broad expanse of the Atlantic Ocean. Catch your breath here and enjoy the view! Beyond this high point, the road swings to the left and begins to descend. As you round the bend, keep your eyes open for a cart track that branches off to the right, heading toward the Tolt. The ride continues on this trail, but we recommend that you continue straight for a short side trip to Miles Pond.

You will continue to follow the main road down toward the pond. This side trip takes you farther inland, and you will be entering a wide, low valley that resembles a large bowl surrounded by a magnificent, rugged, young mountain landscape. As you approach a rocky ridge to the right of the trail, the main road ends. The ride continues in the same direction for a short distance farther, following a cart track toward the pond. This cart track swings around to the right and crosses Miles Brook, at which point the trail may be rather boggy. Beyond the stream, there is a fork in the trail; bear left and continue to Miles Pond. The pond is nestled amid a landscape of scrubby trees and young tamaracks, and is a good location for spotting wildlife, particularly moose.

From the pond, return to the saddle and the high point of the road by retracing your tracks. At the high point the ride continues to the left, following the cart track you looked for earlier that heads toward the Tolt. This left turn may not be terribly clear as it begins across an area scattered with rocks that obscure the path. One sure landmark is a ridge or glacial wall that stretches off to the right, directly across from the trail. The cart track toward the Tolt is directly across from this ridge and follows a grassy and quite rocky path. You will follow it as it curves around to the right side of the Tolt. At the base of the Tolt there is a narrow footpath that climbs to its prominent summit. It is well worth making this short but steep hike to the top. On a clear day you will enjoy a spectacular 360° view of everywhere you've been and everywhere you're going!

From the Tolt, the trail continues downhill, passing through a meadow before deteriorating into a rocky chute that demands some skillful maneuvering. The trail descends to a fence, which it then follows (the fence is on your left), and continues to descend toward Pouch Cove. Some sections of this descent may be awkward, obscured by alders encroaching upon the trail. When you reach a four-way intersection, continue straight. You will find that this is the most obvious path, but there is a grassy cart track branching off on the right and a trail that follows a hairpin turn around to the left.

The trail to the left is worth venturing down if you are riding during berry season. If you choose to explore it, you will cross a rocky and rather wet section of trail before reaching a **Y** intersection and a small bog. Bear left at this junction, and then bear right at the next fork in the trail, following a grassy track to the base of the Tolt and a sprawling raspberry patch. We took a rather lengthy break, in fact, to battle our way into the centre of the thorny tangle of prolific bushes, where we filled a water bottle with berries to enjoy later on in the ride. If you choose to explore this 2.5-km (1.5-mile) out-and-back side trip (1.25 km [0.75 miles] each way), you must simply retrace your way back to the four-way intersection where you ventured off the main trail in order to continue the ride.

Continuing from the four-way intersection, the main trail remains obvious. After a short distance the land around you will begin to open up and you will pass a cart track on the right, a grassy path heading into a meadow garden (also on the right), and a solitary telephone pole with no lines; continue straight at all these landmarks. Beyond the telephone pole, the trail will widen into a graded dirt road. On the left you will pass Paul Shea's turquoise house, a small white house with maroon shutters, and then a gray house. Just beyond the gray house, and before the intersection of paved Evans Road and unpaved Gully Road, turn left down a rocky little chute that descends and almost immediately connects to Gully Road. Bear left when you reach Gully Road.

On the unpaved Gully Road, you will pass a pond on the left, and as the road begins to swing to the right, look on the left for another rocky cart track, which comes just before the intersection of Gully Road and Newell Place. Turn left on this cart track and follow it around a curve to the left. Cross a broad log bridge over a stream, passing a small pond with a duck pen on the right. Beyond the bridge, the path becomes rocky and widens to a double-track trail. Follow the trail as it swings to the right, and bear left at the first fork, passing a grassy trail on the right. This turnoff will bring you almost immediately to another fork in the trail. Bear right at this **Y** intersection. You will ride into a more open area where you will be able to see the Tolt off to the left. Follow the trail around to the right and up a short rise. Turn left and follow a driveway out to a **T** junction with the paved Bauline Road.

Turn right onto Bauline Road, and as the road curves around to the right, turn left up a rocky cart track that heads uphill and begins the middle portion of this ride. This cart track is the first possible opportunity you will have to turn left off of Bauline Road. The trail swings left, up into Lyde's garden, one of many named but unmarked meadow gardens that are dotted through this area outside Pouch Cove. Be sure to pass a trail on the right that heads straight into the woods, and continue riding uphill, following the trail as it swings to the right. There are two short trail options up the steepest part of this hill, at the top of which you will come to a **T** junction. Turn left at this junction and follow the trail as it swings around to the right. Continue to bear right, passing a less distinct grassy trail branching off on the left. A short distance farther, there is another trail branching off on the left. Continue to stay straight, heading west.

You will cross a section of the trail built up with logs placed corduroy-style across the trail. Just beyond this point, the trail emerges into a more open and somewhat boggy meadow area. There is a distinct **Y** in the trail here. Bear right and ride along a grassy trail that then turns back into the woods, veering to the right under some evergreen trees. This stretch of the trail will lead you to a more recently cleared area strewn with slash and complicated by many exposed roots. Forge your way through this area; the trail continues out of the clear-cut and to another meadowlike area that has become the resting place for an old red wreck of a car. Follow the trail straight ahead, heading in a northwest direction. Through a line of trees, you will come to another meadow area, and a grassy trail branching uphill and to the left. Bear right, heading north-northwest and slightly downhill. Having descended that grassy slope, you will come to a **T** junction with a more distinct, rocky cart track.

At the **T** junction with the rocky cart track, turn right and ride over a bridge that crosses a small stream. On the other side of the bridge, bear right up a slope, where a trail joins in on the left. Just beyond this point, you will come to a four-way intersection, where you can look across a large meadow on the right toward the Tolt. The main cart trail runs to your left and right, and there is a less distinct trail continuing straight. Turn right. The trail swings around to the left, and you will want to ride past a trail branching off on the right. Stay on the main trail, passing another grassy trail on the right. As you continue, you will be able to see the town of Pouch Cove to your right. You will ride past several meadow gardens, cross a small plank bridge, and pass a big potato patch on the right before coming to a **T** junction. Turn right here, heading toward some homes on the outskirts of Pouch Cove.

You will descend a short hill and then climb up the other side. The trail then splits at a **Y** intersection. Bear left and ride up to the intersection with another dirt road. Turn left again, this time onto New Road. When you come to a four-way intersection, where Jordan's Lane is straight ahead of you, turn left onto a well-maintained paved road that turns to dirt just a short distance farther. At a fork you will see a dirt trail going through a grassy meadow on the right and the continuation of the gravel road on the left, bordered by a wooden rail fence. Keep to this main gravel road, which will swing around to the right. You will most likely pass by some piles of logs. On our ride along this trail, there was a rather large pile of logs on the left, at a point where you want to follow the trail around a bend to the right. Beyond this bend in the trail you will pass a grassy trail branching off on the right, before you follow the main trail as it heads uphill to the left. At the top of the hill the trail turns sharply again, this time to the right, and leads to the edge of a large field.

From the edge of the field, you must ride straight onto an indistinct, grassy trail that continues directly across the field. Half way into the field, veer to the right, but stay to the left of a big pile of rocks. You should descend toward the woods at the perimeter of the field. Continue bearing right, and ride along the perimeter of the field for just a short distance. You should notice a trail heading into the woods on the left, crossing over an old stone fence. If you were to continue straight past this left turn, you would follow the trail up a rise to the point where it connects back with the trail that went around the right side of the pile of rocks. Should you find yourself at this point, turn around and look for the trail heading into the woods on your right.

Having crossed the gap in the stone fence, you will ride through the woods for a short distance before reaching the perimeter of another grassy meadow. Following a grassy trail that swings down to the left, you will pass a house with a brick facade on the right and descend to a **T** junction with a rocky, gravel cart path. Turn left. Quite soon after turning onto this rocky cart trail, you will cross a brook via a log and plank bridge. A short distance after turning onto this cart track, there will be a trail on the right descending a small hill and crossing over an area of still water. At this junction you can decide to continue the ride out to Cape St. Francis, or cut your trip short and return to the trailhead at the baseball diamond.

The ride to Cape St. Francis continues along the main cart track, along the side of a stone fence. If, however, you choose to return to the trailhead at this point, you will want to turn right, heading downhill slightly and over the patch of still water over the trail. There were some pallets laid down across the water when we rode here. Beyond this wet area, you will climb a steep and rough slope to an open area that affords a terrific view of the ocean on the right. A short distance farther, you will come to a wide, graded gravel road. Turn left. This is Hudson's Lane, which connects at a **T** junction with a paved road. This road, if you were to follow it to the left, continues all the way down to Cape St. Francis. Turning right takes you in the direction of Pouch Cove and back to the trailhead at the baseball diamond, which will be on your left.

Returning to the junction of the cart track and the trail out to Hudson's Lane, for bikers choosing to continue on to Cape St. Francis, the ride begins a challenging, uphill climb on the main cart track. Along the initial stretch of this climb you will pass an opening into a meadow on the left. Stay straight on the main cart track, and follow the trail as it parallels a rock wall on the left. Continue past several trails that branch off to the left. At a fork in the trail, bear right and continue riding up through an old cut. You will climb up through a rocky section of the trail that is best described as a gully. Continue straight, passing a logging road that intersects with the main trail on both the left and the right. From here you will enter a more recently cut area at the top of the ridge, and the trail once again becomes quite grassy. Follow the trail along the ridge, which bends around to the right, out to a four-way intersection with a wide gravel road. This is the main road that runs between Pouch Cove and Cape St. Francis. Turn left to ride out to the lighthouse and high bluffs at the Cape. If you decide at this point to return to the trailhead, turn right and descend steeply, following the road back to the baseball diamond, which will be on your left.

For riders continuing to Cape St. Francis, the route becomes refreshingly easy to follow from this point on. The road is wide and easy to follow all the way out to the Cape. Watch for vehicles on this section of the ride, as this road is accessible to two-wheel-drive vehicles. Some sections of the road are eroded, and others may surprise you with loose gravel and rocks. Ride cautiously, especially along the steep descents. And remember that every downhill you enjoy on the way out to the Cape will become an arduous uphill climb on the return journey! Toward the end of the road you will drop down to a small harbour. Beyond this point, the road climbs steeply for a short distance to the lighthouse. This last section of the road is significantly more eroded and ends at the lighthouse. Enjoy the views, explore the footpaths that lead up to the bluffs, and revel in the beauty of this rugged and remote spot. To return to the trailhead, follow the road all the way back toward the baseball diamond in Pouch Cove, where you began the ride.

Special thanks to Brian Gillett for his willingness to share his knowledge and provide detailed directions to help create this ride.

RIDE 45 • South Side Hills

AT A GLANCE

Length/configuration: 5.5-km (3.5-mile) loop

Aerobic difficulty: Strenuous; you will climb quite steadily for the first half of the ride

Technical difficulty: Advanced; this is an expert rider's playground

Scenery: Beautiful single-track trails through the woods, and one impressive view overlooking the city

Special comments: You can reach this trailhead by bike from downtown St. John's

The South Side Hills create a high ridge overlooking the city of St. John's and its harbour. The topography of the area lends itself to mountain biking, and this ride features quite a bit of climbing for such a short loop. The ride we describe is a challenging 5.5-km (3.5-mile) loop that follows just one variation of the race circuit used by competitive riders in the area. The hard-packed dirt, single-track trails that make up this course are quite unique to this part of

RIDE 45 • South Side Hills

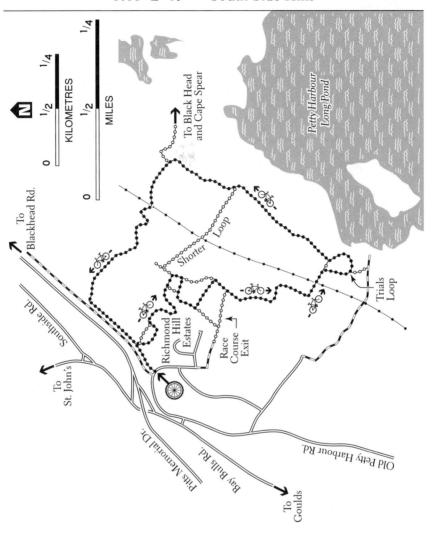

Newfoundland, where virtually all the rides follow extremely rough and rocky terrain. The ride could in no way be described as easy, however, and though the trail conditions are good, the ride is characterized by a constant series of technical challenges. Aerobic fitness is a must, and only riders with exceptional technical skills will be able to make it through this course cleanly.

One of the highlights of this ride is that it can easily be reached by bike from downtown St. John's. The course is part of a network of trails at South Side Hills and the product of many hours of hard work by a few individuals dedicated to the sport of mountain biking. Certain sections of this ride are suited exclusively to expert riders, featuring a variety of obstacles in the style of trials riding. However, the condition of all the trails is very good, and the race circuit is an excellent place for intermediate-level riders to hone their bike handling skills and get a good workout in the process. Equipped with both the topographic map for the area and the series of aerial maps depicting South Side Hills, riders may consider exploring beyond the race circuit described for this ride. In particular, it is possible to ride down to Long Pond, where on warm days you can go swimming, and along trails that head out toward Blackhead and Cape Spear.

General location: The South Side Hills are just south of downtown St. John's, rising up from the water above St. John's Harbour.

Elevation change: You will begin riding at the base of a meadow at approximately 90 m (300 feet), and will climb to approximately 213 m (700 feet) before traversing at that elevation and finally dropping back to 90 m (300 feet). Total elevation gain is approximately 123 m (400 feet).

Season: The best conditions are found from June through September. Avoid riding any of the trails at South Side Hills after heavy rain.

Services: All services are available in nearby St. John's.

Hazards: Some sections of this ride traverse very technical terrain, with steep descents, drop-offs, and trails that seem designed to throw riders headlong into trees or boulders.

Rescue index: Even at the farthest point on this short ride, you will not be far from the residential area of Richmond Hill Estates.

Land status: Crown land.

Maps: The aerial maps for this area indicate the more established trails used along this race circuit. The government topographic map, St. John's 1 N/10, highlights some of the surrounding features in the landscape but does not include any of the trails.

Finding the trail: You can choose to drive or ride to the trailhead at South Side Hills, which is approximately 6.5 km (4 miles) from the centre of St. John's. From downtown, travel west on Water Street. Turn left at a traffic light and cross Waterford River, following signs to Cape Spear. Turn right immediately after crossing the river, and follow South Side Road all the way to its intersection with Route 10, or Bay Bulls Road. Turn left on Bay Bulls Road, and after just a short distance, turn left up Old Petty Harbour Road. You will turn left again almost immediately and follow the pavement uphill and past Richmond Hill Estates. Just past the sign for Richmond Hill Estates, turn left onto a gravel road that continues uphill. If you have driven a car to this point, pull off to the side of the road to park.

Sources of additional information: You may find tips and current information about the race circuit from local riders at either of the two main bike stores in town. Earle Industries is a full-service bike store that also offers mountain bike

Chris Jarret demonstrates the meaning of expert riding on the challenging single-track terrain at South Side Hills.

rentals. The shop is located at the back of an old warehouse at 51 Old Pennywell Road, or you can reach the folks there at (709) 576-1951. Also in town is Canary Cycles, located at 294 Water Street (phone (709) 579-5972).

Notes on the trail: Begin riding uphill on the gravel road. You will follow this road for just a very short distance before turning right on a narrow trail that dips through the ditch on the side of the road. This trail will take you up into a field. Bear right on the trail, and ride up along the edge of the field toward the woods. Bear left at the top of the field, continuing to follow the perimeter until you come to a trail that leads into the woods on the right. Turn right and continue to climb, slowly making your way uphill. The trail becomes quite rocky, and you will continue straight past a single-track trail on the right that may be marked with flagging tape. A short distance beyond this side trail, you will reach a **T** junction with a double-track ATV trail. Turn right at this junction, and then turn right again almost immediately to begin down another narrow, single-track trail through the woods. This detour off the main ATV trail bypasses an area that has suffered considerable damage due to heavy use by ATV riders.

As you descend on the single-track trail, you will pass the other end of the flagged trail you passed on your way up the hill. Continue straight, past this trail on the right, and then past another one on the left. After just a short distance, turn left and head uphill. This particular intersection occurs in an area where bunchberries flourish. Begin climbing, and pass through an area of firs before reaching a four-way intersection with a grassy trail. Continue straight and head up a short, rocky ascent that will force all but the most skilled riders to hop off and hike. You will climb to a **T** junction with the main ATV trail.

Turn right, back onto the main ATV trail, and ride to a **Y** intersection. Bear left here; the right-hand trail option is apparently an exit route off the racecourse and will probably be blocked with a tree or branch. Shortly beyond this junction, you will reach a transmission line. Cross straight over the transmission line, picking up the continuation of the trail on the other side.

Beyond the transmission line, you will come to a **Y** intersection. Here you have the choice of descending to the right and exploring a short but extremely difficult trials loop that reconnects with the main trail a short distance farther up, or of bearing left to continue the ride along the main trail. If you opt for the trials loop, you will drop down the trail to the right and come to a **T** junction. Turn left here (the trail on the right descends to Long Pond). The next portion of the trail features some challenging riding, including a huge rock climb that requires some rather deft maneuvering between closely spaced trees. It is possible to spend a long time in here, tackling each and every obstacle with the hopes of finally passing through this area with no dabs!

You will come to the end of the trials loop at a **T** junction with the main trail. Turn right to continue the ride. Another technical section of the trail lies ahead, and when you reach another **T** junction, you will see a red painted **X** on a white sign to the left. Turn right here, heading uphill slightly. You will climb up to the bottom of a steep rock face, which will be on your left, and along which the trail continues. Beyond this point, you will cross some logs laid down corduroy-style through a bog. This is an area to move through quickly, as mosquitoes hover in droves, awaiting the arrival of new prey.

Beyond the corduroy-log section, you will reach a vague **Y** in the trail that almost looks like a **T** junction. There is an arrow pointing to the left and a vague trail signed to Black Head on the right. Turn left, following the arrow. The next section of the ride meanders through the woods over soft ground and reaches a scenic look-off over the city of St. John's. This view is your warning that you have reached the edge of a lip that drops from this point along a very difficult trail. This hill is one that all but the most experienced riders should consider walking. The descent is steep, riddled with rocks and boulders, and follows a tight path between closely spaced trees. Essentially, there is only one line to follow and no room for error.

At the bottom of the hill you will emerge at the transmission line once again. To your left is the point at which you crossed the transmission line the first time. Turn right, as if to ride beneath the transmission line, but then follow the trail as it veers to the left and heads back into the forest. The trail winds through the woods from here and, at one point, curves sharply around a teepee-like structure. You will enter a more recently cleared area of the woods that seems to be growing in with small firs. Continue to follow the trail, eventually dropping along a very steep slope and down the embankment to a gravel road. Turn left to return to the trailhead, a short distance down the gravel road.

RIDE 46 · Freshwater Bay

AT A GLANCE

Length/configuration: 5-km (3-mile) out-and-back (2.5 km [1.5 miles] each way)

Aerobic difficulty: Extremely strenuous climb back up from Freshwater Bay

Technical difficulty: Advanced; rough and rocky trail conditions along a steep grade

Scenery: Expansive views across the water and out to the high cliffs overlooking Freshwater Bay

Special comments: Hair-raising descent followed by a torturous climb

The trip to Freshwater Bay offers an extended downhill with a few heart-stopping hazards to spice up a rocky ride to the coast. This ride is a favourite among extreme technical enthusiasts and bike store owners of St. John's. Riders enjoy recounting tales of how they hurtled down this rocky gully, and bike store owners look forward to the repairs that follow this excursion, which may include new pulley wheels, derailleurs, brake pads, and the occasional rim. Indeed, this is a 5-km (3-mile) out-and-back ride that can wreak more havoc on your bike components than an entire season of moderate off-road riding.

Despite (or perhaps because of) all of this, Freshwater Bay is one of the most widely talked about and popular rides in the St. John's area. The trail follows a straight rocky slope down to the edge of Freshwater Bay. It features a combination of exposed bedrock, large- to mid-sized boulders, and loose rock. This ride requires that you suspend your disbelief and trust in your bike, your lungs, and your limbs to make your way both down and up the trail. Before embarking on the ascent, take a few moments to take in the view and even check out the *barachois* (lagoon) at the end of the bay. Then, without further delay, retrace your skid marks back up the trail, putting your advanced climbing skills and excellent conditioning to the test.

RIDE 46 • Freshwater Bay

General location: South of St. John's, in the vicinity of the Shea Heights, along the road to Cape Spear.

Elevation change: The 150-m (492-foot) drop to the bay and the return climb of equal distance result in a total elevation change of 300 m (984 feet).

Season: This trail should be ridden in dry conditions between June and September.

Services: All services are available in St. John's. For high performance mountain bike rentals or service, contact Earle Industries, a bike shop located behind a large warehouse at 51 Old Pennywell Road (phone (709) 576-1957).

Hazards: There is one deteriorating bridge with a large gap in the middle, as well as a fault in a large boulder that you must dismount to cross.

Rescue index: Because the trail surface is very unforgiving and because you will have to return to the paved road near the trailhead or to St. John's for assistance, it is strongly recommended that you ride with a buddy.

Land status: The trail is signed as the "Freshwater Bay Hiking Trail" at the trailhead, but it is a public right-of-way on Crown land.

Maps: The trail appears distinctly on government topographic map St. John's 1N/10.

A view of the coast is glimpsed between the pine trees and brush on the trail to Freshwater Bay.

Finding the trail: From downtown St. John's, follow Water Street to a left turn onto Leslie Street. Continue along Leslie Road to Blackhead Road, and turn right at the mural with the whales. On Blackhead Road, continue past Shea Heights, to an intersection with Blackhead Crescent. The trailhead will follow immediately on your left and is marked by a parking area. The sign at the trailhead reads: "Freshwater Bay Hiking Trail."

Source of additional information: To consult with other riders and exchange tales of riding Freshwater Bay, visit Canary Cycle on Water Street in St. John's.

Notes on the trail: Although the ride follows an obvious trail straight down to Freshwater Bay and back again, these directions will prove useful for the simple fact that they provide you with advance warning of the dangerous obstacles on the trail. Stick with us, and you may be able to reduce the risk of injury to you or your bike!

Begin the ride at the fairly wide opening at the eastern end of the parking area. Cross the corduroy bridge, and enter the woods on a hard-packed, narrow, single-track dirt trail. A short distance into the trail, you will reach your first hazard: the dilapidated log bridge. If you dare to begin riding on this dangerous-looking bridge, be aware that about half way across it there is a gap in the wood planks that requires you to dismount—otherwise your front tire will become trapped in the hole and you will find yourself over your handle bars and sprawled on the rocks somewhere. When you arrive safely at the end of the bridge, you can continue riding down a gradual slope with more exposed rocks and small boulders.

Straight ahead, the trail drops off over some rocky ledges that are followed by stretches of loose rock. This stretch of extremely technical terrain is punctuated by the second hazard: a large gap in the bedrock across the trail. It appears rather suddenly near the end of the steep, bouldery section and can completely surprise those who are not looking ahead on the trail. Descend this section slowly, and dismount to cross the gap.

Beyond the gap, you will get your first glimpse of Freshwater Bay. The remainder of the descent is hazard-free but still difficult. You need to stay alert as you continue downhill and pass through the bed of boulders. Emerging from the rocky descent, the trail continues as a grassy single-track toward the bay. It comes to an abrupt halt just before dropping sharply to the shoreline. After spending some time exploring or taking in the view, retrace your tracks up the rocky slope to the trailhead.

RIDE 47 • Petty Harbour

AT A GLANCE

Length/configuration: 17-km (10-mile) out-and-back (8.5 km [5 miles] each way)

Aerobic difficulty: Both the extended technical descent and the arduous climb back from the harbour require good conditioning

Technical difficulty: Advanced intermediate; a long descent and return climb on a rocky old road

Scenery: Barren, rocky coastal terrain and a small fishing village

Special comments: Visit the café in Petty Harbour

As a visitor to St. John's, if you ride no other trail, you should certainly venture down the old road to Petty Harbour. This fishing community is the most easterly in North America, and has become renowned for the wisdom of its long and steadfast commitment to traditional fishing methods. Decades before the Canadian government announced a moratorium on groundfishing, the fishermen of Petty Harbour banned all mass-fishing techniques in an effort to protect their ever-diminishing catches. Unfortunately, it has only been since

RIDE 47 • Petty Harbour

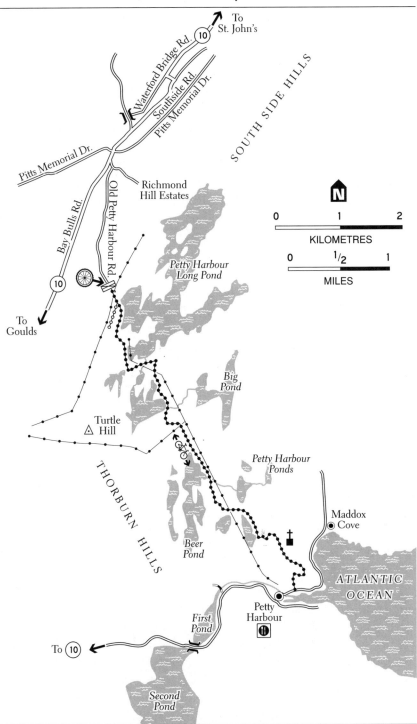

Jodi nears the end of the long climb out of the village of Petty Harbour.

the closing of the fisheries in 1992 that the methods employed by the fishermen of Petty Harbour have received recognition from scientists and legislators as environmentally sound and responsible practices. As you ride from the modern gravel road at the start of this trail to the rocky old road that continues to the harbour, you too will be taking an appreciative step into the past.

The ride descends from the trailhead to the community of Petty Harbour along a 17-km (10-mile) road ideal for mountain biking. On your journey you will pass through desolate barrens, past inland lakes and rocky hillsides, to the dramatic cliffs around the harbour. The old road presents a combination of loose, chunky gravel, exposed bedrock, and small boulders that fat tires can roll over with some skillful maneuvering. The ride is mostly intermediate with some advanced sections where the trail slopes steeply around bends. The return trip, a steady climb for most of the way, requires the strength and endurance of moderate conditioning.

Arriving in Petty Harbour, you can learn about the cod industry and the fishing communities that once depended on it for their livelihood. This history is told in newspaper clippings, photographs and pamphlets available at the Petty Harbour Café and through artifacts kept in the museum. Because the ride to Petty Harbour is demanding in both directions, and the story of the community so worth reviewing, we highly recommend perusing the binders of information at the café. Not only will you be treated to the captivating stories of this community, but you can also sustain yourself for the journey home with a side serving of blueberry cake with rum sauce.

General location: In the vicinity of St. John's, the trailhead is just minutes outside downtown.

Elevation change: On the descent to Petty Harbour you will lose 200 m (656 feet), which you will regain on the climb back to the trailhead. The total elevation change is 400 m (1,312 feet).

Season: Dry conditions are optimal for this ride, as the mostly rocky trail becomes quite slick when wet. The months of July and August are recorded to have the least rainfall, but there may be opportunities to ride in June and September.

Services: Petty Harbour has a museum and a café, but all other requirements should be met in St. John's. This is an ideal ride on which to test a high performance mountain bike, which may be rented from Earle Industries, located at 51 Old Pennywell Road (phone (709) 576-1951).

Hazards: A boggy area midway along the trail could be impossible to cross after a heavy rain or in the early spring.

Rescue index: Beginning on the outskirts of a residential area and descending to the community of Petty Harbour, you are never more than 4 km (2.4 miles) from help at any point on the trail.

Land status: Crown land with restricted road access.

Maps: The trail is clearly marked on the government topographic map St. John's 1 N/10. The trail also appears in *Newfoundland Maps* (map 42, 1N-NE, section D-6; map 46, 1N-SE, section D-1).

Finding the trail: Follow Memorial Highway out of St. John's to the Kilbride exit. From the off-ramp, turn left at the T junction onto Bay Bulls Road. Pass beneath the highway, and after a very short distance, turn left onto Old Petty Harbour Road. Turn right almost immediately, and drive to a gate at the end of the road. There is ample parking in the open area just in front of the barrier.

Source of additional information: The staff and riders who frequent Canary Cycles on Water Street in downtown St. John's will be of some assistance (phone (709) 579-5972).

Notes on the trail: Begin riding on the gravel road beyond the barricade. The road is well graded and becomes more scenic as you approach a wooded lake. At the first Y intersection, bear left, continuing alongside the lake. A short distance farther, the road veers away from the lake, narrows, and becomes rockier as it climbs a short hill. Beyond the crest of the hill, the road descends gradually to a small inlet, which will be on your right. As you near the inlet, the road levels off and bears left, crossing under a pole line. At this point, your view opens up across a patch of classic Newfoundland scenery—rocky, rolling hills to your left, and cliffs that plunge to the water's edge on the right.

As you approach the far end of the inlet, you will reach a fork in the road. Bear left, and enjoy the view out to the ocean from the top of a small knoll. Beyond the viewpoint, follow the road as it descends to the right for a severely eroded descent over large boulders and small- and mid-size loose rocks. The road improves once it levels out, and then a short distance farther, the trail widens and descends to another pond. Here, you are surrounded by grassy hillsides that are crisscrossed by many obvious footpaths. Follow the main trail past a fire pit to the left and through a bog (after a heavy rainfall or early in the spring, this area could be problematic). A path is clearly marked, and offers the driest path of least resistance.

Beyond the bog, you will continue to encounter some short sections of eroded trail as you descend. You will pass a trail on the left that leads into a clearing before reaching two ponds. At the end of the second pond, bear left, continuing to descend. You will pass a chlorine house on the right and a small cemetery up on the hillside to your left. At this point, the road widens and becomes well graded, continuing to descend to Petty Harbour. Nearing the coast, you will be surrounded by views of dramatic bluffs and rocks poised at the top of the surrounding hillsides. As you near Petty Harbour, the gravel road turns to pavement. Brightly-coloured houses nestled in the hills surrounding the harbour characterize your first glimpse of this historic town.

The paved road winds and descends rapidly toward Petty Harbour. Continue all the way to a **T** junction with the main road through town. At this point, you can explore the town at will. Turn right to reach the centre of the community, including the Town Offices, the Museum, and the Petty Harbour Café and Gift Shop. Beyond the café, the road continues past the town wharves to the other side of the small harbour, where you can view the steep little mountains that surround the town and ponder your return trip back up the old road. At the end of your visit, simply retrace your tracks to the trailhead.

RIDE 48 · Shoal Bay

AT A GLANCE

Length/configuration: 14.8-km (9-mile) out-and-back (7.4 km [4.5 miles] each way)

Aerobic difficulty: Intermediate; the ride back up out of Shoal Bay is rigourous

Technical difficulty: Intermediate to advanced; ATV-width trail with sections of severely eroded terrain

Scenery: This ride features a dramatic descent to a stunningly beautiful cove overlooking the ocean

Special comments: Join up with local riders who favour this trail in the winter!

The ride down to Shoal Bay is a popular one, and for good reason. Within relatively close proximity to St. John's, the Shoal Bay trail offers a quick escape to a sheltered, remote cove on the coast. The trail meanders along a rocky old road and then quickly drops through the woods to emerge, abruptly, at a beautiful spot overlooking the Atlantic Ocean. From grassy knolls to flat rocks over which crashing surf cascades, there are numerous places to relax and enjoy the salt air once you reach the water. For visitors to Newfoundland, the scenery is especially dramatic: steep cliffs sweep down to the ocean and whales can often be seen fishing offshore.

Local riders follow this rugged, 14.8-km (9-mile) out-and-back trail in the winter as well as in the summer. Certainly, with snow covering the trail, the rough and eroded trail conditions are somewhat tempered. The ride follows an old road, and during the traditional summer riding season, large rocks and boulders litter certain portions of the trail. The steepest part of the descent to Shoal Bay is particularly jarring, as the road surface has suffered significant deterioration due to erosion. When a pulley wheel on one of our bikes succumbed to the effects of prolonged rattling and disappeared into a mass of rocks and boulders, we were happy to have an engineer as our guide on this ride. He rigged up a temporary fix with nothing more than a zip tie. Along with such trailside savvy, at least intermediate-level skills are recommended for this ride. Furthermore, a good level of physical fitness will hold you in good stead. There is only one way back to the trailhead from Shoal Bay: up the same rigourous trail on which you descended.

General location: Near Goulds, on the southeast shore of St. John's city limits.

Elevation change: You will begin this ride at 107 m (350 feet) above sea level. As you head out toward Shoal Bay, you will reach an elevation of 189 m (620 feet) before descending almost to sea level. For the round-trip ride, total elevation gain is approximately 271 m (889 feet).

Season: Shoal Bay is a trail that local riders use throughout the year, heading out to the water on snow even in the middle of winter.

Services: All services are available in St. John's. Closer to the trailhead, you will find the basics of food and water in Goulds. Due to its proximity to the city, this trail is also accessible by public transit.

Hazards: Exercise caution when riding on the rocks near the shore. There are some large faults, and the surface becomes quite slippery at the water's edge.

Rescue index: This is a popular trail for fishing enthusiasts and ATV riders as well as mountain bikers. There is a good chance that you will encounter other people at some point along the ride. At the farthest point on this trail, down at Shoal Bay, you will be 7.4 km (4.5 miles) from the trailhead and a short distance from Highway 10.

Land status: Crown land.

Maps: The best resource for this ride is the government topographic map Bay

RIDE 48 · Shoal Bay

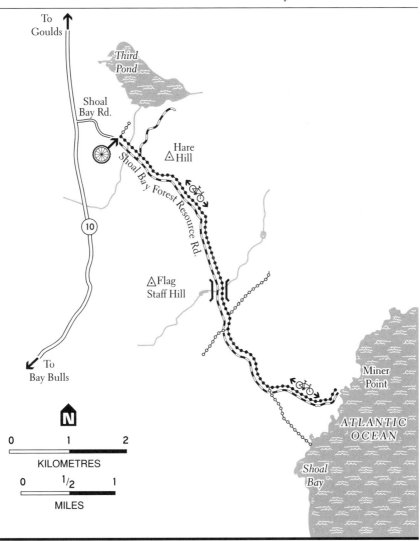

Bulls 1 N/7. Although Shoal Bay itself is not named on the map, the trail is indicated in *Newfoundland Maps* (map 46, sections C-1, D-1, and D-2).

Finding the trail: From St. John's, drive south on NF Highway 10 and follow signs to Goulds. At the junction of Highway 10 and Bay Bulls Highway, turn right onto Main Road. You will pass the Billiard Barn; follow the road around a bend and across a bridge. Continue uphill. As you approach a playground and Veronica's Sewing, Alterations, and Repairs, turn left on Shoal Bay Road. Follow

Dave picks his way between the crevasses on the rocky outcroppings jutting into the ocean at Shoal Bay.

the road to its end at a large cul-de-sac. Park by the side of the road, being sure to leave room for the buses that use this cul-de-sac as a place to turn around.

Sources of additional information: You may be able to seek out local riders who know this ride at one of the bike shops in St. John's. Consider a trip to Earle Industries at 51 Old Pennywell Road (phone (709) 576-1951), or Canary Cycles, at 294 Water Street (phone (709) 579-5972).

Notes on the trail: From the end of Shoal Bay Road, the ride begins down an unpaved, rocky road at the far end of the cul-de-sac. There is a sign at the entrance to this road that identifies it as the Shoal Bay Forest Resource Road. Begin down this road, bearing left almost immediately at a fork. You will descend through a rocky dip before climbing along a slight grade. After the road levels out somewhat, you will reach a distinct fork. Bear right here, following the more well-traveled path. Along this section, the road continues to be fairly flat and is in good condition. Continue straight past a grassy cart track on the left. Farther along the trail, you will descend a short hill and round a bend in the road to the right.

Beyond the bend, you will cross a small wooden bridge over a stream. The road continues uphill from this point, and you will climb for a short distance. As you approach the crest of this hill, you will pass a muddy track branching off on the left. At the crest of the hill, the road flattens out and continues straight ahead for a considerable stretch. After passing two trails on the right that lead up to some cabins, follow the main road around to the left. You will come to an area of exposed bedrock that marks the half way point to Shoal Bay and the beginning of a long descent. The ocean is visible on the horizon from here.

Areas of exposed rock and some boulders, loose rock, and gravel will mark your descent to Shoal Bay. Prepare yourself for a rather bone-rattling ride! At a Y intersection in the trail, bear left. The trail improves slightly from this point, descending the final slope to Shoal Bay along more moderate terrain. When you reach the ocean, you will discover several trails that meander along a meadow-like area along the shore, and that you can ride out to some flat rocks that provide an excellent vantage point from which to enjoy the surf and the surrounding scenery. When you are ready to return to the trailhead, turn back and follow the same route back up to the end of Shoal Bay Road.

RIDE 49 • Kenmount Hill

AT A GLANCE

Length/configuration: Two loops totaling 7 km (4.5 miles) on single- and double-track trails

Aerobic difficulty: Challenging; technical terrain with many short climbs

Technical difficulty: Advanced network of mostly single-track trails

Scenery: Panoramic view of St. John's and a diverse array of trail conditions

Special comments: This network of trails is being expanded every year

This ride at Kenmount Hill traverses advanced single-track that has been developed by a dedicated group of riders in St. John's. They have spent many hours in the woods, using chain saws and their knowledge of riding to build single-track trails that take full advantage of the contours of the hillside. At the time we visited, two loops had been constructed, for a total of 7 km (4.5 miles) of riding. The loops demand advanced-to-expert skills and an excellent level of fitness to ride from start to finish quickly, without a moment's rest.

Located on the outskirts of St. John's in Mount Pearl, the trails make some use of areas cleared around communication towers and of a gravel access road. Most of the trails are very challenging, since they wind tightly through the trees on narrow trails that are webbed with exposed roots and littered with rocks. There are rocky chutes and steep drop-offs that require excellent bike handling

RIDE 49 • Kenmount Hill

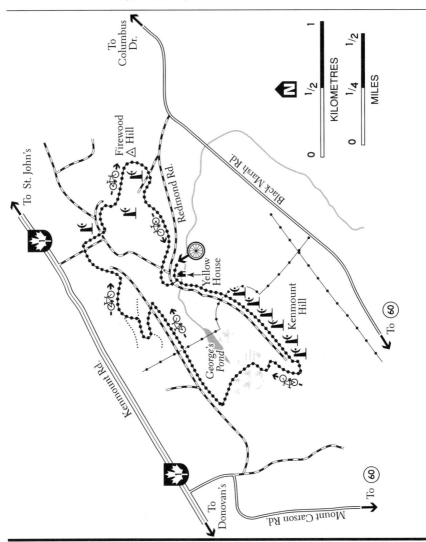

skills on descent and stamina to climb up. The appeal of the area lies in the challenging terrain and proximity to the city, not the scenery. There is one view over St. John's from a radio tower clearing, and you may retrieve a lost treasure from one of the small junkyards you will pedal past, but the rest of the ride follows under power lines and through the woods. But, as we said, who notices such surroundings when one's heart is racing and the adrenaline is flowing?

General location: The trailhead is located in Mount Pearl, just west of St. John's.

Elevation change: The trails at Kenmount Hill are characterized by frequent, short, steep climbs.

Season: The best riding will be found from June to September. Avoid riding any of the trails at Kenmount Hill after heavy rain.

Services: There are no services at the trailhead, but you will find food and beverages in Mount Pearl. All biking needs should be met in St. John's.

Hazards: This is a challenging trail that requires advanced cycling skills. Exercise caution, and head out on these trails accompanied by at least one other rider.

Rescue index: Traffic on the roads near the trails is infrequent, but you can seek help from the houses at the trailhead.

Land status: Crown land.

Maps: There are no maps that include the trails that make up this ride, but you can refer to government topographic map St. John's 1 N/10 for an overview of the area.

Finding the trail: From downtown St. John's, take Water Street west and bear right onto Topsail Road at the first fork. From Topsail Road, turn right onto Columbus Drive, which you will follow to Blackmarsh Road. Turn left onto Blackmarsh Road, and then right onto the unpaved Redmond's Road. Follow the dirt road around a bend to the left, and then park at the side of the road across from a yellow house.

Source of additional information: The riders at Canary Cycle in downtown St. John's will provide you with information on rides in the area (phone (709) 579-5972).

Notes on the trail: Begin the ride by continuing up Redmond's Road toward the radio towers. This initial climb will bring you to the radio towers at the top of the hill, where there is an outstanding view out over St. John's. Continue on the gravel road past the radio towers, and head downhill to the first **T** junction. Turn right at this junction, onto a single-track that is heading downhill. This trail winds tightly through the trees to a bog, which you will have to cross before continuing on the single-track trail. Continue ahead to a **T** junction with a double-track trail. Turn right onto this trail, which is littered with exposed roots and rocks, and ignore the single-track trails branching off to the left. Continue ahead until you arrive at a fork in the trail.

Bear right at the fork, heading into the woods. A short distance along this trail, you will emerge at a field where another trail from the left will merge into the one you are on. Across the field, continue to bear right on this slightly wider single-track, toward a pole line. Once you have crossed under the pole line, you will descend a short hill. At the bottom of the hill, turn into the first single-track on your left. This is another rocky trail with several exposed roots that winds through the woods. It climbs gradually uphill, eventually arriving at a **Y** intersection. Bear right and begin to descend this tightly winding single-track. At a final bend to the left and a short descent, the trail drops down a steep, rocky chute to a single-track trail below.

After a brief stretch on the smooth and level trail, you will arrive at a fork. Follow the left branch, which will take you on another writhing downhill. At a **T** junction at the bottom of the hill, turn right and continue to a double-track trail. Turn left on this double-track, following a more wooded section. Just before the trail seems to deteriorate entirely into a grassy, overgrown, rocky, and hardly discernible trail, turn left onto a single-track running perpendicular to the main trail you have been following. Follow this trail to a **T** junction and turn left.

After turning left, you will ride out to the Red Rock access road. Continue straight ahead, toward the radio tower, past a concrete block resembling the remains of a gated entrance, to a **T** junction. To the right, you will return to the parking area; to the left is the start of another short loop that completes the ride. Turning left, follow the trail to a four-way intersection. Continue straight through the intersection, toward the field and another radio tower. At a fork in the trail past the second radio tower, bear left. The trail will end on the edge of a grassy field that you will continue across, still bearing left. At the opposite end of the field, you will come to a **Y** intersection. Take the option to the left, following a narrow dirt trail. The trail emerges outside a junkyard, and there is a junker car to the right. A short distance farther on the dirt trail, you will connect with a dirt road. Turn right at the road and follow it as it bears left.

Continuing along the gravel road, turn right onto a single-track trail just before it forks. The single-track cuts through some strewn junk (gloves, shirts, plastic bits) and becomes quite soft on the other side as it winds through the woods, carpeted with moss. As you make your way farther into the woods, you will pass through a recently cut area, where you may find logs to cross and stumps to jump. Just before you reach a ditch that climbs up to the road, bear left at a vague fork to avoid a boggy patch. Ride up through the ditch and onto the road. This is Redmond Road, and by turning left, you will ride a short distance back to the parking area.

RIDE 50 • La Manche Bay

AT A GLANCE

Length/configuration: 25-km (15.5-mile) combination (22-km [13.7-mile] loop with spur; spur 1.5 km [0.9 miles] long in each direction)

Aerobic difficulty: Moderate; several rolling hills and one long climb

Technical difficulty: Intermediate; combination of rocky old roads and multi-use trail

Scenery: This ride passes many lakes and ponds, and it includes a glorious descent to a meadow and beach overlooking La Manche Bay

Special comments: Excellent combination of beautiful scenery and varied terrain

Heading out on a hunch with a topographic map, and remembering to pack a delicate blend of patience and determination, you can discover many interesting trails and explore endless kilometres of wilderness terrain on your mountain bike. It is worth acknowledging that without a few individuals with the interest and commitment to embark on this type of excursion, there would not be any off-road riding, let alone guidebooks to refer to when you got a craving for some scenery and exercise. This ride to La Manche Bay can be attributed to a father-and-son mountain biking duo, who have helped extend the mountain biking scene on the Avalon Peninsula beyond the vicinity of St. John's. Their initiative stands as a fine example of how a ride can easily be created using old roads and recreational trails.

This 25-km (15.5-mile) combination features a grassy, wood-lined descent to a beach on La Manche Bay. The ride begins on an abandoned stretch of the Old Trans-Canada Highway, which is now a rocky old road through the woods, and continues on a grassy ATV-width trail on the final descent to the bay. Once you have climbed back up out of the bay, the ride is mostly flat and the return trip follows a converted railroad bed that is part of Trailway Provincial Park. On this section of the gravel-dusted, multi-use trail, you will meander through inland lakes and ponds before you branch off to return to the trailhead. To enjoy the length of the ride and tackle the climb out of the bay, riders should have a good level of fitness.

General location: This ride is located at the westernmost tip of the Avalon Peninsula near Arnold's Cove, approximately an hour and a half west of St. John's.

RIDE 50 • La Manche Bay

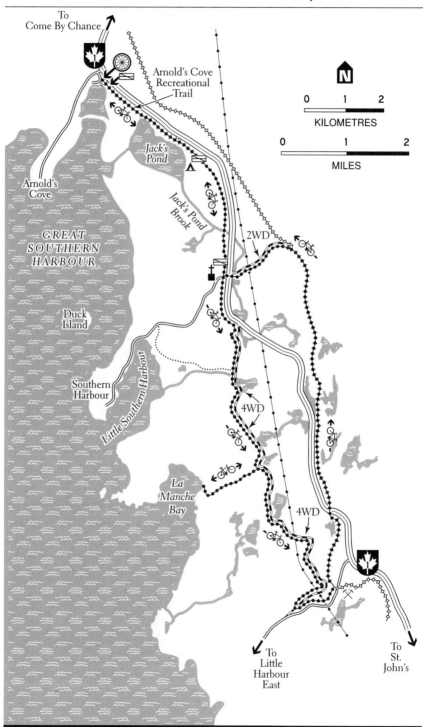

Craggy bluffs and stunning views announce the final descent to the shores of La Manche Bay.

Elevation change: On the way to La Manche Bay, 145 m (475 feet) of elevation is lost. Over one extended climb and several rolling hills on the return trip, the same amount of elevation is gained, resulting in a total elevation change of 290 m (950 feet).

Season: Ideal riding in this area occurs in the dry months of July and August. However, the season may start as early as June and end as late as September in years with little rainfall.

Services: Most services, including camping and accommodations, are available in Arnold's Cove. The closest bike store will be found farther north, in Clarenville.

Hazards: Approximately half way down the outbound trail to La Manche Bay, a section of the trail has been washed out. You will have to dismount and hike your bike across a 1-m (3-foot) gap in the trail, and then resume riding on the other side.

Rescue index: You will never be more than 10 km (6 miles) away from the well-traveled Trans-Canada Highway. Here you can flag for assistance or continue farther along the trail and obtain assistance from the Putt 'n' Paddle Park and Campground in Arnold's Cove.

Land status: The trail makes use of an old road through Crown land as well as government-managed recreational, multi-use trails.

Maps: Refer to government topographic map Dildo 1 N/12. The old road and rail bed are clearly indicated on this map.

Finding the trail: Traveling west on the Trans-Canada Highway from St. John's, take the exit for Arnold's Cove. A short distance from the highway you will come to the Tanker Inn. Turn left into the driveway and continue past the parking area on your right, following a dirt road over a small bridge. Follow the road until it swings sharply to the right. Ahead of you is the trailhead for the Arnold's Cove Recreational Trail. Ample parking is available in front of the barrier at the trailhead.

Source of additional information: We happened upon this ride while visiting with riders in Come By Chance. It is a little-known trail, for which you will have to rely on maps to guide you. However, you can contribute to spreading the news about this ride by sharing your experience with any riders or bike stores you visit on the island.

Notes on the trail: From the parking area, you will begin riding on an abandoned stretch of the old Trans-Canada Highway. The trail is ATV-width and overgrown on either side with alders and fireweed. It begins as a grassy trail and continues as such, apart from a few sections that have become rocky and eroded. Just beyond the first km (0.6 mile) of the trail, you will descend to a four-way intersection of trails. Continue straight through this intersection, crossing the remains of an old bridge and then beginning up a moderate hill. At the end of the climb the trail levels off, and you will pass Jack's Pond on your right.

Beyond the pond, the trail swings away from the water's edge for a short distance. Eventually, you will descend back down to Jack's Pond and the site of the Putt 'n' Paddle park and campground. There is beach access to the water here, as well as an ice-cream and snack hut. Continue straight through the parking area, passing the entrance to the park on the left and following a graded, gravel road toward the camping area. You will ride over a small bridge before the road swings around to the right. Instead of following the road around to the right, bear left and pass through the roped-off entrance for the "Emergency Exit" from the park. At this point you will resume riding along the grassy and patchy gravel surface of the old Trans-Canada Highway.

Eventually, the old Trans-Canada Highway drops down to the new, paved Trans-Canada Highway. Turn right when you reach the pavement and continue riding past the exit to Southern Harbour, which will be on your right. A short distance further along, as the highway curves gradually to the left, turn right onto a gravel road. This is the first and only road you will see past the Southern Harbour exit.

The gravel road continues straight for a short distance, before it appears to be blocked by a pile of gravel and rocks. Make your way through, or around, this obstacle. Beyond it, the road continues straight ahead, though much narrower and more closely shadowed by alders than before. Further along the road you will pass a narrow trail branching off on the right. Shortly after this, you will reach an exceptionally rocky section of the trail and a large pond on the left. For the next couple of kilometres (about 1.2 miles), the trail rolls gently past several more ponds on the left. Ignore several vague offshoots branching off to the left and right. Eventually, the main trail will begin a moderate descent as it curves to the right. At this point you should slow down and prepare to dismount. Ahead of you, the trail drops right down to the edge of a large lake, where a washed-out area requires that you dismount and hike your bike across the gap. Resume riding up the trail beyond the gap. You will climb slightly, and for just a short distance, before reaching a grassy trail branching off on the right. This is the trail down to La Manche Bay; turn right to begin the out-and-back spur to the meadow and beach overlooking the water.

As you make your way down toward the bay, you will pass through a couple of large puddles and drop down several steep and severely eroded sections of the trail. Bear right at a vague fork and continue to descend all the way to a **T** junction with a grassy trail. Turn right and follow the trail all the way down to a meadow, where you will be able to enjoy a stunning view of the beach and bluffs of La Manche Bay. After a stop to take in the view, retrace your tracks up the hill and back to the main trail.

When you arrive at the intersection with the main trail, turn right. You will be following a double-track trail that is relatively flat as it approaches and then winds around a pond to the left. Around the tip of the pond, you will begin a moderate ascent on a gravelly surface. You will pass under a power line and continue ahead. The trail descends gradually and then bends sharply to the right, back under the power line. From here, the trail descends to a **T** junction with a paved road that leads to Little Harbour East. Turn left on the pavement, heading uphill and passing beneath the power lines again. The road swings around to the right and then to the left. You will pass a gravel access road to a quarry on the right and a small pond on the left before reaching the intersection with the abandoned rail bed. The rail bed is easily identifiable and initially follows under a telephone line. Turn left onto this multi-use trail to continue the ride.

Riding along the rail bed, you will first cross a narrow spit over a pond. Farther along, the trail crosses under the Trans-Canada Highway and, for quite a distance, runs parallel to the highway on the other side. At a large pond the trail branches inland to the right, eventually bringing you to a gravel access road on the left. This is the access road to the waste disposal site for Southern Harbour. A short jaunt on this road will return you to the Trans-Canada Highway near the southern tip of Arnold's Cove Recreational Trail. At the highway, turn right and continue on pavement a short distance, heading back to Arnold's Cove Recreational Trail. A red-and-white striped gate on the opposite side of the road marks the opening of this trail. Cross the highway, and follow this trail all the way back to the parking area.

RIDE 51 • Come By Chance

AT A GLANCE

Length/configuration: 8-km (5-mile) loop

Aerobic difficulty: Intermediate; several short but fairly steep climbs

Technical difficulty: Intermediate to advanced; primarily single-track trails

Scenery: Sparsely wooded hillside and barrens overlooking the Come By Chance River

Special comments: "Come by chance, go by choice!"

This race circuit in the town of Come By Chance is proof that mountain bikers exist everywhere and that with a little care and a lot of passion, great trails can be developed in the most unlikely places. Located at the westernmost edge of the Avalon Peninsula, Come By Chance is home to a family of riders who have developed a trail system that draws riders from as far as St. John's for an annual mountain bike race. Part of the attraction is the condition of the trails on this circuit. Unlike most of the trails in and around St. John's, where rocks and baby head–sized boulders turn many riders toward full-suspension bikes, Come By Chance features sweet, hard-packed dirt, single-track trails. With all the challenges of twisty, narrow paths, steep drops, and some areas of rocky terrain, this race circuit is a treat to ride.

The course begins at the edge of a residential area, following an abandoned railroad bed that now serves as a recreational trail. From the rail trail, the circuit cuts down toward the Come By Chance River, then climbs and descends beneath a power line before following an old logging road. A grassy path leads out to a short section of pavement before the ride concludes along a terrific stretch of single-track through a sparsely wooded area with a dense carpet of shrubs and plants. Although the terrain is technically and aerobically quite challenging, this circuit is a great ride for both intermediate and advanced riders. The loop is only 8 km (5 miles) in length and is the perfect arena for developing or polishing your riding skills.

General location: Come By Chance is situated on the western edge of the Avalon Peninsula, approximately 150 km (less than 100 miles) west of St. John's.

Elevation change: You will climb and descend only on short hills, with no significant change in elevation.

RIDE 51 • Come By Chance

Season: Conditions should be good on this trail between June and October. Avoid riding this circuit after heavy rain, to prevent long-term damage to the trails.

Services: Basic services are available in Come by Chance, where a hardware store can furnish many tools and supplies for small repairs.

Hazards: None.

Rescue index: You will never be far from assistance on this trail, which extends only a short distance from a residential area.

ATLANTIC CANADA

A. J. negotiates a drop-off on one of his own freshly cut trails on the Come By Chance race circuit.

Land status: Primarily Crown land, with some distance on a converted, recreational rail trail.

Maps: Maps of this race circuit are distributed every year for the race. However, you may find it difficult to obtain a copy unless you show up the day of the race. The map we have included here, in conjunction with the trail directions, should be adequate to guide you through the course.

Finding the trail: Traveling west on the Trans-Canada Highway from St. John's, turn left at the exit for Come By Chance. Drive down the road for only 1 km (0.6 mile), and just beyond a bend in the road, look for an unpaved gravel access road on the right. This road comes just after the railroad bed crosses the road. Turn right, and follow the road to its end at a small cemetery. There is room to park in a small clearing by the side of the cemetery.

Source of additional information: You may find information about the annual race in Come By Chance in the Newfoundland race schedule.

Notes on the trail: From the cemetery, follow the gravel access road back out toward the main road. After climbing a short rise, you will reach a **Y** intersection.

Bear left, following a short spur that will connect you to the railroad bed. Turn left on the railroad bed, onto a wide, graded recreational trail. Continue straight on the rail trail as it passes beneath a transmission line. You will pass several trails branching off to the left, beneath the transmission line. These trails form a later part of the ride.

Beyond the transmission line, you will ride for some distance before the rail trail ahead of you begins to swing to the left. At this point, look on the left for a narrow single-track trail that begins over a corduroy-style log ramp. There may be some flagging tape marking this turnoff, especially if you ride this circuit soon after a race has been held, but otherwise there are no distinct landmarks. You will descend on this trail, down a short, steep hill. At the bottom of the hill, make a sharp turn to the left. The trail continues over a fairly level area and across some logs before swinging downhill to the right. After this short descent you will ride through an area where logs have been placed corduroy-style over the trail. At the next possible opportunity, cut to the left, riding onto a single-track trail heading uphill. Again, there may be flagging tape in the trees to mark this turnoff.

This next very technical section of the circuit carves a narrow path uphill through the trees. The climb is followed by a tricky, steep descent that ends over a short distance of a roller-coaster terrain. At a **T** junction of single-track trails, you want to be sure to turn left. The trail opens up here slightly, before leading into a gravel clearing and swinging to the left, following a dirt trail. A short distance beyond this point, you will come to a rough four-way intersection beneath the transmission line, just below the rail trail.

The race circuit follows the trail to the left and climbs, beneath the transmission line, back up to the rail trail. When you reach the top, the route simply loops to the right and back down the transmission line along another trail. You will be descending toward the Come By Chance River. At the base of the hill you will reconnect with the four-way intersection; continue along the trail to the left.

From the transmission line, the course follows a wider gravel trail for some distance. When you reach a four-way intersection, bear left and head uphill. At this turnoff there will be a grassy trail over your right shoulder that heads down to the river, and a trail branching off ahead of you and to the right. Bear left again at the first hill through a grassy clearing, and continue straight on a grassy trail. At an intersection with another grassy trail that seems to branch off to the right, bear left up a rocky gully as you proceed uphill. As you come up to the top of the hill, you will enter a clearing where wet, boggy conditions create the perfect habitat for pitcher plants. Veer off to the right at this point, over a series of wooden pallets. The pallets will guide you through a grassy and boggy section of the course. Branch to the right beyond the pallets, and descend slightly. You will come to a little clearing where there is a gravel pit by the side of a paved road. Follow the trail out to the paved road, Shaheen Cresent, and turn left.

From Shaheen Crescent, turn left almost immediately at a **T** junction with another paved road, the main road through Come By Chance. Continue up this road to a red fire hydrant, which is on the right side of the street, just past a mint-green house on the left. At this point you must turn left into a grassy vacant lot and follow a grassy single-track trail that traverses to the far corner of the lot. At the first possible opportunity, and after passing a vague trail on the right, turn left onto a narrow single-track trail. As we made this left turn, we encountered a fallen fir diagonally across the trail. After riding through a small cluster of trees, you will come out in a grassy meadow, behind the mint-green house, and you will want to follow the trail as it swings to the right. Beyond the field, the trail continues through a scrubby meadow of alders, tamarack, fireweed, and grass. The trail is quite narrow, and you will be heading toward a transmission line. Continue straight through an indistinct four-way intersection. A short distance farther, you will come to a scenic look-off over the Come By Chance River. At this point the trail, which is very narrow, curls around to the right and traverses a section of choice single-track. After just a short distance, this trail leads to the clearing and cemetery where you began the ride.

RIDE 52 • Sunnyside

AT A GLANCE

Length/configuration: 14.5-km (9-mile) combination (two 4-km [3.5-mile] loops connected by a spur ridden twice; the spur is 3.25 km [2 miles] each way)

Aerobic difficulty: Intermediate to advanced; mostly undulating terrain with several short but steep climbs

Technical difficulty: Intermediate; varied conditions on old cart tracks include loose rock and some bog

Scenery: From the windswept, barren bluffs of Sunnyside, you'll enjoy views across Bull Arm

Special comments: It really is possible to ride uphill through a bog!

The neighbouring communities of Sunnyside and Come By Chance have as much to offer mountain bikers as their enchanting, whimsical names might suggest. The towns are nestled against a rugged landscape at the tip of Bull Arm, a long, narrow harbour off of Trinity Bay. This landscape can appear daunting to those unfamiliar with Newfoundland's vast expanse of rolling, barren hills, where seemingly endless bogs and multitudes of boulders hint at anything but

RIDE 52 • Sunnyside

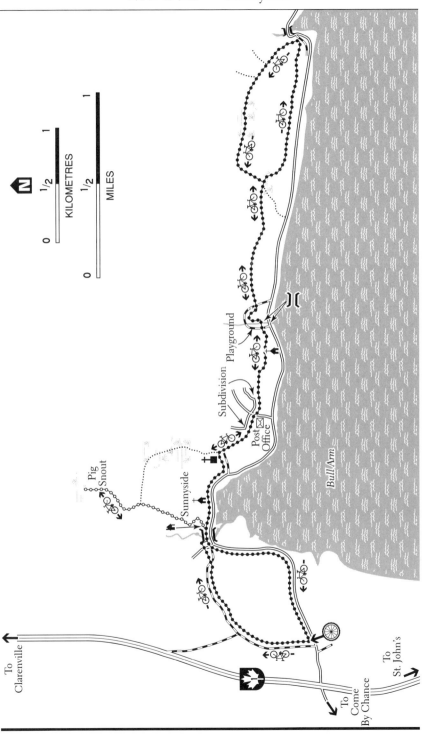

Jodi follows A. J. and Dr. Cleary along an old cart track leading out of the community of Sunnyside to the high bluffs overlooking Bull Arm.

favourable conditions for riding. However, a network of paths and old cart tracks through this area make perfect trails for the likes of mountain bikers eager to explore off-road.

This ride is a classic tour through all the beauty of Newfoundland's rugged landscape. The route is best described as a combination of two 4-km (2.5-mile) loops connected by a spur of approximately 3.25 km (2 miles), which is ridden twice, once in each direction. The total distance for the ride is approximately 14.5 km (9 miles), with the option of adding a total of 2.5 km (1.6 miles) along an out-and-back side trip. Following primarily cart tracks, with the odd stretch along both gravel and paved roads, the ride requires only intermediate-level skills. Due to the number of rather steep climbs, both strength and cardiovascular endurance are required. The highlight of this ride is a hilly path along a high ridge that drops down to Bull Arm. It was in the sheltered waters of Bull Arm that Hibernia, a huge oil rig, was constructed. You will enjoy plenty of views across Bull Arm from various look-offs along the trail. In addition, the optional side trip on this ride leads up to a high mound called the Pig's Snout. The trip is an out-and-back ride to an impressive, sweeping view of the landscape. However, the highlight of the side trip is the uniquely Newfoundland experience of riding uphill through a bog to a point literally surrounded by wet, spongy ground.

General location: Sunnyside is located on the western tip of the Avalon Peninsula, approximately 150 km (less than 100 miles) west of St. John's.

Elevation change: Over constantly rolling terrain, you will gain approximately 122 m (400 feet) of elevation over the entire ride.

Season: The months from June through September provide the best conditions for riding.

Services: Although there are no services at the trailhead, basic services can be found in Sunnyside or the nearby community of Come By Chance. The only source for any bike-related products is a hardware store, so be sure to carry any extra supplies with you, and don't expect to be able to fix any serious breakdowns or replace any specialized parts.

Hazards: At two points in the ride you will descend into a playground where a bridge spans a small stream. Use caution over this bridge, which may be in a state of disrepair.

Rescue index: Although this region feels very isolated, this ride will not take you more than 5 km (3 miles) from the community of Sunnyside.

Land status: Primarily Crown land and established rights-of-way.

Maps: The government topographic maps for this area are 1 N/13 and 1 N/14.

Finding the trail: Driving west on the Trans-Canada Highway from St. John's, turn right at the exit for Sunnyside. Drive just a short distance down the road, until you see a wide, graded, gravel road on the right. Directly opposite this road is the trailhead: a narrow opening between alders that follows the route of the Old Trans-Canada Highway. There is just about enough parking off the side of the road, or up the gravel road on the right.

Sources of additional information: In Newfoundland, almost everyone is a source of information. With respect to this ride, depending on how resourceful you are, you may find yourself duplicating our experiences, riding with a father-and-son team who have explored this area extensively by bike.

Notes on the trail: Begin riding along a rather overgrown path that follows the old route of the Trans-Canada Highway. Alders line both sides of the trail, which is hard-packed, quite rocky, and eroded over some sections. You will be following the trail along a fairly straight course. After some distance, and at the first clear opportunity, turn right at a three-way intersection of trails. You will be turning off the Old Trans-Canada Highway, which continues straight ahead, and following a grassy, sometimes rocky, double-track cart trail.

The cart trail will lead you downhill, toward the community of Sunnyside. As you approach the outskirts of town, you will come to some homes. Follow the most direct route down toward a paved road, respecting the private property you must briefly pass through to get there. You will emerge on pavement at a point near a three-way intersection. The road immediately on the left merely drops down to some homes. Be sure to follow the main road through Sunnyside, bearing left across a small bridge that spans a stream running into Bull Arm. At this point in the ride, you will be beginning the 3.25-km (2-mile) spur that connects the two loops.

Just across the bridge, you will see the Brookside Hospitality Home on the left. The driveway leading up to Brookside continues beyond the house, and is the beginning of the optional side trip you can take up to the Pig's Snout at the end of the ride. Continuing past Brookside Hospitality Home, you will ride through the community of Sunnyside. Pass the Pentecostal Tabernacle on the left side of the road and Foodtown on the right. A short distance past Foodtown, turn left up a gravel access road toward a small cemetery. This road heads uphill between a trailer house and a bungalow, and seems to lead to a tower topped with an antenna. The turnoff is unmarked, but you will know that you have missed it if you continue on the main road and pass a small pier jutting out into the bay on your right.

As you head up the gravel access road, the cemetery will be on your left. Bear right as you approach the crest of the hill, connecting with a trail outside a subdivision. You will come to a junction with a paved road, directly at the point at which the road makes a right angle with itself. Ride straight onto the paved road.

On the paved road, you will ride past the Sunnyside post office on the right. Continue straight through a four-way intersection. Then, as the paved road turns sharply to the left, continue straight onto another cart trail, which branches off the right side of the road across a grassy, barren area. Follow this path, which drops down a very steep bank into a playground. From the playground, carefully cross an old bridge over a small stream and follow the access road out of the park, heading uphill and to the right. As you reach the crest of the hill, turn left and ride toward a worn, narrow, single-track trail that climbs steeply up into the barrens and along the high bluffs overlooking Bull Arm.

As you make your way through this stark, dramatic landscape, follow the most obvious trail over a series of tough climbs. You will eventually descend to a boggy area at the base of a low, ridgelike hill. This point marks the beginning and the end of the second loop of the ride. Keep to the right side of the ridge, and follow a trail that climbs up out of the boggy area and toward Bull Arm. The trail on which you will return to complete this loop is on the left. Be careful not to follow the trail farthest to the right, which merely descends through a small, shale rock slide back down to the main road.

From the high bluff overlooking Bull Arm, the trail continues and will lead you steeply downhill to a dirt road. Turn left when you reach the dirt road, and follow it out to its junction with a paved road. Turning right on this paved road will return you, quite quickly, to the centre of town. To continue the ride, turn left and follow the paved road a short distance to a bridge. Just before the bridge, look for a trail on the left. Bear left onto this trail, which is a rather rough and rutted double-track trail.

At the first fork in this trail, bear left. Then, when you reach a **T** junction, turn left. At a second fork in the trail, there may be some flagging tape in a tree on the right. Continue to bear left here, following the trail that seems to go straight. At the next opportunity, make a sharp left turn onto a new trail, which may also be marked with flagging tape. You will ride through an open, somewhat boggy area as you follow this trail around a low, ridgelike hill, which will be on your left. As you curve around the side of this hill, you will find yourself back at the low-lying boggy area at the beginning of the loop. Bear right up out of the boggy area, and begin riding back along the path you followed in.

You will retrace your route over the hilly, undulating terrain of this portion of the ride. When you drop down the final, steep hill to the access road for the playground, turn right. Ride back down the access road into the playground, and carefully cross back over the bridge again. Follow the same trail that you rode down, back up the steep slope rising from the playground. Continue to follow the trail back toward the residential area and the subdivision, retracing your route on the short stretch of pavement that passes the post office. Continue straight onto the trail you followed out, as the paved road follows a sharp, right-angle turn to the right. You will approach the small cemetery. Bear left, back down the gravel access road to the main paved road through Sunnyside. Follow the pavement back to the entrance to the Brookside Hospitality Home. Here you have the choice of completing the ride and following the pavement back to the trailhead, or of turning up the trail to the Pig's Snout.

For the side trip to the Pig's Snout, turn right up the driveway to the Brookside Hospitality Home. At the end of the driveway you will be able to continue riding along a double-track cart track. Keeping to the main trail, past all side trails on the left and right, you will climb to a small knoll around which bog extends in all directions. At the top of the Snout you are essentially surrounded by bog and cannot proceed any farther. From here, you will be able to appreciate the landscape you have come across. After enjoying the view, simply retrace your route back to the road.

Back on the main road, turn right and ride back across the bridge over the river. At the three-way intersection beyond the bridge, bear left and follow the paved road up toward the Trans-Canada Highway. You will climb on pavement for less than 2 km (1.25 miles) before reaching the trailhead and the wide gravel road directly across from it on the left.

RIDE 53 • Clarenville

AT A GLANCE

Length/configuration: 24-km (15-mile) combination (12-km [7.5-mile] loop with two out-and-back spurs; initial spur 4 km [2.5 miles] each way, second spur 2 km [1.25 miles] each way)

Aerobic difficulty: For fit riders; significant amounts of climbing on two extended ascents

Technical difficulty: Moderate; wide trails with several eroded descents that traverse areas of deep, loose rock

Scenery: This ride climbs through a wooded hillside into rocky, glacially sculpted barrens

Special comments: Spectacular view overlooking Random Island and out toward Trinity Bay

Clarenville is the access town to the Bonavista Peninsula, nestled against a backdrop of low mountains and looking out across Random Island toward Trinity Bay. This 24-km (15-mile) combination ride climbs to a former communications tower site, where sweeping views extend in every direction. Beginning in Clarenville, the ride follows the multi-use trail along a converted railroad bed heading out of town. You will turn off this initial spur (which climbs gradually but steadily) and descend on an eroded cart track, before picking up an old access road and riding up to the top of the former communications tower site. This point is certainly the highlight of the ride, as it offers grand views in all directions. On a clear day, you will be able to look out over Random Island and far across Trinity Bay. The ride concludes with a long, gradual descent from the former communications tower site along the rail trail back into town. Overall, the ride demands intermediate-level biking skills and good cardiovascular endurance.

General location: Clarenville is located off of the Trans-Canada Highway, at the base of three of Newfoundland's easternmost peninsulas: the Avalon Peninsula, the Bonavista Peninsula, and the Burin Peninsula.

Elevation change: You will begin riding from an elevation just above the northwest arm of Random Sound at 23 m (75 feet) above sea level. You will climb to approximately 76 m (250 feet), before descending to 30 m (100 feet), and then turning back uphill to reach the highest point on the ride at the old communi-

RIDE 53 · Clarenville

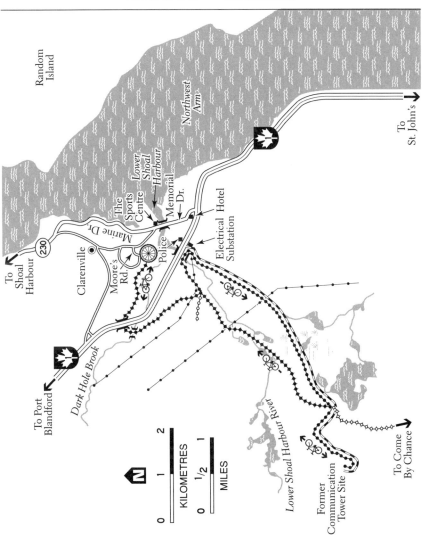

cations site at 274 m (900 feet). From that point, the return ride is all downhill. Total elevation gain for the ride is almost 300 m (1,000 feet).

Season: Good riding conditions can be enjoyed from June through September, with August and July being the warmest and most reliable months for fine weather.

Services: All services are available in Clarenville.

Hazards: Use caution over areas of loose rock, particularly along the rail trail, where heavy ballast can easily take you by surprise and abruptly slow the pace of your descent.

ATLANTIC CANADA

Jodi's victorious arrival at the former communications tower site overlooking Trinity Bay.

Rescue index: From the top of the old communications site, you will be approximately 6.5 km (4 miles) from the nearest source of assistance. It is, however, quite likely that you will encounter other riders or ATVs on this trail.

Land status: Multi-use recreational trail and old access roads with public rights-of-way.

Maps: Topographic maps are available from the government offices building in Clarenville. The two maps relevant to this ride are Random Island 2 C/4 and Tug Pond 2 D/1.

Finding the trail: Traveling west on the Trans-Canada Highway from the Avalon Peninsula, turn right at the first Clarenville exit and begin driving along Memorial Drive. You will cross over a bridge before entering a commercial area and passing The Sports Centre on your right. Bear left at a fork, turning off of Marine Drive, which continues to the right. A short distance beyond this point, turn left on Moore's Road. Follow Moore's Road around to the left. The road soon forks, and the rail trail begins at the middle of the fork. There should be ample space for parking off the road here. The ride begins up the rail trail.

Source of additional information: The staff at The Sports Centre can provide you with additional information about riding and events in the Clarenville area.

The Sports Centre
347 Memorial Drive
Clarenville, NF A0E 1J0
(709) 466-2412

Notes on the trail: The rail trail is easy to follow as it leaves the centre of Clarenville. You will ride beneath the Trans-Canada Highway through a tunnel, and then cross an old railroad trestle. Beyond the trestle, the rail trail begins to climb gradually.

After crossing beneath a power line, begin looking for a four-way intersection that is just a short distance farther up the trail. Here, you will see an indistinct, grassy, double-track trail on the right, and a rougher dirt road on the left. Ahead of you, the rail trail begins to swing to the right. Turn left at this intersection, and begin descending on the unpaved access road, avoiding all side trails. This road will bring you down past a garage, and all the way to the Trans-Canada Highway. Turn right on the Trans-Canada Highway, and pedal on pavement for just a short distance to cross a small bridge. Immediately after pedaling over the bridge, turn right on Plant Road, an unpaved access road overshadowed by an electrical substation. You will begin climbing almost immediately. At a fork in the road, bear left along the less developed road and continue to climb.

The access road is easy to follow and climbs steadily, past several clearings and to a transmission line. Continue straight beneath the transmission line, following the road as it begins to descend. Ride past a road branching off on the left. The trail, which has been bordered by alders, eventually opens up into a more barren landscape, with ponds and bog on both sides. You will pass a small sawmill on the right, and another road branching off on the left. Just beyond this junction, you will come to a four-way intersection with the rail trail. Cross the rail trail and continue straight, following a four-wheel-drive access road that continues to climb to what was once the site of a communications tower. At a fork in the road, bear left and continue riding to the top. From the gravel clearing that remains at the top, you will get a spectacular view of the surrounding area, including Clarenville and Random Island, the White Hills, and the distinct Centre Hill in Summerside.

To continue the ride, descend back to the intersection with the rail trail. Turn left and follow the rail trail all the way back to the trailhead. You will pass the turnoff that took you down to the Trans-Canada Highway on the right. Enjoy the descent!

RIDE 54 • Dunphy's Pond

AT A GLANCE

Length/configuration: 10-km (6-mile) out-and-back (5 km [3 miles] each way)

Aerobic difficulty: Requires a modest level of cardiovascular fitness

Technical difficulty: Suitable for beginning-level riders with good bike handling skills

Scenery: You will ride through boreal forest to the picturesque shore of Dunphy's Pond

Special comments: Dunphy's Pond offers ideal opportunities for swimming and camping

Dunphy's Pond is the largest lake in Terra Nova National Park, and this ride follows one of the few multi-use trails open to riders visiting the park. The trail follows a former access road that creates a 10-km (6-mile) out-and-back ride that provides easy access to the pond and a number of backcountry campsites nearby. Although there is some steady climbing on the way out, this ride is aerobically and technically suitable for all levels. Families and groups of riders will discover this to be an ideal excursion, since the trail is easy to follow and wide enough for two people to ride abreast. Furthermore, Dunphy's Pond is a picturesque site at which to enjoy a picnic lunch or a refreshing swim. For riders seeking more of an adventure, we recommend that you use this trail to begin an overnight trip to the pond and back. Registration is necessary for use of the campsites, and permits can be obtained at the Newman Sound Campground Kiosk or the Marine Interpretation Centre.

The Dunphy's Pond Trail is one of two primary trails open to mountain bikers visiting Terra Nova National Park. The other is Blue Hill West. Our trip to the park coincided with the nesting of a Gos Hawk at one point along the Blue Hill West Trail. Common throughout Newfoundland, these birds can be very aggressive and will chase interlopers away from their nesting sites. As luck would have it, the Blue Hill West Trail offers an ideal nesting habitat for Gos Hawks, and every few years the trail is closed anywhere from June through August. Although we were unable to explore the trail as a result, keep it in mind as an alternative or additional ride to Dunphy's Pond.

General location: Terra Nova National Park, located between Gander and Clarenville on the Trans-Canada Highway.

RIDE 54 • Dunphy's Pond

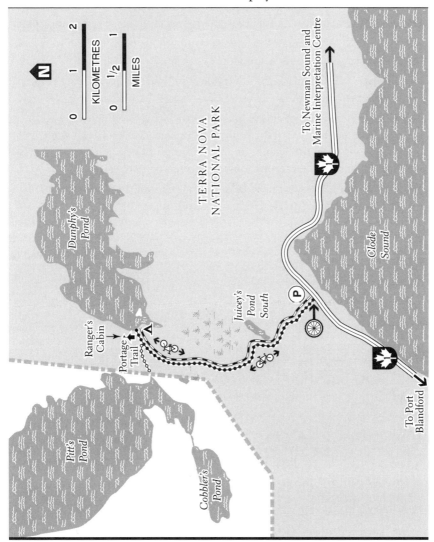

Elevation change: From the parking area at the trailhead, you will be at approximately 30.5 m (100 feet). You will climb gradually to 137 m (450 feet), before descending to the pond at approximately 91.5 m (300 feet). Total elevation change for the out-and-back ride is 304 m (1,000 feet).

Season: The Dunphy's Pond Trail is a relatively dry ride, and conditions should be good from mid-May through October.

Services: The park operates with full services from June through October, though hours are reduced after Labour Day in early September. For bicycle supplies and service, your closest source is in Clarenville.

Hazards: Several of the culverts across this old access road have become exposed.

Rescue index: At the pond, the farthest point on this ride, you will be 5 km (3 miles) from assistance, unless the ranger's cabin is occupied.

Land status: National park; from mid-May to mid-October there is an entry fee for all visitors to the park.

Maps: There are maps of all the trails at Terra Nova National Park available at the park headquarters and at the southern entrance to the park. This ride is easy to follow along its entire length, and you should not need more than the park map to supplement the information we have included here.

Finding the trail: The trailhead is located in the southwest corner of the park, directly off the Trans-Canada Highway. Curiously enough, the trailhead is not well marked in advance, and the sign for the small parking area is difficult to see until you have driven past it. The trailhead is located 27 km (16.7 miles) from the Marine Interpretation Centre. There is enough parking at the trailhead for three or four vehicles.

Source of additional information:

Terra Nova National Park
Glovertown, NF A0G 2L0
(709) 533-2291

Notes on the trail: There is a sign at the trailhead providing some information about the ride and the boreal bird species that you may encounter en route. Begin riding past the gate, along an old access road. The ride follows this road all the way to Dunphy's Pond, so it really is not possible to lose the trail. You will begin riding along a forested, grassy section of the trail. However, as the road begins to climb, you will encounter much rockier trail conditions. Some areas of fairly heavy loose rock and gravel will slow your pace as you ascend a series of gentle but steady grades. Fortunately, the road surface does improve, and at the crest of the hill, you will get a rewarding glimpse of Dunphy's Pond. The descent to the pond is short and fast, and you will arrive at the shore abruptly. There are washroom facilities, several backcountry campsites, and a picnic area nearby, as well as a ranger's cabin. Enjoy the pond before turning back to retrace your route to the trailhead. The return trip is much faster, as you will climb for just a short distance before a long, rolling cruise back downhill to the parking area.

RIDE 55 • Trailway Provincial Park: Gander

AT A GLANCE

Length/configuration: 20-km (12.4-mile) out-and-back (10 km [6.2 miles] each way), with a maze of additional short trails to explore

Aerobic difficulty: Easy; only slight grades along a rails-to-trails recreational trail

Technical difficulty: Wide, graded, crushed-rock surface, suitable for all skill levels

Scenery: A ride through a demonstration forest, past a former town site, and out to Deadman's Pond

Special comments: This ride follows a portion of Newfoundland's Trailway Provincial Park and makes an excellent family outing

The Town of Gander is located at the middle of a section of Newfoundland's Trailway Provincial Park called Cobb's Corridor. The park is being developed through the initiative of a non-profit corporation called the Newfoundland Trailway Council, and will one day extend as a recreational trail from St. John's to Channel-Port-aux-Basques. Following the old Canadian National Railway line, this multi-use trail and park will be Newfoundland's link of the Trans-Canada Trail, a multi-use recreational trail extending 15,000 km (9,300 miles) across the country from St. John's, Newfoundland, to Victoria, British Columbia. Cobb's Corridor is a section of this trail that extends through Gander, traversing 46 km (28.5 miles) between the communities of Benton, to the east, and Glenwood, to the west. As of the time of this book's printing, riders could follow the trail even beyond these points to create a long, 90-km (56-mile) tour between Gambo and Louisport Junction. Further development on the trail will open up even more opportunities for multi-day and long point-to-point excursions between these communities.

This ride begins on the trail in downtown Gander and heads east, through a site that was once developed as a military settlement, out to Deadman's Pond. Much of the ride passes through an area designated as the Thomas Howe Demonstration Forest, and the landscape is a combination of forest and open bog. The trail is wide and well maintained, and provides an easy surface to ride along. There are no significant hills throughout the length of the trail, which makes a perfect outing for families or large groups. In the area of the former town site, a park is being developed, and all the old roads and trails have been exposed.

RIDE 55 • Trailway Provincial Park: Gander

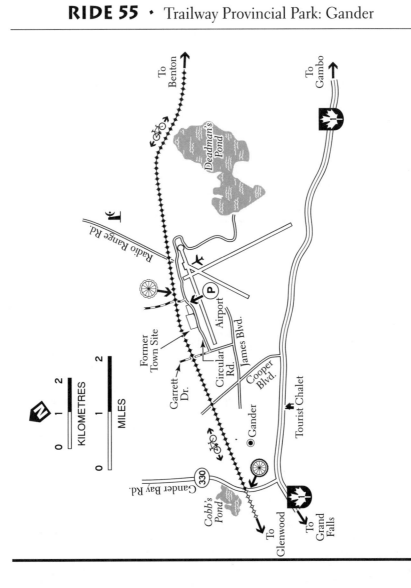

The result is a network of interconnecting trails that can be explored as a short side trip off the railway bed. The park includes a wooden viewing gazebo that is the perfect vantage point from which to watch airplanes taking off and landing at the nearby Gander International Airport. Along with a small playground, this site is sure to be a favourite among younger riders.

General location: Gander is located in central Newfoundland, approximately 76 km (less than 50 miles) west of Terra Nova National Park, and roughly the same distance east of Grand Falls.

Elevation change: This ride follows a recreational trail along an old railroad bed, with virtually no change in elevation.

Season: Trailway Provincial Park is open year-round. The best conditions for cyclists begin in June and continue through September.

Services: All services are available in Gander.

Hazards: None.

Rescue index: This portion of the former railroad never veers too far from the Trans-Canada Highway. From the town of Gander to Deadman's Pond, you will not venture more than 5 km (3 miles) from assistance. For those who choose to extend this ride, assistance can be sought in both Benton and Glenwood.

Land status: This multi-use recreational trail forms part of Trailway Provincial Park.

Maps: The official highway map for Newfoundland highlights the route of the former railroad in red and references it as the Trailway Provincial Park. For a more detailed view of the area, refer to *Newfoundland Maps* (map 25, sections E-1 and F-1). For the most recent information and maps for the trail, stop in at the Tourist Chalet in Gander, located on the Trans-Canada Highway.

Finding the trail: From the Tourist Chalet on the Trans-Canada Highway in Gander, drive west on the highway until you reach its junction with Route 330, Gander Bay Road. Turn right up Route 330, and drive less than 1 km (0.6 mile) before reaching Trailway Park, just before coming to Cobbs Pond on the left. The recreational trail extends toward Glenwood to the left and Benton to the right. Should you wish to plan a shorter ride along the Trailway, the former town site near Gander International Airport makes another good starting point. To reach the site, turn right from the Tourist Chalet on the Trans-Canada Highway and travel east for a short distance. Turn left up Cooper Boulevard, and when you reach a four-way intersection, turn right onto James Boulevard. As you approach the airport on James Boulevard, turn left on Garrett Drive, and continue for less than 1 km (0.6 mile) before turning right on Circular Road. Approximately 1 km (0.6 mile) along Circular Road, you will come to a small parking area and viewing gazebo on the left. To reach the recreational trail from this parking area, backtrack along Circular Road for a very short distance and then turn right down Chestnut Road, one of the former town site roads. Follow Chestnut Road straight to a **T** junction with the rail trail. Turn right to begin riding toward Deadman's Pond and Benton.

Source of additional information: For further information or to find out how to get involved with the development of Trailway Park near your community, contact:

Newfoundland Trailway Council
P.O. Box 306
Gander, NF A1V 1W7
(709) 256-8833

Notes on the trail: Begin riding along the portion of the recreational trail that extends to the right off Route 330 and heads east toward Benton. You will ride through the town of Gander, passing several more sites from which the trail can be accessed and crossing a series of paved roads. The trail heads in the direction of Gander International Airport.

After crossing Cooper Boulevard and Garrett Drive, the trail enters a protected area designated as the Thomas Howe Demonstration Forest. To the right of the trail is the former town site, where a military community of 10,000 residents once thrived. This area is crisscrossed with trails that can easily be explored by bike, and extends up to an unpaved road, Circular Road, that parallels the northern boundary of Gander International Airport.

From the town site, the ride continues to follow the path of the former railroad bed. The route is clear and easy to follow. As you approach Deadman's Pond, some stretches of the trail may be washboarded. The trail opens up through an area of bog, and Deadman's Pond will be visible to the right. Turn around and retrace your route back to Gander, or continue riding for as long as you wish, heading on toward Benton. Outside Benton, there is a small trestle bridge over Burnt Brook.

RIDE 56 • Marble Mountain Summit Trail

AT A GLANCE

Length/configuration: 9-km (5-mile) combination (7-km [4.2-mile] loop with out-and-back spur; spur is 1 km [0.6 mile] each way)

Aerobic difficulty: Advanced; a long steady climb on a dirt road to the top of the mountain

Technical difficulty: Suitable for intermediate and advanced riders with a need for speed

Scenery: Panoramic view over the Humber River Valley from the top of the mountain.

Special comments: Riding a chair lift to the top is not an option

In addition to boasting the best skiing east of the Rockies, Marble Mountain can also lay claim to the longest downhill and most rigorous cardiovascular workout for mountain bikers in Atlantic Canada. The ride to the summit is by far the longest sustained climb and the most elevation gained on a single hill in

RIDE 56 • Marble Mountain Summit Trail

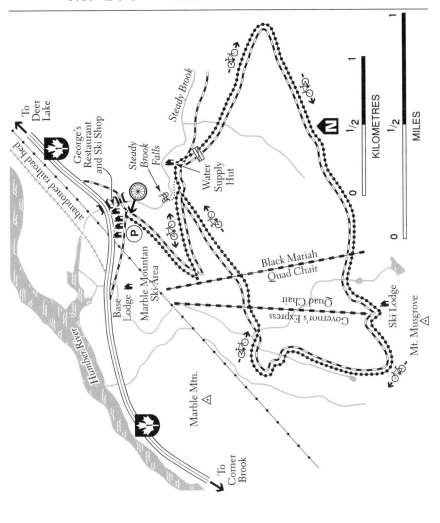

all four provinces. The 450 m (1,700 feet) gained on this ride match, metre for metre, the intensity more typical of trails in Alberta and British Columbia. Furthermore, this climb up Marble Mountain offers equally rewarding views all the way to the top.

The 9-km (5-mile) combination winds up the eastern edge of Marble Mountain and returns riders down its front face on a 7-km (4.2-mile) loop, before reconnecting with the 1-km (0.6-mile) spur to the trailhead. Both the climb and the descent offer a challenge to recreational and competitive riders alike, and the steady climb on loose dirt favours fit riders with good climbing

A view of the Humber River Valley rewards riders who survive the climb to the summit of Marble Mountain.

skills. The descent offers the choice of a technical downhill for truly hard-core riders, or an intermediate cruise on a wide, open road that will satisfy any rider's need for speed. While the descent is the part of the ride most riders will always remember, there are also fabulous views of the Humber River Valley and Humber Arm from the summit.

General location: Just 5 minutes east of Corner Brook, off the Trans-Canada Highway.

Elevation change: Gain 450 m (1,476 feet) on the steady climb to the top, and lose them swiftly on the descent to the parking area. Total elevation change for this ride is 900 m (2,952 feet)

Season: The gravel access road to the summit will permit riding from June to October. However, July, August, and September are the ideal months for riding if you want to avoid even small amounts of rain and fog.

Services: There is a convenience store and service station near the trailhead. All other services are available in nearby Corner Brook.

Hazards: Heed the drainage ditches on the descent or you may find yourself performing inverted aerial maneuvers.

Rescue index: Marble Mountain rises up from the side of the Trans-Canada Highway, and there are shops at the trailhead where you will easily find assistance.

Land status: Public access is permitted on this privately owned ski hill.

Maps: The access road to the top of Marble appears on government topographic map 12 A/13.

Finding the trail: From Corner Brook, take the Trans-Canada Highway east and follow signs for Marble Mountain. The mountain is just a few kilometres outside the city and is clearly signed from the highway. From the exit, continue past the parking lot along a service road, until you reach a small cluster of buildings, which include George's Restaurant and Ski Shop. A short distance past George's, turn right onto a dirt road heading up Marble Mountain. There is a sign for the Western Newfoundland Model Forest Network, as well as an informal parking area that will accommodate a few cars.

Sources of additional information: The Western Newfoundland Model Forest Network distributes a mountain biking brochure through Visitor Information Centres and bike stores throughout the province. It includes a map and other trail suggestions in the Corner Brook area. Contact the Western Newfoundland Model Forest Network at (709) 634-6383, or T & T Cycles, who helped produce the brochure, at (709) 634-6799, for further information.

Notes on the trail: Begin riding up the unpaved access road for Marble Mountain. The road begins on a moderate slope of hard-packed gravel. A short distance up the hill, you will pass a hiking trail on the left that is signed for Steady Brook Falls. Continue straight on the access road, heading toward the chairlift. At the chairlift, ride past the trail on the right that continues under the lift, and bear left on the access road, continuing up a switchback. The grade becomes steeper around the bend to the left, and climbs steadily to an opening at a water supply hut. At the hut you can abandon your bike and take a side trip to a look-off over Steady Brook Falls. The trail to the look-off is just a short distance down the hill to the left. After dropping down the embankment, there is an opening in the woods on the right. A narrow, well-traveled trail leads through the trees to the falls.

Back at the water supply hut, you will continue to climb. Bear right at a fork in the road, continuing uphill past a barrier to vehicular traffic. As you continue up the access road, you can look to your left and see the edge of the road drop off into a forested valley. On your right, a rocky wall that was carved into the mountain when the road was blasted in leads onward and upward. The trail becomes more difficult beyond the barrier, with loose gravel adding more resistance to the climb. Farther ahead, the road switchbacks to the right and presents a short, steep climb on a more eroded slope. Beyond this section, the road levels off briefly, and then resumes climbing more gradually. This section of climbing ends at the top of the quadruple chairlift, where there is a Canadian ski patrol hut and a race board. Having completed nearly two-thirds of the climb, this site offers an opportunity to rest briefly and take in the view of the green and rolling Humber River Valley.

Beyond this point, the road levels off briefly and even offers a short descent. It continues obviously to the left at the next fork, but you will actually branch to the right, continuing toward the second chairlift. Bearing right at the fork, you will descend briefly and cross a small stream before beginning the final climb. The final ascent follows under the new quad and leads up to the ski hut at the top of the hill. The hut has a deck, and it is an excellent spot to stop and view the spectacular coast, forest, and hills that are characteristic of the surrounding Newfoundland landscape. For the return trip, there are two popular options: a hurtling black-diamond descent that is tackled by the downhill racers, and the service road that follows the intermediate blue runs. Unless you have a heavy-duty bike and appropriate padding for such downhills, the latter option is recommended.

To follow the service road, descend a short distance under the chairlift and then bear left, following signs for the three blue-rated ski runs. After crossing the top of the hill the road bends to the right and begins to descend. The initial incline is quite steep, and levels off only slightly as you head toward the mid-section of the hill. At the half way point on the hill, the road begins to level off. At this point, beware of the drainage ditches that appear suddenly as gaps in the gravel surface—caught at a wrong angle, you will find yourself over your handlebars, gazing at the blue skies overhead. Beyond this first drainage ditch, the road curves to the right, and you will traverse the mid-section of the hill. Ignore the more direct routes to the bottom offered by the ski runs, and continue on the service road. You will climb a short hill and eventually emerge back near the water supply hut. Bear left onto the gravel access road, and retrace your tracks on this final descent to the trailhead.

RIDE 57 • Massey Drive

AT A GLANCE

Length/configuration: 24-km (15-mile) combination (one 6-km [3.75-mile] loop and one 18-km [11.25-mile] loop)

Aerobic difficulty: Tough; very little relief from climbing or technical terrain

Technical difficulty: Intermediate to advanced riding on a combination of dirt roads, and double- and single-track trails

Scenery: Watch the rider in front of you get really dirty

Special comments: The maze of trails in and around Massey Drive is an urban biker's paradise

The network of trails in and around the community of Massey Drive offers a sufficient variety of single- and double-track trails to keep beginning to advanced riders occupied. However, no matter what your skill level, you have to be willing to perform several highway crossings to complete the 24-km (15-mile) combination ride described here. For most of the ride, you will follow rocky single- and double-track trails through the woods and under power lines. There are occasional moments of relief from the technical terrain and climbing, during brief stretches on gravel roads and pavement. Local riders favour this circuit because it offers challenging terrain within a close proximity to the city. However, the price of this convenience is the fact that you never lose sight of the power lines, industry, and main transportation routes that service Corner Brook.

The ride begins with a 6-km (3.75-mile) loop on the trails behind the community of Massey Drive, and ends on an extended loop on the other side of the Trans-Canada Highway. Behind Massey Drive is an area dense with intermediate single- and double-track trails that are used for racing and frequented by riders honing their skills throughout the season. As overgrown trails are discovered and resurrected every year, expect to plough through some mud and to battle groping alders along some sections of the trail. The second 18-km (11.25-mile) loop follows sections of single- and double-track trails, mostly under power lines and gravel roads. Adding to the urban feel of this ride are several crossings of the Trans-Canada Highway, and a short stretch that traces the backyards of some houses on your final return to the trailhead. That said, there is no other ride in the area that will offer the technical challenge or the cardiovascular workout of this ride. At the end of the ride you too may find yourself torn between praising its length and variety, and making unfavourable comments about trails that follow pole lines and the incongruity of performing highway crossings on your mountain bike.

General location: West of Corner Brook, off of the Trans-Canada Highway.

Elevation change: Frequent climbs on dirt roads, and single- and double-track trails, for a total gain of 230 m (754 feet).

Season: The Corner Brook area enjoys the warmest and sunniest summer days in Newfoundland. While the boggy sections of the trail are always wet, you can expect to find mostly dry conditions on the rest of the trail from June through September.

Services: All services are available in Corner Brook.

Hazards: You will cross the Trans-Canada Highway several times over the course of this ride. Exercise great caution, ensuring that there is lots of space between the cars that will be approaching from both directions.

Rescue index: Throughout the ride you are never far from the community of Massey Drive or the Trans-Canada Highway.

Land status: All trails traverse Crown land.

RIDE 57 • Massey Drive

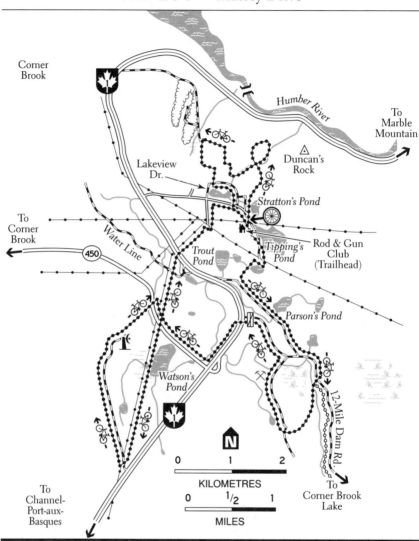

Maps: Some of the trails are highlighted in a map featured in Doug Miller's *Mountain Biking in and around Corner Brook*. You should also refer to government topographic map Corner Brook 12 A/13.

Finding the trail: From Corner Brook, follow signs for the Trans-Canada Highway, heading west toward Channel-Port-aux-Basques. Just beyond the city limits, you will turn left onto Massey Drive, into the town of the same name. Follow Massey Drive to the Bay of Islands Rod and Gun Club, which is located beyond the crest of the hill, where the pavement turns to gravel. Ample parking is available in the area surrounding the lodge.

Source of additional information: Consult Doug Miller's *Mountain Biking in and around Corner Brook* for additional rides and photographs of the trail. The booklet is available at local bike stores.

Notes on the trail: Departing from the Bay of Islands Rod and Gun Club at the end of Massey Drive, backtrack past a few houses along the pavement and turn right onto a dirt trail. Continue straight along the trail to a **T** junction, and bear right. The trail narrows to a single-track and bends sharply to the left. Around the bend, it climbs to a **Y** intersection with two grassy trails. Bear right and continue to the next fork, where you will bear left. A very short distance along the left branch, you will bear right, continuing to follow the somewhat overgrown single-track in a southerly direction. Continue to bear right, past a trail branching off to the left to complete a small loop. At the time of our research, this was a recently resurrected trail and somewhat overgrown. However, the trail surface is in excellent condition, and with more use, this loop will become a favourite, which makes the battle with the groping alders worthwhile.

Back at the start of the loop, continue straight, past the trail you entered on the right, to the next intersection with a grassy trail. The left branch leads back to Massey Drive, and the ride continues to the right. Following the grassy double-track to the right, it narrows to a single-track as you approach a narrow field. There is a worn trail through the field that branches to the right, following its perimeter. Across the field, you will come to a **T** junction with a grassy double-track. Turn right. The trail climbs gradually toward the bush, but as you enter the bush, it narrows to a single-track and winds downhill to the right. A trail merges from the left, and then you round a bend to the left. Around the bend, you will pass through one of the permanently wet areas—crossing a deep puddle. The view of other riders splashing through here is spectacular! The next section of riding features short stretches of more technical terrain. The trail then widens and begins to climb, becoming rockier, until you actually reach a large patch of exposed bedrock. Here, turn left onto a single-track and head back into the bush.

At this point, you will be following a fun stretch of intermediate single-track with just a few exposed roots and rocks. The trail will, however, drop suddenly down a steep hill over a combination of large exposed roots and rocks. At the bottom of the drop you must make a sharp turn to the left, following a single-track trail. You will cross to the left through an open grassy area surrounded by alders and come to a **T** junction. Turn right, following the wider double-track trail. From here, you get a view of a radio tower and begin to descend. The descent will send you hurtling down a gravel slope with a few opportunities to catch some air. Just before the end of the descent, the trail drops off quite steeply, bringing you to a four-way intersection with a grassy trail. If you were to continue straight, you would reach the paved Lakeview Drive and soon arrive at a **T** junction with Massey Drive. Instead, turn left and follow the grassy trail along the edge of a pond. Arriving at the next **T** junction with a gravel road, turn right and descend to Massey Drive.

Turn left at the pavement on Massey Drive and return to the parking area at the Bay of Islands Rod and Gun Club. When the pavement turns to gravel, continue straight, past the lodge, following the wide dirt road. You will pass Tipping's Pond on the left and continue to a large-scale transmission line. With the power line in view, look for two trails branching off to the right. Take the first one, which jogs back up in the direction of your right shoulder. This trail follows the transmission line to a three-way intersection, where you will turn left, away from the transmission line. You will descend from the transmission line on rolling terrain, bouncing over many roots and rocks that are otherwise concealed by boggy mud and grass. At the bottom of the hill you will reach a vague **T** junction. The trail continues obviously to the left, but to the right you can follow a narrower trail to the highway to return to Massey Drive or proceed down to Margaret Bowater Park. To continue on this ride, turn left onto the wide gravel trail and ride to a **T** junction with 12-Mile Dam Road. To the right, the road continues out to the Trans-Canada Highway, but you will turn left onto 12-Mile Dam Road. From this road, you can also complete a 20-km (12.4-mile) loop with Lady Slipper Road (see Ride 59).

Turn left, and follow 12-Mile Dam Road a very short distance. Almost immediately, turn right onto a narrow trail. An enormous puddle is within view from the start of the trail, and you can see that there is only one way to continue. Hanging behind the group, this is another excellent spot to view riders getting soaked and muddy, and sometimes taking an involuntary dip in this small pool. Beyond the puddle, the trail continues as a double-track leading toward the woods. Continuing on the double-track, you will pass a pond, and then a quarry on your right, and you will ride through a clear-cut area. Past the clear-cut, the trail narrows and passes through a row of low-hanging, groping alders. As you approach the end of the alder row, the trail curves to the right, and you will be faced with a steep incline up an embankment, which drops just as steeply over the other side. Over the hump, you will find yourself on a wider gravel road with a grassy median. Turn right. Continuing ahead, you will pass a quarry on the left, and to your right will be the logging road on which you started the loop. At a **T** junction, bear left to continue toward the highway. At the end of the road you will come to a gate that you can either hike your bike over or ride around to the right, following a narrow single-track to the other side. To continue the ride, carefully cross the highway and turn left.

You will ride along the shoulder of the Trans-Canada Highway to the first exit. Turn off the highway at this exit, and continue past Watson's Pond Industrial Park on the left. You will cross over a bridge and then turn left (again crossing the highway) to follow a dirt trail that runs under a power line. This is a rocky dirt trail that begins with a descent and is followed by climbs up two steep hills. At the end of the second hill the trail continues to roll under the power lines to a fork. Bear right at the fork onto a gravel road, which leads to the base of a NewTel communications tower. From the tower, make your way to the narrow single-track trail that runs beneath the telephone line. The trail is quite rocky for a stretch beyond the tower and then continues as a grassy single-track. A final descent brings you to the highway, where you will turn right. Continue along the shoulder for a short distance, and then cross the highway to turn left onto the trail that runs under the power line. This trail is directly opposite the power line under which you rode out to the communications tower. Following under these power lines, you will soon arrive at a **T** junction with a double-track trail. Turning left, you will continue, parallel to the water line that provides power to the mill in Corner Brook, and arrive in downtown. To continue on this ride, turn right.

The double-track trail descends gradually to the right and then swings to the left and crosses a double set of bridges. After the bridges, the trail continues as a gravel road all the way to an orange gate. Skirt around the gate and cross the paved road, continuing up the gravel road signed "Hydro Massey Drive Terminal Station" on the other side. Turn right at the terminal station and, just a short distance beyond, bear left at a three-way intersection of grassy trails, which will take you under the power lines. From this trail, you will turn right under another, shorter power line. At the peach-coloured house, bear left and continue on a trail that traces along the edge of some backyards. A steep, rocky hill drops you to Massey Drive. At the bottom you are directly across from Lakeview Drive, or the end of the first loop. Turn right to return to the parking area at the Bay of Islands Rod and Gun Club.

RIDE 58 · Pinchgut Lake

AT A GLANCE

Length/configuration: 27-km (16.8-mile) out-and-back (13.5 km [8.4 miles] each way)

Aerobic difficulty: Intermediate to advanced; the return trip features one extended climb

Technical difficulty: Intermediate; combination of current and old logging roads

Scenery: Woods and lots of puddles!

Special comments: Ride can be linked with Ride 59 for a longer excursion

Rumour has it that this ride follows a trail that links up with the camp road around Pinchgut Lake. At the time of our research, the ride could easily have been renamed "Where is Pinchgut Lake?" to reflect the fact that no one we encountered had ever actually made it to the lake. Our interest was sufficiently piqued, and in the spirit of leaving no stone unturned, we set out on one

RIDE 58 • Pinchgut Lake

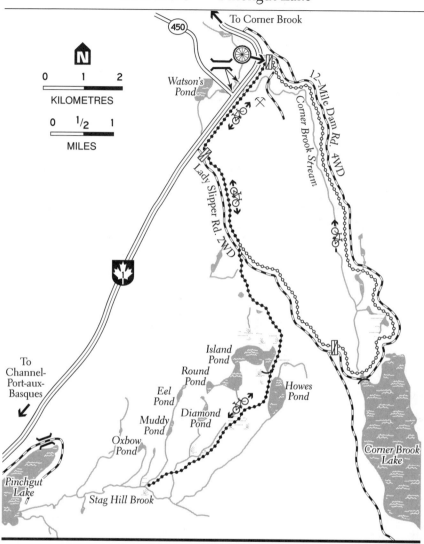

fine evening in August determined to solve the mystery. Accompanied by a large group of enthusiastic local riders, our journey progressed quickly. However, due to circumstances beyond our control at the time, we did not become the first riders to conclude this epic journey at the elusive shores of Pinchgut Lake. Judging from the topographic map of the area, it seems possible to ride out to the lake, if you allow plenty of time to explore the trail in daylight.

Nevertheless, the trail makes a fun ride even without the lake as a destination. The route we describe is a 27-km (16.8-mile) out-and-back that wanders some-

Puddle number 10 of 17 on the Pinchgut Trail.

where close to Pinchgut Lake. Following a series of active and former logging roads, the ride is suitable for intermediate riders and even plucky beginners. The trail surface is hard-packed and predictable, which is good, because a good portion of it lies underwater. This is perhaps the number one reason local riders favour this ride: a series of long, deep puddles guarantees wet feet, at least, and lots of laughs. For those looking to lengthen the ride, create a loop, or merely avoid riding along the paved shoulder of the Trans-Canada Highway at the start, this ride can be combined with Ride 59, Lady Slipper Road–12-Mile Dam.

General location: West of Corner Brook, off of the Trans-Canada Highway.

Elevation change: From the trailhead at 230 m (755 feet), you will climb, gradually at first, and then more steeply, to 400 m (1,312 feet). After a short descent, the trail climbs to the highest point of the ride at 430 m (1,410 feet), and then drops to 270 m (885 feet) as it approaches the area around Pinchgut Lake. Total elevation gain for the out-and-back ride is 320 m (1,050 feet).

Season: As the puddles across this trail apparently never dry out, you can consider conditions on this ride to be acceptable from June through late September.

We suspect that these wet areas of the trail would make the ride an excursion through bug heaven (from the bug's perspective!) in June and July.

Services: All services are available in Corner Brook.

Hazards: Use caution along the side of the Trans-Canada Highway at the beginning of the ride. Also, Lady Slipper Road is used regularly by logging trucks, which have the right-of-way.

Rescue index: At the farthest point on this ride (somewhere near Pinchgut Lake), you will be at least 11 km (7 miles) from the Trans-Canada Highway.

Land status: Crown land and logging roads managed by Corner Brook Pulp and Paper Limited.

Maps: The government topographic map for this area is Corner Brook 12 A/13, and it may prove infinitely more reliable to you than any other resource, equipping you with all the information you will need to guide yourself through this trail.

Finding the trail: The Pinchgut Lake trail begins down Lady Slipper Road, a wide, graded logging road off the Trans-Canada Highway. However, the best place to park a vehicle is at the end of 12-Mile Dam Road. From Corner Brook, head west on the Trans-Canada Highway toward Channel-Port-aux-Basques. After crossing a bridge and rounding a sharp bend in the road, you will pass a distance sign to Channel-Port-aux-Basques. Immediately past this sign, turn left onto 12-Mile Dam Road. The road is gated, but there is ample room to park several vehicles in front of the gate.

Source of additional information: You may want to consider picking up a local trail guide. *Mountain Biking in and around Corner Brook* is a collection of trails and information compiled by Doug Miller.

Notes on the trail: From the parking area at 12-Mile Dam Road, turn left onto the Trans-Canada Highway. Riding along the paved shoulder, you will cross Corner Brook Stream and pass Exit 4 off the highway. When you see a sign for a weigh station, carefully cross to the other side of the highway and turn left on a dirt logging road managed by Corner Brook Pulp and Paper Limited; this is Lady Slipper Road. A steel arm barrier may be lowered across the entrance to this wide, graded logging road, but it can easily be skirted on your bike.

Lady Slipper Road carves a wide path through a barren, rolling landscape of clear-cuts and managed forest. Continue straight on the road for some distance, until the road continues ahead of you up a slight rise and a grassier, older logging road branches off on the right. This fork is the first distinct **Y** you will come to on Lady Slipper Road, and is located just past the 2-km (1.25-mile) marker on the side of the road. There are very few other landmarks, due to the fact that most of the surrounding landscape has been clear-cut. Bear right here, beginning along the Pinchgut Lake trail.

Bear right again almost immediately as you head up the trail, which continues as a fairly well-established double-track trail. After a considerable distance you will come to a clearing, complete with a fire pit, where another trail branches off on the right. Continue straight beyond this clearing, passing another trail branching off on the right just past the fire pit. The trail ahead features a long stretch through a series of puddles that are unusually long and deep. Not only is there no possible way around these puddles, but the dark, cloudy water permits absolutely no glimpse of what lies below. Though initially quite intimidating to the wary and uninitiated, these small ponds can quite easily be traversed if you maintain a steady pace and keep a light, guiding grip on your handlebars.

When you come to a **Y** junction, bear right. A very short distance beyond this fork, you will follow the trail around a bend and over a bridge across a stream. From here, although the path continues to be obvious and easy to follow, the trail becomes technically more difficult and features much rockier and more eroded terrain. Gradually, and then more steeply, the trail also begins to descend. In certain places erosion has left deep, irregular ruts in the trail, and as you ride deeper into the woods, the trail eventually narrows and becomes quite overgrown. For the adventurous, it is possible to continue across a stream and through a much denser part of the woods. Our ride ended just past this stream crossing, where we turned around and raced, single-file, back to the junction with Lady Slipper Road, behind the one rider in the group sporting a white, just-barely-visible-at-night T-shirt.

Back at the junction with Lady Slipper Road, you can choose to turn left and retrace your way back to the trailhead at the end of 12-Mile Dam Road, or to turn right and follow the directions for Ride 59. This option follows Lady Slipper Road to the other end of 12-Mile Dam Road, across a connecting trail at the tip of Corner Brook Lake. The return ride, should you choose this route, is 14.5 km (9 miles), which would bring your trip total to 36 km (22.5 miles).

RIDE 59 · Lady Slipper Road–12-Mile Dam

AT A GLANCE

Length/configuration: 20-km (12-mile) loop on graded gravel, dirt, and paved roads

Aerobic difficulty: Moderate; gradual, mid-sized hills throughout

Technical difficulty: Beginner; smooth, hard-packed surface with some exposed rock

Scenery: View of Corner Brook Lake and rolling, wooded hillsides

Special comments: This beginner ride should not be shunned by advanced riders

Lady Slipper Road and 12-Mile Dam are logging roads that form a popular loop through the heavily forested hills that characterize western Newfoundland. This ride is a fun 20 km (12 miles) that trace a loop through a landscape of rounded, rocky hills and random lakes. The gradual and infrequent climbs make it accessible to all, and fit riders will easily complete the loop in under an hour. The ease of the terrain will enable the most bashful of beginners to successfully complete this popular off-road ride without dismounting, and for the more advanced rider, the sheer speed at which you are able to travel so easily makes up for the lack of technical challenge. Also, the view onto the clear blue Corner Brook Lake and its surrounding, and still forested, hillsides serves as an excellent reminder to even the most hard-core riders of what motivates people to get on a mountain bike in the first place.

General location: A few minutes west of Corner Brook, off the Trans-Canada Highway.

Elevation change: A total elevation gain of 180 m (600 feet) over rolling hills.

Season: Ideal for riding from mid-June to late September.

Services: There are no services at the trailhead. All requirements can be met in Corner Brook.

Hazards: Use caution crossing the Trans-Canada Highway. Give way to logging trucks on Lady Slipper Road.

Rescue index: At the farthest point on the trail, you are 10 km (6 miles) from the highway, and at least 15 km (9 miles) from Corner Brook.

Land status: The roads are public rights-of-way on Crown land that has been leased to private logging companies.

Maps: You will find some of the trails and get a good view of the Massey Drive area by referring to government topographic map Corner Brook 12 A/13. Equipped with this, it is unlikely that you will be unable to find your way out of this network of trails.

Finding the trail: From Corner Brook, travel west on the Trans-Canada Highway toward Channel-Port-aux-Basques. Just outside the city, you will cross a bridge and then pass a mileage sign to Channel-Port-aux-Basques. Immediately after passing the mileage sign, turn left onto 12-Mile Dam Road, an unsigned gravel road with a metal barrier. There is ample room for a few cars at the entrance of the road in front of the barrier.

Source of additional information: You will find some photographs of the trail, as well as a highlighted section of the area topographic map, in Doug Miller's *Mountain Biking in and around Corner Brook*.

Notes on the trail: From the trailhead, turn left onto the Trans-Canada Highway and follow it to Lady Slipper Road. This is a relatively flat ride on the paved shoulder that sets the pace and acts as a warm-up for the ride ahead. After passing through an underpass and climbing a gradual hill, Lady Slipper Road is

RIDE 59 • Lady Slipper Road–12-Mile Dam

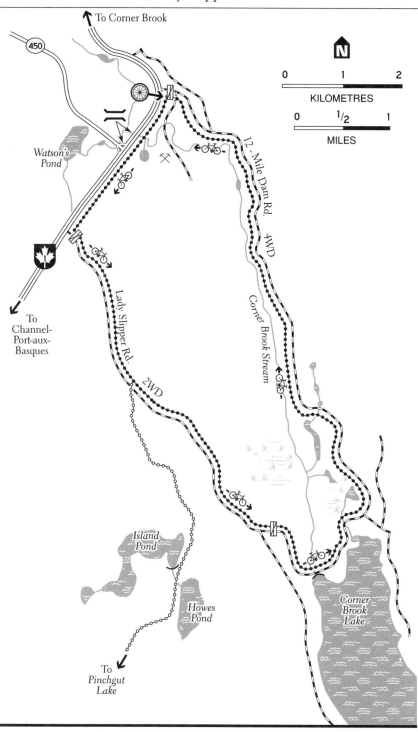

Lady Slipper Road penetrates the vast, barren landscape around Corner Brook Lake.

the first gravel road on the left-hand side. A steel arm barrier may be lowered across the entrance to this wide, well-graded logging road, but it may easily be skirted on your bike.

Lady Slipper Road is carved through a vast, barren landscape, continuing obviously straight ahead. This is an extended climb so gradual, you may hardly notice it. As you climb past the "2km" marker, there is a **Y** in the road. Bear left, continuing past the Pinchgut Lake trail on the right (see Ride 58). Farther along, the road bends to the left for the final stage of the climb. At the crest of the hill you get a view of Corner Brook Lake and begin to descend. On the descent, just past the "5 km" marker, you will turn left onto a narrower gravel road. You will see a sign a short distance down this road for the Corner Brook Water Supply, and pass through an orange gate.

At the end of the descent, a well-maintained wooden bridge crosses the brook that is feeding into Corner Brook Lake. Across the bridge, the trail narrows to an old road that sees only the occasional ATV and regular mountain bike traffic. The trail takes a sharp bend to the left and ascends a small knoll. Beyond the knoll, the trail is walled by alders and has deteriorated to a surface of loose rock and packed dirt. A short distance ahead, there is a short climb on a particularly rocky surface. At the top of the hill the trail becomes slightly grassy, giving it an even more authentic backcountry feel, and levels off. You will continue along this double-track for a few kilometres to a **Y** intersection.

Bear left at the fork, continuing along 12-Mile Dam Road. A rolling stretch of road follows the turn, and eventually takes you through a tunnel of alders. For this stretch, the trail is on a slight uphill grade. Emerging from the alder bushes, you will begin to descend and cruise down a moderate grade to another well-maintained wooden bridge. The trail swoops back up the other side, bringing you up out of the river valley. Still following the main road, you will pass a gravel pit on the left and then arrive at a junction with a gravel road. Bear left, and you will arrive at a gate just before the parking area.

RIDE 60 · Stephenville

AT A GLANCE

Length/configuration: 14-km (8.7-mile) combination (10.8-km [6.7-mile] loop with out-and-back spur; spur is 1.6 km [1-mile] long each way)

Aerobic difficulty: Modest; a mostly flat ride on dirt trails

Technical difficulty: Intermediate riding on a combination of single- and double-track trails with some challenging patches of bog

Scenery: Optional side trip to a high point overlooking Stephenville and the coast

Special comments: While in Stephenville, inquire about additional riding along the cliffs, out of Kippens

Located between Channel-Port-aux-Basques and Corner Brook, Stephenville is the middle child between a historic port on the Strait of Belle Isle and a modern urban centre. The town of Stephenville has maintained its position on St. George's Bay, despite the closing of the military base upon which it was founded, and has since evolved into a pulp mill town with a small commercial centre. The town has established a position among the Corner Brook mountain biking community due to the efforts of local riders, who have built a race circuit and actively promoted riding here.

The race circuit is an 10.8-km (6.7-mile) loop that we extended to a 14-km (8.7-mile) loop with a side trip to a viewpoint overlooking Stephenville and St. George's Bay. It is a mostly flat ride that utilizes gravel roads as well as single- and double-track dirt trails behind the northern extreme of the town's residential area. On this ride you will cross through woods and grassy clearings and negotiate some patches of bog. The riding is most challenging through slick, muddy sections of bog that carefully conceal their water content, as well as rocks and roots under tall grasses. You may find the circuit is relatively easy as a fit,

RIDE 60 • Stephenville

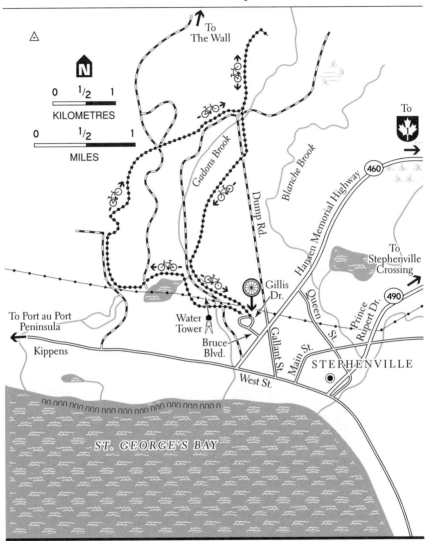

intermediate rider, until you kick into race pace and repeat the circuit a few times, as riders do on race day.

General location: Stephenville is located 77 km (48 miles) southwest of Corner Brook.

Elevation change: Insignificant; small, rolling hills with only one short, steep, rocky climb to the look-off point.

Season: Several patches of bog make this ride more suitable to summer riding, beginning in June and continuing to September.

NEWFOUNDLAND 283

The Stephenville circuit features a variety of terrain and some excellent single-track trails through the woods.

Services: All services are available in Stephenville.

Hazards: None.

Rescue index: The race circuit forms a short loop just beyond a subdivision. You are never more than 6 km (4 miles) from the trailhead and some houses.

Land status: Crown land.

Maps: The trails described in this race circuit do not appear on any map. For an overview of the area, see *Newfoundland Maps* (map 21, sections E-6 and F-6).

Finding the trail: From Corner Brook, take the Trans-Canada Highway west toward Channel-Port-aux-Basques. You will exit onto NF Highway 460 for Stephenville and the Stephenville Airport. Continue straight on Highway 460, which will become the Hansen Memorial Highway. After passing through the second four-way intersection, turn right at the first opportunity onto Bruce Boulevard. Continue straight up the road, and then turn right onto Gillis Drive. You will follow Gillis Drive around a bend to the left and park on the side of the road, near the entrance to a gravel road that branches off to your right.

Source of additional information: You may find riders who have raced on the circuit who can provide you with updated trail information at Play It Again Sports, located at 5 Park Street in Corner Brook.

Notes on the trail: Starting at the dirt road that branches off of Gillis Drive, continue straight toward the power line. When you reach it, turn left on a double-track trail, heading toward a water tower. At the tower, bear left and descend a short hill, and then turn right onto the first trail heading into the woods. This is an ATV-width trail with brief, slick, muddy sections. It will bring you to a fork, where you will bear left on a trail that connects back to the power line. Turn right at the power line and continue to a gravel road that is heading up, on a slight grade, to the right. Turning right on the gravel road, you will pass a beaver brook on the right and continue to a **T** junction at a small, dug-out clearing.

At the clearing, turn right. The road is initially straight, then curves to the left and right. As you wind around the bends, you will pass trails branching off to the left and right. Continue ahead until you can see a large clearing. Just before entering the clearing, turn left onto a grassy single-track trail. There is a short boggy section of trail that is rocky and wet, and then you will come to a fork. At the fork, turn right, following the perimeter of the clear-cut. At the opposite side you will reach a fork in the trail. To the right, the race circuit continues, and to the left, the trail continues out to "The Wall" (an optional out-and-back trip up a mountain that is not part of the race circuit). Bearing right and continuing along the race circuit, you will pass through another open area that has some wet, boggy patches. You will pass an access road on the right and continue ahead to a **T** junction with a wide dirt track. Turn left and continue through an overgrown meadow area, crossing a primitive bridge over a dark, muddy patch of bog. Beyond the bridge, you will come to a **T** junction with an unpaved dirt road that leads to the town dump.

At the dump road you can turn right to continue on the race circuit, or left for a short out-and-back trip to a viewpoint overlooking Stephenville. (We opted for the side trip and traveled a short distance up the road to the left.) Then turn left at a clearing and cross over a heavily rutted area. You will reach a double-track trail and turn right up a steep, rocky slope, to a point overlooking Stephenville. From here, you can also see out to St. George's Bay on the Gulf of St. Lawrence. To finish the ride, retrace your tracks back to the dump road and bear right to continue on the race circuit. You will follow the dump road for nearly a kilometre (one-half mile) before turning right onto a grassy, overgrown single-track trail. Follow the single-track through a small wooded area, and continue straight ahead into a field. Despite the tall grass growing on this trail, the path is fairly distinct and cuts conspicuously across an open field as a wide, grassy double-track. As you cross the field, you will pass a brown building on the right and continue in a direction that seems headed for the water tower. A short distance past the building, you will emerge on a maintained dirt road and pass some homes on the right. Continue straight on the gravel road. This is the same road on which you started out, and in a short distance you will arrive at the trailhead on Gillis Drive.

RIDE 61 • Trailway Provincial Park: Cape Ray

AT A GLANCE

Length/configuration: 38.4-km (24-mile) out-and-back (19.2 km [12 miles] each way)

Aerobic difficulty: This former railroad bed is suitable for all levels of fitness

Technical difficulty: Modest; a few areas of deep, loose rock require some deft maneuvering

Scenery: Gorgeous, sandy beaches to one side and expansive views toward Table Mountain on the other

Special comments: Cape Ray is an interesting destination and makes for a great family or group ride

Starting in Channel-Port-aux-Basques, this ride to Cape Ray follows the right-of-way of the old Canadian National Railway line. The abandoned railroad bed is being developed by the Newfoundland Trailway Council as part of the Trans-Canada Trail. Known as Trailway Provincial Park, the trail will one day stretch 883 km (548 miles), from Channel-Port-aux-Basques to St. John's. This ride begins a section of the route named the Wreckhouse Trail. On a sunny afternoon in August, when the sand dunes and picturesque beaches near Cape Ray make you wonder whether you've been transported down to the Caribbean, it is difficult to imagine the conditions that led to this name. However, winds can blow across this southwestern corner of Newfoundland with gusts of up to 160 km (100 miles) per hour. When the trains were still running, derailments were common along this section of the railroad.

Most of this ride follows the former railroad bed that parallels the coast, heading north from Channel-Port-aux-Basques to Cape Ray. From the community of Cape Ray, the ride continues along Route 408, following a paved road that turns to gravel and leads out to a lighthouse that now serves as a craft shop in the summer. Not far from the lighthouse is the site of a Dorset Eskimo settlement. The Dorset are considered to be among the first people of Newfoundland, living on the shores of the island until the beginning of the first century A.D. The Cape Ray site is the southernmost found to date. It is believed that the Dorsets had a settlement on the Cape from 700 B.C. to A.D. 1400. Although the site was first excavated in the 1960s, much of it has since been covered over in response to concerns about looting. Also, beyond the lighthouse is the beginning of the Cormack Trail, a hiking path that continues north along the coast and makes a great side trip for anyone wanting to stretch their legs on foot before embarking on the return ride to Channel-Port-aux-Basques. The ride to the lighthouse

RIDE 61 • Trailway Provincial Park: Cape Ray

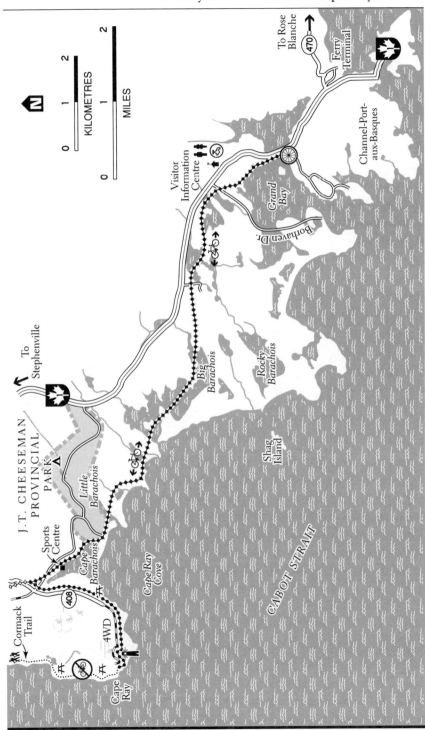

Riding from the lighthouse at Cape Ray, overlooking the Cabot Strait.

covers 19.2 km (12 miles), making the return trip to Channel-Port-aux-Basques a 38.4-km (24-mile) journey. J. T. Cheeseman Provincial Park, located just outside the community of Cape Ray, makes an alternative starting point that provides several options for shortening the ride.

General location: You will be riding between Channel-Port-aux-Basques and Cape Ray, on the southern tip of the west side of Newfoundland.

Elevation change: There is no significant change in elevation along the length of this ride.

Season: Good swimming weather begins at the end of June in Newfoundland. Therefore, the best months to ride this trail are July and August, when you will be able to take advantage of the many swimming opportunities along the way.

Services: Most services are available in Channel-Port-aux-Basques. However, you will not find any bicycle-related services. Be sure to carry an extra inner tube and all the tools you need to fix a flat or make any small repairs. J. T. Cheeseman Provincial Park, on the outskirts of the community of Cape Ray, includes campsites and basic services.

Hazards: None.

Rescue index: Throughout the length of this ride, you will remain within a short distance of the Trans-Canada Highway. J. T. Cheeseman Provincial Park, just outside Cape Ray, is another place where assistance is likely to be found.

Land status: This multi-use recreational trail forms part of Trailway Provincial Park.

Maps: This ride follows the old railroad right-of-way, which is shown in *Newfoundland Maps* (map 35, sections L-5, K-5, and J-5). In addition, the official highway map for Newfoundland highlights the entire route of the former railroad in red, and references it as the Trailway Provincial Park.

Finding the trail: Access to the trail is directly off the Trans-Canada Highway in Channel-Port-aux-Basques, not far from the Hotel Channel-Port-aux-Basques. There is an old caboose parked at the trailhead.

Sources of additional information:

> Southwest Coast Tourism Association
> P.O. Box 2145
> Channel-Port-aux-Basques, NF A0M 1C0
> There is a Visitor Information Centre on the Trans-Canada Highway, just north of the trailhead. For further information about Trailway Provincial Park and its development, contact the Newfoundland Trailway Council at (709) 256-8833.

Notes on the trail: Follow the rail trail as it heads north from the caboose and across Grand Bay. The trail crosses a paved road, Borhaven Drive, a short distance out of Channel-Port-aux-Basques. There may be trucks parked by the trail on the other side of this road. Just look to the right, and you will be sure to find the continuation of the trail. Beyond this point, the trail crosses a service road and then curves gradually around to the left, heading closer to the shore.

As you follow the trail closer to the shore, you will cross a series of causeways. At the end of the second one, over Big Barachois, a network of ATV trails extend to the left toward a beach and some sand dunes. Because any traffic can be damaging to the fragile dune grass of this type of area, be sure to stay on the main trail. Beyond a fourth causeway, you will ride past J. T. Cheeseman Provincial Park on the right. There are changing rooms, outhouses, and beach access from here.

Not far from the provincial park, you will pass Clifford Sheaves Memorial Sports Centre on the left. Just beyond this playing field, you will reach a junction with a paved road. Cross the road and rejoin the trail, which parallels the road for a short distance before reaching a junction with Route 408. At this point you want to leave the rail trail, turning left onto the paved road. Cross a small bridge, and then bear left at a fork, following a sign for Cape Ray Beach and the lighthouse. Continue on the road, which turns to gravel, all the way to the lighthouse on Cape Ray. The gravel road continues a short distance past the lighthouse to a rocky promontory overlooking the Cabot Strait. Spend some time exploring the sites around the lighthouse before setting out on the return trip, which is simply a matter of retracing your tracks back to Channel-Port-aux-Basques.

NOVA SCOTIA

Nova Scotia is one of the most popular travel destinations in Atlantic Canada and enjoys the reputation of being the region's most bicycle-friendly province. Promoting its coastal character and support of a wide variety of outdoor activities, the province boasts of being "Canada's Ocean Playground." This is certainly true for riders, as an extensive system of secondary roads has spurred the growth of touring companies and allowed for the creation of some now-classic road rides and tours, the most well known being the Cabot Trail on Cape Breton Island. Though still outside the main adventure spotlight, mountain biking in Nova Scotia has flourished as a result of the province's development of and commitment to the sport of cycling. In a sense, off-road riding has become a natural extension of the province's passion for two-wheeled travel. Along with many exceptional bike stores throughout the province, clubs offer riders the benefit of organized rides and the provincial race circuit benefits from the support and enthusiasm of such groups.

Though small, the province of Nova Scotia represents a rich diversity of land, people, and plant and animal life. Comprised of a peninsulalike mainland and the adjacent Cape Breton Island, one of the novelties of mountain biking in the province is that so many trails parallel or lead out to the coast. Indeed, no point in the province is more than 56 kilometres (35 miles) from the coast. Along with a dramatic shoreline, Nova Scotia offers riders the experience of exploring a landscape comprised of hard- and softwood forests, salt marshes teeming with wildlife, bogs, and coastal dunes. Thousands of shallow lakes and ponds dot the region, and there is a dramatic contrast between more southerly areas and the northern wilderness of boreal forest and highland barrens.

The area that now makes up the province of Nova Scotia was first inhabited by the Mi'kmaq, many of whom have since returned to their original lands in Cape Breton. John Cabot may himself have landed on Cape Breton Island in 1497, although others claim that his point of contact with the New World was in Newfoundland. The French founded the first permanent European colony in Nova Scotia at Port Royal (now Annapolis Royal) in 1605. This colony was called Acadia and led to further settlements along the shores of the Bay of Fundy, in the region now known as the Annapolis Valley.

Throughout the 1600s, the entire region was the site of numerous French and English hostilities. Possession of Acadia was transferred back and forth between the French and English until 1710, when it was finally appropriated by the British. In 1713 the Treaty of Utrecht confirmed the status of Acadia as a British colony, and it was renamed Nova Scotia ("New Scotland"). The French were left with only a claim to Ile Royal (now Cape Breton Island).

The Treaty of Utrecht forced the Acadians living in newly named Nova Scotia to accept British authority over the region. Between 1713 and 1755 Acadian leaders managed to maintain recognition of their different cultural identity. While refusing to pledge allegiance to the British crown, they also declared that they would remain neutral in the event of a conflict between France and England. Nevertheless, in 1755, eleven years after war was declared in Europe between France and England, the governor of Nova Scotia ordered the expulsion of all Acadians unwilling to pledge their allegiance to England. Thus began one of the most disturbing and tragic events in the history of the province: the deportation of more than 6,000 Acadians.

In the years that followed the Acadian deportation, the British conquered the French fortress of Louisbourg on what is now Cape Breton Island. The Seven Years' War (also known as the French and Indian War) featured continued conflict between the French and English as they competed for dominance in the New World. In 1763 the Treaty of Paris ended the war, and all of present-day Nova Scotia came under the control of Great Britain.

Despite the brutal treatment of the Acadians, the region saw the influx of many people over the years that followed. After the American Revolution, Loyalists moved north and took over much of the land once farmed by the Acadians. Many Acadians eventually returned to Cape Breton Island, where Scottish tenant farmers who were evicted from their lands in the early nineteenth century also landed. The population growth and continued development of the region resulted in the establishment of many of the cart tracks and coach roads that have since formed the foundation of mountain bike trails in the province.

Today, Nova Scotia reflects the cultural diversity of its history in its many small communities, its music, and its art. This diversity is matched by the incredible variety of its landscapes. Indeed, the province can be divided into small areas that represent some of what each of the other Atlantic Provinces offer in abundance. The highlands and rugged wilderness of Cape Breton Island compare to the stunning coastal landscape of Newfoundland. The Annapolis Valley is in many ways reminiscent of the rolling agricultural landscape of Prince Edward Island. Kejimkujik National Park encompasses much of the province's small interior wilderness, and it offers riders an escape to the woods very similar (though on a much smaller scale) to the experience of riding through New Brunswick's north woods. In such a rich and diverse setting, mountain bikers can enjoy some of the most varied riding in Atlantic Canada, and still be in reach of the many opportunities offered in each of the other provinces as well.

THE TRAILS

Of all the Atlantic Provinces, Nova Scotia enjoys the most established and developed network of trails for mountain bikers. There are rides in almost every corner of the province, offering bikers the opportunity to experience the wonderful diversity that describes the province's topography. Within just a few days, it is possible to wander the rugged trails of Cape Breton Island, tackle the challenging single-track in Halifax, or explore the quiet wilderness of Kejimkujik National Park. The trail system enjoys a strong foundation in old coach roads and cart tracks, and also includes park trails, race circuits, mountain bike parks, and trails maintained by local riders. Despite this extensive development, mountain biking in the province awards riders with a sense of remoteness and adventure.

Our tour of Nova Scotia began on Cape Breton Island, where breathtaking coastal scenery is matched by exhilarating biking opportunities. Though much attention is given to roadies who conquer the famed Cabot Trail, mountain bikers can enjoy a quieter yet no less rigourous experience, away from the traffic and crowds of the many tourists who roam the area in the summer. All the riding we explored on Cape Breton Island is in the western part of the island, radiating out from the trails open in Cape Breton Highlands National Park. Riders of all skill levels and ambitions will find trails that take full advantage of the beauty of the landscape, where family and novice rides like Clyburn Valley and Trous de Saumons offer no less appeal than the more advanced expeditions to Lake of Islands or Money Point. Whether your goal is to climb into the vastness of the highlands, ride to a scenic look-off across the water, or take in the beauty of the island from atop a fire tower, the rides on Cape Breton Island will satisfy your every whim.

Although the highest elevations in Nova Scotia are reached in the highlands of Cape Breton Island, heading to the mainland doesn't mean you can't enjoy some rigourous climbing and expansive views. Eigg Mountain is the first ride in the Cobequid/North Shore area of the province, and it features a gradual yet extended climb that rewards riders with sweeping views across the Northumberland Strait toward Prince Edward Island. Farther south, at Wentworth, it is the trails themselves that have won the hearts of riders in search of single-track throughout Atlantic Canada. Closer to the coast, Cape Chignecto offers up spectacular scenery and grand adventures that rival the spirit of Cape Breton Island.

Farther south and west, the Annapolis Valley is a significant destination for mountain bikers, and not only because the region enjoys more sunny days and milder weather than most other parts of Atlantic Canada. Thanks to the vision and the ambition of local riders, extensive trail building in the area has resulted in the creation of Atlantic Canada's first mountain bike park: The Gorge. In Kentville, a visit to Framebreak Bicycles is a must. Not only will you find all you need to pamper your bike, but you will be bound to meet up with some of the many riders in the area, among whom it is always possible to find a guide to introduce you to the labyrinthlike trails in The Gorge.

The riding in the Annapolis Valley area is not simply limited to the network of trails at The Gorge, however. Tours include a ride along the coast in Black Rock and through the historic site of Grand-Pré. Grand-Pré was the principal site of the Acadian deportations and is today a national historic site that stands as a memorial to the Acadian people who were expelled from the region. Mountain bikers can plan a ride to this site along trails that run along the top of dikes constructed by Acadian farmers. Between January and March, bald eagles from Cape Breton Island come to mate in this region and can be seen waiting for fish when the tide comes in. Before leaving the valley, be sure to make your way to Martock Mountain, where one of Atlantic Canada's most talked-about race circuits challenges even the most accomplished riders and features one of the most ruthless downhill courses we have ever encountered.

Continuing through the province, riders can enjoy more coastal scenery and challenging single-track at Delaps Cove, where an old stage coach road has provided the foundation for a series of trails. Farther down the coast, another former stage coach road makes a perfect leg stretch for riders coming into Yarmouth off of the ferry from Maine. Although many visitors to the province simply travel straight to Halifax from Yarmouth, riders will find it well worth stopping to enjoy the beach at the end of the Liverpool-to-Summerville rail trail. Before continuing up the coast toward Halifax, a side trip to Kejimkujik National Park will transport you back to the days when the Mi'kmaq paddled the lakes and waterways of the province's interior.

Halifax can well be considered the hub of mountain biking activity in Nova Scotia. Not only does the city offer up the best in the way of equipment and supplies, but it is home to the largest number of mountain bike enthusiasts and boasts a huge and varied array of trails to choose from. Step into any bike store in the greater Halifax area, and you will learn of club and group rides and meet people who know the trails like their own backyards. One of the best resources for both local and visiting riders is a humourous and detailed collection of maps and trail descriptions put together by Randy Gray, one of the area's best riders and a strong advocate for the sport of mountain biking in the province. The trails we have included for the greater Halifax area can be considered a representative sampling of the many options available to riders of all levels. From the classic excursions offered up by Jimmy's Roundtop and the Lakes Loop, to the mind-boggling single-track at Wrandees, the variety of trails is impressive. Perhaps it is the Lawrencetown Beach ride that best sums up the experience of riding in Nova Scotia, however. From the variety of terrain to the consistent beauty of the land- and seascape, the trail combines the best elements of any ride with a fabulous destination. The Lawrencetown Beach trail could well be said to epitomize the playful spirit and beautiful allure of Canada's ocean playground.

HITTING THE TRAILS

Due to the more established network of trails open to mountain bikers in Nova Scotia, you can actually expect to meet other riders on trails throughout the province. Particularly in the greater Halifax area and in the Annapolis Valley, active mountain biking communities have generated enough interest in the sport to support regular club and group rides. Along with variety, an established race circuit, and dozens of bike shops, Nova Scotia also boasts the only women's mountain bike club we encountered during all our travels.

Although Nova Scotia's proximity to the sea results in a generally moderate climate, the weather can only be described as changeable and unpredictable. High winds are common along the coast, and on many of the rides we have described there is little shelter available from the elements. The best time to ride is from mid-June to mid-September, although excellent conditions can often be enjoyed through November. Before June, conditions are guaranteed to be wet, as snow cover doesn't completely melt until the end of April. After September, cooler temperatures require more clothing but also ensure that you won't be sharing your ride with spring- and summer-loving insects. Fall riding is spectacular but can be complicated by the beginning of hunting season, which in Nova Scotia usually begins the first week in October. Even on Sunday, when hunting is not permitted, it is wise to add as much blaze orange to your outfit as possible. For specific information about the hunting season, contact the Department of Natural Resources.

Many of the rides we have included for Nova Scotia can be identified and highlighted in *A Map of the Province of Nova Scotia*. This book is a valuable resource that offers much more information than the provincial highway map, and makes navigating the province a breeze. In some cases, as we have noted in specific trail descriptions, the maps in this book are sufficient to guide you along the trail. Of even greater value are the topographic maps for the province, available at several locations listed below.

The following list of resources has been assembled to further assist you in your own exploration of Nova Scotia's mountain bike trails:

Nova Scotia Government Bookstore
Box 637
Halifax, NS B3J 2T3
(902) 424-7580
(topographic maps)

The Trail Shop
6260 Quinpool Road
Halifax, NS B3L 1A3
(902) 423-8736
(topographic maps, outfitter)

Tourism Nova Scotia
P.O. Box 130
Halifax, NS B3J 2M7
(800) 565-0000

Cyclesmith
6112 Quinpool Road
Halifax, NS B3L 1A2
(902) 425-1756

Framebreak Bicycles
15 River Street
Kentville, NS B4N 3W4
(902) 679-0611

Singletrack Mudpack
  Nova Scotia Women's Mountain
  Bike Club
c/o Bicycle Nova Scotia
P.O. Box 3010 South
Halifax, NS B3J 3G6
(902) 465-5019

RIDE 62 • Clyburn Valley

AT A GLANCE

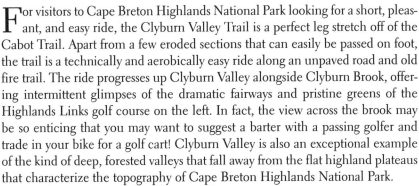

Length/configuration: 9.2-km (5.7-mile) out-and-back (4.6 km [2.8 miles] each way)

Aerobic difficulty: Requires only modest cardiovascular conditioning

Technical difficulty: This ride is suitable for beginning-level riders

Scenery: You'll ride though a spectacular hardwood canyon along the north bank of Clyburn Brook

Special comments: Just think, the golfers put out way more cash than you to enjoy the same scenery!

For visitors to Cape Breton Highlands National Park looking for a short, pleasant, and easy ride, the Clyburn Valley Trail is a perfect leg stretch off of the Cabot Trail. Apart from a few eroded sections that can easily be passed on foot, the trail is a technically and aerobically easy ride along an unpaved road and old fire trail. The ride progresses up Clyburn Valley alongside Clyburn Brook, offering intermittent glimpses of the dramatic fairways and pristine greens of the Highlands Links golf course on the left. In fact, the view across the brook may be so enticing that you may want to suggest a barter with a passing golfer and trade in your bike for a golf cart! Clyburn Valley is also an exceptional example of the kind of deep, forested valleys that fall away from the flat highland plateaus that characterize the topography of Cape Breton Highlands National Park.

This ride is a 9.2-km (5.7-mile) out-and-back jaunt. A nice feature for families or groups involving riders of mixed ability levels is that the ride can easily be shortened by simply turning around at any point. For advanced- or intermediate-level riders seeking a little more adventure, the ride can also be lengthened for a short distance. Beyond the usual turnaround at a small shelter named the "Gold Mine," a neglected portion of the old road continues into the valley. Although this former road seems like the perfect foundation for an excellent mountain bike trail, it is really only possible to follow it for a short distance. Years of erosion due to the ravages of heavy runoff in the spring have caused the trail conditions to deteriorate dramatically. Beyond a certain point, the trail simply becomes unsuitable for riders. The condition of this trail led us to contemplate the plight of trails that, with a little attention, could significantly contribute to the mountain biking opportunities in any area. Perhaps if we were willing to spend $50 to head out on a four-hour ride, our trails would be groomed and maintained like the golf course adjacent to this trail.

RIDE 62 • Clyburn Valley

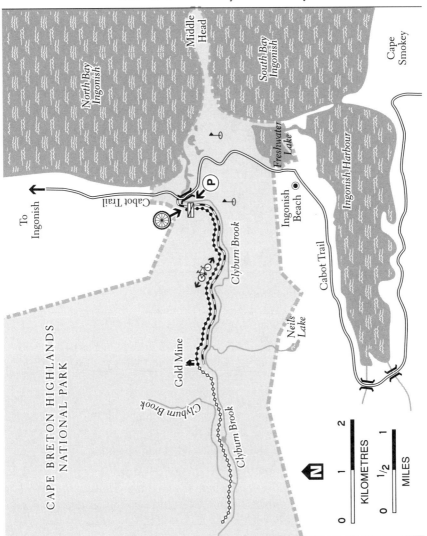

General location: Outside Ingonish, on the east shore of Cape Breton Highlands National Park.

Elevation change: There is no appreciable change in elevation along the entire length of this ride.

Season: June through October; conditions in March, April, and early May are unpredictable, as Clyburn Brook often overflows its banks and floods lower sections of the trail.

Following Clyburn Brook to the old "Gold Mine" shelter at Cape Breton Highlands National Park.

Services: Most services are available in Ingonish, although the nearest source for bicycle service and repair is Sea Spray Cycle in Dingwall. To contact them, call (902) 383-2911 or (902) 383-2732.

Hazards: There really are no hazards on this trail, unless you count the golf carts crossing the bridge over Clyburn Brook at the beginning of the ride. However, riders who choose to continue past the official end of this trail at the "Gold Mine" shelter will encounter rough and severely eroded trail conditions.

Rescue index: At the farthest point on this ride you will be only a few kilometres (a mile or so) from the point where the Highland Links golf course borders one side of the trail. You will almost certainly encounter other people at this point.

Land status: National park; from mid-May to mid-October there is an entry fee for all visitors to the park.

Maps: Detailed topographic maps for Cape Breton Highlands National Park can be purchased at the park gate, where there is a small store and information centre. For this particular ride, the free map offered to all visitors to the park is probably adequate. The Clyburn Valley ride is trail number 24 on the map.

Finding the trail: As you drive north along the Cabot Trail toward Ingonish, the Clyburn Valley Trail is one of the first sites you will come to beyond the park gates. Pass the entrance to Ingonish Campground on your right, and continue for 1.5 km (1 mile). Beyond the campground, you will be able to see the Highland Links golf course. This golf course begins at the Keltic Lodge, also on the right, and extends into the Clyburn Valley, which will be on your left. Look for a parking lot and picnic area on the left, just before the road crosses Clyburn Brook. The trailhead for the Clyburn Valley ride is on the north side of the brook, which you can reach from the parking area by means of a bridge that is also used by golf carts.

Source of additional information:

Cape Breton Highlands National Park
Ingonish Beach, NS B0C 1L0
(902) 224-2306 or (902) 285-2691 (year-round)

Notes on the trail: From the parking and picnic area on the south side of Clyburn Brook, begin by riding across the bridge to the parking area on the other side of the brook. Bear left off of the bridge and ride to a sign at the trailhead, which will direct you down a gated dirt road to the left. As you head out from the trailhead, Clyburn Brook will be on your left. Follow a wide, graded dirt road to a fork and bear right, continuing to follow the main access road. You will soon see the beautifully laid-out fairways and greens of the Highland Links golf course on the other side of the brook. At a second fork in the road, bear right, and continue to follow the wide, graded dirt road to an information sign. The ride continues straight from here, following a less-maintained double-track trail that soon drops to follow the river bank quite closely.

The trail will deteriorate gradually, becoming rockier and presenting a more challenging but rideable combination of exposed rock and sandy soil. This section of the trail is brief, however, and as the path moves inland a bit, you will be riding uphill along a more consistent, grassy, double-track trail through the woods. The forest is intriguing along this section of the ride, as vegetation seems to thrive amid the rocks, boulders, and aging trees. The trail ends abruptly at the top of the hill, at a yellow gate and the site of a small cabin signed as the "Gold Mine." There are some old foundations behind this shelter, as well as an outhouse. We recommend that most riders turn around at this point.

At the "Gold Mine" the trail may or may not be signed as being closed from that point on. Clearly, no maintenance to the trail has been done for some time beyond this spot. However, it is possible to continue riding. The old road follows an obvious path through the woods and across many stream and river gullies. The first of such gullies, Franey Brook, comes just beyond the "Gold Mine" shelter, and is actually spanned by a wooden bridge. Although the brook was dry when we rode here in late August, surrounding debris points to the fact that this brook can rage with high water at other times of the year or after heavy rainfalls. Beyond this bridge, the trail becomes much more difficult. For some distance, you will still be able to follow a rough double-track trail through the woods and over and across numerous rock-strewn river gullies. However, the trail becomes severely eroded, and you should have no doubt about when to call it a day and turn around. Retrace your route back toward the Cabot Trail and parking area.

RIDE 63 • Lake of Islands

AT A GLANCE

Length/configuration: 33-km (19-mile) out-and-back (16.5 km [9.5 miles] each way)

Aerobic difficulty: Requires good endurance

Technical difficulty: An intermediate ride on a rocky old fire road, with a stretch of gravel between the parking area and Lake of Islands trailhead

Scenery: This highland adventure features bog, barrens, and a tremendous view out to Cape Smokey

Special comments: Use the shelter or wilderness campsite at Lake of Islands to create an overnight trip

Cape Breton Highlands National Park is situated in the middle of one of the most scenic destinations in Canada—Cape Breton Island. The dramatic cliffs, forested hills, and rugged highlands draw visitors from all over the world into this area, year-round. Many of the island's attractions can be seen just by driving around the Cabot Trail, a 296-km (185-mile) loop that begins in Baddeck and traces the perimeter of the northernmost peninsula of the island. However, by getting on your bike and heading inland, you can explore and experience far more of this unique area. The Lake of Islands Trail will expose you to the elements of highland terrain, including bog, barrens, random small lakes, and woods. And from a look-off point on the trail, you can see across Ingonish Harbour to Cape Smokey and Smokey Mountain, the highest peak in Cape Breton.

On this 33-km (19-mile) out-and-back trail, you will climb consistently on the outbound trip and enjoy a much swifter ride, downhill, back to the trailhead. The ride begins on an access road before the signed Lake of Islands trailhead. This gravel road has recently been closed to automobile traffic, and you will follow signs to the former Lake of Islands parking area. From there, you will continue on a rocky old road to Branch Pond and Lake of Islands. Beyond Branch Pond, the trail is rougher. It is not maintained and requires a more adventurous spirit. The landscape becomes more exposed, and the trail quite rocky. Pay attention to any possible changes in the weather, and try to avoid being caught in the barrens in fog, wind, or rain. Although the trail requires only intermediate skills, riders should possess above-average endurance and judgment.

General location: Cape Breton Highlands National Park, near the eastern entrance at Ingonish.

RIDE 63 • Lake of Islands

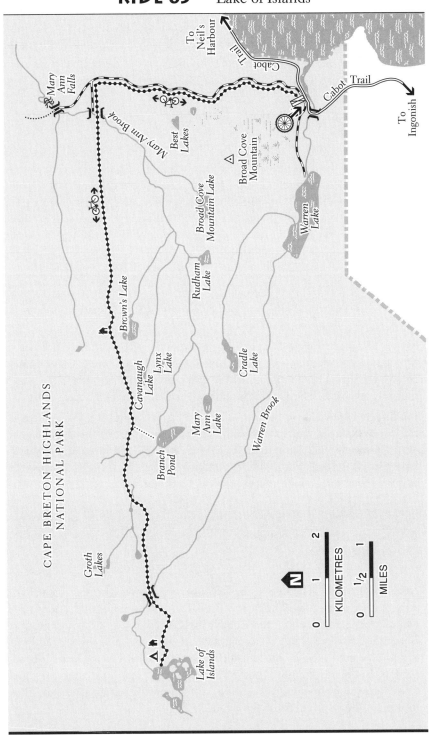

Elevation change: Overall elevation gain for this ride is 435 m (1,425 feet).

Season: Summer is the only season to ride in the park, but even at this time of year, rain, wind, and fog are elements that need to be considered when planning a trip. Early spring and late summer are notable for poor riding conditions; the driest month is July. The months of June and September are runners-up.

Services: There is a grocery and convenience store in Ingonish, and there are many restaurants as you make your way around the Cabot Trail. For bike rentals, guiding, or bike service, contact Sea Spray Cycle in Dingwall (phone (902) 382-2732).

Hazards: Rapid changes in weather could result in reduced visibility due to torrid rains or fog in the barrens. Conditions such as these make it easy to get lost. Also, the exposed, barren landscape poses a risk on clear days, making it potentially very dry and hot. On the final descent on the gravel road, remember that there is a barricade followed by a chain gate as you approach the parking area.

Rescue index: At the farthest extremity of the trail, you are almost 20 km (12 miles) from the front gate and a telephone. However, you are likely to encounter hikers or cyclists at Branch Pond or the Lake of Islands campsite, and assistance may be acquired more readily.

Land status: National park; from mid-May to mid-October there is an entry fee for all park visitors.

Maps: Detailed topographic maps for Cape Breton Highlands National Park can be purchased at the park gate, where there is a small store and information centre. For this particular ride, the free map offered to all visitors to the park is probably adequate. The Lake of Islands ride is trail number 22 on the map.

Finding the trail: Drive on the Cabot Trail to the entrance of Cape Breton Highlands National Park in Ingonish. Beyond the park gates, turn left at the second opportunity, following signs for Warren Lake. Continue past the Warren Lake turnoff immediately to the left, and follow signs for Mary Ann Falls. Park at the gated entrance to the access road to Mary Ann Falls.

Source of additional information:

Cape Breton Highlands National Park
Ingonish Beach, NS B0C 1L0
(902) 285-2691

Notes on the trail: The ride begins beyond a chain across the gravel road to the right of the parking area. The first section of the road winds uphill, and you will continue past a branch to the right, which leads to a group camping area. Beyond a bend to the right, the road takes a sharp curve to the left, and then winds more gently to a scenic look-off across the Atlantic Ocean. From the look-off, the road bends sharply to the left and continues uphill for a short distance. Once you reach the crest of the hill, the road begins a rolling descent to the turnoff for the Lake of Islands trailhead.

David picks his way through the alders on the exhilarating descent from Lake of Islands.

The turnoff comes at the end of this long descent, once the road has leveled off. You will pass a sign before turning left at the first opportunity, onto a gravel road that quickly leads to what was once the parking area for the Lake of Islands trail. There is a sign indicating the start of the trail, which continues straight beyond the end of the gravel road. The trail descends immediately to Mary Ann Brook, which is spanned by a wooden bridge. Continuing on the trail across the bridge, you will begin the lengthy climb to Branch Pond. After gaining close to 100 m (330 feet), the trail levels off briefly in a small clearing. Here the trail becomes a grassy double-track, with sections of loose rock in the middle. A short distance past the clearing, the trail narrows to a single-track through some brush.

Emerging from the brush, the trail turns to loose rock and dirt and resumes climbing. This is a short uphill that opens up and levels off briefly, and then continues to climb two more short hills. Arriving at a larger clearing, the trail appears to branch off to the right, but you will continue to bear left, following the double-track. When we rode, at the clearing there were deposits of red sand and rock from a storm the previous spring—an indication of how forceful the storms can be. Continue a short distance along the double-track, and you will come to a **T** junction. The arrows pointing toward Branch Pond and Lake of Islands direct you to the right, while the look-off point is to the left.

You will get a glimpse of Brown's Lake when you continue to the right, before the trail begins a gradual descent. Almost immediately, you will pass a shelter on the right, and then the trail bends away to the left. This section of trail is quite fun, presenting some small whoop-de-doos and good cruising on a gradual downhill slope. Farther along, you will pass the trail leading to Branch Pond on your left. You get a clear view of Branch Pond at this point, and you can look behind you to a view of the ocean and cliffs. Continue ahead, bearing right, and you will soon descend the rocky double-track to a stream crossing. Ford the stream, and on the other side the trail widens slightly, broadening as the landscape becomes more barren. Entering into the barrens, the trail turns rockier and the landscape resembles that of the Irish highlands, which the first settlers would have recognized. Few trees are able to survive here, but it appears to be an ideal landscape for blueberry and other low-lying bushes.

Follow the rocky trail that is littered with mid-sized boulders to a four-way intersection marked by a cairn. Looking down onto the trail, you will make out an arrow formed from small boulders pointing to the left. Another line of rocks at the entrance to other trails discourages forward- or right-hand travel. Turn left, following the arrow to a crossing at Warren Brook. Typically, this is a bridged crossing, but it had been washed out when we arrived, and a guide rope had been strung across the river. Across the river the trail narrows and makes its way to the Lake of Islands, where there is a shelter and primitive campsite. To return, backtrack to the Lake of Islands trailhead, and then continue to the parking area on the gravel road.

RIDE 64 · Money Point

AT A GLANCE

Length/configuration: 25-km (15.5-mile) combination (16-km [10-mile] loop connected to an out-and-back spur; spur is 4.5 km [2.7 miles] each way)

Aerobic difficulty: Extreme!

Technical difficulty: Intermediate to advanced; primarily dirt roads and cart tracks, with a few extra-steep, eroded descents and climbs that require skilled bike handling

Scenery: Breathtaking coastal views in a rugged and remote location

Special comments: Brace yourself for 370 m (1,213 feet) of elevation gain over 1.5 km

This 25-km (15.5-mile) combination ride traces a 16-km (10-mile) loop up and around Cape Breton Island's northernmost tip. After traversing a high bluff overlooking Aspy Bay, the loop connects to an old road that adds a dramatic, 9-km (5.5-mile) out-and-back excursion to Money Point. Although the ride begins and ends on pavement, most of this trip follows unpaved roads and old wagon tracks. Several severely eroded sections of the trail demand good bike handling skills and at least an intermediate level of technical ability. Furthermore, cardiovascular fitness is a must for anyone hoping to enjoy the ride or merely survive the climb back from Money Point! Be sure to begin this ride early in the day to allow enough time to complete the trip, spend some time down at Money Point, and take in the many breathtaking views.

Between the Bay of St. Lawrence and Aspy Bay, Cape North juts out into the Cabot Strait. The northernmost point on Cape Breton Island, this area epitomizes the extreme nature of the landscape: the flat plateau of a 430-m (1,410-foot) mountain drops away abruptly to the ocean below, offering sweeping views from towering cliffs. Money Point, situated just a few kilometres (a mile or so) southeast of Cape North, also captures the spirit of this rugged and remote region. To reach the point, you will begin by riding along the access road to several communications towers, before plunging downhill on a severely eroded old road to the shore. You will then be able to ride out to Money Point on a wagon track that runs along a narrow, grassy strip of land at the base of the cliffs. The surf can pound the shore along this portion of the coast, as evidenced by the remains of an old wharf and the wreck of the *Kismet II*, a ship that ran aground here during a snowstorm in 1955. In addition to a new lighthouse, you will ride past the remains of the old lighthouse and several old foundations to buildings long-since abandoned.

General location: Money Point is located near the northernmost tip of Cape Breton Island, not far from the village of Bay St. Lawrence, in Victoria County.

Elevation change: From the highest point on this ride at approximately 366 m (1,200 feet), the final descent to Money Point involves inching your way or plummeting straight down an extremely steep and very eroded old road to the shore. The return trip up this hill involves a fairly torturous climb that, in addition to a long, gradual ascent at the beginning of the ride, contributes significantly to the roughly 609 m (2,000 feet) of elevation gain for this ride.

Season: Reasonable riding conditions can be enjoyed from June through September, although there are times when it is impossible to escape from the wind, rain, and fog that characterize the summer weather conditions of Cape Breton Island. July is generally the driest month, but keep in mind that the weather here can be quick to change at any time of year, and that it will most likely be colder and more windy once you reach Money Point.

Services: Bay St. Lawrence offers the basics of food and water. Bicycle service and repair can be sought in Dingwall, a small town situated on Aspy Bay, a few kilometres (a mile or so) northeast of the town of Cape North. There, Sea Spray

RIDE 64 · Money Point

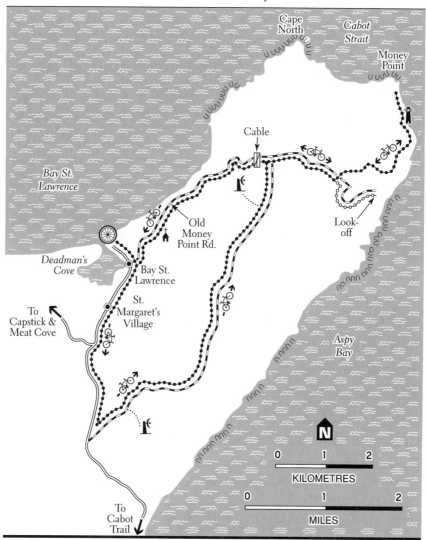

Cycle offers bike care and maintenance, in addition to a variety of guide services and tours. Contact them at (902) 383-2911, or off season at (902) 383-2732.

Hazards: Be sure your brakes are in good working order for the final descent to Money Point! On the return ride, at the time we visited here, there was a street cable across the trail at the top of the old Money Point Road, just before the descent back to the government wharf.

Rescue index: At Money Point, the farthest point on this ride, you will be approximately 9 km (5.5 miles) from the community of Bay St. Lawrence. Although you

A dramatic view across Bay St. Lawrence captures the spirit of the epic ride to Money Point.

may find other people on the trail, it is wise to be prepared for the possibility of encountering no one. Pay close attention to the weather, and allow plenty of time for this ride. If looming clouds or a setting sun creep up on you, turn around immediately.

Land status: This ride follows public rights-of-way, along a combination of paved and unpaved roads and a rocky old wagon track.

Maps: The roads that make up this ride are clearly indicated in *A Map of the Province of Nova Scotia* (map 36, sections E-3 and E-4). For a more detailed representation of the area, refer to the government topographic map Dingwall 11 K/16.

Finding the trail: We began this ride from the government wharf in Bay St. Lawrence, approximately 15 km (9.3 miles) from the Cabot Trail. To get to the wharf, turn off the Cabot Trail in Cape North. Drive north on an unnumbered road to the community of Bay St. Lawrence. You will pass a turnoff to Capstick and Meat Cove on the left, before arriving in Bay St. Lawrence. The government wharf is approximately 500 m (three-tenths of a mile) beyond St. Andrew's Church. You will find plenty of space to park at the wharf.

Source of additional information: For tales about Money Point and the surrounding area, you may want to pick up a copy of *Mountain Bike Nova Scotia*, a 1996 Nimbus publication by Geoff Brown and Kermit Degooyer.

Notes on the trail: From the parking area at the government wharf, turn right up the paved road on which you drove in and head south, back toward the Cabot

Trail. At the first split in the road, continue straight. The road on the left (old Money Point Road) is the one on which you will complete the ride, and it's paved at this end. Continue straight at the next junction, following the sign for the town of Cape North and passing the paved road branching off to the right toward Capstick and Meat Cove. Just beyond this junction, the road swings sharply to the left and continues climbing gradually. You will ride past a small, open, gravelly area on the left, before coming to a few garage buildings, also on the left. Just beyond these buildings, and before the main road begins to descend slightly, turn left up a wide, graded dirt road.

You will begin to climb immediately, and very steeply. Although wide and fairly well maintained, this road is made slightly more technically challenging by virtue of some eroded gullies. Your reward for this first climb is a tremendous view across Bay St. Lawrence to the left. Continue to follow the road as it twists its way uphill. The worst of this first climb is over when you pass a communications tower on the right. Be sure to stick to the main road, riding past all driveways and side trails. Beyond the tower, the road actually descends slightly, before cutting sharply to the right. Another dazzling view of St. Margaret's Village and Deadman's Cove awaits you on the left here. Then, as you ride out of the curve, look right for a dramatic view over Aspy Bay.

The road continues along the top of the mountain, bordered on both sides by scrubby trees that betray the harsh weather conditions in this area. Although you may catch views to the left and right through clearings off the side of the road, this relatively level stretch of the ride is really quite closed in by the trees on either side.

Stay straight when you come to a road that leads up to a series of communications towers on the left. A short distance farther, you will pass another road on the left that leads up to a coast guard station. Beyond this last offshoot, the main road deteriorates into a track with a grassy median and descends to a **T** junction with the old Money Point Road. The ride out to Money Point continues to the right. To the left is the road you will take on your return to the government wharf in Bay St. Lawrence.

After turning right onto the old Money Point Road, you will descend through a dip in the road and then climb a short distance to a **Y** intersection. The route to Money Point follows the power lines along the road that descends to the left. However, you may want first to head up the road to the right, which leads into a clearing that was once the site of a microwave tower. Should you choose to explore this short side trip, make your way to the far end of the clearing at the end of the road. Leave your bike at the edge of the clearing and follow any one of a few footpaths that lead to the edge of the awe-inspiring cliffs that sweep down toward Aspy Bay. This view serves well as a reminder of the elevation you will lose on the way down to Money Point as you continue the ride. When you've had your fill of the view, descend back to the last intersection, and turn right to head down the road to Money Point.

As you follow the power lines down the old Money Point Road, you will be riding on a double-track road with a grassy median. Four-wheel-drive accessible for the first 300 m (less than one-tenth of a mile), the road drops to a small clearing that serves as a turnaround for vehicles. This is the point of no return, as the road that continues from here plunges straight down to the ocean. This descent is treacherous, strewn with flinty rocks and loose boulders and unbelievably steep.

At the bottom of the hill you will find yourself in a grassy meadow at the edge of the ocean, where a wagon track extends both left and right. A short distance to the right is the site of the *Kismet II* shipwreck. The ride continues to the left, following the edge of the coast toward the lighthouse. Past the lighthouse, the trail continues a short distance farther, up to a grassy knoll that offers a dramatic view of the point.

Naturally, there is only one way to leave Money Point by bike. Steel yourself for the grueling trip back up the old road. The turnaround offers brief respite before the remainder of the climb. Turn right when you finally reach the **Y** intersection at the top of the climb. You will drop back through the small dip in the road. Continue straight, past the road you followed in on the left and up to a tremendous view overlooking Bay St. Lawrence and Deadman's Cove. There may be a cable across this road before it begins a steep and eroded descent to the community of Bay St. Lawrence. As you make your way down, the condition of the road will gradually improve until you reach pavement. Ride past Burton's General Store, and then turn right to return to the government wharf, where you parked.

RIDE 65 · Trous de Saumons

AT A GLANCE

Length/configuration: 13-km (8-mile) out-and-back (6.5 km [4 miles] each way)

Aerobic difficulty: Suitable for all fitness levels; only short climbs

Technical difficulty: Easy; double-track trail with short sections of rough terrain toward the end of the ride

Scenery: This ride parallels the Cheticamp River up a sheltered valley of Acadian forest

Special comments: Pools on the Cheticamp River attract anglers fishing for Atlantic salmon

Trous de Saumons is an easy, 13-km (8-mile) out-and-back ride along a former road. Hard-packed and well graded along most of the route, the trail includes only a few sections of exposed and loose rock, where erosion has dete-

RIDE 65 • Trous de Saumons

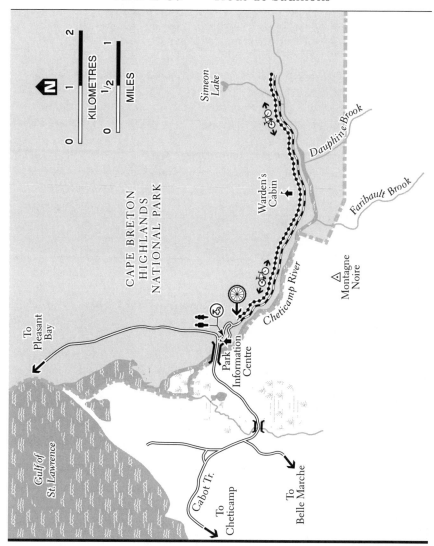

riorated the trail surface. Fortunately, these conditions exist only after the trail reaches a warden's cabin 3.5 km (2 miles) into the ride. Up to this point, the ride is suitable for novices and makes a great 7-km (4.3-mile) round-trip for families or group excursions involving riders of mixed skill levels. Beyond the warden's cabin, the trail becomes both technically and aerobically more difficult. A deteriorating trail surface and several short but steep hills require slightly higher skill and fitness levels.

French for "salmon pools," the name of this ride describes the deep lagoons that make the Cheticamp River a favourite destination among anglers. Only fly fishing is permitted on the river, where people come to try their luck casting for Atlantic salmon. Following the river inland from where it empties into the Gulf of St. Lawrence, you will ride into an ever-narrowing valley along the base of the its northern slope. Along the first section of the ride, the trail lies in the shadow of Montagne Noire, which looms over the river from the southern side of the valley. Farther up, the trail enters a narrow ravine before steep cliffs literally force the end of the trail.

General location: North of Cheticamp, in the southwest corner of Cape Breton Highlands National Park.

Elevation change: Although there is no appreciable gain in elevation on this ride, you will find the return trip slightly faster, as you experience the gentle slope back down toward the ocean.

Season: Mid-May to late October. Note that the lower section of this ride is likely to be wet in the spring, as runoff from the highlands causes the Cheticamp River to swell.

Services: With the exception of a bike store, you will find all services in Cheticamp, just a short distance south of the trailhead. Basic services, including water and washrooms, are even closer to the trailhead, at the Cheticamp Information Centre. For bike rentals, service, or tour guides and information, contact Sea Spray Cycle in Dingwall at (902) 383-2911 or (902) 383-2732.

Hazards: Bikers may encounter a few isolated eroded spots on the trail, particularly toward the end of the ride.

Rescue index: At the farthest point on this ride, you will be 6.5 km (4 miles) from the very busy Cheticamp Information Centre near the trailhead. Chances are good that you will encounter other trail users as well.

Land status: National park; from mid-May to mid-October there is an entry fee for all park visitors.

Maps: Detailed topographic maps for the park can be purchased at the Cheticamp Information Centre, located just inside the park boundary. For this particular ride, the free map offered to all visitors to the park is probably adequate. The Trous de Saumons trail is number 2 on the map.

Finding the trail: Enter the park on the Cabot Trail, heading north from Cheticamp. After crossing the Cheticamp River, and just before the entrance kiosk for the park, turn right into the parking area for the Park Information Centre. The trailhead for Trous de Saumons is located past the parking area.

Source of additional information:

Cape Breton Highlands National Park
Ingonish Beach, NS B0C 1L0
(902) 224-2306 or (902) 285-2691 (year-round)

Notes on the trail: From the parking area behind the Cheticamp Information Centre, follow a road through the campground and toward the group camping area. Ride past a "Department Vehicles Only Beyond This Point" sign, and be sure to continue past a road that heads uphill on the left. Although there is a sign marking the Trous de Saumons trail, it is small and not very obvious. There is a metal gate at the trailhead, beyond which the trail continues as a wide, hard-packed path.

You will climb a small hill before quickly descending on the trail, which begins through a pretty hardwood forest. The trail is clear and easy to follow, and meanders through the woods like a pathway through a vast park. You will cross two small bridges before coming close to the river, which will be on your right. Take some time to stop at this point and look out across the first of a series of salmon pools. There is an observation area here, where the patient and keen-sighted may catch a glimpse of the elusive Atlantic salmon.

Beyond this first salmon pool, the trail climbs to the crest of a hill. A warden's cabin is situated by the side of the trail here. It is beyond this point that the trail conditions become more difficult. As the valley narrows, so does the trail. If you do continue farther up the trail, you will pass Chance's Pool just beyond the warden's cabin. A few kilometres (a mile or so) farther up the trail, you will ride into a clearing. A large boulder toward the end of this clearing prevents bikers from continuing any farther. Turn around here to return to the trailhead and parking area.

RIDE 66 · Pembroke Lake

AT A GLANCE

Length/configuration: 32-km (20-mile) out-and-back (16 km [10 miles] each way)

Aerobic difficulty: Several long climbs and descents make this a strenuous ride

Technical difficulty: Basic; well-maintained forestry roads with some areas of loose gravel

Scenery: Deep, forested valleys and the rugged, barren landscape of Cape Breton's highlands

Special comments: We hope you are met by our friends Alexander and Keith at the end of this ride!

The ride up to Pembroke Lake is a short but strenuous climb on a wide gravel road. Beyond the lake, this ride continues inland and taps into a vast network of forestry roads that are used extensively by snowmobile clubs in the

RIDE 66 • Pembroke Lake

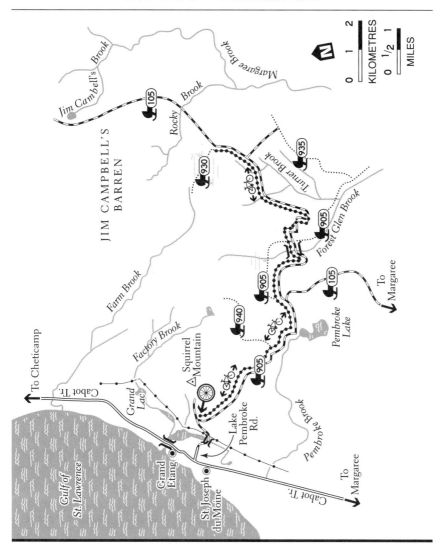

winter and by ATV riders in the summer. Thanks to these organized groups, the roads are well marked and mapped and offer endless kilometres of riding to fat-tire enthusiasts. Be prepared to turn some heads, however: the sight of mountain bikers returning from this hilly terrain is enough to generate at least an offer of a cold post-ride beverage, if not an invitation for a dinner of deer stew. It is likely that anyone you meet will be impressed (or dumbfounded) by your willingness to set out on these roads under your own power. Although they require only the basics of good bike handling skills, solid cardiovascular con-

Ruthie and Evanger cruise by the calm waters of Pembroke Lake.

ditioning is a must. Nevertheless, the rewards are many, and whether you are looking for wildlife, the chance to explore the rugged interior of Cape Breton Island, or simply an escape in and out of deep, forested valleys, this area has much to offer.

The ride we describe is a 32-km (20-mile) out-and-back excursion that will consume all of either a morning or an afternoon. However, the network of trails you will be following offers unlimited options for both shortening or lengthening the ride, particularly for the sake of exploring some of the side trails and interconnecting snowmobile routes. Riders should be cautioned that not all of the snowmobile trails depicted on the maps of the area can be traversed in the summer: bogs, rivers, and streams cannot always be negotiated by mountain bike. For example, Snowmobile Trail 930, which is shown as a link trail to Trail 940, is not a maintained or even passable trail in the summer. If the spirit of adventure moves you to explore beyond the route we have described, be sure to carry plenty of water and extra food. Be aware that the weather can change quickly, and never ride beyond the point that you will be able to comfortably turn around and retrace your path back to the trailhead.

General location: Inverness County, just a few kilometres (a mile or so) south of the southern boundary of Cape Breton Highlands National Park.

Elevation change: From where you begin this ride, at approximately 90 m (300 feet), you will immediately climb to 335 m (1,100 feet) at Pembroke Lake. From the lake, although you will climb a few small hills, you will essentially descend back down to 213 m (700 feet) at the crossing of Forest Glen Brook. From there, you will climb steeply and then more gradually to the highest point on the ride, at 425 m (1,400 feet). The total elevation gain for the round-trip ride is just over 600 m (almost 2,000 feet).

Season: The roads that this ride follows should be in good condition from May through October. In the winter, most of the roads are used as snowmobile trails.

Services: Most services are available on nearby Highway 19, with the exception of bicycle service and repair. The closest source of bike-related goods and services is at Island Eco-Adventures in Baddeck (phone (902) 295-3303).

Hazards: Keep your eyes and ears open for the few four-wheel-drive vehicles that may be on these roads. Remember too that it can be very easy to follow roads for long distances in one direction. Be sure to always allow enough time to safely make your way back again. As with all the rides on Cape Breton Island, bring food, water, and extra clothing. Additionally, carry tools and plenty of extra inner tubes to ward off the possibility of a flat along one of the fast, rocky downhills.

Rescue index: You will be more than 16 hilly km (10 miles) from assistance at the half way point on this ride.

Land status: These forestry roads penetrate the Crown lands south of Cape Breton Highlands National Park and Jim Campbell's Barren.

Maps: There is a wonderful snowmobile trail map put out by the Inverness, Victoria Counties Trails Federation. Although the map provides little in the way of detail and no indication of the status of the trails in the summertime, it does give a comprehensive outline of the snowmobile trail system throughout Cape Breton Island. We miraculously obtained a copy of this map partway through our ride, after a chance encounter with a group of kind snowmobile enthusiasts who were scouting out the trails by truck in the summer. However, you can plan ahead and obtain a copy of the map from:

Inverness, Victoria Counties Trails Federation
P.O. Box 828
Cheticamp, NS B0E 1H0

Additionally, many of the roads in this area are indicated in *A Map of the Province of Nova Scotia* (map 37, sections A-4 and B-4).

Finding the trail: From Inverness, head north on the Cabot Trail toward Cheticamp. In the community of St. Joseph du Moine (before you reach Grand Etang), look on the right for a paved road that is signed for Pembroke Lake and is referred to as Lake Pembroke Road. Turn right, and the pavement will end just before the road swings around to the right. Continue on the unpaved portion of the road, which will descend before rounding a bend to the left and crossing a small brook. From the brook, the road continues uphill and crosses beneath a transmission line. Pull over, and park on the left at the first **Y** in the road. The ride begins up the fork on the right.

Sources of additional information:

Inverness Recreation and Tourism Department
P.O. Box 179
Port Hood, NS B0E 2W0
(902) 787-2278

Victoria County Recreation Department
P.O. Box 370
Baddeck, NS B0E 1B0
(902) 295-3231

Notes on the trail: From where you have parked, begin riding up the right fork in the road. For the first kilometre (0.6 mile), you will be climbing very steeply. Beyond that point, you will continue to climb, but more gradually than at first. Pass a double-track, grassy jeep trail on the left, and then, just a short distance farther, pass another logging road on the left. Continue to follow the main road, past a road descending on the right. Beyond this offshoot, the climbing levels off a bit, although the road continues to twist and turn. When we rode here, a sizable log pile to the right of the road was posted as "Hector's Log Pile." Keep to the main road, passing another trail branching off to the right beyond the log pile.

You will come to an indistinct three-way intersection of snowmobile trails approximately 4 km (2.6 miles) into the ride. At this point, Snowmobile Trail 940 North is signed along a grassy trail to the left. Continue straight here, following the main road, which is signed as Trail 905 South. A short distance from this point, you will come into your first view of Pembroke Lake. The road curves around the left side of the water, affording good views of the length of the lake.

Continuing on the road beyond Pembroke Lake, you will come to another snowmobile sign. To the left, Trail 905 is signed to Forest Glen and follows a much more overgrown, grassy double-track trail. Straight ahead on the main road is Trail 105. Continue straight for just a short distance, after which you will come to a significant intersection of wide, graded logging roads. There is another snowmobile sign at the middle of this junction: Trail 105 South, heading toward Margaree, continues uphill to the right; and Trail 105 North drops downhill to the left. The road you have ridden up is signed to Grand Etang. Bear left at this intersection, descending on Snowmobile Trail 105 North and heading in the direction of Jim Campbell's Barren.

What begins as a gradual descent eventually heads straight down into a deep valley. The gravel road seems built for speed at this point: it is wide, well signed, and free of obstacles. The view is stunning: heavily forested, flat-topped hills fall away dramatically into valleys that follow the winding paths of streams and brooks. A few sharp bends in the road are signed and will force you to slow your descent somewhat. As you approach the valley floor, you descend steeply before crossing Forest Glen Brook.

Beyond Forest Glen Brook, a steep climb on loose gravel awaits—time to sweat back all the elevation you just lost! You will climb up to a four-way intersection of snowmobile trails, where you will want to continue straight on Trail

105 North. To the left is Trail 905 to Forest Glen, and to the right, the 905 continues to Margaree Valley. The landscape changes around this intersection, showing signs of recent tree harvesting operations. Beyond the intersection, you will be faced with a rather significant climb.

Toward the end of your climb, you will pass a double-track logging road branching off on the right. This road is less distinct than the main road, on which you want to continue climbing. A short distance farther, you will reach a bit of a plateau. Continue past an old logging road branching off on the left, and then pass two more, also on the left. The road continues with less severe, more undulating hills. You will pass another logging road on the left as the road swings around to the right. Just past this intersection, the main road swings back to the left and descends over a small brook. You will pass another logging road that branches off over your right shoulder. All these logging roads are rather vague and indistinct, so it is very easy to follow the trail, which keeps to the main road.

Beyond the last brook crossing, you will approach the highest point of the ride and pass an improved dirt road branching off to the right, perpendicular to the main trail. This road is signed as Trail 935 to Rocky Brook. Continue straight on the main road, climbing ever so gradually to the 425-m (1,400-foot) mark. At this point, the road surface deteriorates and becomes extremely rough and rocky for a short distance, before descending slightly and passing a road branching off on the right. Once again, keep to the main trail. You will reach the snowmobile trail junction with Trail 930 on the left at exactly 16 km (10 miles). Unless you have the energy to continue farther, turn around here and retrace your route down, up, and down again to the trailhead. Overall, the return trip feels faster than the way out. If you do plan to explore this area further, be sure that you are carrying a map, plenty of food and water, and extra clothing!

RIDE 67 · Cape Mabou

AT A GLANCE

Length/configuration: 31-km (19-mile) loop

Aerobic difficulty: Intermediate to advanced; extended climbs on dirt roads at moderate grades

Technical difficulty: Intermediate riding on dirt and old woods roads

Scenery: Ocean bluffs and cultivated highlands

Special comments: A must-see off of the Cabot Trail

RIDE 67 • Cape Mabou

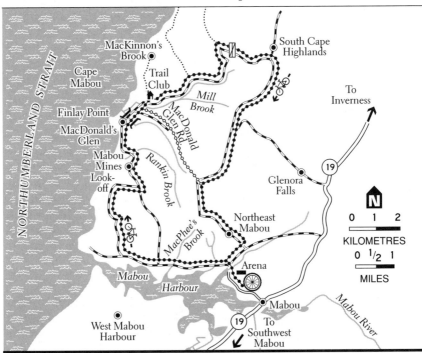

The ride at Cape Mabou is situated in the heart of Scottish country, off the Ceilidh (pronounced "kay-lee") Trail on Cape Breton Island. The history of Scottish settlement here is reflected in the names of the area's geographical landmarks and cultivated highlands. You will explore the features and history of the area on this 31-km (19-mile) loop, which begins along the coast, is bordered by small farms, and then travels inland on wooded trails. You will pass former town sites and ride through a glen before returning through the farm fields to the trailhead.

Cape Mabou is situated along the western edge of the Cape Breton highlands, a rugged and beautiful region characterized by deep, narrow valleys and steep hillsides. This trail includes several extended climbs, which you may find increasingly challenging over the course of the 31-km (19-mile) loop. The terrain is varied, including well-maintained dirt roads, rocky double-track trails, and old gravel roads. It is a fun ride, suitable for anyone with beginner to intermediate stamina and bike-handling skills. Your excursion can also include a side trip to Sight Point. This option offers a challenging hike up to the edge of the cliffs overlooking the Northumberland Strait, to what is said to be one of the best views in Nova Scotia. If you choose this side trip, by the time you return to your bike and complete the ride, you will have propelled yourself over 50 km (30 miles) in one day.

Turning inland from the coast, the trails at Cape Mabou follow narrow valleys along streams, woods, and old pastureland.

General location: In the vicinity of Mabou, on the west side of Cape Breton Island in Inverness County.

Elevation change: The longest climb, at the beginning of this ride, gains 155 m (508 feet) of elevation. Over subsequent moderate hills, you will gain an additional 325 m (1,066 feet), for a total gain of 480 m (1,574 feet) throughout the ride.

Season: Rain is the biggest threat to riding in this area and can be highly unpredictable. July and September are considered the driest months, although the riding season may begin as early as June and continue to October.

Services: Although the town of Mabou has an excellent bakery and café, bicycle service is more difficult to come by. The nearest shops are to be found in Baddeck or on the mainland in Antigonish.

Hazards: Sections of loose rock on the double-track trails provide little traction and require good bike-handling skills, especially on the descents.

Rescue index: A small population is scattered throughout the area, but riders should be prepared to return to the parking area or nearby Mabou for assistance.

Land status: Dirt roads and old roads through private pastures and Crown land in the highlands.

Maps: All roads appear in A *Map of the Province of Nova Scotia* (map 33, sections B-4 and C-4). Refer also to government topographic map, Lake Ainslie 11 K/3.

Finding the trail: Traveling toward Cape Breton Island on the Trans-Canada Highway from the mainland, cross the Canso Causeway to Port Hastings. Across the bridge, follow NS Route 19 north (Cabot Trail) for approximately 60 km (36 miles) to Mabou. There is only one opportunity to turn left in Mabou, just beyond the bakery and café. Continue for a short distance after this turn, to an arena on the right-hand side of the road. There is plenty of parking available here.

Sources of additional information: Consult Michael Haynes' *Hiking Trails of Nova Scotia* for additional information on the hiking side trip, or contact the Cape Mabou Trail Club (General Delivery, Inverness, NS B0E 1N0) for information about the status of the trails in the area. For other rides in the area, refer to a brochure called *Trails of Inverness County*, available at Visitor Information Centres throughout the province.

Notes on the trail: Departing from the arena just west of Mabou, turn right and continue on the paved road. You will cross a bridge over Northeast Cove and then continue past several cow pastures. The road will briefly approach the shores of Mabou Harbour before continuing inland. After crossing MacPhee's Brook, you will pass a road on the right and continue toward the mouth of Mabou Harbour, where the road crosses two inlets, bridging the first and hugging closely to the shores of the second. After the second inlet, you will reach an intersection where the ride continues up the road to the right. However, for a quick side trip, turn left and ride down to the public wharf located near the mouth of Mabou Harbour.

Continuing the ride up the road to the right, you will begin an extended climb to a look-off across Mabou Mines and the Northumberland Strait. This is a steady climb and over the course of 2.5 km (1.5 miles), you will gain roughly 155 m (508 feet) of elevation. The road follows the rocky, jagged coast, offering views over the cliffs to the Northumberland Strait on one side and inland to the pastoral highlands on the other. From the look-off, you can see out to Finlay Point and up toward the highlands into which you will continue the ride. Beyond the look-off, follow the road as it curves around to the right, heading inland, and descend through the woods to a **T** junction. Turn left at the **T** junction, following a wide, gravel road heading north. Almost immediately on the left, you will pass a road that descends to Mabou Mines, the site of a coal mine that operated for just a few years in the early 1900s. The village that grew up around the mine was abandoned when the mining company shut down, and if you venture down this road you will discover that nothing remains of the town. The coast is worth exploring, however, and the site makes for a beautiful and interesting side trip.

Beyond Mabou Mines, the hard-packed dirt road descends gradually. You will pass the access road to a wharf on your left as well as several homes. Continue on the main road, crossing a bridge over Rankin Brook before reaching an intersection with a gravel road on the right. This road is the MacDonald Glen Road and, although it looks like a driveway, the road actually continues up past a white house with green trim.

The ride continues straight at this point, heading toward Mill Brook, but you can significantly shorten your ride with an optional right turn onto the MacDonald Glen Road. Glen Road continues as a double-track trail. The trail descends to a bridge, and then climbs up into a small clearing. Keep to the main trail beyond this point, passing several old logging roads on the left. The trail gradually deteriorates, becoming rougher and more overgrown. After a short distance, the grassy surface is liable to become quite wet and rocky, as the trail flirts and trades places with a small stream. After the trail and the stream split, a tough climb will lead you up to a crossroads. A wide gravel road continues straight and to the left at this point, and there is a vague, grassy trail that leads to the right. The shortcut continues straight, descending along the dirt road to a **T** junction in Northeast Mabou. Turn right at this **T** junction, following another road to another **T** junction with the main road through Mabou. Turn left here, crossing Northeast Cove to return to the trailhead at arena.

Back on the main ride, continue straight past the MacDonald Glen Road and descend toward Mill Brook. This section of the road is sheltered by trees and continues in very good condition on hard-packed dirt. Bear right past a vague trail on the left and cross the bridge over Mill Brook. You will quickly come to the Mabou Post Road trailhead, marked with a bulletin board providing information about the trails managed by the Cape Mabou Trail Club. Pass this trailhead on your left and continue straight on the dirt road.

You will pass a rough, dirt road branching off to the right as you follow the main road, climbing gradually up into MacIsaac's Glen. You will then descend to a clearing where apple trees grow and a beaver dam has created a pool in MacIsaac's Glen Brook. Here, you will cross a bridge and begin climbing up the other side of the narrow valley. Keep to the main road as you climb, passing all the hiking trails signed for Sight Point and MacKinnon's Brook, as well as Fair Alistair's Mountain along the Mabou Post Road. The road continues just a short distance further before crossing another bridge. Beyond the bridge, the road continues uphill to a sharp curve to the right, at which point there is a gate across the road and an overgrown trail on the left that leads to Sight Point.

Follow the main road around to the right, passing the trail on the left and continuing past the gate. You will be heading uphill for a short distance before the road levels off and comes to a **T** junction with another dirt road just south of the community of South Cape Highlands. Turn right here, beginning a section of the ride that passes through a former Scottish settlement. You will notice old foundations off the side of the road, and the remnants of abandoned farms scattered throughout the fields. Follow this dirt road to a three-way intersection marked by snowmobile trail signs. Here, the Glenora Falls Road descends to the left and another dirt road continues straight ahead. Continue straight, following the relatively level road past several logging roads branching off on both the left and right. Further along, the road begins to descend. At a sharp bend in the road to the left, you will pass the other end of the MacDonald Glen Road on the right. Keep to the main road, descending all the way to a **T** junction with a dirt road in Northeast Mabou. Turn right, and continue down the road a short distance to a **T** junction with the main road you started on. Turn left and cross the bridge over Northeast Cove to return to the parking area at the arena.

RIDE 68 · River Denys Mountain

AT A GLANCE

Length/configuration: 19.3-km (12-mile) loop

Aerobic difficulty: Modest; comfortable climbs and descents

Technical difficulty: Mixed; graded dirt roads and a final stretch along a more rugged cart track

Scenery: Wooded countryside that tells the history of early settlement in the area

Special comments: A fire tower near River Denys Mountain offers spectacular views on clear days

The ride up River Denys Mountain is a pleasant and rewarding one, offering access to an old community church, as well as to a fire tower that provides panoramic views of the surrounding countryside, including views of Bras d'Or Lake and the Nova Scotia mainland. This 19.3-km (12-mile) loop is technically easy for the most part, following graded gravel roads and double-track trails. The ride does conclude over slightly more difficult terrain, with a short descent along a rough cart track that has suffered some damage due to flooding. You will need less than half a day to complete this ride, allowing you plenty of time to wander around the Saint Margaret of Scotland Church that now stands in solitary testament to the community that once existed here. From the church, your ride can continue as a pilgrimage to the fire tower near River Denys Mountain. There, you can add your own name to the fire tower walls as you search for the inscription of two great adventurers: Ruthie and Evangerswish.

RIDE 68 • River Denys Mountain

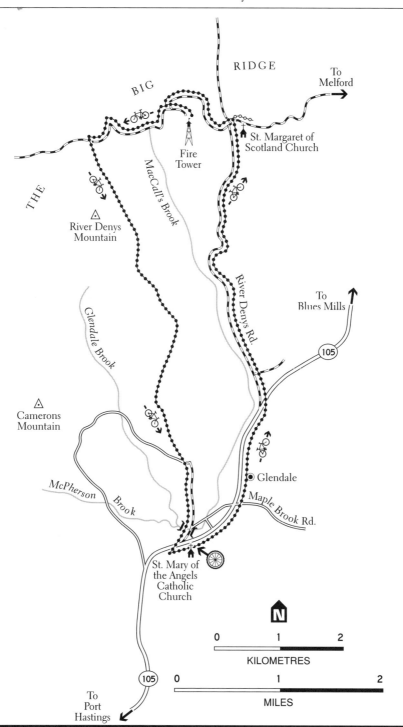

Racing along an old cart track in the final descent from River Denys Mountain.

From the fire tower, it is possible to gaze out over a seemingly endless series of low, rolling hills and forested countryside. The view is spectacular on a clear day, stretching out to St. George's Bay to the west and to Bras d'Or Lake to the east. Furthermore, the rural and potentially confusing nature of the landscape will be apparent from this vantage point: you will notice that the area is crossed by old cart tracks, newer logging roads, trails marked for snowmobiles in the winter, and farm roads that wander far from the beaten track. Although this ride is relatively straightforward, it is important to carry a compass and a detailed topographic map in case you either choose to wander or inadvertently drift farther into the confusing network of roads and trails.

General location: River Denys Mountain is in Glendale, approximately 25 km (15.5 miles) northeast of the Canso Causeway, on Highway 105.

Elevation change: From where you begin this ride, you will be at an elevation of approximately 60 m (200 feet). You will climb to roughly 334 m (1,095 feet) at the fire tower. The elevation change over the course of the loop is approximately 550 m (1,800 feet).

Season: Riding conditions are suitable from June through October. Be aware that the last leg of this ride descends along a cart track susceptible to wet conditions in the early spring and after heavy rainfall.

Services: There are no services at the trailhead, and Highway 105 offers little more than gas stations and convenience stores. For access to all other services, travel south to Port Hastings or Port Hawkesbury.

Hazards: Be aware that this region is covered with a maze of old roads and trails that can be confusing to follow. If you choose to climb to the top of the fire tower near River Denys Mountain, use care on the rather steep, narrow ladder.

Rescue index: You will not travel more than 10 km (6 miles) from Highway 105.

Land status: This ride follows gravel roads and cart tracks with public rights-of-way.

Maps: The River Denys Mountain ride is outlined in a map brochure entitled *Trails of Inverness County*, which can be obtained through the Visitor Information Centre in Port Hastings. In addition, all the trails that form this ride appear in *A Map of the Province of Nova Scotia* (map 34, sections D-2, D-1, C-1, and C-2).

Finding the trail: Travel north from Port Hastings on NS Highway 105. You will pass through the communities of Queensville and Kingsville before reaching Glendale. The ride begins from the Catholic Church of Saint Mary of the Angels in Glendale, which will be on the right side of Highway 105 as you approach it from the south.

Sources of additional information: There is a Visitor Information Centre in Port Hastings that is well signed and located immediately off of the Canso Causeway. There, you can pick up a copy of a guide entitled *Trails of Inverness County* and ask for any more recent information. Alternatively, write and ask for a copy of the guide (a folded pamphlet with very basic maps):

Inverness County Tourism Department
P.O. Box 179
Port Hood, NS B0E 2W0

Notes on the trail: From the parking lot of Saint Mary of the Angels Catholic Church, turn right onto Highway 105 and begin riding up the paved road. Ride past the intersection of Maple Brook Road and continue straight on the highway, keeping your eyes open for River Denys Road on the left. You may notice a large green sign indicating River Denys Mountain. Carefully cross Highway 105 and turn left up the unpaved River Denys Road.

River Denys Road is a wide, well-maintained, graded gravel road that climbs gradually into the hills. Almost immediately after turning onto the road, continue straight past a gravel road on the right that is marked with snowmobile signs. Farther up the road, you will ride past a grassy track on the right, a snowmobile trail branching off on the left, and a grassy double-track road to a cabin also on the left. Keep to the main road at all these junctions. River Denys Road will eventually level off before a short descent to a **T** junction with another unpaved road.

At this **T** junction you will notice a small, painted snowmobile trail sign on the left. The ride continues to the left, following the signs toward Snowmobile Trail 104, and the 505 Alpine Club Trails, Port Hastings, Port Hawkesbury, food, gas, and lodging. However, for a short side trip to the Saint Margaret of Scotland church, turn right.

The side trip to the church involves a short ride down the main gravel road. As you follow this road around to the right, you will ride past a road branching downhill on the left. The church is a short distance beyond this junction, on the right. A row of white-painted stones by the side of the road lead up to the church itself, and a small, old graveyard stretches toward the woods out back. You can see the fire tower, your next destination, from this site. To resume the ride, backtrack to the **T** junction with the snowmobile trail signs.

As you approach the junction with the snowmobile trail signs, simply follow the road you are on around to the right. You will pass River Denys Road, the way you came up, on the left. A short distance around the bend in the road, a recent clear-cut opens up views of the rolling countryside to your right. Continue straight at this point, past a clearing that serves as a logging yard and a logging road that branches off on the right. Just beyond the logging area, the road curves gently to the left, whereupon you will see a very distinct gravel road that leads up to the fire tower. Turn left and ride up this access road to the fire tower. There is a small cabin at the foot of the tower, where you might find our friend John O'Brian. With his help and the reassuring security of harnesses, we proceeded up to the look-off at the top of the tower. After paying homage to Ruthie and Evangerswish, we were able to gaze out across the rolling, wooded countryside through which we had been riding. If you are able to make this journey on a clear day, you will be able to see the southern reaches of Bras d'Or Lake as well as the Nova Scotia mainland.

From the fire tower, follow the access road back down to the main road and turn left. Bear left again almost immediately, past an offshoot on the right. Keeping to the main road, which is the most distinct route, pass one logging road branching off on the left, and then another one a short distance farther on. Follow the main road as it swings to the right and then curves back to the left. Immediately after this, you will come to a three-way intersection that almost looks like a **T** junction. Turn left onto a grassy double-track trail.

From the **T** junction, you will begin heading down a less maintained four-wheel-drive road that quickly becomes overgrown and enters the woods. Bear left at the first fork in this trail, following the snowmobile trail markers. A short distance farther, the trail narrows significantly beyond a small clearing that has unfortunately been used as a dumping ground for old household items. Continue onward, passing several vague offshoots that appear at irregular intervals on both sides of the main trail. You will most likely encounter occasional wet patches and large, stagnant puddles covering deep wallows of thick mud. This old road will lead you deeper into the woods, changing from a hard-packed trail through an open area overgrown with alders to a mossy woods trail ducking through a forest of old, dead, and new growth.

A couple kilometres (a mile or so) down this old road, you will descend along a portion of the trail that, when we rode it, had been eroded to the point that a narrow gully had been created by a stream. The trail surface is very rocky along this section of the ride, and you will have to pick your way down to a large steel culvert, beyond which the trail gradually improves. Past the culvert, the trail merges into a more maintained gravel road. There is a gate on the right, a trail branching off on the left, and homes a short distance farther on. Continue heading downhill, passing Apple Tree Farm on the right. Follow the road out to a **T** junction with an unpaved, red gravel road and turn left. This is MacInnis Road. At the next **T** junction, turn right and cross a brook over a bridge to Highway 105. Turn right on Highway 105 and return to the church, where you parked.

RIDE 69 · Eigg Mountain

AT A GLANCE

Length/configuration: 24-km (15-mile) loop

Aerobic difficulty: Moderate; the ride begins with a steady, gradual climb

Technical difficulty: Easy; a combination of double-track trails, logging roads, and some pavement

Scenery: Several beautiful views, especially along the final downhill stretch

Special comments: Arisaig Provincial Park includes walking trails that descend to the ocean

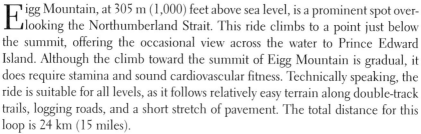

Eigg Mountain, at 305 m (1,000) feet above sea level, is a prominent spot overlooking the Northumberland Strait. This ride climbs to a point just below the summit, offering the occasional view across the water to Prince Edward Island. Although the climb toward the summit of Eigg Mountain is gradual, it does require stamina and sound cardiovascular fitness. Technically speaking, the ride is suitable for all levels, as it follows relatively easy terrain along double-track trails, logging roads, and a short stretch of pavement. The total distance for this loop is 24 km (15 miles).

The ride up Eigg Mountain begins from Arisaig Provincial Park in Antigonish County. The park overlooks the Northumberland Strait and includes a campground, picnic sites, toilets, water, and an interpretive centre that provides geological information about the region. Arisaig is a popular destination among geologists because of the number of fossils that can be viewed from the shore

RIDE 69 • Eigg Mountain

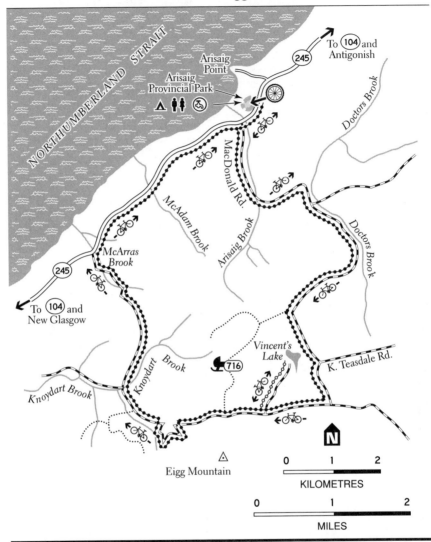

below the park. In fact, the area boasts one of the world's best, exposed sections of Silurian rocks, which date back 438 to 408 million years. After your ride, it is well worth stretching out along the boardwalk and walking to the beach, where you may find examples of these four-million-year-old fossils in the sedimentary rock.

General location: Arisaig Provincial Park is located northwest of Antigonish.

Elevation change: From Arisaig Provincial Park, you will climb steadily to

Climbing up Eigg Mountain beneath a canopy of birch trees overshadowing Doctors Brook.

approximately 285 m (935 feet) on Eigg Mountain. Total elevation change for the complete loop is roughly 570 m (1,870 feet).

Season: Riding conditions are suitable from late May through October.

Services: All services are available in Antigonish.

Hazards: You will cross a bridge of questionable stability along the initial uphill climb to the top of Eigg Mountain. Toward the end of the ride, watch your speed, as well as possible traffic, on a long, winding descent that includes a couple of tight turns.

Rescue index: At the half way point in this loop, you will be about 10 km (6 miles) from assistance.

Land status: You will be following an old wagon track and a series of logging roads through Crown lands.

Maps: This ride can be found in A *Map of the Province of Nova Scotia* (map 29, section B-3).

Finding the trail: To reach Arisaig Provincial Park from Antigonish, head west on NS Highway 245. Bear left at a fork when you reach the ocean, and continue through the small town of Arisaig. You will pass a road on the right that descends to Arisaig Point. The park entrance is clearly marked and will be on your right. There is parking available at the trailhead for the interpretive centre, which is adjacent to the outhouse and water pumps.

Source of additional information: Stop in and see the folks at Peak Performance Bicycle Shop on the Post Road in Antigonish (phone (902) 863-6722).

Notes on the trail: From the parking area at Arisaig Provincial Park, ride back out to Highway 245 and turn right. After passing one road branching off to the left, turn left on the unpaved MacDonald Road. This road crosses Arisaig Brook and then narrows considerably. At this point, you will be riding in the shadows of the steep walls of sedimentary rock that rise high above the road, creating dramatic slopes of crumbling rock and a dark, tunnel-like atmosphere. You will cross Arisaig Brook again before coming to a **Y** in the road. Bear right at this fork.

Beyond the fork, continue on the main trail for some distance. You will pass a road heading uphill to the left. You will then round a bend to the left and pass a driveway on the left. You will ride past two houses, one on either side of the road, before arriving at a point in the road where a double-track road branches off to the left, heading uphill. Bear right past this road and begin a short, gradual descent. You will pass grassy trails branching off either side of the road at irregular intervals; keep to the main road, which is obvious and easy to follow. Beyond a clearing on the left, you will cross a wooden bridge over Doctors Brook. Past the bridge, there is another **Y** intersection. Bear right onto the less distinct, grassy trail. When we pedaled this ride, there were several small white signs with a red mountain bike stencil marking this route.

Turning right past Doctors Brook takes you along a very pretty section of this ride. You will be in the woods, a combination of hard- and softwoods that are spectacular in the autumn, and the trail often comes very close to the brook. The most startling characteristic of this portion of the ride is how quiet it is; the canopy of branches and leaves seems to muffle even the gentle sound of the brook. The trail climbs steadily but gradually along a hard-packed trail. You will cross an old culvert, which now looks like a wooden frame strewn with stones, before coming to a rickety wooden bridge across the brook. Use caution across this bridge, which may not prove stable enough to ride over.

As you approach the top of the climb, you will pass an open, clear-cut meadow on the right. A grassy trail branches to the right into this cleared area, but be sure to continue up the main trail. A short distance beyond this point, you will come to a **T** junction with a major logging road. Turn left. At this point, you will be leaving behind the shade of the tall, old hardwoods along Doctors Brook and entering a landscape created by the timber industry. The logging roads along the top of Eigg Mountain have opened up the previously dense forest. While this has dramatically altered the landscape and forced riders to endure the heat of the sun, it has also opened up some views and increased the opportunities to spot wildlife. We were lucky enough to watch the graceful movements of a deer bounding off into the trees as we quietly rolled along one of these roads.

After turning onto the first logging road, ride past another double-track logging road branching off to the left. Continue straight on the main road, and pass the signed K. Teasdale Road, also on the left. At a **T** junction with another major logging road, turn right. You will climb a short distance before entering a cleared area with a logging road branching off to the left. Continue straight past this road, and descend a short slope before looking for another logging road, this one branching off the main trail to the right. At this junction, the ride continues straight on the main logging road. However, the road on the right will take you down to Vincent's Lake, a worthwhile side trip that offers several good rest and snack spots.

If you opt to take this trip, follow the road straight past a left offshoot. On your right, you will notice a water-filled channel that is actually an old canal. For the humourous story surrounding this abandoned project, you may want to refer to Geoff Brown and Kermit Degooyer's *Mountain Bike Nova Scotia*. Ride alongside the canal to where the trail curves around to the left. Here, a short, steep slope straight ahead of you leads into a grassy area, where you can see the lock to the canal and Vincent's Lake in the distance. Although you can follow the main trail out to the lake a short distance farther on, the route becomes muddy and there are no ideal places to stop and linger by the lake. When you have finished exploring, turn right, back onto the main logging road.

Continuing on the main logging road beyond the side trip to Vincent's Lake, you will ride through a recently logged area that boasts a fine network of snowmobile trails, judging from all the signs. A short distance farther on, you will pass a road branching off on the right that is signed for snowmobiles as Trail 716. Continue on the main road, passing an offshoot on the left just before the road enters the woods and begins to descend. At this point along the ride, you will pass a sign that reads: "Caution: Steep Descent." Indeed, it is all downhill from here!

A short way along the descent, you will pass an opening that affords a tremendous view across the Northumberland Strait to Prince Edward Island. Beyond this opening, the descent is long and winding, and follows a rocky old road around several sharp bends and over a few culverts. You will cross one bridge, passing a right offshoot just beyond it. At a clearing and three-way intersection, continue straight, passing a bridge on the left and following a sign for McArras Brook. From here, the trail is easy to follow. You will pass several side trails branching off in both directions, cross another bridge, and pass a logging yard before reaching a **T** junction with Highway 245. Turn right and ride on pavement back to Arisaig Provincial Park, which will be on your left.

RIDE 70 • Wentworth

AT A GLANCE

Length/configuration: 18-km (11-mile) loop

Aerobic difficulty: Intense; significant climbing on technical single-track terrain

Technical difficulty: Intermediate to advanced; mostly single-track trails, with some short stretches on double-track trails and logging roads

Scenery: Panoramic view of the Wentworth Valley

Special comments: Lots of single-track!

When we asked riders in southern New Brunswick to name their favourite place to ride, Wentworth, Nova Scotia, was clearly the winner. Once you have ridden here, chances are good that you will add Wentworth to your own list of best places to ride in Atlantic Canada. This 18-km (11-mile) loop begins from the yard of the youth hostel perched on the lower part of the hill at Wentworth Station. Behind the hostel is a network of trails used by bikers, hikers, cross-country skiers, and orienteering buffs. They are primarily single- and double-track trails that wend, weave, and wind around the hill. There are dozens of options for creating rides of varying lengths, which you might like to explore as you become more familiar with the area.

The best way to learn the trails at Wentworth is to follow someone who has already been there, or in the absence of a guide, to equip yourself with this guidebook and the orienteering map available at the hostel. The ride described here is suited to intermediate and advanced riders with a good fitness level. The terrain is characterized by tight, narrow trails riddled with roots and rocks. You will climb steadily off the start of this ride to a look-off point, and continue on rolling terrain for the remainder. Although it may seem impossible *not* to get lost in the maze of trails, you will discover that all the side trails are short and interconnected, enabling you to quickly reorient yourself. If you do get confused, stop for a minute and refuel with a snack or a beverage, and then retrace your tracks to a familiar intersection before you resume riding.

General location: Wentworth is located 50 km (30 miles) northwest of Truro, Nova Scotia. It is also approximately the same distance south of Moncton, New Brunswick.

Elevation change: On the first climb to the look-off point, you will gain 125 m (410 feet). On several rolling hills and one moderate climb, you will gain an

RIDE 70 • Wentworth

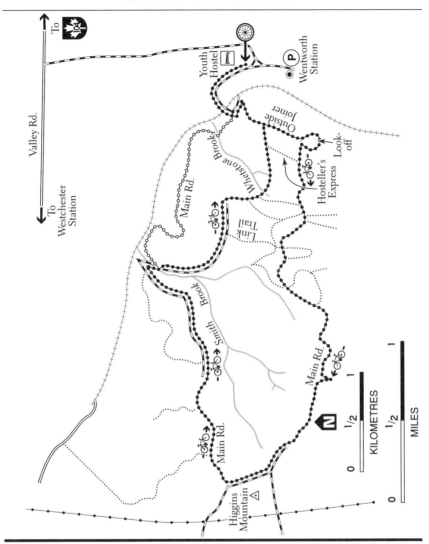

additional 150 m (492 feet), for a total of 275 m (902 feet) of elevation gained throughout the ride.

Season: Trail conditions are best from late June to September, but in years of minimal rainfall, riding may begin as early as late May, and continue through the end of October. In the fall, you can bet the foliage will be spectacular.

Services: There is a youth hostel at the trailhead that will provide information and offers accommodation. As there are no other services at the trailhead, all further needs should be met prior to your departure. The nearest bike stores are found in Truro or Moncton.

Hazards: Watch for hikers and other trail users.

Rescue index: Your most likely source of assistance is the hostel, never more than 10 km (6 miles) away.

Land status: Crown land.

Maps: Government topographic map Oxford 11 E/12 provides an overview of the area, but an excellent orienteering map can be purchased at the hostel.

Finding the trail: From Truro, travel north on the Trans-Canada Highway toward Wentworth. Before the intersection with NS Highway 246, turn left onto Valley Road. From Moncton, New Brunswick, travel south on the Trans-Canada Highway and turn right onto Valley Road after the intersection with Highway 246. From Valley Road, turn left onto Wentworth Station Road, just before the pavement turns to gravel. Unless you have plans to stay at the hostel, continue heading uphill on the gravel road and park in the cul-de-sac across from the CN rail lines.

Source of additional information:

Wentworth Hostel
R.R. #1
Wentworth, NS B0M 1Z0
(902) 548-2379

Notes on the trail: Begin the ride by dropping back down the hill to the hostel and turning left up its driveway. The ride begins behind the house, along a mowed trail through an old orchard. Following the mowed trail, you will come to a set of train tracks, which are still in use and should be crossed with caution. The trail beyond the tracks veers around to the left, and then around to the right, heading uphill and into a small field. Blueberries line the edge of the field, and you may be tempted to stop if you are riding in mid-summer. From the edge of the field, you will want to ride up to the left, until you reach a small sign pointing to the right. Following this sign, you will begin up a short, steep climb. When you come to a three-way intersection, continue straight, following a sign for the look-off. Still climbing, but not much farther along the trail, you will come to a second three-way intersection of single-track trails. Bear right at this junction, and continue to follow signs for the look-off. At a fork in the trail, just a short distance farther, bear left. When you come to a second fork in the trail, bear left again, still following signs for the look-off.

You will be riding along a fairly technical section of the trail when the look-off will appear on your left. It is a bare outcropping of granite that offers a panoramic view to the south across the Wentworth Valley. Continuing past the look-off, you will traverse more of the same technical single-track before reaching a junction. The trail to the right provides a quick route back to the hostel, but the ride continues to the left, following a single-track trail signed the "Outside Loop" (or

The shaded, single-track trails that wind up and around Higgins Mountain offer fabulous views of Wentworth Valley.

the "Outside Joiner" on the orienteering map). Entering the main section of cross-country ski trails, you will pass various offshoots to the left and right. Continue to bear left, following the main trail. When you reach another intersection offering a shortcut to the hostel, bear left again. Farther along, you will reach a junction with an established logging road—which appears on the orienteering map as the "Main Road"—to the left, and another trail to the hostel on the right. Turn left on the "Main Road."

You will follow the "Main Road" as it climbs gradually and narrows to a single-track trail. It winds across the top of the hill, bringing you to the western edge of the trail system. The terrain is rolling and heavily foliaged for this stretch of the ride. You will follow the trail as it bears gently to the right, passing all the offshoots to the left and right. After passing a large stretch of open land on your left, bear right sharply with the trail, still following the "Main Road." This section of double-track brings you to another logging road. Through a small clear-cut area, ride in a northwesterly direction, and continue as the road narrows to a double-track trail. This trail will take you to the edge of a field. Ignore the right-hand branch of the road and bear left, riding uphill on what continues to be a double-track trail. The road eventually opens up on a blueberry barren, at which point you will see power lines ahead of you. It is said that on a clear day, if you follow the power line, you can see the Confederation Bridge connecting Prince Edward Island with the mainland.

To continue the ride, turn right on the first dirt trail. Now traveling north, you will pass an old forest and dead clear-cut. Almost immediately, you will want to bear right at a fork in the trail. You will still be following a double-track trail. After a slight descent, the trail swings to the right and connects with a single-track trail. From this single-track trail, you will emerge at a clearing, where you will bear left onto a logging road. The road descends moderately, along a hard-packed surface initially, before the grade becomes steeper and the surface conditions deteriorate to loose gravel and rock. As the road approaches the railway tracks, you will have to turn sharply to the right before crossing them. This descent to the tracks is quite lengthy, and one on which our guide reached peek speeds of about 60 kph (36 mph) while we hung on to our brakes to maintain a more sane 35 kph (21 mph).

At the bottom of the hill you have two options: take the first left and follow the "Main Road" back to the hostel, or continue ahead on the gravel road, back up the mountain into the area of cross-country ski trails. Returning on the "Main Road" is the flatter, easier-to-follow option. On our return up the mountain, we looped around several cross-country ski trails that were not well suited to mountain biking, before finally connecting with the trail that returns to the hostel. We recommend exploring this option once you are more familiar with the area. On the "Main Road" you simply continue ahead and bear right at the first **Y** intersection. The gravel trail continues all the way back to the hostel, and then you can retrace your tracks along the gravel road to the parking area.

RIDE 71 • Cape Chignecto

AT A GLANCE

Length/configuration: 14.5-km (9-mile) point-to-point (14.5 km [9 miles] one way, and then a vehicle shuttle)

Aerobic difficulty: Moderate; the ride begins with a long climb on a gravel road, followed by frequent steep climbs on rocky hills

Technical difficulty: Easy to intermediate; wide, gravelly dirt roads and double-track old roads with challenging descents and climbs

Scenery: Lush brook valleys and dramatic cliffs at Spicer's Cove

Special comments: Excellent destination for a multi-day adventure combining biking and hiking

We inadvertently arrived at Cape Chignecto Provincial Park during its sixth week of operation. Impressed by the scenery along the park's coastline, we were easily persuaded by the park staff at the entrance to ride its only bike trail. Equipped with the park's detailed brochure, we were able to appreciate the scenery and the geological significance of the topography on our ride to Spicer's Cove. Ridden point-to-point with a vehicle shuttle, the ride is 14.5 km (9 miles) in length. It is an intermediate double-track trail that follows the old Eatonville Road, with frequent climbs and descents. The ride requires good physical fitness for the first hill, on which you will gain 200 m (660 feet), and on subsequent hills, where you will frequently lose and regain up to 100 m (330 feet).

Riding along the old Eatonville Road, you will be introduced to some of the remarkable features of the landscape's development. The descents that immediately swoop back up rocky slopes at brook crossings are evidence of recent faults and fractures that occurred in the underlying bedrock. They are young, just like the riders to whom they will appeal! Another notable feature is a stretch of large, exposed rock that you ride over as you approach Spicer's Cove. Here, glaciers once carved their trademark grooves and striations into the exposed rock that can still be identified on the surface. Finally, arriving at the cove, you will be met by dramatic red cliffs overlooking Chignecto Bay. Created by volcanic eruptions, these cliffs have stood sentry over the waters of the bay for about 400 million years. Enjoying the scenery and terrain of this ride does not require a geologist's eye, but acknowledging its geological significance provides further appreciation for the role of the park in preserving another part of our natural history.

General location: Cape Chignecto forms the westernmost point of Cumberland County and is located approximately 80 km (50 miles) southwest of Amherst.

RIDE 71 • Cape Chignecto

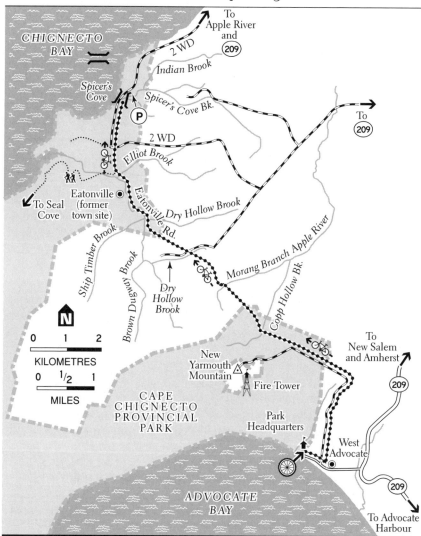

Elevation change: Over the course of the first rolling climb, you will gain 200 m (656 feet) in elevation. Through a series of climbs that follow frequent descents into brook valleys, you will gain another 200 m (656 feet), for a total elevation gain of roughly 400 m (1,312 feet).

Season: The park is open from June through October, conveniently coinciding with prime riding season.

Services: There is a convenience store not far from the park entrance, and in Advocate Harbour there is a small grocery and convenience store at a service station, as well as a campground with a café. There are no bike stores within a reasonable proximity to the park.

Hazards: There are several deteriorating bridges at brook crossings and across the Eatonville River. These bridges are unsafe for bike travel, and you will be required to dismount before crossing.

Rescue index: There are a few houses along the Eatonville Road, but riders concerned about their safety should register at the park entrance.

Land status: Provincial park.

Maps: A detailed map of the trail appears in the Cape Chignecto Provincial Park brochure, available at the entrance to the park. The trail also appears in *A Map of the Province of Nova Scotia* (map 13, sections A-1 and A-2).

Finding the trail: Cape Chignecto Provincial Park is located 45 km (28 miles) west of Parrsboro, and 80 km (50 miles) southwest of Amherst. To reach the trailhead, take exit 4 off the Trans-Canada Highway in Amherst and follow NS Highway 2 heading south toward Parrsboro. You will drive through Springhill and to the outskirts of Parrsboro, where you will turn right onto NS Highway 209, heading west. Follow Highway 209 through the small community of Advocate Harbour. Beyond Advocate Harbour, Highway 209 turns sharply to the right and heads north, away from the coast. Just beyond this bend in the road, turn left onto a secondary road that leads to West Advocate and the entrance to Cape Chignecto Provincial Park. Continue straight to reach the park entrance and the Red Rocks parking area.

If you plan on riding the trail as a one-way point-to-point, you will want to leave a vehicle at the endpoint as well. To reach the endpoint at Spicer's Cove, leave the park and drive back out to Highway 209. Turn left on Highway 209, heading north toward New Salem and Apple River. Past New Salem, as Highway 209 approaches Apple River, bear left and drive west toward West Apple River. The road will turn to gravel, and you will pass an airfield on the left. A short distance further, you will cross a bridge over the South Branch of the Apple River. The road will take you through West Apple River and past West Beach on Pudsey Point. Continue on the gravel road all the way to Spicer's Cove, where you will find space to park on the left just before the bridge across Spicer's Cove Brook.

Source of additional information: Between June and October you can contact the park at (902) 392-2085. At other times of the year, contact:

> District Office
> Department of Natural Resources
> P.O. Box 428, Parrsboro
> Cumberland County, NS B0M 1S0
> (902) 254-3241

Notes on the trail: Departing from the Red Rocks parking area, backtrack along the road you drove in on and turn left at the first opportunity, following

At the northern end of the old Eatonville Road, a dirt road continues along the shores of the Bay of Fundy.

signs for the Chignecto Variety Store. The pavement turns to gravel beyond the store, and there is a short stretch of flat road before you begin an extended climb. The climb begins gradually and then becomes a series of moderate hills over which you gain significant elevation. Beginning to climb the second hill, you will pass a recent clear-cut on the right and a small clearing on the left. The road bends to the left and then snakes around to the right, offering a view into the valley of Dewis Brook.

The gravel road progresses around the bend and continues to climb. It levels off for a short distance before ascending the final lip. Up top, you will pass a logging road on the left and a clearing on the right as the road narrows and becomes hard-packed dirt. Here you are entering an area where, it is believed, the forest has never been logged. After climbing a short hill, the road levels off and brings you to a meadow. Continue past the meadow to a fork in the road. The left branch leads to the fire tower on New Yarmouth Mountain, which affords tremendous views of the Bay of Fundy and makes a good side trip. The main trail follows the branch to the right, continuing along the old Eatonville Road toward Spicer's Cove.

Just past the branch to Yarmouth Mountain, the gravel road ends and the Eatonville Road continues as a double-track trail. At this point you will begin to descend, the grassy trail punctuated by some exposed rocks and potentially wet in places. The trail becomes more eroded as you make your way down and, about half way through the descent, you will cross over a wooden, bridged culvert. Carry on past a trail signed "Old Brush Arbour" on the right-hand side, and continue downhill toward Copp Hollow Brook. Exercise caution along this portion of the descent, in anticipation of the deteriorating bridge you will have to cross over the brook.

Immediately after crossing Copp Hollow Brook, you will begin to climb. As you near the top of this climb, you must cross another brook and hurdle over some railway ties before the grade becomes more gradual. Across another small, wooden, bridged culvert, you will reach the top of the hill. At the top the trail bends to the left and begins another short climb. There may be some wet sections, and there are two wooden, bridged culverts to cross before you reach an opening. The trail levels off for a short period, before you descend an eroded, rocky hill that swoops back up immediately. This gully accommodates seasonal flow of the Morang Branch of the Apple River, which means there may be a stream here in the spring.

As the trail levels off, it bends gently around to the right and then to the left. It then climbs gradually before dropping off along another rocky descent to a four-way intersection with a red dirt road. The trail on which you have descended veers to the right at this intersection. However, you will cross straight over the dirt road and reconnect with the trail on the opposite side. It begins with a short climb, followed by a section of very loose rock and gravel. The trail then dips, dropping on loose rock down to a brook and climbing back up the other side. As you descend, the trail deteriorates further, and ATV users have created a short detour to the left, around the rubble of large, loose boulders. Beyond the rubble, you will cross a deteriorating wooden bridge (stay left!) over Dry Hollow Brook, and then climb up the other side.

At the top, continue ahead to a four-way intersection with a gravel road. Cross the road and continue on the trail to a meadow on your right. Past the meadow, the trail begins to descend gradually and washes out as the grade increases. An ATV track merges into the trail on the left as you descend into the woods. At the bottom of the hill you will cross Hollow Brook on a small wooden bridge, and then bear left onto an ATV track at a fork (if you miss the fork, you will head up the driveway to a cottage). This is a short stretch of grassy double-track that may be overgrown in sections. It will bring you to an iron bridge over the Eatonville River. At the time of our research, there were several gaps in this bridge and the remaining slats were rotting and unstable, making riding across it unsafe and impossible.

Cross the bridge on foot, and then resume riding on the ATV track. A short distance along, you will come to a wooden bridge that crosses the Eatonville River a second time. This one is in excellent condition, and the view down the river is quite picturesque. Across the bridge, the trail is slightly wider and follows along Eatonville Brook for a short distance. After a brief section in the woods, you will cross Elliot Brook on another wooden bridge that is in need of some repair. Just past this bridge, you will come to a vague **T** junction. The narrow trail branching off to the left links up with the coastal hiking trail and is signed "To Spicer's Cove and Red Rocks." Bear right at this junction, following the main trail. A steep climb awaits you, one that is made even more challenging by the eroded channels and loose rock in the lower extremity. On the final third of the climb, the trail conditions improve considerably, and as you crest the hill you will continue along a wide, easy, grassy trail through the woods. When you reach a grassy clearing, continue straight on a rough, gravel road and pass a two-wheel drive, red gravel road on the right. This road on the right is part of a network of logging roads that leads back out to Highway 209.

The final stretch of the ride to Spicer's Cove continues along the rough, gravel road. You will ride across sections of large, exposed bedrock, where it is interesting to note fine, deep grooves in the stone; these are glacial scars that attest to this area's fascinating geological history. The few houses you pass along the way are all that remain of the once-thriving community of Eatonville. This area was home to 350 people, several lumber mills, and a shipyard. Past the final house, the trail begins to descend more steeply and will bend to the right for the final descent to the sandy shores and 400-million-year-old cliffs of Spicer's Cove.

RIDE 72 · Martock

AT A GLANCE

Length/configuration: 6.5-km (4-mile) race circuit comprised of two connected loops

Aerobic difficulty: Strenuous; the initial climb up Martock Mountain is severe

Technical difficulty: Much of this single-track circuit demands precise bike handling skills

Scenery: Mountainside views and winding trails beneath a canopy of dense forest

Special comments: Brave Martock's infamous downhill and test yourself on awe-inspiring trails through an old gypsum mine!

Martock Mountain, a popular ski destination in the winter months, boasts one of the most challenging mountain bike courses on the Nova Scotia race circuit. This ride is a tough 6.5-km (4-mile) course that begins with a loop up and down Martock Mountain and concludes with a second loop through a primarily wooded area at the base of the mountain. The trails are primarily single- and double-tracks that incorporate all the features of a good race circuit: tough climbs, exhilarating downhills, and skill-testing technical terrain. Because the course is relatively short, riders of all skill levels can explore their own limits on

RIDE 72 • Martock

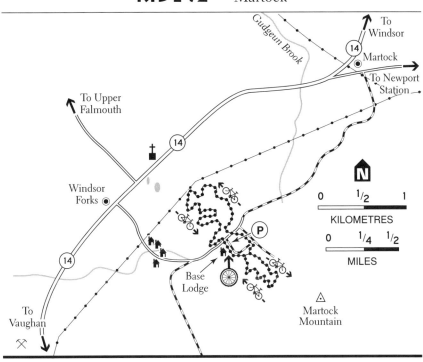

this ride. Furthermore, there are some options along the course that will give novice riders the chance to bypass some of the most technically and aerobically challenging sections of the ride. Two features of the course stand out: the famous single-track downhill run on the mountain, and the technically outrageous trails that follow a twisted and precarious path through an old gypsum mine. Adorning the entrance to one section of single-track through the old mine is a virtually complete deer skeleton. Understanding the sense of humour that added this touch to the trail may be your first step in successfully clearing the course!

Martock Mountain operates its lifts during several weekends in October and offers bike-and-hike day passes. This is perhaps the most mountain-biker-friendly thing anyone does in Atlantic Canada, and it reflects Martock's commitment to expanding recreational opportunities at the mountain throughout the year. For riders looking for the best places to enjoy fall foliage, this is a great time of year to visit Martock and take in the splendour of the season from the top of the mountain. Call the lodge to find out when this Festival of Colours takes place.

General location: Martock is located off of Route 14, about 8 km (5 miles) from Windsor.

Elevation change: You will gain roughly 250 m (820 feet) along the length of this ride, which features a rather monumental climb at the start of the course and many short, steep climbs through the latter section.

Season: This course is open to riders from June to November. Avoid riding the trails at Martock during or after heavy rainfall, when slick conditions will make many sections of the race circuit nearly impossible to ride.

Services: All services are available in nearby Windsor. In addition, the ski lodge at the base of the mountain is frequently open during the summer.

Hazards: Ski lift and snowmaking equipment line the first loop of this course. Many deep sinkholes lie in wait along the second portion of the course, a product of the gypsum mine that once operated here.

Rescue index: You will never ride more than 2 km (1.25 miles) from assistance.

Land status: Private ski resort.

Maps: The only map that might supplement the one we have included here is the one printed each year for the races. There may or may not be a map of the course posted at the base lodge.

Finding the trail: Take Exit 5A off of the Trans-Canada Highway (NS Highway 101) in Windsor. Follow signs to Windsor and Martock, driving down Wentworth Road to a four-way intersection with O'Brien Street. Turn left at this intersection, continuing to follow signs to Martock. Bear left through an intersection with King Street, and then turn right on Route 14 East. Drive for approximately 7 km (4.4 miles) on Route 14 before turning left on Martock Road. Follow this access road up toward the mountain, turning into the parking area at the base lodge on the right. The race circuit begins in front of the main lodge.

Source of additional information:

Ski Martock
R. R. #3
Windsor, NS B0N 2T0
(902) 798-9501
www.martock.com

Notes on the trail: As you look up at the mountain from the parking area, begin your ride along the left-hand side of the main lodge and descend past it, along a dirt access road. Follow the access road toward the base of the mountain, and continue to follow it as it swings to the left and crosses beneath the chairlift. You will ride over an exposed pipe as you pass under the chairlift. Beyond the chairlift, bear right onto an indistinct grassy track that traverses the main ski trail and passes beneath the lighting equipment. Follow this trail over to the second farthest ski run on the left, and continue climbing. You will have reached the half way mark of the ascent as the access road swings toward the right and evens out into a more level run that traverses the mountain and separates the lower half of the mountain from the upper half. At this point, you can choose to follow the

Sarah skillfully winds her way between the trees and whoop-de-dos on the Martock race circuit.

novice racecourse and traverse the slope, heading in the direction of the T-bars. If you choose this option, ride to the T-bars and connect with a single-track trail heading downhill to your right. Alternatively, you can follow the expert course along a trail that traces a path up a slight rise over to the next ski run and then heads uphill. Although this second portion of the climb begins gradually, it will slowly and surely suck the wind right out of you. After following a grassy switchback up the ski run, you will be breathlessly relieved to finally reach a headwall, at which point the trail cuts into the woods on the right and connects with a hard-packed dirt trail that descends beneath the T-bar.

The downhill portion of this first loop follows the T-bar, descending along a challenging single-track trail through the trees. Pick a line and head downhill! Steep, tight turns, exposed rock and roots, and sudden drop-offs all contribute to the expert rating of this downhill challenge. Partway down the mountain you will come to a grassy area, just past a blue-gray–coloured cabin. This is the point at which the expert course reconnects with the novice course. Bear left, crossing beneath the T-bar and picking up the continuation of the single-track trail in the woods.

The trail will cross back and forth beneath the T-bar a few times before it emerges from the woods and cuts across two ski runs, heading in the direction of a small pond. Your final drop down the mountain will take you along a single-track trail, across a couple of hills, through a small wooded area, and out onto a beginner ski run. You will zigzag down this trail and cross beneath the chairlift line. Continue straight from this point, heading toward the T-bar hut, before making a sharp right turn and curving back onto the main access road. Ride past the pond, keeping it on your left, and then turn left up a dirt driveway beneath a transmission line. You will follow this road back up into the parking lot.

As you reach the edge of the parking lot, cut to the left and head diagonally across the parking lot, toward the unpaved road on which you drove in to reach the mountain. Cross the road, and turn into a sandy opening to enter the cleared, grassy area on the other side. Head straight through the middle of this field, toward the trees at the far edge. You will find a trail into the woods to the right of a rather large and distinct pine tree. Follow this trail to the first four-way intersection, where there is another large, distinguished-looking pine tree on the left. A less used, grassy trail connects with the main trail on the left, and if you look straight ahead down the main trail, you can make out another trail that branches off to the left a short distance beyond. This second trail on the left is the route that you will take at the completion of the loop you are about to make. To begin the loop, turn right and descend on a dirt trail into the woods. There will be a small stream down a bank to your left.

You will soon ride out of a heavily shaded hemlock forest and into a clearing that is loaded with blackberry bushes and even boasts a few apple trees. There is a **Y** in the trail at this point. The left fork is part of the novice race circuit, and the right, which is longer and more difficult, is the route that the expert races follow. Bear right for the longer loop, which is also the more obvious of the two trails. A short distance farther into this clearing, you will come to another **Y** in the trail. Bear left here; the right-hand spur leads into a corn field. Ride through a small wooded area, over some exposed roots, and bear right through some alders as you pass an indistinct trail branching off on the left. Continue to bear right, heading up a small slope into the woods. A short distance farther, you will come to the first part of an old gypsum mine that forms the most technically challenging section of the circuit. There are tall hemlocks throughout this area, and the trail, though firm, twists and snakes over a series of tight turns, dips, and humps. To each side of the trail there will be sinkholes that we can vouch for being every bit as deep as they look! One false move, and you will find yourself and your bike literally swallowed up by one of these holes. You will negotiate a short section of this terrain before the trail evens out for a stretch. You will then climb back into the woods, winding through trees and in between sinkholes. You will cross a narrow bridge between two sinkholes, and just after the trail follows a sharp curve to the left, you will come out of the woods and onto a transmission line.

Beneath the transmission line lies a grassy path that stretches to both the left and the right. Turn left. You will follow the transmission line for just a very short distance before turning left onto a narrow single-track trail back into the woods. This left turn is easy to miss, and it comes just before the trail beneath the transmission line dips downhill slightly. Back in the woods, you will ride along a carpeted single-track trail with lots of exposed roots. Enjoy this brief stretch of carefree riding; it ends quickly as you ride beneath a tree to which the skeleton of a deer has been attached. From this point on, you are in enemy territory. The sinkholes through this portion of the gypsum mine increase in depth to up to 6 m (20 feet). The trail follows tight, tough, and very technical terrain through the trees and across exceedingly narrow bridges of land between the sinkholes. The trail turns sharply to the left a short distance farther, and all but the most accomplished of riders will hesitate over the many equally treacherous-looking options for riding through an area that has more sinkholes than riding surface.

You will eventually emerge from the gypsum mine and enjoy a short stretch of flat single-track that ends at a **T** junction with a wide dirt trail. Bear left, and then turn right almost immediately to follow a trail that heads back into the woods. There may be branches placed in the trail at this intersection, directing you along the correct route. This is also the point at which the expert and novice courses reconnect. If you were to turn left and continue along the wide, dirt trail, you would come out at the clearing at the beginning of the gypsum mine section of the ride, and the point at which the expert and novice courses diverge.

Continuing the ride, you will come to a bit of a clearing and reach an indistinct **T** junction with a wide grassy trail. Bear right. Continue riding straight, past a grassy offshoot on the right. At a second **T** junction with a wider grassy trail, turn left. At most of these turns the route will be obvious because of the pattern of wear on the trails. A short distance farther, at a broken-off pine tree, bear left around the turn downhill, passing a vague trail that branches off to the right. Just beyond this turn, you will cross a wet area that may be built up with logs and the occasional pallet. This area is followed by a slight climb, beyond which the trail widens. Continue straight past a rough cart track that creates a four-way intersection, and then bear left, following an arrow and passing another rough cart track that branches off to the right. Just beyond that intersection, bear right (the left trail is blocked with trees), and then turn right onto a single-track trail. If you ride past this right-hand turn and continue straight, you will very quickly arrive at the huge pine tree that marks the very first four-way intersection of this portion of the ride.

From the right-hand turn onto the single-track trail, you will pass a trail over your right shoulder. Continue straight, and then turn sharply to the left at a **T** junction of sorts with a logging road. There is a clear-cut area on the right, and there will be logs placed in the trail at such an angle as to direct you around to the left and along a single-track trail. Just beyond that point, you will reach a three-way intersection. Continue straight. You will climb up to the edge of a sandpit, which will be on your right. As you continue riding, the access road to Martock Mountain and a transmission line will be straight ahead of you. Follow a trail to the left, around a curve into the woods. At a **T** junction just beyond that curve, bear right and ride toward a small cabin. Pass a trail that branches off over your right shoulder, and head back into the clearing in front of the ski lodge. Cross the road and finish your ride back in the parking lot, or head toward the right side of the lodge and cut back over to the left to begin the circuit again.

Note: Martock recently developed a new network of cross-country ski trails. These trails will have altered the landscape along the second portion of this race circuit considerably. Although much of the race circuit will remain the same, we recommend that you pick up a copy of the cross-country ski trail map, which will outline the new trails. The good news is that this development should also improve the riding opportunities on the mountain, making more trails accessible to a greater number of people.

RIDE 73 • Grand-Pré Dikes

AT A GLANCE

Length/configuration: 16-km (10-mile) combination (11-km [6.9-mile] loop with an out-and-back; spur is 2.5 km [1.5 miles] long each way)

Aerobic difficulty: Requires only a basic level of fitness

Technical difficulty: Easy riding on smooth double-track dirt trails and paved roads

Scenery: Rich farmlands, salt marshes, and the dramatic shore cliffs of the Minas Basin shoreline

Special comments: The Grand-Pré National Historic Site is worth a visit

This ride across the Grand-Pré Dikes to the Grand-Pré National Historic Site speaks volumes about the history of Atlantic Canada and its Acadian culture. The Grand-Pré Dikes were built by the first French settlers in the early 1700s. These settlers established the foundations of Acadian culture and identity. In the mid-1700s, as conflict escalated between the British and the French, relations between the British and the Acadians deteriorated. When Nova Scotia became a British colony, the Acadians were expelled and dispersed among British colonies to the south. The Grand-Pré National Historic Site commemorates the Acadians of the Minas Basin and their eventual deportation.

While the site offers an elaborate history of the people and the area, the symbol of Acadian identity is everywhere on this part of the peninsula. Adopted from

RIDE 73 • Grand-Pré Dikes

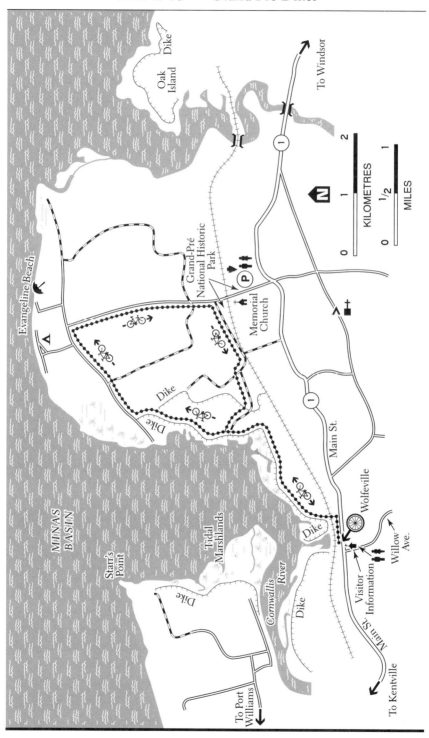

Riding between tidal marshland and fertile farmland along the top of the dikes in Grand-Pré.

Henry Wadsworth Longfellow's poem that immortalized the deportation, the name "Evangeline" symbolizes the Acadians' struggle for survival. Today, her name retains its symbolic status and appears as a preface to almost every service on the peninsula. The popularity of the poem also succeeded in drawing a number of American tourists to the area in the 1800s, possibly contributing to the establishment of Grand-Pré and the Annapolis Valley as the popular tourist destination it is today.

For much of this 16-km (10-mile) ride, you will be riding along the top of the Grand-Pré Dikes, which were constructed to enable farmers to cultivate the rich soil of the marshlands by keeping the tidal waters at bay. At present, 815 hectares (2,013 acres) of farmland below sea level are protected behind 8.6 km (5.3 miles) of dikes. The trail is wide enough, almost jeep width, that you can enjoy the view without fear of inadvertently toppling over the edge. The wide double-track trail has an excellent riding surface of hard-packed dirt with some grassy sections. From this unique vantage point, you can see across the Minas Basin to the Blomidon Cliffs *and* survey the farmers working the fertile soil of the marshlands.

General location: Approximately one hour north of Halifax on the Evangeline Trail, in the Annapolis Valley.

Elevation change: Minimal; there are only a few very short hills.

Season: Short of heavy rainfall that would make the upper dikes trails slick with mud, conditions for this ride should be good most of the summer season, beginning as early as May and continuing through October.

Services: Food and accommodation are available in Wolfeville, where you will also find Valley Stove and Cycle, located at 234 Main Street (phone (902) 542-7280). Another source for bicycle service and rentals is Framebreak, located in nearby Kentville at 15 River Street (phone (902) 679-0611).

Hazards: Although the trails on the top of the dikes enjoy the status of public rights-of-way, all of the land and farm roads surrounding the dikes are private property.

Rescue index: Throughout the ride, you will likely encounter other people, be it riding along the dikes, at the national historic site, or in Wolfeville. Help is always close at hand.

Land status: Private land surrounds the dikes, but the trail on the top of the dikes is a public right-of-way.

Maps: Refer to A *Map of the Province of Nova Scotia* (map 13, section E-5).

Finding the trail: Traveling west on NS Highway 101, take Exit 10 to Wolfeville. The exit will bring you to Route 1, where you will turn left, still following signs to Wolfeville. As you approach downtown, the Visitor Information Centre will be on your left-hand side on Willow Street, which runs perpendicular to Main Street. Ample parking will be found at the information centre and on the street.

Sources of additional information: The Wolfeville Visitor Information Centre has maps and extensive information about the area. Contact them at (902) 542-7000, or at wolftrsm@glinx.com.

Notes on the trail: Departing from the Visitor Information Centre in Wolfeville, turn right on Main Street. Continue along Main Street a short distance to the Randall Museum. Directly across from the museum, turn left onto a narrow, tree-lined pathway between two buildings. This is a short corridor that connects the start of the dikes with downtown Wolfeville. At the end of the pathway you will pass through a pedestrian gate and cross a set of railway tracks. Continue ahead, following the dirt trail that leads up onto the dike. This dirt double-track trail continues for the length of the dike.

Tracing the edge of the Minas Basin, you will be looking out on the renowned tidal marshlands on your left. Farther out, at the tip of the basin, you can just barely make out the Blomidon Cliffs. To the right are the fertile lands that French settlers began to farm in the early 1700s. Continue along this hard-packed dirt trail, ignoring all the drop-offs to the farm roads. After the final bend to the left, the trail continues straight to its end. At the far end, on a clear day you will get a good view of the Blomidon Cliffs on the distant side of the basin. Even from this distance they are spectacular. Soon the trail ends, however, and you will connect with a dirt access road that is lined with trees. Continue straight on this dirt road to a **T** junction with a paved road.

Turn right on the paved road, and continue past another access road to the dikes on the right. You will pass a small white church on the right before approaching a stop sign at a three-way intersection. Turning left here would take you to Evangeline Beach, a great destination for a side trip on a sunny day. To continue the ride, follow the paved road straight through this intersection, then follow it as it bends to the right a short distance further on. A good distance farther along this road, you will pass an entrance to the dike road on the right; to the left there is a panel providing some information on the farmlands. A short distance beyond the entrance, you will arrive at the Grand-Pré National Historic Site. The parking area is on the left-hand side of the road, where you will find picnic tables and washrooms. You may also obtain information here and pay the entrance fee to tour the site.

To return to Wolfeville, exit the parking area and head back down the paved road to the large blue sign with factual information on the dikes and the commemorative plaque. Turn left to enter the dirt access road. There are fields on either side and a caution sign advising people to enter at their own risk. The goal now is to make your way expediently toward the dike and avoid encountering any heavy farm machinery! The ride through the farm fields is likely to be uneventful, but do give way should you encounter any farm equipment. Continue along the dirt road, past a road branching off to the left. As you advance, the road will curve to the right and wind through the fields. When the road straightens, you will approach a fork where you will bear left, away from a cow pasture. At a **T** junction with another dirt road, climb the embankment and continue to the left, toward Wolfeville, on the double-track dirt trail that follows the top of the dike. At the end of the dike, cross the railroad tracks and ride back down the gravel path to Main Street. Turn right to return to the Visitor Information Centre, just a short distance ahead on Willow Street.

RIDE 74 · Annapolis Valley Time Trial Loop

AT A GLANCE

Length/configuration: 14.5-km (9-mile) combination (3.8-km [2.4-mile] spur connected to a 6.9-km [4.3-mile] loop)

Aerobic difficulty: Modest; the ride features climbs along only short, steep hills

Technical difficulty: Novice; primarily double-track trails with some more challenging single-track sections

Scenery: Largely forested trail that reaches the Cornwallis River at the site of a bird sanctuary

Special comments: This circuit is featured at the Annapolis Valley Mountain Bike Festival

Featured every year at the Annapolis Valley Mountain Bike Festival, the Time Trial Loop is a fast-paced, 14.5-km (9-mile) combination ride. The ride we describe is only slightly modified from the actual race loop, beginning from downtown Kentville and including a short side trip down to the bank of the tidal Cornwallis River. The route begins and ends with a 3.8-km (2.4-mile) spur along the recreational trail through downtown Kentville. This portion of the ride links up with a 6.9-km (4.3-mile) loop that includes a combination of single- and double-track trails through the woods. The ride is suitable for all levels of mountain bikers; making for a fast, rolling race circuit for advanced riders or an excellent introduction to off-road and single-track riding for novices. Most of the trails are hard-packed dirt, with some stretches that feature more sandy conditions. From fast cruising along the recreational trail to tight turns and whoop-de-doos along the single-track trails, this ride presents a broad range of riding conditions.

General location: Kentville, in the Annapolis Valley region of Nova Scotia.

Elevation change: Between the Cornwallis River and the multi-use recreational trail, you will climb only short, steep hills along a few sections of single-track trail.

Season: Late May through early October; the Annapolis Valley is the warmest part of Nova Scotia.

Services: All services are available in Kentville. This ride begins and ends at Framebreak Bicycles, where you can fill up your water bottles and chat with local riders about other places to ride in and around Kentville. Framebreak is also the central meeting point for club rides and both co-ed and women-only organized group rides.

Hazards: None.

Rescue index: You will never be far from assistance, since this ride stays within close proximity to secondary roads and residential areas.

Land status: Recreational trail and paths open to mountain bikers.

Maps: We could find no adequate map of this ride.

Finding the trail: As you drive into Kentville, turn down Cornwallis Avenue from Main Street. Pass Webster Street on the left and a small information centre, also on the left. Bear left on Aberdeen Avenue instead of following Cornwallis Avenue over a bridge across the Cornwallis River. Almost immediately after turning onto Aberdeen Avenue, bear right onto River Street. Framebreak Bicycles will be directly on your right.

Source of additional information:

Framebreak Bicycles
15 River Street
Kentville, NS B4N 1H9
(902) 679-0611

RIDE 74 • Annapolis Valley Time Trail Loop

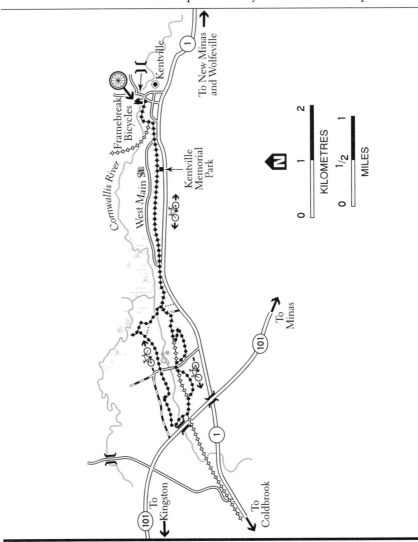

Notes on the trail: From Framebreak, turn right and follow the unpaved continuation of River Street to a gravel road that will connect you with the abandoned railroad bed that now serves as a recreational trail. This first portion of the rail trail is somewhat indistinct and will take you past some old brick buildings. Cross West Main Street after just a short distance, and pick up a more established section of the trail on the other side. You will pass the playing fields of Kentville Memorial Park on the left of the trail.

Beyond the park, the trail continues past two homes on the right. The main road out of Kentville is just on your left here. Cross the access road that serves as a driveway to the two homes, and immediately begin looking for a narrow single-track trail branching off to the left. Turn left here for a short stretch of single-track that will pop you back out on the rail bed just a short distance farther up. Bear left, back onto the recreational trail.

You will very quickly come to a cart track that crosses the trail. Continue straight for the beginning of the loop portion of the ride; the cart track trail to the right is the path along which you will complete the loop. Again, immediately after passing the cart track, turn left off the rail bed. Head up a small hill onto a trail that will take you to a cul-de-sac at the end of a dirt road. You will see a small, brown, brick building here. Turn right toward a street light and follow another single-track trail back into the woods. When you reach the crest of a hill on this wide single-track trail, turn right onto a narrow trail that will take you on a roller-coaster–like loop through the woods. This portion of the trail will connect back with the wider single-track trail at a **T** junction. Turn right, and continue riding through a beautiful forest of softwoods and ferns.

You will descend a short hill, at the bottom of which there is a spring on the right. When you come to a **T** junction with a wide, graded dirt road, turn right. After just a short distance, you will arrive at a four-way intersection where the road, which continues straight, is bisected by the rail bed. Turn left on the rail bed. Almost immediately, you will turn left again, back onto a single-track trail for which you will need an easy gear.

This trail will take you uphill toward some homes on the left. There is a trail that descends on the left, but be sure to bear right. You will round a bend to the right and descend before climbing again, this time into a recently cleared area. A short distance farther, you will be facing a downhill that seems to head toward the rail bed. Drop to a **T** junction with the rail bed and turn left once again. Continue straight on the rail trail, all the way to the site of an overpass for Highway 101.

Just before the overpass (which we found makes a great shelter during a rainstorm!), you will come to a four-way intersection of trails. Turn right to complete the Time Trial Loop, following a wide, sandy trail through a low dip that is followed by a short, steep climb. Be aware that there are two options for climbing this hill, and that the right is more extreme than the left. Beyond the climb, you will be following a fairly wide trail along the top of the embankment that drops to Highway 101 on the left. Ride straight through the first four-way intersection you come to, and then take the next right, following a trail that heads back into the woods. As a reference, this trail comes at a point where you can see a road sign for Berwick, Middleton, and Bridgetown off of the highway.

You will descend on this trail, riding away from the highway through a pine forest and down to a gravel clearing. Make a sharp turn to the right at the edge of this clearing, turning onto another sandy trail. There are homes in this area and you will notice, in particular, one on the left with a swimming pool. Keep to the main trail, and ride past a trail on the left that heads into a grassy lawn. Continue straight past several offshoots that appear to lead to some homes on the left. The main trail is obvious, carving a wide and sandy path through the trees. At a split in the trail, bear left. You will find yourself on a paved road called

Marie Drive. After passing some homes on both sides of the road, you will come to a four-way intersection. Continue straight.

When you reach the end of the pavement at a large field, continue on a grassy path along the right-hand perimeter of the field. This path will lead you back into the woods, where it becomes a wide dirt trail. Pass a trail branching off on the left, and ride up to a four-way intersection of trails. Continue straight. Bear left as you approach a **Y** in the trail, and almost immediately, bear left again at a second **Y**. You will descend for a short distance and pass a grassy trail that you will notice over your left shoulder.

Beyond this point, the Time Trial Loop continues straight, rounding a bend to the right and descending. However, there is a trail on the left that passes beneath tall pines and leads to a bird sanctuary at the edge of the Cornwallis River. If you opt to take this short side trip, turn left off the main trail and ride through the forest of tall pines. Follow the trail around to the right at a vague **T** junction, where a less distinct trail branches off to the left. You will come to another, more distinct **T** junction a short distance farther. Here, a grassy trail bends around to the right, and a short trail to the left drops to a marsh. From the scenic viewpoint at the marsh, you will be looking out over the Cornwallis River, where a trail development program is under way to create a network of multi-use trails.

From this scenic look-off, turn around and continue straight past the first intersection you come to (passing, on the right, the trail that you rode in on). Continue straight on the trail, passing some white buildings on the right. After a short distance, you will reconnect with the Time Trial Loop. Bear left to continue straight along the main trail. You will ride across a wooden bridge, and the trail will then curve around to the left quite sharply, passing some apple trees. A short distance beyond this point, you will reconnect with the rail bed. Turn left on the rail bed, and follow it straight back to the centre of town.

RIDE 75 · The Gorge

AT A GLANCE

Length/configuration: 4-km (2.5-mile) loop with a maze of additional trails to explore

Aerobic difficulty: Moderate to advanced; many short but severe climbs on technical terrain

Technical difficulty: Primarily advanced single-track trails

Scenery: An upside-down, turned-around jumble of trees, roots, rocks, ledges, ravines, and streams

Special comments: We spent an hour and a half playing on less than 5 km (3 miles) of trails!

The Gorge is a mountain bike park that is the creation of some of the most extreme riders in the Wolfville and Kentville areas. Leading the construction of trails in this park is the owner of Framebreak Bicycles. His preference for "sick" and "sweet" single-track has been fully indulged in The Gorge. Designed as a training ground for all levels of riders, the park features a broad range of technically and aerobically challenging terrain. The trail system is primarily single-track, with some connecting stretches on wider, grassy double-track trails. A ride through The Gorge is an intense experience, particularly when you find yourself following its creator through mazelike single-track, over log piles, down extreme drops, through rocky little stream beds, up treacherous banks and ledges, and across trails that teach you all there is to fear about off-camber riding. Of course, Brian is also the first person to tell you that you can ride anything, and if you can lure him out for a ride he'll show you that it can be done and encourage you to stretch your limits. Chances are good that you'll consider yourself a better rider at the end of the day.

The ride we describe here is actually one variation of the novice race circuit at The Gorge. The trails for this 4-km (2.5-mile) loop circle the upper perimeter of The Gorge, then zigzag across "Crazy Creek" several times. Throughout the ride, you can opt to continue on the novice trails or branch off and explore some of the expert sections of The Gorge. The expert trails follow the creek bed more closely, climbing and descending the steep banks of The Gorge and passing through the sweetest and sickest obstacles in the park.

General location: The Gorge lurks in the town of Kentville in the Annapolis Valley, less than two hours north of Halifax.

Elevation change: The Gorge is aptly named, and for a relatively small area, you will find yourself negotiating many steep drops and ascents back and forth across "Crazy Creek." Overall elevation change will vary according to the route you pick through the park but will never amount to any significant gain.

Season: Late spring through fall; avoid riding these trails after heavy rainfall, to reduce the damaging impact of erosion.

Services: All services are available in Kentville.

Hazards: The trail system at The Gorge demands respect. There are areas in the park where only the most accomplished bikers will be comfortable riding. Ride within your range, particularly if you are new to the trails. Be aware that hikers also use the trail system. The top portion of this ride passes a barbed wire fence that is very clearly marked.

Rescue index: The trails at The Gorge are bordered by a residential area and never extend far from the main road through Kentville.

Land status: City land.

Maps: The map we have included in this book is as good as it gets!

Finding the trail: In Kentville, ride or drive west out of downtown, heading toward Coldbrook. Keep in mind that Main Street in Kentville is one way and that you have to follow Webster Street to a **T** junction with Main Street before you will be able to turn right. As you leave the downtown area, bear left and continue traveling on Park Street. You will very quickly come to a ballpark on the right, which is Kentville Memorial Park. Continue on Park Street for just a short distance before turning up the first road you come to on the left. There is a small medical facility at the corner here, and you will be able to see a walkway behind it that connects with a dirt trail coming out of the woods. This dirt trail is the one on which you will ride out at the completion of the ride. To begin the ride, continue up the paved road to an abandoned condominium development and cul-de-sac. There is space to park here, behind the buildings, if you choose to drive up to this point. You will also see a hiking sign. The ride begins up a dirt access road that continues uphill, to the left of the condo development.

Source of additional information:

Framebreak Bicycles
15 River Street
Kentville, NS
(902) 679-0611

Notes on the trail: From behind the abandoned condo development, follow the dirt access road up to its first fork and bear left. Almost immediately, you will pass a single-track trail entering the woods on the left. This trail is the beginning of the expert circuit and, for those interested, features a challenging drop into a deep gully from which an equally challenging trail rises up on the other side. Called the "Stadium," this spot makes an exciting vantage point from which to

RIDE 75 · The Gorge

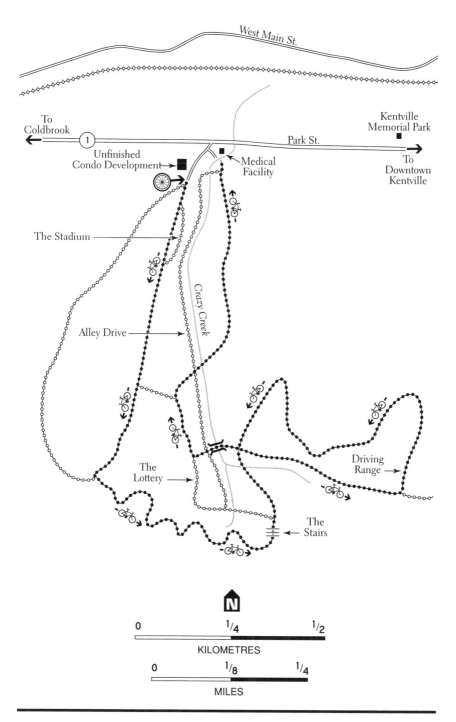

watch riders plummet to undignified heaps off the edge of the trail. To warm-up over less rigourous terrain, continue following the wide grassy trail.

At a fork in the grassy trail, bear left. You will ride past an access trail that leads into the centre of The Gorge on your left. Continue riding along the wide, grassy, double-track trail until it veers around to the right slightly and a single-track trail branches off to the left in between some alders. Turn left onto this trail, the first stretch of single-track, which is tight and twisty, coiled between trees and rocks and areas of exposed roots. You will come to a small log pile referred to as "The Stairs" at a point where the trail turns left into the woods. There is a well-marked, barbed-wire fence along the perimeter of the trail here, which will be on your right.

Follow the trail over the log pile, and continue past another narrow trail branching off to the left. This trail is called the "Lottery" and is one of the expert trails. Keep to the main trail, which descends over some small whoop-de-doos to cross "Crazy Creek." You will drop quite steeply to cross the creek, climbing to a four-way intersection on the other side. Turn right here, following a trail that heads back uphill along the small ridge overlooking the creek. The trail straight ahead of you at this intersection is the one on which you will complete this loop, and the trail to the left, which begins with a series of palettes over the creek, is the one you will follow out of The Gorge after completing this first loop.

A short distance beyond this first climb, you will reach a potentially confusing intersection, where logs have been laid in an attempt to direct riders toward the correct trail. Bear right here. If you look to the left, you will be able to make out the trail on which you will return to this junction later in the ride. Turning right will connect you with a wider double-track trail. Cruise along this fast stretch of the ride until you come to a log across the trail. In case this landmark has been moved, you may also want to watch for a small wooden sign in a large tree on the left side of the trail. This sign has a bicycle chain adorning it. Turn left here, off the double-track trail and back onto some more technical terrain in the woods that is referred to as the "Driving Range."

The "Driving Range" is a moderate descent that crosses a big whoop-de-doo before reaching a small creek bed. The trail crosses the creek bed and then swoops uphill to the left. You will traverse a particularly rocky area, climbing gradually to a point where you can make out the double-track trail you followed into this part of the woods on your left. The trail curves around to the right here. After another view of the double-track trail on the left, you will cross another small creek bed before heading back uphill. Along this short climb, you will notice that logs have been laid on the downslope of the trail so as to prevent it from washing out. The trail then follows the stream bed downhill to the right for a short distance. You will then return to the junction where the double-track trail on which you began this loop is immediately to the left. Bear right here, heading back down toward "Crazy Creek" and the major four-way intersection.

Turn right at the four-way intersection, heading over a few wooden palettes to cross "Crazy Creek." Follow the trail as it heads up a rise on the other side of the creek and then curves around to the right. On the left side of the trail, you will pass the other end of the "Lottery." One other point of interest: an expert trail called "Alley Drive" begins here, dropping off the wooden palettes and heading down and alongside "Crazy Creek." This trail is one we fondly remember for plunging straight into the abyss of The Gorge. It is an extreme expert trail, and definitely one to save for a day when your senses are sharp and your skills are at their prime.

After crossing the creek and passing the "Lottery" on your left, you will traverse the bank that rises from "Crazy Creek." You will pass another trail branching off to the left, which is one end of an access trail that reconnects with the grassy double-track trail you followed at the beginning of the ride. Continue along the main trail, traversing the slope over a series of whoop-de-doos, until it finally curves around to the right and drops, quite steeply, back down to "Crazy Creek." Cross the creek, over another palette, and climb the other side, following the trail as it makes its way along the creek bank to the left. The trail from this point on is very easy to follow and passes through a more recently cleared area before descending and finally emerging in the small parking area of the brick medical building. To return to the parking area (where you can also re-enter The Gorge), turn left and follow the paved road back up to the condo development and the trailhead.

RIDE 76 · Black Rock

AT A GLANCE

Length/configuration: 29-km (18-mile) loop

Aerobic difficulty: Rigourous climbing on dirt roads over two mountains

Technical difficulty: Beginner riding on paved and dirt roads, with some intermediate sections on double-track trails through the woods

Scenery: Orchards, woods, and coastal views

Special comments: Good cruising on the downhills

This ride begins near the lighthouse at Black Rock Beach on the Bay of Fundy. Beginning your ride from this scenic site may tempt you to advance no further—after all, what could possibly offer more in the way of scenery than this spectacular coast? Indeed, across the road from the trailhead, ancient rocky shores will invite you to roam at your leisure, scrutinizing the lava rock and searching for marine life. However, on this 29-km (18-mile) loop, you will gain an enlightening perspective on the area by climbing to great heights from which you will be able to survey your surroundings. You will travel from the coast, up over the North Mountain, and down the other side into the Annapolis Valley. There you will ride through rich orchard lands before returning to the coast.

The ride follows mainly dirt roads and double-track trails through the woods, with some connecting stretches on pavement. While the majority of the ride is technically easy and follows graded dirt roads, the trails through the woods feature rocky climbs and descents that require intermediate skills. You will encounter the first of such climbs and descents as you cross North Mountain at the beginning of the loop. To return to the trailhead, you will then have to climb Burgess Mountain, from which you will descend quickly back down to the coast. These are the two main climbs of the loop, over which you will gain 400 m (1,300 feet). At the highest point you will have a spectacular view out to the Bay of Fundy, over the Minas Basin to Cape d'Or, and you might even catch a glimpse of Cape Chignecto. Riders heading out with a strong set of legs and a healthy pair of lungs will enjoy this ride immensely.

General location: The trailhead is approximately 20 km (12 miles) west of Kentville.

Elevation change: A total of 425 m (1,400 feet) are gained on two extended climbs and a few short hills.

Season: Riding can begin as early as April, but expect a lot of mud on the double-track trails. Conditions will improve considerably by June and continue to be good through October.

Services: All services are available in Kentville, including a full service bike shop, Framebreak, located at 15 Water Street (phone (506) 679-0611).

Hazards: You will encounter sections of loose rock and generally eroded conditions on the dirt roads and double-track trails. Exercise caution as you approach all descents.

Rescue index: The ride often follows or intersects well-traveled dirt and paved roads, where you can flag down assistance. You can also seek assistance at the farms and houses you pass on the trail.

Land status: The roads and double-track trails on this ride are all public rights-of-way.

Maps: Refer to A *Map of the Province of Nova Scotia* (map 13, section B-4).

Finding the trail: From Kentville, follow NS Highway 101 west. Take Exit 14, and continue west on Highway 1 toward Cambridge and Waterville. From Waterville, follow the signs to Black Rock, continuing north through a four-way intersection. You will cross Cornwallis Road and then Highway 101. At a four-way intersection with Highway 221, continue straight, following signs to Black Rock. Arriving at Canada Creek, bear left, following the road along the shore, toward the Black Rock light. At the stop sign, turn right and follow the

RIDE 76 • Black Rock

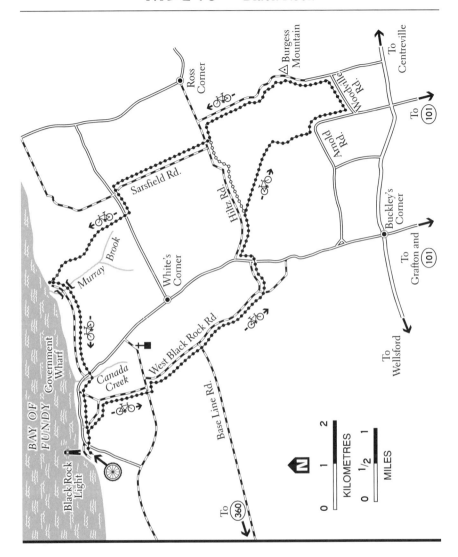

gravel road to the light. Park on the left side of the road, across from the light in a small cul-de-sac.

Source of additional information: This ride is also described in Geoff Brown and Kermit Degooyer's *Mountain Bike Nova Scotia*.

Notes on the trail: From the parking area, ride back out to the main dirt road, and turn left. Follow the road as it bends sharply to the right and continues uphill (you will return on the road branching off to the left). At the end of the

Preparing for a rough descent over the eroded terrain of North Mountain.

climb and after a short flat stretch, you will come to a three-way intersection. Bear right and continue riding to a **T** junction. At this junction, Harbourville is signed to the right and Waterville is indicated to the left. Turn left toward Waterville, and continue riding along a wide dirt road. You will proceed a short distance up this road before turning right at the first opportunity and continuing uphill. Following this dirt road, you will pass Baseline Road and then a sheep farm before arriving at a **Y** intersection. Bear left at the fork, still following a dirt road, and continue to a **T** junction with a paved road. At the **T**, turn left and ride on the pavement for a short distance to Hiltz Road. Turn right onto Hiltz Road, and ride for approximately 1 km (0.6 mile) to a point where a double-track trail branches off to the right. At this point, you may continue the ride along this double-track trail, or create a shorter loop back to Black Rock by continuing straight on Hiltz Road. If you choose to ride this shorter loop, follow the directions below, starting at the junction of Hiltz Road and Sarsfield Road.

Turning right onto the double-track trail that branches off Hiltz Road will lead you into the woods. Trees border both sides of the grassy median on this old road, and you will ride past a grassy side trail on the left. You may have to negotiate a muddy area with several large puddles as you make your way into the woods. The bugs in this section can be quite fierce in the spring and early summer, which should prompt you to pick a line and continue straight without meandering or further damaging the trail. Beyond the muddy section, you will begin an extended downhill over a bed of loose, exposed rock. You will emerge from the old road at a lumberyard and a **T** junction with a gravel road. Bear left, and continue to descend to a **T** junction with Arnold Road. Turn left onto this paved road and begin the ride through apple orchard country.

You will ride on pavement alongside a series of apple orchards until you come to Woodville Road. Turn left onto this paved road, and continue past a pear orchard. You will ride by the Foote Family Farm and eventually come to a three-way intersection. Turn left at the intersection, heading toward Burgess Mountain. As you begin the climb, the paved road will turn to gravel. The climb is broken up into two hills, the first being the steeper, more challenging one, and the second a moderate but more extended climb. You will crest the road up Burgess Mountain at 205 m (675 feet) and get a glimpse of Cape d'Or across the Minas Channel. From here the road descends, bringing you to a **T** junction with a more easterly portion of Hiltz Road. Turn left onto Hiltz Road and ride for a short distance, before turning right at the first opportunity onto Sarsfield Road.

Turning right onto Sarsfield Road, you will climb briefly before beginning a stretch of effortless cruising. As you descend, you may catch another glimpse of Cape d'Or in the distance. At the end of the downhill you will arrive at a four-way intersection with a paved road. Turn left onto the paved road, following the sign to Black Rock. A short distance along this road, watch for the house numbered 470 on the left. Directly across from this house is a dirt track branching off on the right. Turn right onto this double-track to continue to descend toward Black Rock. After passing a double-track trail heading into a clearing on the left, the trail will begin to veer slightly in the same direction. The Bay of Fundy comes clearly into view, and you will descend to a primitive campsite at Murray Brook. Follow the sharp turn to the left, away from the campsite, and continue across a bridge. Beyond the bridge, continue straight through a small clearing, to a three-way intersection with a gravel road. Bear right and follow the gravel road straight. At the next **T** junction, turn right onto a paved road. You will pass the Canada Creek government wharf, and then the road will swing around to the left and continue uphill. The pavement turns to gravel, and at the sign indicating you are entering Black Rock, continue straight, past a road branching up to the left. At a **T** junction, turn right to return to the Black Rock light and parking area, just a short distance farther on the right.

RIDE 77 • Delap's Cove

AT A GLANCE

Length/configuration: 8.5-km (5.25-mile) combination (a 2.25-km [1.4-mile] loop and a 2-km [1.25-mile] loop joined by a spur; spur is 2.1 km [1.3 miles] each way)

Aerobic difficulty: Modest; short but challenging climbs on technical terrain

Technical difficulty: Intermediate to advanced riding on single-track trails

Scenery: Lots to view: an old settlement, a waterfall, and the Bay of Fundy

Special comments: Save this ride for a clear, dry day, when the views will be smashing!

The trail system at Delap's Cove has been developed around the Shore Road Trail, an old road that traverses rolling, intermediate-level terrain and easily accommodates both hikers and bikers. The Shore Road Trail connects two loops: the Bohaker Trail, which is closest to the parking area, and Charlie's Trail, which begins just over two km (approximately 1.75 miles) from the parking area. Both loops favour fit riders and are characterized by tight turns and short, steep climbs that require good bike handling skills. Bikers looking for advanced single-track riding will enjoy the rocky, rooty trails that hug the shore of the Bay of Fundy. However, the small area in which these trails are contained and the fact that hikers flock to the area throughout the summer prevents Delap's Cove from being a technical rider's paradise. While there are some limitations to the biking here, we consider it a worthwhile destination because the trails offer unique coastal riding and the interpretive signs along the trails provide valuable insight into the human and geological history of Nova Scotia.

This ride is an 8.5-km (5.25-mile) combination that begins along the Shore Road Trail, following it all the way out to the access point for Charlie's Trail. Charlie's Trail is a 2-km (1.25-mile) loop that, though slightly shorter than the Bohaker Trail, features some advanced single-track riding. The ride traces this loop in a counterclockwise direction, passing several look-off points on the coast before turning back inland. Before completing the loop, you will pass the remains of a settlement where interpretive signs tell the story of the 70 inhabitants who received land claims here after the American Revolution. From Charlie's Trail, you will retrace your tracks along the Shore Road Trail to its junction with the Bohaker Trail. This trail is a slightly longer loop at 2.25 km (1.4 miles), but it features slightly less difficult terrain. You will ride this loop in a clockwise direction, following a series of interpretive signs that describe the

RIDE 77 · Delap's Cove

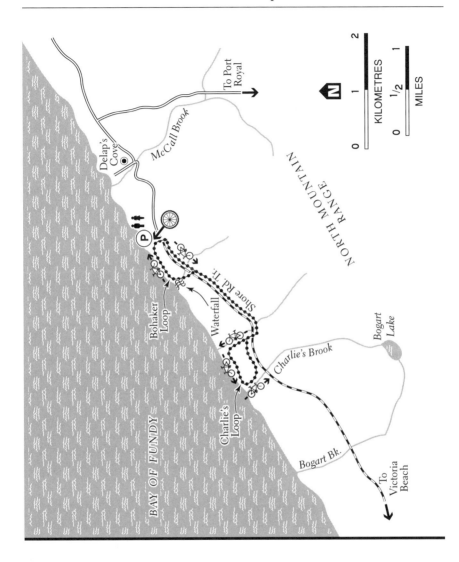

formation and geological history of the rocky shore. The trail offers several spectacular views across the Bay of Fundy as well as a look-off at the top of Bohaker Falls.

General location: Outside Annapolis Royal, 30 km (18 miles) west of Digby on the Bay of Fundy

Elevation change: Other than a few short, steep climbs, there is no dramatic change in elevation.

Season: Ideal riding conditions exist between June and August. Foggy and wet days should be avoided, as the exposed roots and rocks become very slippery and almost impossible to ride when wet.

Services: The parking area has outhouses, a picnic table, and maps of the area. Other services are available in Annapolis Royal, and the nearest bike store is located in Kentville.

Hazards: There is a steep, unforgiving downhill at the beginning of the Bohaker Trail. Consider walking down this steep hill, which includes a sharp turn to the left, as failure to make the turn will send you over the edge of the trail and into the forested valley of Sloan's Brook.

Rescue index: Because this is a popular destination, you can probably look to hikers or other bikers for assistance on the trail. Other sources of help will be found in nearby Annapolis Royal or at houses in the vicinity of the trailhead.

Land status: The trails are on Crown land managed by the Annapolis County Recreation Department.

Maps: The trail map posted on the information board at the trailhead is the only one that exists. However, the trails are well signed, which should prevent you from getting lost. The government topographic maps Digby 12 A/12 and Granville Ferry 21 A/13 do not display the trails, but they will orient you to the area.

Finding the trail: From Annapolis Royal, take NS Highway 1 across the causeway to Granville Ferry. There, turn onto Parkers Cove Road, heading toward the Bay of Fundy. Continue to a **T** junction at the shoreline, and turn left toward Delap's Cove. Follow the road until the pavement ends, where a road sign will direct you down a steep dirt road on the left to the parking lot at the trailhead.

Source of additional information: The area is managed by the Annapolis County Recreation Department, which can be reached at (506) 532-2334.

Notes on the trail: Begin on the Shore Road Trail to the left of the Bohaker trailhead. The grassy old road starts off relatively flat, with lots of exposed rock. Continue straight ahead, past the first signed entrance to the Bohaker Trail. A short distance along, there is a significant dip in the trail, immediately followed by another entrance to the Bohaker Trail on the right. Continue on the old road to a **Y** intersection. At the fork, bear right, ignoring the grassy offshoot to the left.

You will descend a rocky slope to a small bridge over a brook. Cross the brook at the bottom of the dip, and then swoop back up the other side. The climb is steep and somewhat longer than the descent, on loose rock. At the top the entrance to Charlie's Loop is just a short distance along on the right-hand side. The entrance should be signed on the opposite side of the trail, and there is also a noticeable gap in the woods. Turn right onto the narrow length of single-track, and continue along a stretch of tightly twisting turns, clumps of entangled roots, and a scattering of small boulders. Proceed just a short distance to a **Y** intersection and bear right. This intersection marks the beginning of the loop, which you will ride in a clockwise direction.

Tight, technically difficult trails wind through the woods at the edge of Delap's Cove.

From the **Y** intersection you will follow the trail down a gradual hill. After this descent, you will cross a rocky stream bed and come to a signed junction for a look-off point. Abandon your bike and walk the short distance to the shore, to a view over the Bay of Fundy. Back at your bike, you will follow the left arm of the trail. This section of trail follows closely along the bluffs overlooking the Bay of Fundy and becomes more technically challenging. In addition to gnarly knots of thick, exposed roots, there may even be fallen trees (if the trail hasn't been cleared) that cross the trail at chest level, requiring you to dismount to pass underneath. There are several look-off points along this trail, and shortly after the second optional branch to the shore, the trail widens and becomes smoother through a stretch of coniferous woods.

At this point the trail bends to the left, heading inland. You will climb a grassy trail alongside Charlie's Brook, which will bring you past the remains of a stone foundation (see the interpretive panel). Across from this site is a hiking trail that descends to the small brook. Beyond the foundation, you will pass a shed, and then veer left again into the woods on a single-track trail. This trail begins with a climb that is made challenging by the exposed roots and rocks, as well as by the steep pitches. At the top it descends again almost immediately into a small rock garden, and then climbs up the other side. Another short climb follows, before the trail descends and merges with the trail you came in on. Bear right, and continue back out to the Shore Road Trail.

At the **T** junction with the Shore Road Trail, turn left, back toward the parking area. At the first signed entrance to the Bohaker Loop, turn left onto the single-track trail. The entrance may be marked by a cairn, and you will enter the woods on a narrow single-track trail with many exposed roots and rocks. Bear right on this trail and begin a descent. Exercise extreme caution when descending this steep slope, as there is an unforgiving drop-off at the end of the hill that requires a sharp turn to the left if you are to stay on the trail. Because you cannot see the end of the hill from the top, it is highly recommended you dismount and walk this section, at least for the first time. Around the bend, the trail continues to descend more gradually. Continue straight on the trail, past a wooden bridge on your right that leads straight back up to the parking area. You will cross the second bridge you come to, following the trail as it winds alongside the brook.

As you ride along this section of the trail, you will pass several interpretive signs, so do not be surprised if you encounter groups of hikers. At the first **T** junction it is again worthwhile to abandon your bike and cross the bridge to access the look-off point. This look-off at Bohaker Falls is one of the most impressive on these trails. Back at your bike, you will now head to the right, following the trail toward the Bay of Fundy. The trail widens slightly and presents a sharp turn to the left, down a short slope that sets you on course for the ride to the rocky shore.

You will arrive at another look-off with a bench overlooking the bay. There is an interpretive sign about the geology of the area, dating the basalt back three hundred million years. The rugged shore of the Bay of Fundy is officially termed a "Rocky Shore" that has a number of distinct characteristics. Continuing ahead, you will gain a full appreciation for the definition as you pick your way through the many projecting rocks. As you round the bend, heading inland, there is a wooden footbridge with steps built into it. The steps will make most of us walk, which is advisable, given the number of hikers you are likely to encounter here. (To avoid this section, you can retrace your tracks from the look-off and return on the Shore Road Trail.) Beyond the bridge, you will arrive at a **Y** intersection with a sign for Charlie's Trail. Turn left, and return to the parking lot on the slightly wider single-track trail.

RIDE 78 · Fire Tower Trail

AT A GLANCE

Length/configuration: 18-km (11-mile) out-and-back (9 km [5.5 miles] each way)

Aerobic difficulty: Modest; gradual climb to the fire tower

Technical difficulty: Easy; the trail follows gravel and dirt access roads

Scenery: Magnificent hardwood forest and access to the shores of Puzzle Lake and North Cranberry Lake

Special comments: If you dare to climb it, the fire tower makes a great look-off

The Fire Tower Road in Kejimkujik National Park is one of the longest trails open to mountain bikers and is a wonderful way to explore the park's interior. This ride is an easy 18-km (11-mile) out-and-back trip on a combination of gravel and dirt roads. Although the trail climbs to a fire tower, it does so gradually, making this an excellent all-levels ride suitable for groups and families. The fire tower is one of the very few places in the park where you can enjoy a view across the rolling hills and many lakes of this part of Nova Scotia. Of course, to reach the view, you have to scale the ladder that runs up the middle of the spindly metal tower! At the top, you can perch rather precariously below the tiny cage that is kept locked and gaze out over the vast Kejimkujik Lake and surrounding hills.

For riders who don't mind leaving their bikes, this ride also offers some fun short hikes from the main trail. The fire tower road crosses two portage trails, which provide access to several of the park's many lakes. Between Puzzle Lake and North Cranberry Lake, Portage B provides very quick access to views across either lake. Farther into the ride, Portage E crosses the trail and connects Minards Bay on Kejimkujik Lake with top of Mountain Lake. At 2 km (1.25 miles) Portage E is the longest in the park, and carries the name Big Hardwoods Carry. Following this trail in either direction creates a 2-km (1.25-mile) jaunt out to the water and back. Heading along the trail to the right is especially beautiful, as you will follow a narrow, hard-packed footpath through one of the few old growth hardwood stands in the park. As you approach the lake, this trail drops quite steeply before opening out across Minards Bay.

General location: Kejimkujik National Park, which is situated between the South Shore and the Annapolis Valley.

RIDE 78 • Fire Tower Trail

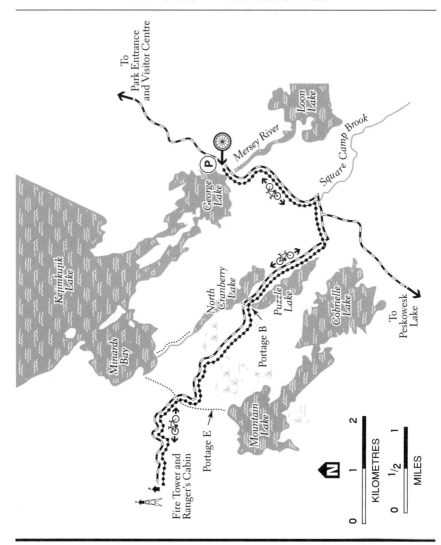

Elevation change: You begin this ride at the parking area off the main park access road at approximately 91 m (300 feet). The trail climbs gradually to 122 m (400 feet), and then continues up to the fire tower at 152 m (500 feet). Total elevation gain for the out-and-back ride is a modest 61 m (200 feet).

Season: The park is open year-round, with full services up and running from late June to Labour Day (the first weekend in September). Conditions for this ride are good from June through October. Autumn is a spectacular time of year at the park. Not only does the landscape boast all the vivid red, yellow, orange, and gold colours of fall foliage, but there are fewer insects and fewer people with whom you have to share the trails.

Services: From late June to Labour Day, services at the park include camping, an information centre, rest rooms, and a canteen. Bicycles can be rented at Jakes Landing.

Hazards: Use extreme care if you decide to climb the fire tower, which is a precarious-looking structure with a steep, narrow, metal ladder that goes to the top. Note that the small cage at the top of the tower is locked, and that the tower is unsafe in winds above 50 kilometres (30 miles) per hour.

Rescue index: At the fire tower, the farthest point on this ride, you will be 9 km (5.5 miles) from the parking area at the end of the park access road. During the summer months, and especially on weekends, it is likely that you will encounter other park users on the trail or in the parking area. During quieter times, assistance may be as far away as the Visitor Centre at the entrance to the park, approximately 19 km (12 miles) up the road from the trailhead and 28 km (17.5 miles) from the fire tower.

Land status: National park; there is an entrance fee for all visitors to the park.

Maps: This ride follows the fire tower road, which is indicated as Trail #16 on the free map handed out at the Visitor Centre. It is also possible to buy a more detailed, topographic map of the entire park at the Visitor Centre. The government topographic map is Kejimkujik 21 A/6.

Finding the trail: Follow the park access road from the Visitor Centre all the way down to Mersey River. The road will change from pavement to gravel approximately 11 km (7 miles) from the park entrance. From mid-June to Labour Day, there is a gate preventing vehicles from traveling beyond the Mersey River. There is a parking lot and picnic area on the right before the river.

Sources of additional information: Pop into the Visitor Centre or the campground kiosk for answers to any questions you might have during your visit to the park. It is worth asking for an update on all the trails open to mountain bikers, as further development might expand the opportunities. For information prior to your trip or to make campsite reservations, contact the park at:

Kejimkujik National Park
Maitland Bridge, NS B0T 1N0
(902) 682-2772

Notes on the trail: From the parking area near Mersey River, begin the ride by continuing down the park access road, crossing a bridge over the river, and (if you are riding between mid-June and Labour Day) passing by the gate restricting vehicular access. You may notice signs for Portage O, which connects George Lake and Loon Lake along the southern bank of the river.

Beyond the bridge, the road climbs slightly, and then traverses the top of a low hill. This hill, or drumlin, is actually a glacial deposit. Because of the rich, well-drained soil in these deposits, hardwoods flourish here. Continue on the road to Square Camp Brook, where you will cross a small bridge. Just a short distance beyond this bridge is the turnoff for the fire tower trail on the right. Turn right onto a dirt road at this junction, branching off from the park access road, which continues straight on toward Peskowesk Lake.

The first part of the fire tower road begins along a narrow ridge between Puzzle Lake, which will be on your left, and North Cranberry Lake, which you will see on the right, a short distance farther up the trail. At the top of Puzzle Lake you will cross over Portage B, a footpath for canoeists that spans the short distance between the two lakes. It is well worth the effort to walk down the path in either direction and look out over the lakes.

Continuing past Portage B, the trail travels through a combination of woods and open bog. You will climb, ever so gradually, for approximately 3 km (1.8 miles) to where Portage E crosses the road. You may want to leave your bike at this intersection and walk along the footpath to the right. A short hike will drop you down to Minards Bay on Kejimkujik Lake.

The ride continues beyond the intersection with Portage E, climbing more steeply over the last few kilometres of the trail to the fire tower. The tower and a warden's cabin stand in a small clearing overshadowed by trees. The only view to be had is from climbing the ladder to the top of the tower, a worthwhile endeavour on a clear day. From the fire tower, follow the same route back to the parking area.

RIDE 79 · Mushpauk Lake

AT A GLANCE

Length/configuration: 10-km (6-mile) out-and-back (5 km [3 miles] each way)

Aerobic difficulty: For all fitness levels; no significant climbs

Technical difficulty: Easy; a great introduction to off-road riding

Scenery: Pass through an old homestead down to an old dike on Mushpauk Lake

Special comments: Bring a topographic map and explore the trails branching off of this old coach road

Mushpauk Lake can be reached by biking along the remains of an old coach road that once ran between Quinan and the town of Pubnico on the coast. Having deteriorated considerably since the last farms were abandoned, the road makes an excellent introduction to the type of terrain common to off-road riding: exposed rocks, puddles, muddy ruts, grassy double-track, and short climbs and descents. All of these elements combined make this an interesting ride, without demanding a high level of technical skill. Furthermore, because of the relatively short length of the trail, this ride makes a great outing for families or groups with riders of all fitness and ability levels.

Between Quinan and Mushpauk Lake, the old coach road will take you past an abandoned homestead. Apple trees, stone fences, and the remains of a foundation are all that remain at the site now. Farther along the trail, old stone fences actually border the old road before it opens out into a meadow overlooking Mushpauk Creek. This is a beautiful spot for a picnic, and you can ride over a bridge to reach the site of an old stone and earth dike at the top of Mushpauk Lake.

General location: This ride begins in Quinan, a small community 25 km (15.5 miles) east of Yarmouth, Nova Scotia.

Elevation change: There is no appreciable change in elevation along the length of this ride.

Season: Conditions for this ride are best from June through October. Be prepared for lots of puddles in the spring and after heavy rainfall.

Services: All services are available in Yarmouth.

Hazards: Be sure to deck yourself out in bright colours during the fall hunting season, when this road and the surrounding land become quite busy with hunters.

Rescue index: At the farthest point on this ride you will be only 5 km (3 miles) from the main road and the houses that form the community of Quinan.

Land status: Public right-of-way bordered on both sides by private land.

Maps: The old coach road along which this ride follows is shown in A *Map of the Province of Nova Scotia* (map 5, section C-3). For more detailed information, refer to the government topographic map for Tusket 20 P/13.

Finding the trail: From Yarmouth, follow NS Highway 103 east to Exit 33. Turn left on Highway 308, and head toward Springhaven and Quinan. Approximately 14.5 km (9 miles) from the exit, you will pass a sign for Spring-Haven Canoe Outfitting. A few hundred metres (less than two-tenths of a mile) beyond the sign, you will come to St. Agnes Catholic Church and a community hall on the right. There is a parking lot immediately before the church. The trailhead, though unmarked, is in the far right (west) corner of the lot.

Sources of additional information: There is a brochure published by the Yarmouth County Tourist Association that describes several hiking trails in the area. Mushpauk Lake is Trail #2 in this brochure, which can be picked up at the

RIDE 79 • Mushpauk Lake

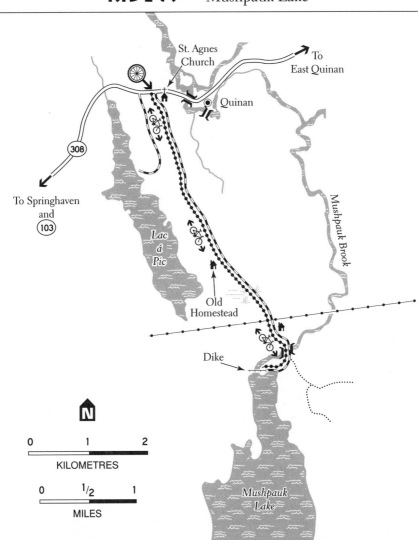

Yarmouth Tourist Bureau, located just up from the ferry terminal. For further details or information on the area, contact:

Yarmouth County Tourist Association
P.O. Box 477
Yarmouth, NS B5A 4B4
(902) 742-5355

Notes on the trail: Ride to the far right corner of the parking area and pick up the old road. You will want to stay straight on this road, all the way to Mushpauk Lake. Although there are no significant turns or bends in the road, you will pass a number of ATV trails branching off on both sides, especially over the first kilometre (0.6 mile). Also at the beginning of the trail, you may notice a good number of "Keep Out" notices. Posted by the side of the road, these signs mark the properties on either side of the road and do not apply to the road itself, which follows a public right-of-way.

The first section of the road may be rutted and interrupted by big puddles. You will also notice, through the trees to the right, that there is a gravel road that runs parallel to the trail. This is a relatively new road that leads out to Lac à Pic, where several cottages are located. There are ATV trails connecting the newer road with the old coach road, and many trail users go back and forth on the roads to avoid the worst of the puddles.

The abandoned farm sits at the top of the first rise along the trail. Look for some old apple trees, which will signal the site. The foundation of a house is still evident in the field, which is enclosed by old stone fences. Beyond this site, you will descend a gentle slope. Continue straight past another road, which branches off on the right, and through an area that has been cleared and planted with firs. You will continue for some distance through this area, passing an open bog before entering the trees for a short distance and then crossing beneath an electrical power line.

Beyond the power line, you will pass an old house or shed to the left of the trail. A short distance beyond this building, the road seems to resume its character of days gone by: old stone fences border both sides of the trail, which is wide and carpeted in needles from the spruce trees towering high overhead. You will quickly emerge in a meadow that drops to the bank of Mushpauk Creek. There are more old fruit trees here, and the road continues as a grassy doubletrack trail toward a bridge across the creek. We disturbed two great blue heron as we rode up to the bridge, which is certainly the most picturesque site at which to pause for a break or picnic.

To continue the ride to the old dike, cross the bridge and pick up a grassy trail on the other side. Keep following the trail to the right, passing two trails branching off to the left. Beyond the second of these two trails, the path you want to follow may be obscured by the low branches of some firs. Nevertheless, by following the trail continuously to the right, you will wrap around to the top of Mushpauk Lake and find yourself riding up on a bed of needles to the old stone and earth dike. This is also a beautiful spot, and the lake invites anyone interested in a swim.

Mushpauk Lake marks the end of the ride, and unless you have come equipped with a topographic map and the desire to explore some of the other trails that continue beyond the dike, turn around and retrace your route back to the trailhead.

RIDE 80 • Liverpool–Summerville Rail Trail

AT A GLANCE

Length/configuration: 28-km (17.4-mile) out-and-back (14 km [8.7 miles] each way)

Aerobic difficulty: Easy; former railroad bed that features only gradual grades

Technical difficulty: Basic; graded, gravel rail trail suitable for all levels

Scenery: Wooded corridor between Liverpool and the Atlantic Ocean

Special comments: Plan on a side trip to Summerville Beach Provincial Park for a swim

This ride follows the path of a multi-use trail between the towns of Liverpool and Summerville. The trail was the first rails-to-trails conversion opened in Nova Scotia and was part of a successful community initiative to develop the rights-of-way of the former Canadian National Railway for recreational purposes. Opened in 1990, the trail now features a small nature park at the trailhead in Liverpool and creates a narrow wilderness corridor in which opportunities to spot wildlife abound. Furthermore, the trail provides a scenic, off-road alternative for accessing Summerville Beach, where a saltwater lagoon makes a swim impossible to resist.

The trail, like most converted railroad beds, features a smooth, crushed-rock surface and no technically challenging terrain. The distance between Liverpool and Summerville Beach is approximately 14 km (8.7 miles), making this a 28-km (17.4-mile) out-and-back ride. Riders of all fitness levels will enjoy the relatively flat ride out to the beach, passing several picnic and resting spots on the way. Although the trail ends rather suddenly at a junction with Highway 3, a short 1.5-km (1-mile) ride on pavement will take you out to the beach for a refreshing post-ride swim. For families or anyone looking for a shorter ride, the rail trail can also be accessed closer to Summerville. A few suggestions for alternative starting points have been noted on the map, although none offer the convenience of a designated parking area.

General location: Between Liverpool and Summerville Beach, on the South Shore.

Elevation change: There is no significant change in elevation along the length of this ride.

Season: This ride follows a trail open to year-round recreation. Riding is most

RIDE 80 • Liverpool–Summerville Rail Trail

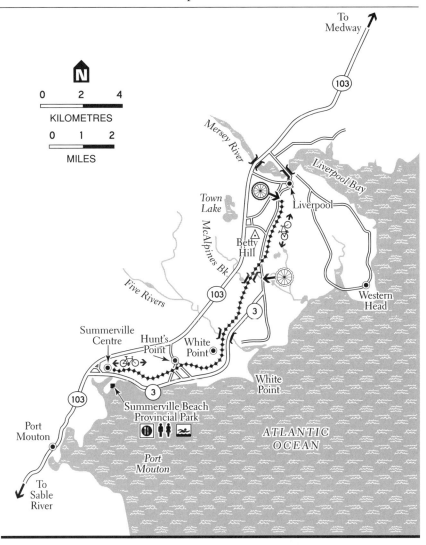

common between June and September, but weather permitting, conditions should be good as early as May and through the end of October.

Services: All services are available in Liverpool, including those found at the All Seasons Sports and Bike Shop, located on the outskirts of town at 151 Bristol Avenue (phone (902) 354-4311). In Summerville you will find basic services at the provincial park, as well as gas, accommodations, and a restaurant.

Hazards: This trail crosses Highway 3 at McAlpines Brook, just 3 km (1.9 miles) from the Liverpool trailhead. Use caution at this road crossing, as well as at the

Boulders mark the beginning of the rail trail between Liverpool and Summerville Beach.

Summerville end of the trail, if you choose to ride the short distance on Highway 3 to the beach. If you are riding this trail in the fall, be sure to outfit yourself with as much blaze-orange gear as you can find. Although hunting is prohibited on the trail, private land borders the route on either side.

Rescue index: Between Liverpool and Summerville, you will always be within a short distance from Highway 3. This area is a popular vacation destination in the summer, so you are likely to encounter other people on the trail.

Land status: Provincial trail.

Maps: The railroad right-of-way that this ride follows appears in A *Map of the Province of Nova Scotia* (map 16, sections B-2 and A-3).

Finding the trail: Access to the trail is easiest in Liverpool, where there is a small parking area at the trailhead. From downtown, drive out on NS Highway 3, heading south toward Yarmouth. Still inside the town limits, look for West Street on your left. The Queens County municipal office building is located just beyond this intersection and will be your signal if you miss the turn. Turn left down West Street, where you will find the trailhead, a parking area, and the beginning of a self-guided nature walking tour. If you are accessing the trail in

Summerville, follow the signs for the trail off Highway 103. You will drive down Highway 3 for approximately 1.6 km (1 mile), passing Summerville Beach Provincial Park on the right before reaching the signed entrance to the trail on the left. There is no space to park a vehicle at this end of the trail.

Source of additional information: A detailed description of this trail can be found in *Hiking Trails of Nova Scotia* by Michael Haynes.

Notes on the trail: Begin riding south on the rail trail, heading away from downtown Liverpool. At an intersection with Bog Road you will find an information panel that provides a map of the trail. This map is useful for identifying points along the trail to mark your progress. The trail itself is easy to follow along its entire length.

Just 3 km (1.8 miles) into the trail, you will come to an intersection with Highway 3. After crossing the road, you will cross a reconstructed railway bridge over McAlpines Brook. This intersection can also be used as an alternative access point to the trail. From this point on, the road will be on your left, though the trail curves inland and away from the road for the next km (0.6 mile). After this stretch of trail, the most remote along the entire ride, you will begin to notice houses on the left.

The half way point on this ride comes at the second bridge. This one crosses Five Rivers and signals your approach to White Point. In White Point the trail and Highway 3 run virtually side-by-side, providing another opportunity for riders looking for a shorter ride to access the trail. Beyond White Point, the trail turns inland again, curving around to the right. The spruce and pine that stood by the side of the beginning of the trail give way here to an area of abandoned fields and overgrown alders.

In Hunts Point, just 4 km (2.5 miles) from Summerville Beach, the trail crosses three roads in rather quick succession. At each road intersection, large boulders preventing vehicular access to the trail will block your path. Another set of boulders will signal your arrival at the end of the trail, outside Summerville. There is another information panel posted here. To continue on to the beach, turn right on Highway 3 and ride just 1.5 km (1 mile) to the entrance of Summerville Beach Provincial Park. Retrace your tracks for the return trip, which may take somewhat longer due to the slight incline in the trail back to Liverpool.

RIDE 81 • Jimmy's Roundtop

AT A GLANCE

Length/configuration: 28.5-km (17.7-mile) combination (1.6-km [1-mile] spur, ridden twice, connects to 25.3-km [15.8-mile] loop)

Aerobic difficulty: Moderate; only rolling hills

Technical difficulty: Intermediate; primarily rough old roads, cart tracks, and logging roads

Scenery: Barren, glacial landscape and wooded area along a series of lakes

Special comments: Popular ride due to its proximity to downtown Halifax

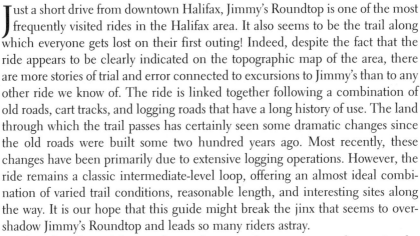

Just a short drive from downtown Halifax, Jimmy's Roundtop is one of the most frequently visited rides in the Halifax area. It also seems to be the trail along which everyone gets lost on their first outing! Indeed, despite the fact that the ride appears to be clearly indicated on the topographic map of the area, there are more stories of trial and error connected to excursions to Jimmy's than to any other ride we know of. The ride is linked together following a combination of old roads, cart tracks, and logging roads that have a long history of use. The land through which the trail passes has certainly seen some dramatic changes since the old roads were built some two hundred years ago. Most recently, these changes have been primarily due to extensive logging operations. However, the ride remains a classic intermediate-level loop, offering an almost ideal combination of varied trail conditions, reasonable length, and interesting sites along the way. It is our hope that this guide might break the jinx that seems to overshadow Jimmy's Roundtop and leads so many riders astray.

The ride at Jimmy's begins along a short spur that connects to a large, triangle-shaped loop, for a total distance of 28.5 km (17.7 miles). The ride is most often ridden (or attempted) in a counterclockwise direction. Beginning down the Old Halifax Road, you will ride toward a small community at the base of Coolen's Hill, which falls in between the villages of Seabright and Glen Margaret, on Highway 333. From Coolen's Hill, you will pick up the Old St. Margaret's Bay Road and ride inland toward Big Five Bridge Lake, before turning left and heading north across the barren, glacial landscape of Jimmy's Roundtop. Of course, for variety, you can ride the loop in the opposite direction, and for a shorter ride, you may want to use the road across Jimmy's Roundtop to create a 12-km (7.5-mile) out-and-back trip.

General location: You will begin this ride from Hubley, in Halifax County. Jimmy's Roundtop lies west of the city of Halifax and overlooks St. Margaret's Bay.

RIDE 81 • Jimmy's Roundtop

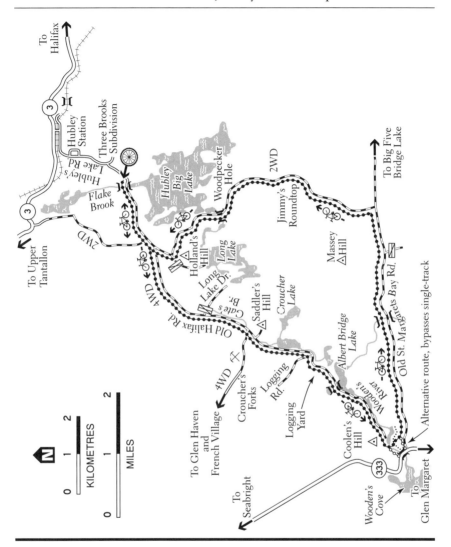

Elevation change: You will begin this ride at approximately 61 m (200 feet) at Flake Brook. You will gain only 38 m (125 feet) over the course of the first section of the ride, which descends close to sea level at the bottom of Dolly's Pond. From there, you will gain 104 m (340 feet) over several hills, to reach Jimmy's Roundtop at an elevation of 104 m (300 feet). You will complete the ride by descending and climbing back up out of Woodpecker Hole, which brings the total elevation gain for the ride to 165 m (540 feet).

Season: June through October. Note that conditions are likely to be wet along certain portions of this ride in the spring and after any rainfall.

Services: All services are available in Halifax.

Hazards: Due to recent development in the area, the nature and condition of some of the trails used along this ride may have altered since we rode here. Although the trail is clearly marked on the government topographic map, the actual route may not be the most obvious. In particular, the first turnoff onto the Old Halifax Road is inconspicuous, and the linkup between the Old Halifax Road and the Old St. Margaret's Bay Road is unclear. Be sure to carry a topographic map, in case you find yourself questioning the correct route.

Rescue index: You will not venture more than 5 to 7 km (3 to 4.2 miles) from assistance. At the farthest point on the trail, between the junction of the Old St. Margarets Bay Road with the last section of the ride and Jimmy's Roundtop, you will be riding along the sections of the ride that are easiest to follow. As a result, assistance should never be too difficult to find.

Land status: A combination of private and Crown land; the trail uses public rights-of-way that follow the Old Halifax Road and a portion of the Old St. Margaret's Bay Road, and traverse the barrens across Jimmy's Roundtop.

Maps: The best map of this area is the government topographic map Halifax 11 D/12. In addition, the route can be outlined in *A Map of the Province of Nova Scotia* (map 20, sections D-5, C-5, and the bottom strip of the map that actually forms the top of map 21, sections C-1 and D-1).

Finding the trail: Follow NS Highway 103 west out of Halifax. Take Exit 4 off the highway, and drive west on Route 3 for 2.5 km (1.5 miles). Turn left at a large sign for the Three Brooks subdivision, across from a pizza place and general store. Cross an abandoned railroad bed and immediately turn right. Continue to follow the signs for Three Brooks, turning left down Hubley's Lake Road, and following the paved road to its end, approximately 2.5 km (1.5 miles) from the old railroad crossing. There is room to park off to the side of the road.

Sources of additional information: This ride is one of many featured in a photocopied series of maps and trail descriptions assembled by Randy Gray. The information is gathered under the title *Mountain Bike Trails for Halifax and Vicinity* and can be purchased at most of the bike stores in Halifax. In addition to finding Randy's guide there, we found the folks at Cyclesmith to be particularly helpful:

Cyclesmith
6112 Quinpool Road
Halifax, NS B3L 1A2
(902) 492-1759

Notes on the trail: Begin riding along the wagon track that extends beyond the road you drove in on. You will cross a small bridge over Flake Brook. The wagon track is sandy and strewn with rocks, and there may be large puddles across the trail. You will pass two abandoned cars and a narrow side trail to the left, before reaching a junction with a wide, unpaved fire road. Continue straight onto the fire road, which also branches back up to the right. Stay straight on this road for a short distance, and at the crest of a slight hill, as the road curves a little to the left, bear right onto a less distinct trail. This turn comes exactly 2 km (1.25 miles) into the ride and, though not obvious, is the first possible turnoff to the right. There may be flagging tape marking this junction, which is where you will finish the loop.

This trail is the Old Halifax Road. Built two hundred years ago, it is now overrun with alders. You will follow this old road almost all the way down to Coolen's Hill, which overlooks St. Margaret's Bay. During the spring and after heavy rainfall, every dip along the first portion of the road will fill with water. Continue straight past an offshoot on the right that looks like a logging road. A short distance beyond this point, you will reach a junction with Long Lake Drive. There is a gate across this road, which is on your left. Continue straight, following an improved gravel road.

Ride along the gravel road for approximately 1.2 km (0.75 miles). As it follows a curve around to the right, heading toward Croucher's Forks, look for a narrow trail that continues straight. Bear left onto this trail, which begins a rather rough, wet, and rutted course across Gates Brook and up along the base of Saddler's Hill. Continue straight, past another road that seems to go off to the left, uphill. You will descend along this trail, crossing a brook over what looks like a small, rocky causeway. Continue straight over another brook just a short distance farther. Just past this second brook, stay to the right of a large boulder to cross a small wooden ramp that leads up to a logging road.

Continue straight down this logging road. When we rode here, the area was being cleared and the trail progressed across a rough, rutted logging yard still covered with slash. Since then, logging activity has ceased and the condition of the trail may have improved. Also, the wooded areas along this section of the trail may no longer exist! Be sure to stay straight through this portion of the ride, passing any old or new trails branching to the left or right. After just a few kilometres (a mile or so), you should find yourself on the wooden bridge between Brine's Little Lake on the right and Albert Bridge Lake on the left.

Beyond the bridge, the trail condition should improve. Wooden's River runs parallel to the trail on the left, and the bank boasts a beautiful array of mosses and ferns. As you approach Coolen's Hill, look on the left for a rocky, narrow trail descending to the stream. There is an old wooden railroad trestle here that crosses the water at the base of Dolly's Pond. At this point, you can opt to cross the bridge and link up with the unpaved Old St. Margaret's Bay Road, along a series of narrow trails through the woods. However, these trails can be rather difficult to follow. As an alternative, you can choose to follow the Old Halifax Road out to its junction with Highway 333. Turn left on Highway 333, and cross the bridge over Wooden's River. Almost immediately, turn left up a dirt road. When you reach another dirt road that branches uphill to the right perpendicular to the road you are on, turn right and begin to climb. This is the beginning of the Old St. Margaret's Bay Road. You will ride up past a house and some old barns.

Toward the top of the hill, you will pass a trail on the left; this is the trail you would have come out on had you crossed the old trestle bridge at Dolly's Pond. Continue straight on the Old St. Margaret's Bay Road.

If you choose to cross the old trestle bridge, you will see a trail to the right, and another one continuing straight ahead. Follow the trail straight ahead, which follows the bank alongside Dollys Pond. After just a short distance, turn right and follow a smaller trail up a hill. This trail may be flagged, and it follows a fairly obvious path through the woods. However, the going is tough, and most riders will find themselves walking their bikes up the hill. Be sure to stay straight along this trail, passing any offshoots. Although the distance is short, it may seem like a long time before you come to a **T** junction with an unpaved old road. This is the Old St. Margaret's Bay Road. Turn left to continue the ride.

Following the wide, obvious path of the Old St. Margaret's Bay Road, you will be riding east, into the more barren landscape that characterizes the inland portion of this ride. There is some climbing along this trail, and some of the slopes are rough and rocky from erosion. You will cross a brook over a primitive ramp bridge and pass a small clearing on the left. A short distance farther, you will pass an offshoot on the right that is barred by a green gate. Soon after the gate, you will come to another road branching off to the left at a right angle. This is where you turn off the Old St. Margaret's Bay Road and head north, up and across Jimmy's Roundtop. Turn left, passing an abandoned car that marks this intersection.

From this point, the ride follows the obvious path of a rocky old road, all the way back to the beginning of the loop. You will cross a bridge and ride up to Jimmy's Roundtop across a barren landscape of rock, huge granite boulders, and scrubby pine trees. Although you never gain much elevation, even at the top of Jimmy's, you will enjoy expansive views across the relatively flat terrain. Follow the main road toward Hubley Big Lake, which will be off to your right as you descend into Woodpecker Hole. You will pass an offshoot on the left.

Beyond the bridge at Woodpecker Hole you will gradually climb up Holland's Hill. You will pass an offshoot on the left that leads to Long Lake. Continue straight again, past an offshoot on the right. The road will curve around to the left and climb more steeply. Continue to follow the main road as it curves around to the right, passing a grassy trail on the left that descends to Long Lake. A short distance beyond this point, the road begins to descend slightly and you will pass the trail along which you began the ride on the left. Continue up the road for a short distance, before bearing right onto the wagon track that leads back to Flake Brook at the trailhead.

RIDE 82 · Lakes Loop

AT A GLANCE

Length/configuration: 25-km (15-mile) loop

Aerobic difficulty: Strenuous; consistent climbing on rolling terrain with steep and moderate hills

Technical difficulty: Intermediate; rocky old roads with wet, muddy sections

Scenery: The area is mostly wooded with many small lakes

Special comments: Suitable for group rides

The 25-km (15-mile) Lakes Loop begins on the popular Anderson Road trail that connects with the French Village and other trails within the Halifax area. There are endless possibilities for riding in the land surrounding the city, and many of the trails can be connected to each other if you don't mind crossing a highway or cutting through the parking lot of a Sobey's grocery store to do so. The striking contrast between thrashing about on trails in the woods and making your way through a concrete jungle to the next stretch of trail is a common attribute among urban rides, and one that you will experience on this loop. Heading out on this ride, anticipate being seduced by an ice-milky cone from Dairy Queen, and be prepared to get repeatedly wet and muddy.

The Lakes Loop is a long ride that passes through a variety of terrain, including densely wooded forests and lake areas, clear-cuts, and strip malls. The trails follow bone-rattling old roads, hilly transmission lines, and graded gravel roads. There are views of small lakes throughout the ride, and a panoramic view out to the ocean from a high point beneath a transmission line. Frequent climbing and technical terrain make this a challenging excursion that is best suited to intermediate riders with a good fitness level.

General location: West of Halifax, near St. Margaret's Bay.

Elevation change: The terrain is consistently rolling. There are regular short-to-moderate climbs and descents that add up to roughly 520 m (1,700 feet) of total elevation gain.

Season: Most riders in the Halifax area hit the trails in May. At this point in the season, the Anderson Road and French Village sections of this trail can be ridden as out-and-back rides. However, the section of the Lakes Loop that passes through the bog, connecting the far ends of these trails, is not recommended for riding until early July. Riding on all trails can usually continue through October.

RIDE 82 · Lakes Loop

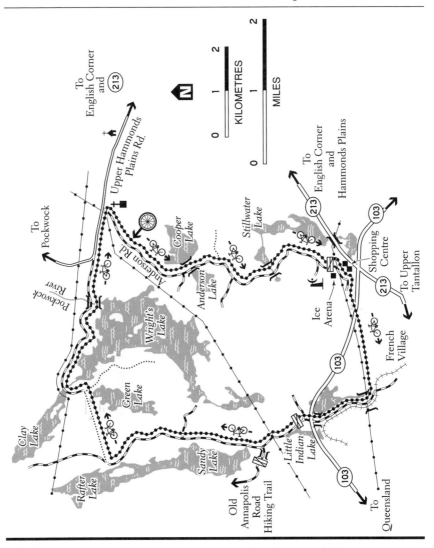

Services: All services are available in Halifax. Any snacking needs not anticipated at the start of the trail may be met at the Dairy Queen or the Sobey's you will pass midway through the ride!

Hazards: From the radio tower at the top of the hill on Anderson Road, you will follow a long descent on a gravel road that ends at a gate at the bottom. Also, at two points later on this ride, you must cross Highway 103.

Rescue index: At the farthest points from the trailhead, you will cross a major highway and emerge at a shopping centre. You are never far from assistance on this trail.

Nancy and Laura living the good life at the beginning of an epic tour of the Lakes Loop.

Land status: All of the trails pass through Crown land.

Maps: Your best resources are government topographic maps Halifax 11 D/12 and Mount Uniacke 11 D/13.

Finding the trail: From Halifax, take Bayers Road out to NS Highway 102. Travel north on Highway 102 to Exit 3B, signed for Route 213 west, or Hammonds Plains Road. Follow the exit ramp around to the right, and cross beneath the highway. Continuing on Hammonds Plains Road, you will pass through several residential areas. Just before a pizza restaurant, bear right onto Upper Hammonds Plains Road. You will pass the Emmanuel Baptist Church of Upper Hammonds Plains and the town community centre on the right. A short distance farther, turn left onto Anderson Road. As you descend, you will pass the community cemetery on the left. A short distance farther the pavement ends. Park in the gravel area at the end of the pavement.

Source of additional information: For a guide to the trails that make up this ride and other trails in the Halifax area, consult Randy Gray's booklet *Mountain Bike Trails for Halifax and Vicinity*, which is available at most Halifax bike shops.

Notes on the trail: Begin riding on the unpaved portion of Anderson Road, which begins as a four-wheel-drive–accessible road. It is littered with protruding boulders, which deteriorate to sections of loose rock. A short distance from the trailhead, you will descend an eroded section of the road before it evens out and then curves to the right. Around the bend, Cooper Lake is barely visible to the left but will become more apparent as you approach the first fork. Bear left at the fork, following a grassy trail that continues parallel to the lake through the woods. After crossing a small plank bridge over a stream, you will begin to climb a rocky slope. Beyond the crest of the hill, the road is level and mostly dirt, with just a few loose rocks and boulders.

Farther along the trail, a short descent is followed by a short climb that brings you to a **Y** intersection with an ATV track to the left and an old road to the right. Bear right, following the old road. You will pass through a rolling section with a few wet patches, which could be very wet but still passable in the spring. Beyond this stretch, you will come to another **Y** intersection. Bear left to continue following the old road; the trail to the right is fairly indistinct and will come to an abrupt end. After bearing left, you will descend a rocky gully to cross a culvert at the bottom of the slope before climbing a short hill. At the top, the trail immediately descends again and crosses a small brook. There is an old log bridge over the brook, and the trail narrows and climbs on the other side.

The trail levels out for a short distance and curves to the right through an open sandy area, beyond which you are faced with a moderate climb into a more forested area. At the completion of that climb you will pass through a muddy section that is followed by another short climb. At the end of the short climb you will descend and cruise for a brief stretch, before arriving at "Gadget Hill." It is not unlikely that riders have lost or have had to replace several gadgets in descending this steep, rocky slope from the other direction. Conversely, faced with having to climb this hill, a motorized gadget would be a welcomed attachment for your bike. The climb, though short, is remarkably steep, and made more challenging by large, protruding boulders.

At the top of the hill, the double-track continues ahead. A short distance along the trail, you will arrive at **T** junction with a loose gravel road. There is a radio tower to the right, and you will turn left to descend to the end of the Anderson Road trail. At the bottom of this gravel hill you will approach a gated fence. Watch your speed heading downhill, as the gate is not very visible at the bottom. To continue the ride, squeeze past the gate, through a narrow opening between the trees and a telephone pole. Beyond this point, you will emerge beneath a power line overlooking a main highway pull-off. Follow the continuation of the gravel access road to a four-way intersection with a paved road. Continue straight, and ride through a paved lot behind a large Sobey's building. Turn left between two buildings in the shopping plaza and head toward the main parking lot. The area around the main parking lot was under development when we rode here. As a result, we can only suggest that, no matter what structures may block your path, you make your way across the parking area to the right and toward the transmission lines behind the shopping area.

When we rode here, a dirt road led up an extremely steep hill to a trail beneath the transmission lines.

When you reach the top of the hill, and the trail beneath the transmission lines, bear left. You will descend a short hill, and then cross a large puddle before climbing an embankment to Highway 103. Disregard the short paved stretch through the shopping development: this highway crossing is, as one of our guides noted, a somewhat less-than-ideal aspect of the ride. Carefully cross the highway, waiting for a good space between cars and lots of time for you and any other riders to cross. You will pick up the trail under the transmission lines on the other side of the road.

At this point, you are embarking on the portion of the ride that follows the French Village Trail. This trail follows the transmission lines just north of French Village, located near the head of St. Margaret's Bay. Descend the embankment under the transmission line, and follow the trail as it climbs a short hill where a large boulder sits. From here, you can look out and enjoy a glorious view of St. Margaret's Bay. Continuing under the transmission lines, you will ride through a series of descents and climbs. The trail is a combination of rocky double-track and single-track, with a wet section at the beginning of the first descent. At the end of the final descent you will drop into a wet grassy area littered with some large rocks. Turn left here, and ride through a rock garden to reach a **T** junction with a gravel road. Turn right onto the gravel road.

Continue along the gravel road over two railway bridges. This will bring you to a **T** junction with another gravel road, where you will turn right. Following this gravel road, you will pass Mill Lake, a small dam, and a gatehouse on the right. Follow the road past a smattering of small buildings and a pump station that make up the Bowater Eastern Region Woodlands Office. Bear right over a small bridge, and continue out the main driveway to another intersection with Highway 103. Once again, cross the road with caution and reconnect with the Bowater logging road on the other side. As you begin up the road on the other side, you will pass another road branching off to the right before coming to a sign for the Old Annapolis Road Hiking Trail.

Beyond the sign for the hiking trail, you will pass through an orange metal gate. Notice the warning about the logging trucks you may encounter on this road as you pass through the gate. Continue along the main logging road, ignoring any offshoots. You will pass Little Indian Lake on the left. Then, after crossing beneath the transmission line and passing a dirt trail on the right, you will come to a fork in the road. To the left, the Old Annapolis Road Hiking Trail begins beyond a metal gate. Bear right, keeping to the main logging road. Beyond the fork, the logging road crosses a small bridge over a white pipe and heads up a short rise. Still following the logging road, you will pass many side trails to the left and right.

This portion of the ride follows a long, rolling stretch of road. After the first hill, you will descend to a scenic point overlooking Sandy Lake. As you continue past this point and begin to ascend, you will pass the site of an old gravel pit on the left. Descending again, you will arrive at a more recent gravel pit on the right. Continue straight, climbing gradually to the crest of another small hill and passing a logging road on the right. Eventually you will ride past a very large, recently dynamited gravel pit on the right. Up a small rise beyond this site, you will ride into a more recently logged area. As you descend beyond this point, watch for a narrow ATV track on the right-hand side. The trail may be obscured by overgrown alders and bushes but is, nevertheless, fairly distinct. There may or may not be flagging tape marking the entrance to this trail. Turn right on this trail, which will take you all the way back to Upper Hammonds Plains Road.

Entering the ATV track, the trail begins on a soft, needled bed. You will cross a stream bed where there was once a log bridge and then start to climb. The trail levels out, bringing you to a grassy area before you enter a bog. There will be a long section of puddles in which you will sink up to your chain ring—at least. Some of the wet sections over this next kilometre (0.6 mile) have had corduroy-style logs or wooden flats laid across them; presumably ATV riders have placed them there to avoid getting stuck in the mud. Beyond the puddles, you will descend a rocky hill and continue through a forested stretch of trail. You will pass Wright's Lake on the right, and there is a grassy spur off the main trail, leading to the water's edge.

Continue on the ATV track, which will curve sharply to the left, passing what looks like an old apple orchard. The trail nears Clay Lake on the left, and then crosses beneath a power line. Continuing onward, you will pass a trail branching off to the left. Then the trail will open up, closely following the edge of Wright's Lake, which will be on your right. You will ride over a wooden culvert and up into a small clearing by the water's edge. Re-entering the woods, the trail becomes smoother and then crosses a deteriorating culvert, where there is a small bog on the left. Beyond the bog, there is another rocky hill to climb and a final puddle to pass through. The trail continues to a bridge over the Pockwock River, and you will pass a double-track trail with a "No Trespassing" sign on the left. The final climb brings you to a **T** junction with Upper Hammonds Plains Road. Turn right onto the paved road, and begin to descend. To return to the parking area, turn right at the first opportunity onto Anderson Road. Enjoy the continued descent on the pavement that will swiftly return you to the trailhead.

For our friend Nancy Austin and the women riders in Halifax whose tire-tracks we followed on these trails.

RIDE 83 · Shad Bay

AT A GLANCE

Length/configuration: 10-km (6-mile) out-and-back (5 km [3 miles] each way)

Aerobic difficulty: Basic; a short ride with short, manageable hills

Technical difficulty: Hard-packed dirt trail with exposed rocks suitable for plucky beginners and intermediate riders

Scenery: Holmar Marsh Lake is a restful spot at the end of the trail

Special comments: Bring your fishing rod!

The ride along the Shad Bay trail is a short, 10-km (6-mile) out-and-back on a rolling, rocky old road. It has all the components of a traditional mountain bike ride: mud, roots, and rock packed into a short double-track trail that can be managed by most riders. In fact, we recommend this ride to beginners wanting to develop their skills in climbing and descending rocky slopes or in ploughing through mud holes. You will find the hills are long enough to present a challenge, but they end before you become too frustrated or exhausted. The wide trail and space between the rocks make it possible to plan and pick your path, and the ride is short enough that beginners will experience minimal frustration. The mostly forested outbound trail ends with a rewarding view at Holmar Marsh Lake—an ideal spot to simply take in the view or try to catch a trout for dinner!

General location: Southwest of Halifax, toward Peggy's Cove.

Elevation change: On the outbound trip you will gain 100 m (328 feet) on a rolling climb and then descend a short hill as you approach Holmar Marsh Lake. On the return trip you will have a short climb back from the lake and then descend to the parking area. The total change in elevation is roughly 240 m (787 feet).

Season: The driest months are July and August, but you may begin riding in June and continue through October.

Services: There are no services at the trailhead, but all services are available in Halifax.

Hazards: Because you are departing from the clubhouse of an archery club, you should exercise caution and make yourself known as you make your way along the initial stretch of the trail into the woods (also the archery practice area).

RIDE 83 · Shad Bay

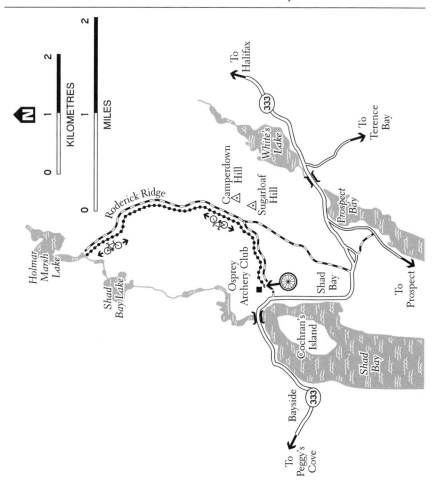

Rescue index: You may not encounter other riders or archers on the trail, so you may have to return to the trailhead or the main road to find help.

Land status: The trail is on private land, but public access is permitted.

Maps: The trail appears clearly in *A Map of the Province of Nova Scotia* (map 21, section D-1).

Finding the trail: From Halifax, exit onto St. Margaret's Bay Road from the Armdale Rotary. This road will take you past Teddy's Motor Inn and a Green

Gables convenience store. Follow signs for Peggy's Cove, taking the first exit and bearing left on NS Highway 333. Continue along Highway 333 to Shad Bay. A short distance outside Shad Bay, you will see signs for the Osprey Archery Club on the right side of the road. There is a parking area farther along the road at the trailhead.

Source of additional information: This and other trails in the Halifax area are contained in Randy Gray's booklet *Mountain Bike Trails for Halifax and Vicinity*, available at most Halifax bike stores.

Notes on the trail: Continuing beyond the parking area, the trail is a wide, dirt track that heads into the woods. Ignore the first branch to the right and make your way through an area of exposed rocks and roots that poses a greater challenge to your bike handling skills that anything you will encounter later on the trail. Beyond the rock garden, the ride starts up a gradual slope that continues for the first kilometre (0.6 mile). The slope varies from nearly flat to short, steep sections, and levels temporarily at a boggy section. Crossing the bog to the left, you will find that some wood has been laid in a corduroy fashion to make the swampier areas passable. After crossing the bog, you will begin another rocky climb.

Upon completion of the second climb, you will have doubled your elevation gain since the end of the last climb—a total 70 m (230 feet) on two short, steep hills. At the top the trail becomes slightly easier, with fewer exposed rocks and a less densely forested landscape. The flat stretch ends shortly, and you will begin the descent to Holmar Marsh Lake. The descent is gradual and is made only moderately challenging by the combination of small boulders and exposed rock over which you will roll en route. At the bottom the trail bends to the right around the lake and begins to narrow. There are more exposed roots on this brief section of trail, which will entirely disappear beyond the look-off point. Enjoy the view, and then retrace your tracks to the parking area. Remember, the return ride begins with a short climb, but then it is all downhill!

RIDE 84 • Wrandees

AT A GLANCE

Length/configuration: 10 km (6 miles) of many interconnecting loops

Aerobic difficulty: Advanced; even short, steep climbs are tough amid the terrain at Wrandees

Technical difficulty: Extreme; this is paradise for expert riders or gluttons for punishment

Scenery: In the wooded slopes on the edge of Long Lake, watch for riders capable of cleaning these trails

Special comments: It may be hard to believe, but there are riders out there who can ride all this stuff!

"Wrandees" is a network of single-track trails in Halifax that is legendary for its extreme terrain. Utilizing the natural growth patterns in the forest, the trails have not been cut, but instead have been traced between the trees and established only through use. We knew that we were in for a good ride when a local rider talked us through the trail system and pointed out various landmarks on our map: an infamous boulder drop-off, Tracy's ACL Corner, and a section of trail named "Warranty Claim." Though they may seem to be arranged in a labyrinth at times, the trails are actually a series of loops that can be ridden in a veritable plethora of ways. At some trail junctions you may find arrows that indicate which direction will take you deeper into the trail system ("in loop"), and which direction will provide an escape or quick exit ("out loop"). In total, there are approximately 10 km (6 miles) of trails. Don't be fooled by the seemingly harmless distance, though: these trails really are all single-track, and it can take upwards of three hours to ride everything (and that is if you're having a good day).

The good news is that these trails, by virtue of the number of riders who actually progress inward, become more and more difficult the farther in you ride. Therefore, you can begin with the outer, "easier" trails, and move farther into the trail system once you've mastered them. Furthermore, because the trails cover just a small piece of land between St. Margaret's Bay Road and Long Lake, it is virtually impossible to get lost. The wooded terrain is a perfectly sweet getaway from the bustling summer crowds in downtown Halifax, and much of the ride keeps you in view of Long Lake. Be prepared for tight, narrow trails; steep drop-offs; rocks and boulders; and masses of exposed roots. Unless you're an expert rider with exceptional bike handling skills, be prepared to dismount frequently.

RIDE 84 • Wrandees

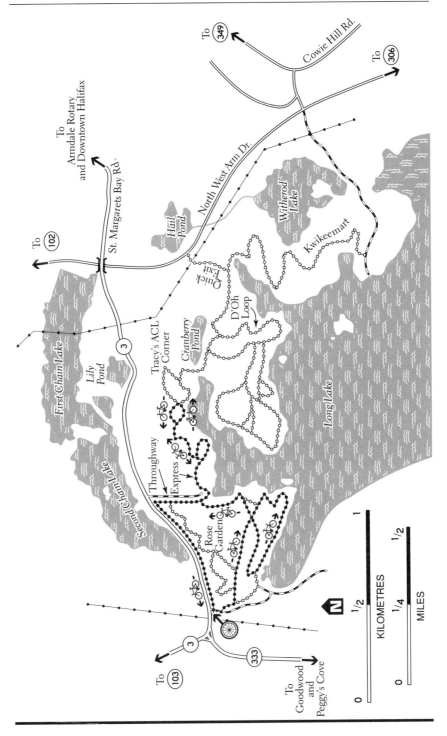

General location: Southwest of downtown Halifax, just a short distance from the Armdale Rotary. Wrandees' trails are sandwiched in between St. Margaret's Bay Road and Long Lake.

Elevation change: You will climb and descend steep but very low hills, over which the elevation change is insignificant.

Season: These trails should be in good shape from June through September. Avoid riding during or after any rainfall and in early spring, when some areas are particularly wet and susceptible to damage. In particular, the trail that goes past Witherod Lake from Cowie Hill can be extremely wet in the springtime.

Services: All services are available in Halifax.

Hazards: Everywhere; the trail is littered with drop-offs and jagged rocks.

Rescue index: The trails at Wrandees are always within close proximity to St. Margaret's Bay Road, Prospect Road, or Northwest Arm Drive. In addition to many other riders, you will usually encounter hikers and other trail users.

Land status: Undeveloped provincial park.

Maps: Check out Randy Gray's booklet *Mountain Bike Trails for Halifax and Vicinity*. Most of the bike shops in Halifax sell copies of this comprehensive guide to exploring all the possible riding areas in and around the city. The government topographic map for this area is Halifax 11 D/12, though it is helpful only in defining the boundaries of the trail system, which does not appear on the map.

Finding the trail: Wrandees is located close enough to downtown Halifax that many riders simply ride to the trailhead. Whether riding or driving, from downtown Halifax you want to follow signs to NS Highway 3, also named St. Margaret's Bay Road. By following these signs, you will reach the Armdale Rotary, which may very well be the most frightening part of this ride. From the rotary loop, continue to follow signs for Highway 3, or Bay Road, as it is abbreviated on the signs. You will drive past Teddy's Motor Inn and a Green Gables convenience store. Continue straight beyond a residential area, across Northwest Arm Drive, and through a set of traffic lights. Just beyond a "Welcome to Halifax" sign with the Citadel clock on it, turn in to a small gravel lot on the left side of the road, just before the turnoff for Peggy's Cove, which is Route 333. The gravel lot is just across from a small sign for Exhibition Park.

Sources of additional information: We suggest you do a tour of all the bike shops in Halifax before setting out for Wrandees. Talk to as many people as possible so that you'll be equipped with all the tales of glory and woe you will need to sustain yourself for your own personal adventure at Wrandees.

Notes on the trail: From the parking area, ride down a short slope and cross a shallow stream coming out of a culvert that goes beneath St. Margaret's Bay Road. This trail will connect you to a double-track trail heading south, away from the main road. You will ride just a few metres (several feet) along the double-track trail before turning left onto a single-track trail heading into the woods. Although this

Sarah approaches on a deceptively clean stretch of single-track at Wrandees.

trail is inconspicuous, its entrance has been enhanced by the addition of some crushed stone. You will begin by climbing, gradually and for no great distance, along a good introductory stretch of single-track. Exposed roots, rocks, and boulders litter the narrow corridor that forms this trail.

Just a short distance into this trail, you will come to a small sign: "Welcome to a biking and hiking trail built by cyclists for everyone." This is the only sign we have ever encountered that encourages hikers to give cyclists the right-of-way! Continue past this sign to a fork in the trail. Bear right along the more significant, and ultimately more difficult, trail. There is a sign here as well, indicating that this area is part of a provincial park. Keep to the main trail as it bends around to the left, and find yourself atop an area of exposed rock from which the only escape is a hair-raising drop-off. This is a preview of the type of terrain you can expect to find along the entire length of this trail system. In whatever fashion you choose, bear right across the rock, and make your way past a tree and down the face of the boulder to reach a four-way intersection of trails. Turn right to begin the lower loop of this section of the trail system, referred to as the "Rose Garden."

As you pick your way through the "Rose Garden," you will encounter more classic single-track terrain: roots, rocks, and boulders all packed into a narrow, twisty trail. When you drop so that you can see Long Lake ahead of you through the trees, you will find yourself at an intersection of trails. There is a fairly significant single-track trail continuing around to the left at this point, another one continuing straight, and a much narrower trail branching off to the right. Follow the trail around to the left. This next section of the trail is the lower portion of the "Rose Garden," and it closely follows the shore of Long Lake, which will be on your right.

Follow the full length of the lower "Rose Garden" loop, along the shore of Long Lake. You will ride through a few open areas beneath tall pine trees, where fallen needles create a soft carpet beneath your tires. You will also pass several trails branching up to the left, leading back and deeper into the woods. When you arrive at a fire pit, you will know that you have reached the portion of the trail that juts out into the water. There is a small island just off the mainland here. Follow the trail as it wraps up to the left. You will continue to hug the shore, and the trail is noticeably narrower along this stretch. When you come to a vague **T** junction with a slightly wider, more significant single-track trail, bear right. You will traverse a rather rough section of trail beyond this point, picking your way through a damp and rather nasty rock garden. From here, you will climb up to another little opening, where the water will be directly on your right. The trail swings around to the left again crosses a low log jump, and you will want to ride past a trail branching off to the right. A short distance farther, you will come to a fork. Turn left. You will very quickly find yourself back at the first four-way intersection, at the point at which the upper and lower "Rose Garden" loops connect.

At this major four-way intersection of the "Rose Garden" loops, turn right. You will ride back down toward the water and come to a **T** junction. Turn left. Note that the trail on the right is a continuation of another trail you passed by just before reaching the four-way intersection. Continue to follow the trail along the water's edge, passing a narrow trail branching up into the woods on the left. A short distance beyond this intersection, you will pass by another trail branching up to the left, at the site of a large boulder that is split down the middle and looks like a large dinosaur egg. Bear right here. You will ride through a muddy area, before reaching a **T** junction with a wide, obstacle-free trail called "Throughway," which marks the outer perimeter of the "Rose Garden."

Turning left at this junction will take you straight out to St. Margaret's Bay Road, a short distance up. There are also several trails branching off this main route to the left, heading back into the "Rose Garden" and offering all sorts of opportunities for farther exploration. Alternatively, and if you feel ready to venture farther into the trail system, turn right and follow the "Throughway" down to a small dam at the edge of Long Lake. Follow the trail beyond this point, heading back into the woods. You will reach an intersection of trails that marks the first loop along this portion of the ride. Both trails reconnect a short distance farther down. The right-hand trail, the "Throughway," is more difficult and follows the shore of Long Lake. The left trail, "Express," turns inland and is technically easier. Our ride took us to the left at this point, along a blissfully rideable stretch of single-track. You will then reach a four-way **X** intersection. This intersection marks the point at which the first and second loop along the "Throughway" intersect. We continued straight at this point, heading downhill for a short distance toward the water, before following the trail back into the woods, heading uphill and around to the left. You will quickly come to a clearing atop a small knoll that is actually an area of exposed bedrock fringed by trees.

From the knoll, it may be difficult to immediately make out the trails. There is one to the left that begins through two large pine trees and that will reconnect you to the four-way **X** intersection. The other trail, which continues the ride, heads out straight across the bedrock and down a small drop into a gully. In following this trail, you will climb up out of the gully on the other side before reaching a fork in the trail. When we rode this trail, there was a blue arrow pointing down and to the right here. Turn right, and prepare yourself for a challenging stretch of riding. You will follow the trail back down toward the water, before heading up to another small knoll where exposed bedrock creates a clearing. There is a narrow trail heading away from the clearing to the left, and a wider trail that continues beyond the edge of the bedrock to the right. Following the trail to the right will connect you with the more difficult loops at Wrandees: the "D'Oh Loop," "Where's My Burrito?" "Warranty Claim," and "Blood, Sweat, and Beers." You can also take this right-hand trail and then continue to bear left at every subsequent intersection to ride out of the trail system along the "Quick Exit" trail.

Alternatively, follow the trail to the left to complete the series of loops along the "Throughway" and return to the "Rose Garden." You will first drop back into the gully before reaching a fork. Bear left here. Follow the trail back to the first of the two small knolls you visited on the way out. Head across the bedrock and bear right, traveling between two pine trees. The trail to your left as you ride across the bedrock is the trail on which you rode up. Before you know it, you will be back at the four-way **X** intersection. Continue straight to ride the lower portion of this loop. At the next trail junction, turn left to head back toward the concrete dam. Follow the wide, smooth trail up to a **T** junction with the paved St. Margaret's Bay Road, and turn left to return to the trailhead and parking area.

RIDE 85 • Lawrencetown Beach

AT A GLANCE

Length/configuration: 32-km (20-mile) loop

Aerobic difficulty: Requires only basic conditioning

Technical difficulty: Suitable for all skill levels

Scenery: Coastal vistas, salt marshes, and wooded, inland lakes

Special comments: End your ride with a swim and lunch from Marie's fish & chip van!

From the glorious views stretching across the Atlantic Ocean at Lawrencetown Beach, this ride turns inland and traces a scenic, counterclockwise loop around Porters Lake and Lawrencetown Lake. The ride follows a combination of abandoned railroad bed, some pavement, and an unpaved, rough, old cart track. The trails are technically easy, and there are no dramatic changes in elevation, making this a suitable ride for anyone who feels comfortable with the 32-km (20-mile) distance.

Along the first portion of the ride, pretty, grassy verges turn the trailside along the abandoned railroad bed into a showy display of wildflowers. Farther into the ride, you will cruise along a short stretch of pavement between the rail trail and an old cart track, accompanied by refreshing breezes off of Porter's Lake. The cart track follows a bumpy path through the woods and meanders past scenic outcroppings at Goose Lake. Then, beyond another short stretch of pavement between Minesville and West Lawrencetown, you will hook back up with the rail trail. Riding over an old railroad trestle across West Marsh, will give you a close-up view of a salt marsh teeming with the activity of birds and insects, particularly at low tide. If you're lucky, the surf will be up when you return to Lawrencetown Beach, and surfers will be riding the waves that have made this beach so popular. From beginning to end, this ride passes through an enchanting, ever-changing landscape that is sure to delight gearheads and recreational riders alike. The moderate terrain ensures that you will have a chance to enjoy every view and finish the ride with enough energy to take to the waves yourself!

General location: Lawrencetown Beach is located on NS Highway 207, approximately 16 km (10 miles) east of Dartmouth.

Elevation change: Following an abandoned railroad bed for much of the way, there is no significant change in elevation along the length of this ride.

RIDE 85 • Lawrencetown Beach

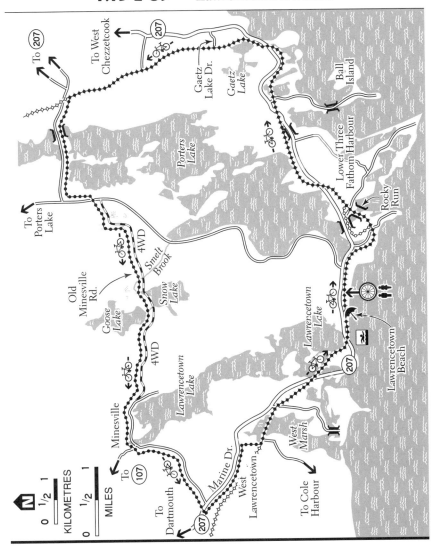

Season: Suitable riding conditions should exist from June through October. We recommend this ride in late August, when the chill of the ocean has been tempered and warm, sunny afternoons create the perfect opportunity for a post-ride swim.

Services: There are rest rooms, changing rooms, and a snack shop at the beach. All other services can be found in both Dartmouth and Halifax.

Hazards: A railroad trestle over Rocky Run, a reversible tidal rip, is in poor repair and is missing several cross timbers. All riders must walk their bikes, or choose to ride on Highway 207 and bypass the bridge altogether.

Rescue index: You will never be more than a few kilometres (a mile or so) from assistance.

Land status: The right of way along the abandoned railroad bed is owned by the Department of Natural Resources. Additionally, you will pass through Lawrencetown Beach Provincial Park and along an old road with public access.

Maps: All the roads and trails that connect to make up this ride are indicated in *A Map of the Province of Nova Scotia* (map 24, sections C-5 and B-5). For more detailed information, consult the government topographic map for the area, which is West Chezzetcook 11 D/11.

Finding the trail: Drive east on NS Highway 207 from Dartmouth, and continue all the way to Lawrencetown Beach Provincial Park, which is approximately 16 km (10 miles) from the city. The entrance to the park is well signed and is on the right side of the road. Drive to the far side of the parking area, beyond the rest room and changing facilities, where you will find plenty of parking close to the trailhead.

Source of additional information: A variation of this ride is described in *Mountain Bike Nova Scotia*, a guide to off-road cycling written by Geoff Brown and Kermit Degooyer.

Notes on the trail: Between the parking area at Lawrencetown Beach Provincial Park and the beach itself, there is a wooden boardwalk constructed over a former railroad bed. To reach the trailhead for this ride, walk along the boardwalk to its end, a short distance from the rest room and changing facilities. The rail trail begins at the end of the boardwalk, at which point you can begin riding, keeping the beach on your right and Highway 207 on your left.

A short distance from the park, the trail crosses the driveway to Moonlight Beach Inn. It then narrows to a single-track path that drops suddenly into a little rocky cul-de-sac. Beyond this point, it widens to a double-track trail. You will cross another driveway before the trail narrows again, through an area of low alders. You can see the ocean from this point, and the view makes this a pleasant part of the ride, the edge of the trail filled with an abundance of wildflowers.

You will cross a paved road, which leads from Highway 207 down to Half Island Point. (This is the road that you should follow if you choose to make a detour around the railroad trestle across Rocky Run.) Clear and easy to follow, the rail trail continues to Rocky Run, a reversible tidal rip over which an old railroad trestle still stands. However, the bridge has been barricaded, due to an obvious lack of maintenance. Although the supporting structure is still intact, several cross ties are missing from the bridge. All riders must walk their bikes across the bridge, using extreme caution and stepping with care. The trail continues on the other side, passing the tiny fishing village of Lower Three Fathom Harbour. A short distance from the bridge, the trail crosses a paved road and heads into the woods.

If you decide that the bridge across Rocky Run is unsafe to cross, backtrack to the last intersection with the paved road to Half Island Point. Turn right, and

On a warm day, the old Minesville road is an ideal place to stop for a swim at Goose Lake.

ride to a **T** junction with Highway 207. Turn right on the highway, and cross Rocky Run on a paved bridge. You will be able to see the railroad trestle across the water to your right. Just beyond the bridge, turn right on another paved road and ride just a short distance to where the rail trail crosses the road in Lower Three Fathom Harbour. Turn left to reconnect with the rail trail and continue the ride.

From Lower Three Fathom Harbour, you will follow the trail for a short distance before reaching Highway 207. Cross straight over the road. The trail on the north side of Highway 207 will cross a private driveway. At this point it becomes slightly narrower than your average double-track trail, although it remains easily passable. Over the next few kilometres (several miles), you will follow the trail across several driveways, through a couple of sudden deep dips, and along areas overgrown with alders. Then you will cross back over Highway 207. Pick up the rail trail on the other side and continue straight, crossing a paved road that leads to a fishermen's reserve on Ball Island.

Continuing on the rail trail, you will cross another driveway. You will pass a small cove to the right of the trail, and Highway 207 is visible as it parallels the trail on the left. A short distance farther, you will cross back over Highway 207 and pick up the rail trail on the other side. This portion of the trail is much wider; it appears to have been graded, and all the old ballast has been removed. You will cross Gaetz Lake Drive and several driveways before continuing past a paved cul-de-sac. At the first paved road that creates a four-way intersection with the rail bed, turn left, heading in the direction of Middle Porters Lake.

You will cross a one-lane bridge over open water on this road, which you will follow to a **T** junction with another paved road. Turn left, and ride on pavement until you reach the paved Old Minesville Road, which is signed. Turn right on this road and follow it to a small cul-de-sac where the pavement ends. Continue on the unpaved portion of the road, which deteriorates into an old cart track.

At a **Y** in the trail, bear left. The road on the right is more like a logging road. Not much distance farther on, you will pass a bog on the right. The road at this point may be rather wet terrain but remains entirely passable. Keep to the main trail, passing any side trails or logging roads branching off on either side. You will cross a stream over a bridge with corduroy logs, and just a short distance farther, there will be another corduroy-style bridge at a point on the trail where you are able to look down over Snow Lake on your left. Again, stay straight on the main road and continue to Goose Lake, which will be on your right.

Beyond Goose Lake, you will descend on a rocky trail to a **T** junction with a paved road, passing a house on your way. There is a large block of mailboxes placed here on the right. Turn right on the paved road, and ride past Minesville River Lane on your left. Continue straight, past a pair of roads branching off on the right, until you come to a **T** junction with Highway 207. Turn left, and head east on Highway 207 until you come to West Lawrencetown Road. Turn right, and ride down the road until you come to where the old railroad bed crosses the road.

Turn left on the old railroad bed, and squeeze past some boulders that have been placed so as to prevent motorized vehicles from accessing the trail. This initial stretch of the trail may also be quite overgrown with alders. However, there is no mistaking the former railroad bed, and after a very short distance, you will be riding across West Marsh, a beautiful salt marsh area that is crossed at one point by an old bridge. Beyond the marsh, you will enter an area of single-track rail trail riding, where alders have virtually overrun the railroad bed. Make your way through this leafy alley and continue straight across a paved road.

The next road you cross is Highway 207. Continue on the trail across another bridge; Lawrencetown Lake will be on your left, and you will be approaching Lawrencetown Beach ahead. Cross Highway 207 one more time to reach the entrance of Lawrencetown Beach, where you began the ride. Enjoy the rewards of warm sand, high surf, and Marie's fish and chips!

APPENDIX: METRIC CONVERSION

Though many of Canada's metric signs and measures include handy conversions for the visiting Yank, it's not something you want to count on—especially out on the trail, where missing a turn can cost you hours of backtracking.

All measurements in this book include both metric and standard values, but just in case, here's a few general conversion tips, plus some examples.

Kilometres and Miles

1 kilometre = 0.62 mile (or about two-thirds of a mile). To convert kilometres to miles, you can approximate by multiplying total kilometres by 0.6. To go back the other way and get kilometres, multiply total miles by 1.6.

Kilometres	Miles
1	0.62
2	1.24
5	3.1
10	6.2
15	9.3
20	12.4

Metres, Yards, and Feet

1 metre = 1.09 yards = 3.28 feet.

Metres	Yards	Feet
1	1.09	3.28
10	10.9	32.8
100	109	328
500	546	1,640
1,000 (1 km)	1,093	3,280

Temperature: Celsius and Fahrenheit

This is the tricky one. Strictly speaking, degrees Celsius = (degrees Fahrenheit minus 32) multiplied by $5/9$. However, unless you have a slide rule in your brain, don't stake your comfort level on your math skills. Below is a handy chart that will let the nonmetrically inclined figure out Celsius weather forecasts.

°Celsius	°Fahrenheit
40	104
35	95
30	86
25	77
20	68
15	59
10	50
5	41
0 (freezing)	32 (freezing)

GLOSSARY

This short list of terms does not contain all the words used by mountain bike enthusiasts when discussing their sport. But it should serve as an introduction to the lingo you'll hear on the trails.

ATB	all-terrain bike; this, like "fat-tire bike," is another name for a mountain bike
ATV	all-terrain vehicle; this usually refers to the loud, fume-spewing three- or four-wheeled motorized vehicles you will not enjoy meeting on the trail—except, of course, if you crash and have to hitch a ride out on one
blaze	a mark on a tree made by chipping away a piece of the bark, usually done to designate a trail; such trails are sometimes described as "blazed"
blind corner	a curve in the road or trail that conceals bikers, hikers, equestrians, and other traffic
blowdown	see "windfall"
bollard	a post (or series of posts) set vertically into the ground which allow pedestrians or cyclists to pass but keep vehicles from entering (wooden bollards are also commonly used to sign intersections)
braided	a braided trail condition results when people attempt to travel around a wet area; networks of interlaced trails can result and are a maintenance headache for trail crews
buffed	used to describe a very smooth trail
Carsonite sign	a small, thin, and flexible fiberglass signpost used to mark roads and trails (often dark brown in color)

catching air	taking a jump in such a way that both wheels of the bike are off the ground at the same time
cattle guard	a grate of parallel steel bars or pipes set at ground level and suspended over a ditch; cows can't cross them (their little feet slip through the openings between the pipes), but pedestrians and vehicles can pass over cattle guards with little difficulty
clean	while this may describe what you and your bike won't be after following many trails, the term is most often used as a verb to denote the action of pedaling a tough section of trail successfully
combination	this type of route may combine two or more configurations; for example, a point-to-point route may integrate a scenic loop or an out-and-back spur midway through the ride; likewise, an out-and-back may have a loop at its farthest point (this configuration looks like a cherry with a stem attached; the stem is the out-and-back, the fruit is the terminus loop); or a loop route may have multiple out-and-back spurs and/or loops to the side; distance for a combination route is for the total distance to complete the ride
cupped	a concave trail; higher on the sides than in the middle; often caused by motorcycles
dab	touching the ground with a foot or hand
deadfall	a tangled mass of fallen trees or branches
decomposed granite	an excellent, fine- to medium-grain, trail and road surface; typically used in native surface road and trail applications (not trucked in); results from the weathering of granite
diversion ditch	a usually narrow, shallow ditch dug across or around a trail; funneling the water in this manner keeps it from destroying the trail
double-track	the dual tracks made by a jeep or other vehicle, with grass, weeds, or rocks between; mountain bikers can ride in either of the tracks, but you will find that whichever one you choose, no matter how many times you change back and forth, the other track will appear to offer smoother travel
dugway	a steep, unpaved, switchbacked descent
endo	flipping end over end
feathering	using a light touch on the brake lever, hitting it lightly many times rather than very hard or locking the brake

GLOSSARY

four-wheel-drive	this refers to any vehicle with drive-wheel capability on all four wheels (a jeep, for instance, has four-wheel drive as compared with a two-wheel-drive passenger car), or to a rough road or trail that requires four-wheel-drive capability (or a one-wheel-drive mountain bike!) to negotiate it
game trail	the usually narrow trail made by deer, elk, or other game
gated	everyone knows what a gate is, and how many variations exist upon this theme; well, if a trail is described as "gated" it simply has a gate across it; don't forget that the rule is if you find a gate closed, close it behind you; if you find one open, leave it that way
Giardia	shorthand for *Giardia lamblia,* and known as the "backpacker's bane" until we mountain bikers expropriated it; this is a waterborne parasite that begins its life cycle when swallowed, and one to four weeks later has its host (you) bloated, vomiting, shivering with chills, and living in the bathroom; the disease can be avoided by "treating" (purifying) the water you acquire along the trail (see "Hitting the Trail" in the Introduction)
gnarly	a term thankfully used less and less these days, it refers to tough trails
graded	refers to a dirt road that has been smoothed out by the use of a wide blade on earth-moving equipment; "blading" gets rid of the teeth-chattering, much-cursed washboards found on so many dirt roads after heavy vehicle use
hammer	to ride very hard
hammerhead	one who rides hard and fast
hardpack	a trail in which the dirt surface is packed down hard; such trails make for good and fast riding, and very painful landings; bikers most often use "hardpack" as both a noun and adjective, and "hard-packed" as an adjective only (the grammar lesson will help you when diagramming sentences in camp)
hike-a-bike	what you do when the road or trail becomes too steep or rough to remain in the saddle
jeep road, jeep trail	a rough road or trail passable only with four-wheel-drive capability (or a horse or mountain bike)
kamikaze	while this once referred primarily to those Japanese fliers who quaffed a glass of sake, then flew off as human bombs

in suicide missions against U.S. naval vessels, it has more recently been applied to the idiot mountain bikers who, far less honorably, scream down hiking trails, endangering the physical and mental safety of the walking, biking, and equestrian traffic they meet; deck guns were necessary to stop the Japanese kamikaze pilots, but a bike pump or walking staff in the spokes is sufficient for the current-day kamikazes who threaten to get us all kicked off the trails

loop — this route configuration is characterized by riding from the designated trailhead to a distant point, then returning to the trailhead via a different route (or simply continuing on the same in a circle route) without doubling back; you always move forward across new terrain but return to the starting point when finished; distance is for the entire loop from the trailhead back to trailhead

multi-purpose — a designation of land which is open to many uses; mountain biking is allowed

off-camber — a trail that slopes in the opposite direction than one would prefer for safety's sake; for example, on a side-cut trail the slope is away from the hill—the inside of the trail is higher, so it helps you fall downhill if your balance isn't perfect

ORV/OHV — a motorized off-road vehicle (off-highway vehicle)

out-and-back — a ride where you will return on the same trail you pedaled out; while this might sound far more boring than a loop route, many trails look very different when pedaled in the opposite direction

pack stock — horses, mules, llamas, etc., carrying provisions along trails

point-to-point — a vehicle shuttle (or similar assistance) is required for this type of route, which is ridden from the designated trailhead to a distant location, or endpoint, where the route ends; total distance is for the one-way trip from the trailhead to endpoint

portage — to carry your bike on your person

pummy — soil with high pumice content produced by volcanic activity in the Pacific Northwest and elsewhere; light in consistency and easily pedaled; trails with such soil often become thick with dust

quads — bikers use this term to refer both to the extensor muscle in the front of the thigh (which is separated into four parts) and to maps; the expression "Nice quads!" refers always to

	the former, however, except in those instances when the speaker is an engineer
runoff	rainwater or snowmelt
scree	an accumulation of loose stones or rocky debris lying on a slope or at the base of a hill or cliff
side-cut trail	a trail cut on the side of a hill
signed	a "signed" trail has signs in place of blazes
single-track	a single, narrow path through grass or brush or over rocky terrain, often created by deer, elk, or backpackers; single-track riding is some of the best fun around
skid road	the path created when loggers drag trees through the forest with heavy equipment
slickrock	the rock-hard, compacted sandstone that is great to ride and even prettier to look at; you'll appreciate it even more if you think of it as a petrified sand dune or seabed (which it is), and if the rider before you hasn't left tire marks (from unnecessary skidding) or granola bar wrappers behind
snowmelt	runoff produced by the melting of snow
snowpack	unmelted snow accumulated over weeks or months of winter—or over years—in high-mountain terrain
spur	a road or trail that intersects the main trail you're following
squid	one who skids
stair-step climb	a climb punctuated by a series of level or near-level sections
switchback	a zigzagging road or trail designed to assist in traversing steep terrain; mountain bikers should not skid through switchbacks
talus	the rocky debris at the base of a cliff, or a slope formed by an accumulation of this rocky debris
tank trap	a steep-sided ditch (or series of ditches) used to block access to a road or trail; often used in conjunction with high mounds of excavated material
technical	terrain that is difficult to ride due not to its grade (steepness) but to its obstacles—rocks, roots, logs, ledges, loose soil . . .
topo	short for topographical map, the kind that shows both linear distance and elevation gain and loss; "topo" is pronounced with both vowels long

GLOSSARY

trashed — a trail that has been destroyed (same term used no matter what has destroyed it . . . cattle, horses, or even mountain bikers riding when the ground was too wet)

two-track — see "double-track"

two-wheel-drive — this refers to any vehicle with drive-wheel capability on only two wheels (a passenger car, for instance, has two-wheel drive); a two-wheel-drive road is a road or trail easily traveled by an ordinary car

waterbar — an earth, rock, or wooden structure that funnels water off trails to reduce erosion

washboarded — a road that is surfaced with many ridges spaced closely together, like the ripples on a washboard; these make for very rough riding, and even worse driving in a car or jeep

whoop-de-doo — closely spaced dips or undulations in a trail; these are often encountered in areas traveled heavily by ORVs

wilderness area — land that is officially set aside by the government to remain natural—pure, pristine, and untrammeled by any vehicle, including mountain bikes

windchill — a reference to the wind's cooling effect upon exposed flesh; for example, if the temperature is minus 12 degrees Celsius and the wind is blowing at 32 kilometres per hour, the windchill (that is, the actual temperature to which your skin reacts) is minus 36 degrees; if you are riding in wet conditions things are even worse, for the windchill would then be minus 59 degrees!

windfall — anything (trees, limbs, brush, fellow bikers . . .) blown down by the wind

INDEX

Adair, Larry, 129
Adair's Wilderness Lodge, 126, 137
Advance ride recommendations, *xxv*
Adventure High, 153
Aerobic difficulty information, 1
America by Mountain Bike map legend, *xii*
Annapolis County Recreation Department, 366
Annapolis Valley Time Trial Loop
 map of, 352
 ride through, 350–54
Anne's Land Heritage Roads
 map of, 173
 ride through, 172–74
Archer's Alley
 map of, 17
 ride through, 16–22
Atlantic Canada. *See also* New Brunswick; Newfoundland; Nova Scotia; Prince Edward Island (PEI)
 flora and fauna of, *xix–xxi*
 geography of, *xix*
 history and people of, *xvii–xix*
 hitting the trails tips for, *xxi–xxiv*
 joy of mountain biking in, *xviii, xxiii*
 maps of, *x, xi*
 weather of, *xxi*
Atlantic Mountain Bike Championships, 159
Austin, Nancy, 390

Baie Verte Lake, 91
Bay of Fundy, 142, 338
Baymount Outdoor Adventures, 105
Bay St. Lawrence, 305
Beaumont
 map of, 95
 ride through, 94–98
Beginner ride recommendations, *xxv*

Bennett Brook
 map of, 115
 ride through, 114–17
Bike Trails for Halifax and Vicinity (Gray), 382
Bird life, *xxi*
Bishop, Jodi E., *xxiv*
Black Rock map, 361
Bonshaw
 map of, 184
 ride through, 183–86
Bouctouche
 map of, 86
 ride through, 85–87
British Columbia Provincial Parks Department, 2
Brookvale
 map of, 176
 ride through, 175–79
Brookvale Provincial Park, 177, 178
Brown, Geoff, 305, 329, 361, 402
Bull Arm, 250
Bungay's Bicycle & Snowboard Shop, 96
Bunker's Hill
 map of, 23
 ride through, 22–28

Cabot, John, *xvii*, 197
Cabot Strait, 287
Camping ride recommendations, *xxvi*
Canada Map Office, 6
Canary Cycles, 201, 222, 230, 237
Cape Breton Highlands National Park, 294, 296, 297, 300, 309
Cape Chignecto
 map of, 336
 ride through, 335–40
Cape Mabou
 map of, 316
 ride through, 315–20

INDEX

Cape Mabou Trail Club, 318
Cape Tryon lighthouse, 166–167
Caraquet
  map of, 73
  ride through, 72–76
Cartier, Jacques, *xvii*, 198
Cellular phones, 9–10
Centennial Park
  map of, 100
  ride through, 99–102
Centre Echo Restigouche, 66
Charlotte's Shore Heritage Roads
  map of, 181
  ride through, 180–83
The City of Fredericton Trail Guide, 30
City of Saint John Parks Department, 145
Clarenville
  map of, 255
  ride through, 254–57
Clyburn Brook, 296, 297
Clyburn Valley
  map of, 295
  ride through, 294–97
Coastal ride recommendations, *xxvi*
Coello, Dennis, 9
Come By Chance
  map of, 245
  ride through, 244–48
Come By Chance race circuit, 199, 246
Corner Brook Lake, 280
Cripps Hill
  map of, 124
  ride through, 123–29
Cyclesmith, 293, 382

Degooyer, Kermit, 305, 329, 361, 402
Delap's Cove
  map of, 365
  ride through, 364–68
Department of Environment & Lands, Lands Branch (Newfoundland), 201
Department of Natural Resources (Nova Scotia), 337
Destination Newfoundland and Labrador, 201
Doctor's Brook, 327, 328
Double-track trails. *See also* Single-track rides
  around Poley Mountain, 121

Double-track trails *(continued)*
  in Hillsborough, 104
Drinking water supply, 7–8
Ducks Unlimited Musquash Marshaland Trail, 147–51
Dunphy's Pond
  map of, 259
  ride through, 258–60

Earle Industries Ltd., 201, 204, 221–22, 230, 234
East Coast Trail Association, 209
Eigg Mountain
  climbing up, 327
  map of, 326
  ride through, 325–29
Elmira Confederation Trail
  map of, 194
  ride through, 192–96
Equipment/tools, 8–9
Etiquette, 6–7
"Evangeline" (Longfellow), 348

Falcon Orienteering Club, 104–5
Family ride recommendations, *xxvi–xxvii*
Faust, Jeff, 10
Fire Tower Trail
  map of, 370
  ride on, 369–72
First-aid kit, 9
Flora and fauna, *xix–xxi*
Fluid requirements, 7–8
Framebreak Bicycles, 293, 349, 353, 356
Fredericton Trails Coalition, 30, 31
French Fort Cove map, 77
French Fort Cove Trail, 76–80
French River
  map of, 165
  ride through, 164–68
Freshwater Bay
  map of, 225
  ride through, 224–27
  view of, 226
Frying Pan Lake, 145
Fundy Model Forest, 126
Fundy Model Forest Network, 132
Fundy National Park, 109, 113, 116
The Fundy Trail
  map of, 140

The Fundy Trail *(continued)*
  ride on, 139–42
Fundy Trails Council, 141

Gaspereau Trail, 91–93
Gillett, Brian, 219
"Gold Mine" shelter (Cape Breton Highlands National Park), 296
Goose Lake, 405
Goose River
  map of, 107
  ride through, 106–10
The Gorge
  map of, 357
  ride through, 355–59
Grand Manan Island, 151–55
Grand Manan/Southern Head
  map of, 152
  ride through, 151–55
Grand-Pré Dikes
  map of, 347
  ride through, 346–50
Gray, Randy, 382, 387, 393, 396
Gros Morne National Park, 200

Hale, Sarah L., *xxiv*
Harrigan Lake, 146
Haynes, Michael, 318, 379
Hazards, 2
Higgins Mountain, 333
Hiking Trails of Nova Scotia (Haynes), 318, 379
Hillsborough
  map of, 103
  ride through, 102–6
Historic sites ride recommendations, *xxvii*
Hitting the trails
  in Atlantic Canada, *xxi–xxiv*
  information tips contained in, 7–9
  in New Brunswick, 14–15
  in Newfoundland, 200–201
  in Nova Scotia, 293
  in Prince Edward Island, 159–60
Homestead Trail
  map of, 169
  ride through, 168–71
Humber River Valley, 266
Information Centre (Caraquet Trail), 75
Intermediate ride recommendations, *xxv*

International Mountain Bicycling Association (IMBA), 6–7
Inverness County Tourism Department, 323
Inverness Recreation and Tourism Department, 314
Inverness Victoria Counties Trails Federation, 313
Irving Eco-Centre, 85, 87
Island Eco-Adventures (Baddeck), 313
Island Trails, 160

Jarret, Chris, 222
Jessome's Source for Sports, 42
Jimmy's Roundtop
  map of, 381
  ride through, 380–84

Kedgwick Forestry Museum, 61
Kejimkujik National Park, 369, 371
Kenmount Hill
  map of, 236
  ride through, 235–38
Kouchibouguac
  map of, 82
  ride through, 81–84
Kouchibouguac National Park, 81, 84
Kouchibouguac National Park's Visitor Information Centre, 83

Lady Slipper Road–12-Mile Dam
  map of, 279
  ride through, 277–81
Lake of Islands
  map of, 299
  ride through, 298–302
Lakes
  Baie Verte, 91
  Corner Brook, 280
  Dunphy's Pond, 258–60
  Frying Pan, 145
  Goose, 405
  Harrigan, 146
  Marven, 110–14
  Mushpauk, 372–75
  Pembroke, 310–12
  Silver, 90
  Spruce, 150

INDEX

Lakes Loop
  map of, 386
  ride through, 385–90
La Manche Bay
  map of, 240
  ride through, 239–43
  view of, 241
Land status, 2–3
Lawrencetown Beach
  map of, 401
  ride through, 400–404
Le Canotier, 39
Le Sentier Petit Temis
  map of, 38
  ride through, 37–40
Liverpool–Summerville Rail Trail
  map of, 377
  ride through, 376–79
Logging companies, 2
Longfellow, Henry Wadsworth, 348
Loop ride recommendations, *xxvii*

McAskill, J. Dan, 163, 189
MacQuarrie, Kate, 163, 189
Macqueen's Bike Shop & Travel, 157–58, 160
Mann Siding–Whites Brook Trail, 59–62
A Map of the Province of Nova Scotia
  Black Rock map in, 360
  Cape Chignecto map in, 337
  Cape Mabou map in, 318, 327
  Eigg Mountain map in, 327
  Grand-Pré Dikes map in, 349
  Jimmy's Roundtop map in, 382
  Lawrencetown Beach map in, 402
  Liverpool–Summerville Rail Trail map in, 378
  map resources within, 293
  Money Point map in, 305
  Mushpauk Lake map in, 373
  Pembroke Lake map in, 313
  River Denys Mountain map in, 323
  Shad Bay map in, 392
Maps. *See also The New Brunswick Atlas; specific rides.*
  America by Mountain Bike map legend, *xii*
  Atlantic Canada, *x, xi*
  listed, *xiii–xiv*

Maps *(continued)*
  New Brunswick, *x*
  Newfoundland, *xi*
  Newfoundland Maps as resource for, 230, 233, 283
  Nova Scotia, *x*
  obtained from Canada Map Office, 6
  topographic series of, 3–6
Marble Mountain, 266
Marble Mountain Summit Trail
  map of, 265
  ride through, 264–58
Martock
  map of, 341
  ride through, 340–46
Martock Mountain, 340, 341
Martock race circuit, 343
Marven Lake
  map of, 111
  ride through, 110–14
Massey Drive
  map of, 270
  ride through, 268–73
The Mighty Salmon
  map of, 130
  ride through, 129–35
Miller, Doug, 199, 270, 271
Miramichi City Community Recreational Department, 78
Moncton Mountain Bike Club, 96
Money Point
  map of, 304
  ride through, 302–7
Mont Farlagne
  map of, 41
  ride through, 40–44
Morell–St. Peter's Confederation Trail
  map of, 187
  ride through, 186–89
Mountain Bike Nova Scotia (Brown and Degooyer), 305, 329, 361, 402
Mountain Bike Tour Map and Guide brochure (Fundy Model Forest Network), 132
Mountain Bike Trails for Halifax and Vicinity (Gray), 382, 387, 393, 396
Mountain Biking in and around Corner Brook (Miller), 199, 270, 271
Mountain ride recommendations, *xxvi*

INDEX

Mount Carleton Provincial Park, 53
Mount Carleton Recreational Loop
  map of, 51
  ride on, 50–54
Mount Carleton Summit Trail
  map of, 55
  ride on, 54–58
Mt. Scio House, 204
Murphy, Bea, 196
Mushpauk Lake
  map of, 374
  ride through, 372–75
Musquash–West Saint John Trails, 147–51

National Topographic Series (NTS), 3, 4–5
Nature Trails of Prince Edward Island (McAskill and MacQuarrie), 163, 189
New Brunswick. *See also* Atlantic Canada
  all about trails in, 12–14
  Archer's Alley ride, 16–22
  Beaumont ride, 94–98
  Bennett Brook ride, 114–17
  Bouctouche ride, 85–87
  Bunker's Hill ride, 22–28
  Caraquet ride, 72–76
  Centennial Park ride, 99–102
  Cripps Hill ride, 123–29
  described, 11–12
  French Fort Cove ride, 76–80
  The Fundy Trail, 139–42
  Goose River ride, 106–10
  Grand Manan/Southern Head ride, 151–55
  Hillsborough ride, 102–6
  hitting the trails tips for, 14–15
  Kouchibouguac ride, 81–84
  Le Sentier Petit Temis ride, 37–40
  map of, x
  Marven Lake ride, 110–14
  The Mighty Salmon ride, 129–35
  Mont Farlagne ride, 40–44
  Mount Carleton Recreational Loop ride, 50–54
  Mount Carleton Summit Trail, 54–58
  Odell Park ride, 28–31
  Poley Mountain ride, 118–23
  Porter's Pacer ride, 44–50

New Brunswick *(continued)*
  resource list on, 15
  Restigouche River ride, 62–67
  Rockwood Park ride, 143–46
  Sentier NB Trails
    Grand Manan/Southern Head, 151–55
    Sackville–Port Elgin, 88–93
    West Saint John–Musquash Trails, 147
  Sugarloaf Mountain ride, 68–71
  Tour of Lisson Settlement ride, 135–38
  Wollastook ride, 32–36
The New Brunswick Atlas. See also Maps
  on Bunker's Hill, 24
  as map resource, 15
  on Mont Farlagne, 42
  on Restigouche River Trail, 65
  on Sentier NB Trail railroad route, 61
  on Tour of Lission Settlement, 137
New Brunswick Multi-Use Trail System, 141
The New Brunswick Multi-Use Trail System Trail Guide, 149
New Brunswick Tourism, 53, 57
New Brunswick Trails Council, Inc., 61, 90, 149
Newfoundland. *See also* Atlantic Canada
  all about trails in, 198–200
  Clarenville ride, 254–57
  Come By Chance ride, 244–48
  description and history of, 197–98
  Dunphy's Pond ride, 258–60
  Freshwater Bay ride, 224–27
  hitting the trails tips for, 200–201
  Kenmount Hill ride, 235–38
  Lady Slipper Road–12-Mile Dam ride, 277–81
  La Manche Bay ride, 241–43
  map of, xi
  Marble Mountain Summit Trail ride, 264–68
  Massey Drive ride, 268–73
  Petty Harbour ride, 227–31
  Pinchgut Lake ride, 273–77
  Pippy Park ride, 202–6
  Pouch Cove ride, 211–19
  resources available on, 201
  Shoal Bay ride, 231–35

INDEX

Newfoundland. *(continued)*
  South Side Hills ride, 219–24
  Stephenville ride, 281–84
  Sunnyside ride, 248–53
  Torbay Coast ride, 206–11
  Trailway Provincial Park
    Cape Ray, 285–88
    Gander, 261–64
Newfoundland Maps, 230, 233, 283
Newfoundland Model Forest Group, 199
Newfoundland Trailway Council, 263
New London Bay, 170
North Mountain, 362
Nova Scotia. *See also* Atlantic Canada
  all about trails in, 291–92
  Annapolis Valley Time Trial Loop ride, 350–54
  Black Rock ride, 359–63
  Cape Chignecto ride, 335–40
  Cape Mabou ride, 315–20
  Clyburn Valley ride, 294–97
  Delap's Cove ride, 364–68
  described, 289–90
  Eigg Mountain ride, 325–29
  Fire Tower Trail ride, 369–72
  The Gorge ride, 355–59
  Grand-Pré Dikes ride, 346–50
  hitting the trails in, 293
  Jimmy's Roundtop ride, 380–84
  Lake of Islands ride, 298–302
  Lakes Loop ride, 385–90
  Lawrencetown Beach ride, 400–404
  Liverpool–Summerville Rail Trail ride, 376–79
  map of, x
  Martock ride, 340–46
  Money Point ride, 302–7
  Mushpauk Lake ride, 372–75
  Pembroke Lake ride, 310–15
  River Denys Mountain ride, 320–25
  Shad Bay ride, 391–93
  Trous de Saumons ride, 307–10
  Wentworth ride, 330–34
  Wrandees ride, 394–99
Nova Scotia Government Bookstore, 293
Novice ride recommendations, *xxv*

Odell Park
  map of, 29

Odell Park *(continued)*
  ride through, 28–36
Official Travel Map (Tourism New Brunswick), 85
Old Eatonville Road (Cape Chignecto), 338
Old Minesville Road (Goose Lake), 403
Out-and-back ride recommendations, *xxvii–xxviii*
Outside Expeditions, 160, 166

Parks Canada, 171
Peak Performance Bicycle Shop, 328
PEI Cycling Association, 160
Pembroke Lake
  map of, 311
  ride through, 310–15
Petty Harbour
  map of, 228
  ride through, 227–31
Pinchgut Lake
  map of, 274
  ride through, 273–77
Pinchgut Trail, 275
Pippy Park
  map of, 203
  ride through, 202–6
Play It Again Sports, 201
Point-to-point ride recommendations, *xxviii*
Poley Mountain
  map of, 119
  ride through, 118, 119–23
Poley Mountain Resorts Ltd., 120
Port Elgin–Sackville Trails, 88–93
Porter, John, 47
Porter's Pacer
  map of, 45
  ride through, 44–50
Pouch Cove
  map of, 212
  ride through, 211–19
Prince Edward Island (PEI). *See also* Atlantic Canada
  all about trails in, 157–59
  Anne's Land Heritage Roads ride, 172–74
  Bonshaw ride, 183–86
  Brookvale ride, 175–79

INDEX 419

Prince Edward Island (PEI).*(continued)*
  Charlotte's Shore Heritage Roads ride, 180–83
  described, 156–57
  Elmira Confederation Trail, 192–96
  French River ride, 164–68
  Homestead Trail, 168–71
  Morell–St. Peter's Confederation Trail, 186–89
  resources available on, 160
  restricted trail access in, *xxii*
  Souris Confederation Trail, 189–92
  Tignish–Alberton Confederation Trail, 161

Race circuits recommendations, *xxv*
The Radical Edge, 15, 18, 24
"Red Mud Cup" race circuit, 158–59
Rescue index, 2
Restigouche River
  map of, 63
  ride through, 62–67
Rides. *See also* Maps; Trails
  beginner to advanced recommendations listed, *xxv*
  first-aid kit for, 9
  hitting the trail tips for, 7–9
  race circuits recommendations, *xxv*
  special interest recommendations listed, *xxv–xxvii*
  topographic maps for, 5–6
  trail descriptions for, 1–3
  trail etiquette during, 6–7
  using cellular phones during, 9–10
Ritchie, Sean, 106
River Denys Mountain
  map of, 321
  ride through, 320–25
"The Rock," 199. *See also* Newfoundland
Rockwood Park
  map of, 144
  ride through, 143–46
Rules of the Trail (IMBA), 6–7

Sackville–Port Elgin Trails, 88–93
Salt & Fir (Fundy National Park visitor guide), 112
Scenery, 2

Scenic Heritage Roads of Prince Edward Island, 175, 183, 195
Seasons, 2
Sea Spray Cycle, 296, 300, 309
Sentier NB Trails. *See also* New Brunswick
  the Fundy Trail
    map of, 140
    ride through, 139–42
  Sackville–Port Elgin
    map of, 89
    ride through, 88–93
  West Saint John–Musquash
    map of, 148
    ride through, 147–51
  Whites Brook–Mann Siding
    map of, 60
    ride through, 59–62
Sentiers Peninsule Acadienne, 75
Services available, 2
Shad Bay
  map of, 392
  ride through, 391–93
Shoal Bay
  map of, 233
  ride through, 231–35
  rocky crevasses along, 234
Silver Lake, 90
Singletrack Mudpack (Nova Scotia Women's Mountain Bike Club), 293
Single-track ride recommendations, *xxvi*
Ski Martock, 342
Smith, Ed, 105
Smith, Luella, 105
Smooth Cycle, 158, 160, 178, 184

Souris Confederation Trail
  map of, 190
  ride through, 189–92
Southern Head cliffs, 154
South Side Hills
  map of, 220
  ride through, 219–24
Southwest Coast Tourism Association, 288
Special interest ride recommendations, *xxv–xxvii*
The Sports Centre, 256
Spruce Lake, 150

Stephenville
  map of, 282
  ride through, 281–84
Sugarloaf Mountain
  map of, 69
  ride through, 68–71
Sugarloaf Mountain Provincial Park, 68–69, 70
Summerville Beach, 378
Sunnyside
  map of, 249
  ride through, 248–53
Sydor, Alison, 1

Terra Nova National Park, 258, 260
Tignish–Alberton Confederation Trail
  map of, 161
  ride through, 161
Tools/equipment, 8–9
Topographic series maps, 3–6. *See also* Maps
Tor Bay, 208
Torbay Coast
  map of, 207
  ride through, 206–11
Tourism New Brunswick, 85
Tourism Nova Scotia, 293
Tourism PEI, 160
Tour of Lisson Settlement
  map of, 136
  ride through, 135–38
Trail aerobic difficulty information, 1
Trail elevation changes, 2
Trail etiquette, 6–7
Trail hazards, 2
Trail land status, 2–3
Trail length/configuration information, 1
Trail names, 1
Trail rescue index, 2
Trails. *See also* Maps; Rides
  about New Brunswick, 12–14
  about Newfoundland, 198–200
  about Nova Scotia, 291–92
  about Prince Edward Island, 157–59
  at a glance information on, 1–2
  category information on, 2–3
  description outline for, 1–4

Trails. *(continued)*
  hitting the trail tips for, 7–9
  recommendations for special interests, *xxv–xxviii*
Trail scenery information, 2
Trail seasons, 2
Trail services, 2
The Trail Shop, 293
Trails of Inverness County brochure, 318, 323
Trail technical difficult information, 1–2
Trailway Provincial Park
  Cape Ray
    map of, 286
    ride through, 285–88
  Gander
    map of, 262
    ride through, 261–64
Trans-Canada Trail initiative, *xxii*
Trans-Canada Trail ride recommendations, *xxvii*
Treaty of Utrecht (1713), *xvii–xviii*
Trinity Bay, 256
Trous de Saumons
  map of, 308
  ride through, 307–10

Valley Stove and Cycle, 349
Victoria County Recreation Department, 314

Water supply, 7–8
Water supply safety, 8
Weather, *xxi*
Wentworth
  map of, 331
  ride through, 330–34
Wentworth Hostel, 332
Wentworth Valley, 333
West Saint John–Musquash Trails, 147–51
Whites Brook–Mann Siding Trail, 59–62
Wilderness ride recommendations, *xxvi*
Wildlife, *xx*
Wolfeville Visitor Information Centre, 349

Woolastook
    map of, 33
    ride through, 32–36
Woolastook Recreation Park, 34
Wrandees
    map of, 395
    ride through, 394–99

Yarmouth County Tourist Association, 374

ABOUT THE AUTHORS

Superheroes have soared through the ether of the North American Zeitgeist for the better part of the twentieth century—as we approach the twenty-first with anxious giggles, why should the next hundred years prove any different? Indeed, if Ruthie and Evangerswish have anything to say about it, the year 2000 will see landscapes from the Atlantic to the Pacific made accessible to mountain bikers everywhere. **SARAH HALE** and **JODI BISHOP**, like most superheroes-to-be, failed to notice their amazing powers of balance, control, and need we say, crash recovery, until mountain biking tested their natural abilities to the limit.

Then, out of the blue, like a rider hurtling ass over teakettle, their destinies socked them right in the kisser, and they knew what trails fate had blazed for them. Were it not for their intrepid alter-egos, Sarah and Jodi might not have achieved the summit of Bunker's Hill, or wrestled the Mighty Salmon to the shore, or survived the deceptively treacherous stretches of converted rail bed confronting the prospective tamer of Atlantic Canada's wilds. Perhaps you, too, will discover your superbiker persona as you climb onto your bike and pedal up the hills that await you.

—*The Scarlet Pumpernickel*